SIMPLER
COURSE FOR FIRST
EXAMINATIONS

BY

A. RUSSON

AND

L. J. RUSSON, M.A.

LONGMAN

LONGMAN GROUP LIMITED

London

Associated companies, branches and representatives
throughout the world

ISBN 0 582 36168 0

2 075781 21

First published 1955
2nd edition 1969
5th impression 1975

Printed in Great Britain by Richard Clay (The Chaucer Press), Ltd.,
Bungay, Suffolk

PREFACE

The *Simpler German Course* is designed to meet the needs of those who might find the *Complete German Course* too elaborate at their stage but who nevertheless wish to reach the standard required for passing German at Ordinary level in the General Certificate of Education.

In the grammatical section those parts of German grammar that could be omitted at this stage have been omitted, and a simpler presentation has been made of certain paragraphs, in particular of those dealing with word-order and indirect speech. The principle of word-lists has been retained, but the number of words has been reduced considerably, and the longer lists broken up into more manageable groups. The sentences in the exercises designed to give practice in vocabulary and grammatical construction have deliberately been made short, and the prose passages for translation into German have been carefully graded, beginning with very simple passages of English. The section devoted to Free Composition is on very much the same lines as in the *Complete German Course*, somewhat more help, however, being given to the pupils.

The passages chosen for translation, comprehension and reproduction are a good deal simpler than those in the *Complete German Course*. They are arranged in an order corresponding roughly to their length and difficulty.

We hope that our choice of poems will commend itself. Whilst remaining within the range of comprehension of sixteen-year-old children they are, we believe, none of them without some merit as poetry.

The " model " answers given to the questions set to test the comprehension of a German prose passage will, it is hoped, give pupils a clearer idea of what is required of candidates who have to answer a comprehension test and should help them to avoid the sort of mistake that examiners cannot help but penalize. It must be emphasized, however, that questions set to discover how well a passage of German has been understood are fairly difficult questions and require time and consideration of the text before they can be suitably answered. They are, in fact, not the sort of questions that are designed necessarily to lead to the ability to reproduce in German the passage that has been read. For this purpose more straightforward questions of the type of „ Was machte A. ? " „ Was machte er dann ? " „ Wie war er ? " are clearly more appropriate, and are easily devised by the teacher.

We venture to suggest that prose compositions can be made a more profitable exercise than it sometimes is, and one needing less correction by the teacher, if pupils are expected only to *prepare* a prose composition for home-work, making full use of the notes and vocabulary and perhaps writing down a rough translation. This transla-tion, if done, will be collected the next day at the beginning of the lesson, rapidly glanced through and the prose com-position will be gone over again in class, no more than ten or fifteen minutes being devoted to this. The pupils will then be asked to write out a translation in class either with their books open or from the dictated English. It has been our experience that this method ensures a real effort being made to assimilate the vocabulary and idioms needed for prose composition.

Finally, we should like to express our gratitude to the many who have helped us in the composition of this book, and in particular to our friends Mr. I. D. McIntosh, former Headmaster of Fettes College, Edinburgh, and the late Dr. Otto Benecke, former Generaldirektor der Max Planck Gesellschaft zur Förderung der Wissenschaften, who have made countless valuable suggestions.

A. R.
L. J. R.

Winchester, 1954

ACKNOWLEDGMENT

GRATEFUL thanks are due to the Reclam-Verlag, Stuttgart, who have granted permission to reproduce extracts from *Das Recht der Frau* by Ludwig Fulda.

CONTENTS

SECTION I
GRAMMAR

SECTION II

SENTENCES AND PHRASES ON GRAMMATICAL POINTS

SECTION III

ENGLISH PROSE PASSAGES FOR TRANSLATION

SECTION IV

FREE COMPOSITION

SECTION V

GERMAN PROSE EXTRACTS

SECTION VI

GERMAN VERSE FOR TRANSLATION OR FOR EXERCISES IN COMPREHENSION

VOCABULARY

ABBREVIATIONS AND SIGNS USED

A	accusative ; governs accusative.
AD	governs accusative and/or dative.
adj.	adjective.
adv.	adverb.
AG	governs accusative and genitive.
cf.	compare.
cond.	conditional.
conj.	conjunction.
D	dative; governs dative.
e.g.	for example.
etc.	etcetera.
f. or *fem.*	feminine.
fig.	figuratively.
fut.	future.
G	genitive; governs genitive.
i.e.	that is.
imper.	imperative.
impf.	imperfect.
ind.	indicative.
intr.	intransitive.
irr.	irregular.
lit.	literally.
m.	masculine.
N	nominative.
n.	neuter.
Nr.	*Nummer* (= number).
o.s.	oneself.
p.	page.
pers.	person; personal.
pf.	perfect.
pl.	plural.
plpf.	pluperfect.
prep.	preposition.
pres.	present.
pron.	pronoun.
S.	*Seite* (= page).
s.	strong verb.
s.b.	somebody.
sing.	singular.
s.th.	something.
subj.	subjunctive.
tr.	transitive.

* conjugated with *sein*.
(*) conjugated with *sein* or *haben* according to meaning.
§ paragraph.
> becomes.
+ plus.
- inserted between prefix and verb indicates that the verb is separable.

SECTION I

GRAMMAR

WORD ORDER[1]

1. **Main Clauses**

(a) Statements:

In a statement consisting of one **main** clause the FINITE VERB is always the **second** idea:

1	2	3	4	5
Er	**liest**	mir	die Zeitung	vor.
He	*reads*	*to me*	*the paper*	*aloud.*
Jeden Tag	**hat**	er	die Zeitung	vorgelesen.
Every day	*has*	*he*	*the paper*	*aloud read.*

(b) Questions:

(i) In questions introduced by an interrogative adverb, adjective or pronoun (e.g. *wann? welcher? wer?*) the FINITE VERB is always the **second** idea:

1	2	3	4	5
Wann	**wird**	er	die Zeitung	lesen?
When	*will*	*he*	*the paper*	*read?*

(ii) In questions asking for the answer " yes " or " no " the FINITE VERB is always the **first** word:

1	2	3	4	5
Hat	er	ihr	die Zeitung	vorgelesen?
Has	*he*	*to her*	*the paper*	*aloud read?*

(c) Commands:

In commands the FINITE VERB is always the **first** word:

1	2	3	4	5
Lesen	Sie	sie	jeden Tag	vor!
Read	*(you)*	*it*	*every day*	*aloud.*

Note. **All** infinitives, past participles and separable prefixes stand **last** in main clauses.

[1] The " English " renderings of the German examples in §§ 1–4 are given in the word order of the original in order to show more strikingly the difference between English and German in this respect.

1

2. Compound Sentences

In a sentence consisting of two or more **main** clauses (i.e. in a **compound** sentence) the FINITE VERB is the **second** idea in each clause. Such main clauses are usually joined by a co-ordinating conjunction. (See § 6.)

1	2	3	4	1	2	3	4
Er	**setzte**	sich,	aber	(er)	**sagte**	nichts.	
He	*seated*	*himself*	*but*	*(he)*	*said*	*nothing.*	
Er	**setzte**	sich,	und	dann	**las**	er	Briefe.
He	*seated*	*himself*	*and*	*then*	*read*	*he*	*letters.*
Er	**setzte**	sich,	denn	er	**war**	müde.	
He	*seated*	*himself,*	*for*	*he*	*was*	*tired.*	

3. Subordinate Clauses

In a **subordinate** clause the FINITE VERB is normally the **last** word except when there are two infinitives in the clause:

	Wenn	er		die Zeitung	**liest,** ...	
	When	*he*		*the paper*	*reads* ...	
But	Wenn	er	sie	**hätte**	lesen	können, ...
	If	*he*	*it*	*had*	*read*	*been able to*

Note. A subordinate clause is introduced by any one of the following:

(*a*) A subordinating conjunction. (See § 7 (*a*).)

(*b*) An interrogative pronoun, adjective or adverb in indirect questions. (See § 7 (*b*).)

(*c*) A relative pronoun. (See §§ 58-61.)

4. Complex Sentences

(*a*) When the main clause precedes the subordinate clause the FINITE VERB stands **second** in the **main** clause and **last** in the **subordinate** clause:

Er	**liest**	die Zeitung,	wenn	er	nach Hause	**kommt.**
He	*reads*	*the paper*	*when*	*he*	*home*	*comes.*

Note. When the main clause introduces direct speech there is no change in the normal word order:

Dann	sagte	er:	„ Ich	bin	müde."
Then	*said*	*he:*	*" I*	*am*	*tired."*

(*b*) When the subordinate clause, or when direct speech, precedes the main clause the FINITE VERB stands **first** in the **main** clause, i.e. there is inversion of subject and verb:

			1	**2**		
Als	er	**zurückkam,**	**war**	er	sehr	müde.
When	*he*	*back came*	*was*	*he*	*very*	*tired.*

Da er faul **ist** und nicht **arbeitet, macht** er keine Fortschritte.

As he lazy is and not works   makes he no   progress.

„ Ich | bin | müde", | **sagte** er.
I | *am* | *tired,* | *said*   *he.*

5. Order of Words within the Clause

(a) Direct and Indirect Objects:

(i) If both objects are **nouns** the **indirect** (=dative) precedes the **direct** (= accusative):

           1   **2**
Er gab dem Mann das Buch.   *He gave the book to the man.*

(ii) If both objects are **personal pronouns** the **direct** precedes the **indirect:**

          1   **2**
Er gab   es   ihm.   *He gave it to him.*

(iii) If one object is a personal pronoun and the other a noun, the **pronoun,** whether accusative or dative, comes **first:**

          1   **2**
Er gab   es   dem Mann.   *He gave it to the man.*
Er gab   ihm   das Buch.   *He gave the book to him.*

(b) Adverbs and Adverbial Phrases:

(i) The normal order of precedence is:

1. Adverbs of **Time.** 2. Adverbs of **Manner.** 3. Adverbs of **Place.**

       1   **2**   **3**
      TIME   MANNER   PLACE
Er fährt jeden Tag mit dem Zug zur Schule.
He goes to school every day by train.

(ii) The adverb, unless it is the first word in the sentence, is preceded by all pronouns:

Gestern hat er sich sehr amüsiert. ⎫
Er hat **sich** gestern sehr amüsiert. ⎬ *He enjoyed himself yesterday.*
                    ⎭

Ich gab **ihm** gestern das Buch.	*I gave him the book yesterday.*
Ich gab **es ihm** gestern.	*I gave it to him yesterday.*

(*c*) **Position of** *nicht:*

  (i) In a negative **main** clause *nicht* immediately precedes the past participle, infinitive(s), separable prefix or predicative adjective. If none of these is present *nicht* is the last word.

Ich habe ihn **nicht** gesehen.	*I have not seen him.*
Ich kann ihn heute **nicht** sehen.	*I can't see him to-day.*
Sehen Sie sich **nicht** um!	*Don't look round.*
Es ist heute **nicht** kalt.	*It is not cold to-day.*
Ich sehe ihn **nicht.**	*I don't see him.*

  (ii) In a negative **subordinate** clause *nicht* precedes the finite verb. If there is a past participle, infinitive(s) or predicative adjective, *nicht* precedes these:

Wenn ich es **nicht** tue, . . .	*If I do not do it . . .*
Wenn ich es **nicht** getan hätte, . . .	*If I had not done it . . .*
Wenn Sie **nicht** kommen können, . . .	*If you cannot come . . .*
Wenn es heute **nicht** kalt wäre, . . .	*If it were not cold to-day . . .*

  (iii) If a particular word in the sentence is to be negatived *nicht* immediately precedes the word:

Das ist **nicht mein** Buch.	*That is not **my** book.*
Ich kann ihn **nicht heute** sehen.	*I can't see him **to-day.***

(*d*) **Position of reflexive pronoun:**

  (i) In a **main** clause *sich* etc., immediately follows the finite verb:

Er setzt **sich** auf den Stuhl.	*He sits down on the chair.*

  (ii) In a **subordinate** clause *sich* etc., usually immediately follows the subject of the clause:

Da er **sich** nicht amüsiert hat, . . .	*Since he didn't enjoy himself . . .*

(e) After exclamations and interjections there is **no** inversion of subject and verb:

Ja, das ist wahr.	*Yes, that is true.*
Ach! das wußte ich nicht.	*Oh! I didn't know that.*

(f) For word order with separable verbs, see § 95 (b).

CONJUNCTIONS

6. Co-ordinating Conjunctions (cf. § 2)

und	*and*	aber	*but, however*
denn	*for*	sondern	*but, on the contrary*
oder	*or*		

7. Subordinating Conjunctions and Interrogatives (cf. § 3)

(a) Subordinating Conjunctions:

als	*when, as, than*	ohne daß	*without*
als ob	*as if, as though*		*(+ gerund)*
(an)statt daß	*instead of*	seit ⎱	*(ever) since*
	(+ gerund)	seitdem ⎰	*(temporal)*
ausgenom-men, wenn	*except when*	sobald	*as soon as*
		so daß	*so that (result)*
bevor ⎱ ehe ⎰	*before*	solange	*as long as*
		trotzdem	*despite the fact*
bis	*till, until*		*that*
da	*since, as (causal)*	während	*while, whereas*
damit	*so that (purpose)*	weil	*because*
daß	*that, so that*	wenn	*if, when, when-ever*
indem	*as, by*		
	(+ gerund)	auch wenn	*even if, even when*
nachdem	*after*		
ob	*whether, if*	wenn ... nicht	*unless*
obgleich	*although*	wie	*as (manner)*

(b) Interrogative Adverbs, Adjectives and Pronouns introducing indirect questions (cf. §§ 41, 55-57, 105 (b)):

wann	*when*	wer	*who*
wie	*how*	welcher	*which*
etc.		etc.	

8. Some Difficult Conjunctions

as:

> **Da** er große Eile hatte, blieb er nur kurze Zeit.
> *As (=since) he was in a great hurry he only stayed a short time.*
> **Als** er ins Zimmer kam, drehte er das Licht an.
> *As (=when) he came into the room he turned on the light.*
> **Wie** du siehst, habe ich geschlafen.
> *As (= in the way that) you see, I have been asleep.*

but:

> Es ist nicht kalt, **aber** ich friere.
> *It is not cold but I am freezing.*   *(=I, however, am freezing.)*
> Ich fahre **nicht** mit dem Wagen, **sondern** gehe zu Fuß.
> *I do not go by car but (=on the contrary) walk.*
>
> Sie ist **nicht** schön, **sondern** häßlich.
> *She is not beautiful, but (=on the contrary) ugly.*

Note. Sondern is to be used when **all** the following conditions are fulfilled:

> (a) The first statement must be in the negative.
> (b) The second statement must contradict the first.
> (c) Each statement must have the same subject.

if:

> **Wenn** du Lust hast, kannst du mitkommen.
> *If you care to you can come with us.*
>
> Ich weiß nicht, **ob** ich Zeit habe.
> *I do not know if (= whether) I have time.*

since:

> **Da** er klug ist, lernt er schnell.
> *Since (=as) he is clever he learns quickly.*
> **Seitdem** er die Schule verlassen hat, hat er keine Stelle gehabt.
> *Ever since (=since the time) he left school he has not had a job.*

so that:

> Gib mir einen Bleistift, **damit** ich schreiben kann.
> *Give me a pencil so that (= in order that) I can write.*
> Es hörte auf zu regnen, **so daß** wir ausgehen konnten.
> *It stopped raining, so that (=with the result that) we could go out.*

when:

Wenn ich ihn sehe, werde ich mich freuen.
When I see him I shall be glad. (A future event.)

Wenn ich ihn sehe, freue ich mich.
When (=whenever) I see him I am glad.

Wenn ich ihn sah, freute ich mich.
When (= whenever) I saw him I used to be glad.

Als ich ihn sah, freute ich mich.
When I saw him I was glad. (**One** occasion in the **past.**)

Sobald (or **nachdem**) Sie ihn gesehen haben, kommen Sie
zurück.
When(= as soon as) you have seen him, come back.

Ich weiß nicht, **wann** er kommt.
I don't know when he's coming. (Indirect question.)

Kaum hatte er begonnen, **da** wurde er unterbrochen.
Scarcely had he begun when he was interrupted.

Es gibt Augenblicke, **in denen** (or **wo** or **da**) es schwer ist.
There are moments when it is difficult.

9. Adverbial Conjunctions

also		(je)doch	*yet, however*
daher		kaum	*hardly*
darum	*therefore, (and) so*	sonst	*otherwise, or else*
deshalb			
so		trotzdem	*in spite of that*
auch	*also, and, too*	übrigens	*moreover, anyhow*
auch . . . nicht	*nor, not . . . either*		
		unterdessen	*meanwhile*
außerdem	*besides*		

Note. When adverbial conjunctions begin a sentence **inversion** of
subject and verb usually takes place:

Auch arbeitet er **nicht.**   *Nor does he work.*

10. Correlative Conjunctions

bald . . ., bald	*now . . . now*
entweder . . . oder	*either . . . or*
je . . ., desto	*the (more) . . . the (more)*
nicht nur . . ., sondern auch	*not only . . . but also*
sowohl . . . als auch	*both . . . and*
weder . . . noch	*neither . . . nor*

(*a*) Connecting two clauses:

Bald regnet es, **bald** schneit es.
Now it rains, now it snows.

Weder hat er uns geschrieben, **noch** hat er uns besucht.
He has neither written to us nor visited us.

Entweder sagst du es ihm, **oder** ich tue es.
Either you tell him or I shall.

Je älter man wird, **desto** klüger wird man.
The older one gets the shrewder one becomes.

(*b*) Connecting two subjects, objects or predicative adjectives, with one verb, or two verbs with one subject:

Sowohl er **als auch** sie sind dort.
Both he and she are there.

Weder er **noch** wir können es tun.
Neither he nor we can do it.

Es gibt **entweder** Tee **oder** Kaffee.
There is either tea or coffee.

Sie ist **nicht nur** schön, **sondern auch** mutig.
She is not only beautiful but also brave.

THE ARTICLES

11. Declension of the Definite Article

	sing.			pl.
	m.	f.	n.	m.f.n.
N.	der	die	das	die
A.	den	die	das	die
G.	des	der	des	der
D.	dem	der	dem	den

12. Declension of the Indefinite Article and its Negative

	sing.			sing.			pl.
	m.	f.	n.	m.	f.	n.	m.f.n.
N.	ein	eine	ein	kein	keine	kein	keine
A.	einen	eine	ein	keinen	keine	kein	keine
G.	eines	einer	eines	keines	keiner	keines	keiner
D.	einem	einer	einem	keinem	keiner	keinem	keinen

13. **Use of the Definite Article**

The **definite article** is normally required:

(*a*) Before abstract nouns:

    Die Zeit vergeht schnell.   *Time passes quickly.*

(*b*) When a proper noun is preceded by an adjective:

    Das moderne Deutschland.   *Modern Germany.*

(*c*) In quotations of prices:

    2 Mark **das** Pfund, **das** Stück.   *2 marks a pound, each.*

(*d*) Before names of rivers, mountains, lakes, streets and squares :

    Der Rhein; **die** Themse.   *The Rhine; the Thames.*

(*e*) Before names denoting periods of time and meals, especially when governed by a preposition:

    Der Herbst; **der** August.   *Autumn; August.*
    Im Herbst; **im** August; **am** Montag.   *In autumn; in August; on Monday(s).*
    In **der** Nacht; nach **dem** Frühstück.   *At night; after breakfast.*

(*f*) Before names of parts of the body and of clothing when these refer to the subject of the sentence and are **not** qualified by an adjective:

    Ich hob **die** Hand.   *I raised my hand.*

But   Er öffnete seine müden Augen.   *He opened his tired eyes.*

(*g*) As in (*f*) above, the possessor being indicated by the dative pronoun (cf. § 96):

    Er hat **mir das** Leben gerettet.   *He saved my life.*

(*h*) Before names of countries and provinces which are feminine or plural:

    Die Schweiz; **die** Niederlande.   *Switzerland; Holland.*

But   Deutschland; Preußen.   *Germany; Prussia.*

(*i*) In certain stock phrases (cf. also §§ 81 and 82):

    In **der** Schule; in **der** Stadt.   *In, at school; in town.*
    Im Bett; aus **dem** Bett.   *In bed; out of bed.*
    In **der** Tat.   *Indeed, in fact.*
    Im allgemeinen.   *In general, as a rule.*
    Zur Schule; **zur** Kirche.   *To school; to church.*
    Mit **der** Bahn; mit **der** Post.   *By rail; by post.*

14. **Omission of the Article**

(a) After *sein, werden* and *bleiben* the article may be omitted before nouns denoting a person's profession or nationality:

Er ist Deutscher.	*He is a German.*
Er will Arzt werden.	*He wants to become a doctor.*
Er blieb Soldat.	*He remained a soldier.*

Note. If such nouns are qualified by an adjective the article is required:

Er ist ein berühmter Arzt.   *He is a famous doctor.*

(b) The partitive article (**some, any**) is usually not translated except by *kein* when this is the only word showing that the sentence is negative:

Ich habe Brot.	*I have **some** bread.*
Hast du Brot?	*Have you **any** bread?*
Haben Sie Eier gekauft?	*Did you buy **any** eggs?*
Ich trinke nie Milch.	*I never drink **any** milk.*

But   Ich habe keine Milch.   *I haven't **any** milk.*

(c) Common expressions which do not contain the article:

Er hat guten Appetit.	*He has a good appetite.*
Wir haben Besuch.	*We have a visitor (or visitors).*
Er hat (großen) Durst.	*He is (very) thirsty.*
Er hat keinen Durst.	*He is not thirsty.*
Er hat keine/große Eile.	*He is in no/a great hurry.*
Der Krieg war zu Ende.	*The war was over (at an end).*
Er hat (großen) Hunger.	*He is (very) hungry.*
Er hat Kopfschmerzen.	*He has a headache.*
Ich habe (keine) Lust.	*I (don't) feel inclined to.*
Du hast recht,[1] unrecht.[1]	*You are right, wrong.*
(Es ist) schade.[1]	*It is a pity.*
Er hat Schmerzen.	*He has a pain.*
Er ist in guter (schlechter) Stimmung.	*He is in a good (bad) mood.*

[1] These nouns are now written with small letters.

NOUNS

15. The Declension of Nouns

	IA Pl. not modified	IA Pl. modified	IB Pl. not modified	IB Pl. modified	IC Pl. not modified	IC Pl. modified	II (WEAK)	IIIA (MIXED)	IIIB (MIXED)
	(10)		(3)	(10)					(10)
MASCULINE									
Sing. N.	Tag	Sohn	Geist	Wald	Onkel	Apfel	Mensch	Staat	Name
A.	Tag	Sohn	Geist	Wald	Onkel	Apfel	Menschen	Staat	Namen
G.	Tag(e)s	Sohn(e)s	Geistes	Wald(e)s	Onkels	Apfels	Menschen	Staat(e)s	Namens
D.	Tag(e)	Sohn(e)	Geist(e)	Wald(e)	Onkel	Apfel	Menschen	Staat(e)	Namen
Pl. N.	Tage	Söhne	Geister	Wälder	Onkel	Äpfel	Menschen	Staaten	Namen
A.	Tage	Söhne	Geister	Wälder	Onkel	Äpfel	Menschen	Staaten	Namen
G.	Tage	Söhne	Geister	Wälder	Onkel	Äpfel	Menschen	Staaten	Namen
D.	Tagen	Söhnen	Geistern	Wäldern	Onkeln	Äpfeln	Menschen	Staaten	Namen
	(10)	(30)				(2)			
FEMININE									
Sing. N.	Trübsal	Stadt	None	None	None	Mutter	None	Frau	None
A.	Trübsal	Stadt				Mutter		Frau	
G.	Trübsal	Stadt				Mutter		Frau	
D.	Trübsal	Stadt				Mutter		Frau	
Pl. N.	Trübsale	Städte				Mütter		Frauen	
A.	Trübsale	Städte				Mütter		Frauen	
G.	Trübsale	Städte				Mütter		Frauen	
D.	Trübsalen	Städten				Müttern		Frauen	
	(1)	(1)	(3)			(1)		(7)	(1)
NEUTER									
Sing. N.	Tier	Floß	Kind	Haus	Fenster	Kloster	None	Bett	Herz
A.	Tier	Floß	Kind	Haus	Fenster	Kloster		Bett	Herz
G.	Tier(e)s	Floßes	Kind(e)s	Hauses	Fensters	Klosters		Bett(e)s	Herzens
D.	Tier(e)	Floß(e)	Kind(e)	Haus(e)	Fenster	Kloster		Bett(e)	Herzen
Pl. N.	Tiere	Flöße	Kinder	Häuser	Fenster	Klöster		Betten	Herzen
A.	Tiere	Flöße	Kinder	Häuser	Fenster	Klöster		Betten	Herzen
G.	Tiere	Flöße	Kinder	Häuser	Fenster	Klöster		Betten	Herzen
D.	Tieren	Flößen	Kindern	Häusern	Fenstern	Klöstern		Betten	Herzen

Note. The approximate number of nouns, excluding compound nouns, in the various groups is given where this is not large.

16. Notes on the Gender of Nouns

(a) Masculine:

(i) Names of seasons, months and days (§ 48) and of points of the compass, e.g. *der Herbst, der Mai, der Montag, der Norden.*

(ii) Nouns, not ending in *-t*, that form the stem of verbs, e.g. *der Besuch* (from *besuchen*). They belong to Group IA. (Exceptions: *das Bad, Bild, Kleid, Knie, Spiel, Urteil, Ziel.*)

(iii) The suffixes *-ig* and *-ling*, e.g. *der König, der Frühling.* These belong to Group IA.

(iv) Most nouns ending in *-en*, e.g. *der Morgen.* (Exceptions: *das Eisen, das Zeichen*; all infinitives used as nouns; and all diminutives in *-chen.*) These belong to Group IC.

(b) Feminine:

(i) Names of most fruits and trees, e.g. *Birne, die Eiche.* (Exceptions: *der Apfel* and nouns ending in *-baum.*)

(ii) Nouns ending in *-t* forming the stem of verbs, e.g. *die Antwort.* (Exception: *der Rat.*)

(iii) All nouns ending in the suffixes *-ei, -ie, -ik, -in, -ion, -heit, -keit, -schaft, -tät* and *-ung*, e.g. *die Musik, die Königin, die Schönheit, die Zeitung.*

(iv) The vast majority of nouns ending in *-e*, especially abstract nouns, e.g. *die Farbe, die Brücke.* (Exceptions: masculine nouns belonging to Groups II and IIIB; neuter nouns belonging to Group IIIA.)

Note. The suffix *-in* added to certain masculine nouns (particularly to those ending in *-er*) gives the feminine equivalent of them, e.g. *Lehrer > Lehrerin; Bauer > Bäuerin.* Such nouns usually modify the vowel if possible. (See § 18 (c) (ii).)

(c) Neuter:

(i) Names of continents and of most towns and countries (see § 25), e.g. *das alte Berlin, das moderne Frankreich.*

(ii) Names of most metals, e.g. *das Eisen, das Gold.* (Exceptions: *der Stahl, die Bronze.*)

(iii) All infinitives used as nouns (see § 19 (c) (i) (β)), e.g. *das Lesen.*

(iv) The suffixes *-chen* and *-lein*, e.g. *das Brötchen, das Fräulein.*

Note. The suffixes *-chen* and *-lein* form diminutives, e.g. *Brot > Brötchen, Frau > Fräulein.* Such diminutives usually modify the vowel if possible.

17. Masculine Nouns

(a) Group IA (Strong):

(i) Declined like **Tag(-e)**, i.e. plural not modified:

Abend, *evening*
Arm, *arm*
Augenblick, *moment*
Autobus,[1] *bus*
Bahnsteig, *platform*
Befehl, *command, order*
Berg, *mountain, hill*
Besuch, *visit, visitor(s)*
Bleistift, *pencil*
Blick, *glance, view*
Blitz, *lightning*
Brief, *letter*
Dom, *cathedral*
Erfolg, *success*
Feind, *enemy*
Film, *film*
Fisch, *fish*
Fortschritt, *progress*
Freund, *friend*
Frühling, *spring*

Geburtstag, *birthday*
Handschuh, *glove*
Herbst, *autumn*
Hund, *dog*
König, *king*
Kreis, *circle*
Krieg, *war*
Mittag, *midday, noon*
Monat, *month*
Mond, *moon*
Nachmittag, *after-noon*
Nachteil, *disadvantage*
Ort, *place*
Preis, *price; prize*
Ring, *ring*
Ruf, *shout; reputation*
Schein, *light; ticket; banknote*
Schirm, *umbrella*
Schreibtisch, *desk*
Schritt, *step, yard*

Schuh, *shoe, boot*
Sieg, *victory*
Sinn, *sense*
Stein, *stone*
Stern, *star*
Stoff, *stuff, material*
Tag, *day*
Teil, *part, share*
Tisch, *table*
Unterschied, *difference*
Versuch, *attempt; experiment*
Vorteil, *advantage*
Weg, *way, road*
Wein, *wine*
Wert, *value, worth*
Wind, *wind*
Wirt, *landlord, host*
Zweck, *purpose, use*
Zweig, *branch*

(ii) Declined like **Sohn (–̈e)**, i.e. plural modified:

Anfang, *beginning*
Anzug, *suit*
Arzt, *doctor*
Ausdruck, *expression*
Bahnhof, *station*
Ball, *ball*
Baum, *tree*
Einkauf, *purchase*
Fall, *case; fall*
Fluß, *river*
Fuß, *foot*
Gast, *guest, visitor*
Gegenstand, *object, subject*
Grund, *reason*
Gruß, *greeting*

Hals, *neck*
Hof, *court, yard, farm*
Hut, *hat*
Kampf, *fight, struggle*
Kopf, *head*
Korb, *basket*
Markt, *market*
Obstbaum, *fruit-tree*
Plan, *plan*
Platz, *seat; square; room*
Raum, *space, room*
Rock, *coat, skirt*
Saal,[2] *(big) room, hall*
Satz, *sentence; jump*
Schrank, *cupboard*

Sohn, *son*
Spaziergang, *walk*
Stock, *stick*
Strumpf, *stocking*
Stuhl, *chair*
Sturm, *storm, gale*
Traum, *dream*
Turm, *tower*
Umschlag, *envelope*
Vorschlag, *suggestion*
Weihnachtsbaum, *Christmas tree*
Wunsch, *wish*
Zahn, *tooth*
Zahnarzt, *dentist.*
Zug, *train; feature*

---

[1] Plural: *Autobusse.*   [2] Plural: *Säle.*

(b) **Group IB (Strong):**

    (i) Declined like **Geist(-er)**, i.e. plural not modified:

Geist, *mind, spirit*

    (ii) Declined like **Wald(-̈er)**, i.e. plural modified:

Gott, *god*	Mund, *mouth*	Reichtum, *wealth*
Mann, *man, husband*	Rand, *edge, rim*	Wald, *wood, forest*

(c) **Group IC (Strong):**

    (i) Declined like **Onkel(-)**, i.e. plural not modified:

Arbeiter, *workman*	Haufen, *heap, crowd*	Rücken, *back*
Ausländer, *foreigner*	Himmel, *sky, heaven*	Schatten, *shadow,*
Briefträger, *postman*	Kaiser, *emperor*	*shade*
Dichter, *poet*	Käse, *cheese*	Schlüssel, *key*
Diener, *servant*	Kellner, *waiter*	Schriftsteller, *writer*
Einwohner, *inhabitant*	Koffer, *suit-case, bag*	Schüler, *schoolboy*
Enkel, *grandson*	Körper, *body*	Sommer, *summer*
Fehler, *mistake; flaw*	Kuchen, *cake*	Spiegel, *mirror*
Felsen, *rock*	Künstler, *artist*	Teller, *plate*
Finger, *finger*	Lehrer, *teacher*	Verkäufer, *shop*
Flügel, *wing; piano*	Löffel, *spoon*	*assistant*
Führer, *leader, guide*	Morgen, *morning*	Wagen, *cart,*
Gepäckträger, *porter*	Onkel, *uncle*	*car(-riage)*
Gipfel, *top (of hill)*	Redner, *speaker*	Winter, *winter*
Händler, *tradesman*	Richter, *judge*	Zweifel, *doubt*

    (ii) Declined like **Apfel(-̈)**, i.e. plural modified:

Apfel, *apple*	Großvater, *grand-*	Mangel, *lack, defect*
Boden, *ground, floor*	*father*	Mantel, *coat, cloak*
Briefkasten, *letter-box*	Hafen, *harbour*	Ofen, *stove*
Bruder, *brother*	Kasten, *box*	Vater, *father*
Garten, *garden*	Laden, *shop, shutter*	Vogel, *bird*

(d) **Group II (Weak)**, declined like **Mensch(-en, -en):**

Note. Nouns in this group ending in *-e* in the nominative singular add *-n* only.

Gefährte, *companion*	Kamerad, *comrade*	Neffe, *nephew*
Held, *hero*	Löwe, *lion*	Prinz, *prince*
Herr,[1] *gentleman,*	Matrose, *sailor*	Schurke, *scoundrel*
master, lord, Mr.	Mensch, *man, person*	Soldat, *soldier*
Junge, *boy, lad*	Narr, *fool*	Student, *student*

[1] Adds *-n* in the singular, *-en* in the plural.

(e) **Group IIIA (Mixed)**, declined like **Staat(-(e)s, -en)**:

Bauer,[1,2] *peasant, farmer*	Schmerz,[3] *pain, ache*	Staat, *state*
Nachbar,[1,2] *neighbour*	See,[1] *lake*	Vetter,[1] *cousin*

(f) **Group IIIB (Mixed)**, declined like **Name(-ns, -n)**:

Friede,[4] *peace*	Glaube,[4] *belief*	Wille,[4] *will*
Gedanke, *thought, idea*	Name, *name*	

(g) **Masculine Nouns normally used only in the Singular:**

Appetit, *appetite*	Norden, *north*	Strand, *shore, beach*
Dank, *thanks*	Osten, *east*	Süden, *south*
Donner, *thunder*	Rauch, *smoke*	Tabak, *tobacco*
Durst, *thirst*	Regen, *rain*	Tee, *tea*
Hunger, *hunger*	Schnee, *snow*	Verkehr, *traffic*
Kaffee, *coffee*	Sonnenschein, *sun-shine*	Westen, *west*
Lärm, *noise, din*		Zorn, *anger*
Mut, *courage*	Stolz, *pride*	Zucker, *sugar*

18. Feminine Nouns

(a) **Group IA (Strong):**

     (i) Declined like **Trübsal(-e)**, i.e. plural not modified:

Erlaubnis,[5] *permission*	Kenntnis,[5] *knowledge*	Trübsal, *affliction*
Finsternis,[5] *darkness*		

     (ii) Declined like **Stadt(⸚e)**, i.e. plural modified:

Angst, *fear*	Kuh, *cow*	Mitternacht, *mid-night*
Ankunft, *arrival*	Kunst, *art*	
Bank, *bench*	Luft, *air*	Nacht, *night*
Brust, *breast, chest*	Lust, *desire*	Not, *need, distress*
Hand, *hand*	Macht, *power*	Stadt, *town, city*
Hauptstadt, *capital*	Maus, *mouse*	Wand, *(inner) wall*
Kraft, *strength*		

(b) **Group IC (Strong)**, declined like **Mutter(⸚)**:

Mutter, *mother*	Großmutter, *grand-mother*	Tochter, *daughter*

---

[1] Adds -s in genitive singular and -n in plural.
[2] Also declined weak.   [3] Adds -es in genitive singular.
[4] Rarely used in the plural.   [5] Plural, -nisse.

(c) **Group III** (**Mixed**), declined like **Frau(-en)**:

> *Notes.* (1) Nouns of this group ending in *-e*, *-er* and *-el* only add *-n* to form the plural.
>
> (2) Many nouns of this group can, because of their meaning, only be used in the singular.

(i)

(α)

Absicht, *intention*	Flasche, *bottle*	Hütte, *cottage, hut*
Antwort, *answer*	Frau, *woman, wife,*	Insel, *island*
Arbeit, *work*	*Mrs.*	Jacke, *jacket*
Art, *kind*	Freude, *joy*	Jahreszeit, *season*
Bahn, *rail, path*	Furcht,[1] *fear*	Jugend,[1] *youth*
Bank, (*money*) *bank*	Gabel, *fork*	Karte, *card, map*
Bibliothek, *library*	Geburt, *birth*	Kartoffel, *potato*
Blume, *flower*	Gefahr, *danger*	Katze, *cat*
Briefmarke, *stamp*	Gegenwart,[1] *present*	Kirche, *church*
Brücke, *bridge*	(*time*), *presence*	Klasse, *class*
Butter,[1] *butter*	Gelegenheit, *oppor-*	Küche, *kitchen*
Ecke, *corner*	*tunity*	Lage, *situation*
Erde, *earth, ground*	Geschichte,	Lampe, *lamp*
Fahrkarte, *ticket*	(*hi-*)*story*	Mahlzeit, *meal*
Fahrt, *journey*	Hälfte, *half*	Mark,[1] *mark* (*coin*)
Familie, *family*	Heimat, *home*	Mauer, (*outer*) *wall*
Farbe, *colour, paint*	Hilfe, *help*	Meile, *mile*
Feder, *feather; pen*	Hitze,[1] *heat*	Menge, *crowd, lot*

(β)

Milch,[1] *milk*	Schule, *school*	Treppe, *staircase,*
Mitte, *middle*	Schulter, *shoulder*	*stairs*
Mühe, *trouble*	Schwester, *sister*	Tür, *door*
Musik,[1] *music*	Seite, *side; page*	Uhr, (*o'*)*clock, watch*
Nachricht, *news*	Sonne, *sun*	Ursache, *cause*
Nase, *nose*	Sprache, *language*	Vergangenheit,[1] *past*
Natur, *nature*	Straße, *street, road*	Wahl, *choice, election*
Nichte, *niece*	Stunde, *hour; lesson*	Weile,[1] *while*
Pflicht, *duty*	Summe, *sum* (*of*	Weise, *manner, way*
Polizei, *police*	*money*)	Welt, *world*
Post,[1] *post* (*-office*)	Suppe, *soup*	Wiese, *meadow*
Postkarte, *postcard*	Tafel, (*black-*)*board*	Woche, *week*
Rose, *rose*	Tante, *aunt*	Wolke, *cloud*
Sache, *thing, matter*	Tasche, *pocket*	Zeit, *time*
Scham,[1] *shame*	Tasse, *cup*	Zeitung, *newspaper*
Schrift, *writing*	Tat, *deed*	Zigarette, *cigarette*
Schublade, *drawer*	Tinte, *ink*	Zukunft,[1] *future*
Schuld, *guilt; debt*	Träne, *tear*	

[1] Only used in the singular.

(ii) **Derivatives** from **masculine nouns** by the addition of **-in** (pl., **-innen**) and modification of vowel usually, if possible, e.g. **Arzt>Ärztin, Lehrer>Lehrerin**:

Arbeiterin, *work-woman*	Freundin, (*girl*) *friend*	Lehrerin, *school-mistress*
Bäuerin, *peasant-woman*	Heldin, *heroine*	Nachbarin,[1] *neighbour*
	Kaiserin, *empress*	Prinzessin,[2] *princess*
Enkelin, *grand-daughter*	Kellnerin, *waitress*	Schülerin, *schoolgirl*
	Königin, *queen*	Studentin, *girl-student*

(iii) **Derivatives** from **adjectives**:

(α) By the addition of **umlaut** (if possible) and **-e** (see § 30 (*b*) (i)):

Ferne, *distance*	Kälte,[3] *cold(ness)*	Stärke, *strength*
Größe, *size*	Nähe, *vicinity*	Stille, *stillness*
Güte,[3] *goodness*	Schwäche, *weakness*	Wärme,[3] *warmth*

(β) By the addition of **-heit** (see § 30 (*b*) (ii)):

Dunkelheit, *darkness*	Gesundheit, *health*	Schönheit, *beauty*
Freiheit, *freedom*	Krankheit, *illness*	Wahrheit, *truth*

(γ) By the addition of **-keit** (see § 30 (*b*) (iii)):

Dankbarkeit, *gratitude*	Schwierigkeit, *difficulty*	Wirklichkeit, *reality*
Fähigkeit, *ability*		

(iv) **Derivatives** from **nouns, adjectives** or **verbal nouns** by the addition **-schaft**:

Bekanntschaft, *acquaintance*	Freundschaft, *friendship*	Landschaft, *landscape*
Eigenschaft, *quality*	Gesellschaft, *company, society, party*	Leidenschaft, *passion*

(v) **Derivatives** from **verbs**:

(α) By the omission of the last letter of the infinitive, e.g. **eilen>Eile** (see § 87 (*b*), weak verbs):

Bitte,[4] *request*	Liebe, *love*	Reise, *journey*
Decke, *blanket, ceiling*	Pfeife,[4] *pipe, whistle*	Ruhe,[3] *rest*
Ehre, *honour*	Pflanze, *plant*	Sorge, *care* (=*concern*)
Eile,[3] *haste, hurry*	Rede, *speech*	Stelle, *place, spot*
Folge, *consequence*	Regel, *rule*	Stimme, *voice; vote*
Frage, *question*	Reihe, *row, series*	Strafe, *punishment*

[1] Note no modification of vowel. [2] Note irregularity.
[3] Only used in the singular. [4] Derived from strong verb.

(β) By adding **-ung** to the stem of the infinite, e.g.
ändern>änder->Änderung:

(Cf. § 87 (c), weak verbs.)

Änderung, *alteration*   Ordnung, *order(-liness)*   Sammlung, *collection*
Bildung, *formation,*   Prüfung, *examination*   Stimmung, *mood*
  culture, education   Rechnung, *bill*   Störung, *disturbance*
Handlung, *action;*   Regierung, *reign;*   Übung, *practice*
  shop; business   *government*   Wirkung, *effect*
Hoffnung,[1] *hope*   Rettung, *rescue*   Wohnung, *flat*
Meinung, *opinion*   Richtung, *direction*   Zeichnung, *drawing*

(Cf. § 95, compound verbs.)

Bedeutung, *meaning*   Erkältung, *cold*   Unterhaltung, *con-*
Bemerkung, *remark*   Erklärung, *explana-*   *versation*
Bewegung, *movement*   *tion, declaration*   Verbindung, *connec-*
Einladung, *invitation*   Erzählung, *tale*   *tion*
Erfahrung, *experience*   Übersetzung, *transla-*   Vorbereitung,
Erholung, *recovery*   *tion*   *preparation*

19. Neuter Nouns

(a) **Group IA (Strong):**

(i) Declined like **Tier(-e)**, i.e. plural not modified.

Abteil, *compartment*   Geschenk, *gift,*   Pferd, *horse*
Bein, *leg*   *present*   Problem, *problem*
Beispiel, *example*   Gesetz, *law*   Pult, (*master's*) *desk*
Bier, *beer*   Gewicht, *weight*   Recht, *right, justice*
Boot, *boat*   Haar, *hair*   Schaf, *sheep*
Brot, *bread, loaf*   Heft, *exercise-book*   Schicksal, *fate*
Ding, *thing*   Jahr, *year*   Schiff, *ship*
Dutzend, *dozen*   Jahrhundert, *century*   Spiel, *game, play*
Flugzeug, *aeroplane*   Kinn, *chin*   Stück, *piece; play*
Frühstück, *breakfast*   Königreich, *kingdom*   Tier, *animal*
Gedicht, *poem*   Konzert, *concert*   Unglück, *misfortune*
Gefühl, *feeling*   Mal, *time, occasion*   Urteil, *judgment*
Gegenteil, *opposite*   Maß, *measure*   Werk, *work*
Geheimnis,[2] *secret*   Meer, *sea, ocean*   Wort, *word*
Gericht, *lawcourt;*   Paar, *pair, couple*   Ziel, *aim, destination*
  dish   Paket, *parcel, packet*
Geschäft, *business*   Papier, *paper*

[1] Adds *-nung* to the stem.   [2] Plural, *-nisse.*

(ii) Declined like **Floß(⸚e)**, i.e. plural modified:
Floß, *raft*.

(b) **Group IB (Strong):**

(i) Declined like **Kind(-er)**, i.e. plural not modified:

Bild, *picture*	Gesicht, *face*	Kleid, *dress, frock*
Ei, *egg*	Gespenst, *ghost*	Licht, *light*
Feld, *field*	Glied, *limb*	Lied, *song*
Geld, *money*	Kind, *child*	Mitglied, *member*

(ii) Declined like **Haus(⸚er)**, i.e. plural modified:

Bad, *bath*	Gras, *grass*	Schloß, *castle, palace*
Blatt, *leaf*	Gut, *estate*	Streichholz, *match*
Buch, *book*	Haus, *house*	Tal, *valley*
Dach, *roof*	Holz, *wood*	Taschentuch, *hand-*
Dorf, *village*	Huhn, *chicken*	*kerchief*
Fach, *(school) subject*	Land, *land, country*	Volk, *people, nation*
Glas, *glass*	Rad, *wheel; bicycle*	Wirtshaus, *inn*

(c) **Group IC (Strong):**

(i) Declined like **Fenster(-)**, i.e. plural not modified :

(α)

Badezimmer, *bath-room*	Knie, *knee*	Theater, *theatre*
Eßzimmer, *dining-room*	Mädchen, *girl; maid*	Ufer, *bank, shore*
	Märchen, *fairy-tale*	Viertel, *quarter*
Fenster, *window*	Messer, *knife*	Wasser, *water*
Feuer, *fire*	Mittel, *means*	Wohnzimmer, *sitting-room*
Fräulein, *Miss*	Möbel, *(piece of) furniture*	Wunder, *wonder, miracle*
Gebäude, *building*	Opfer, *victim, sacrifice*	Zeichen, *sign*
Gemüse, *vegetable(s)*	Schlafzimmer, *bed-room*	Zimmer, *room*
Klassenzimmer, *classroom*		

(β) **Infinitives** used as **nouns:**

Note. Most of these nouns have no plural.

Aussehen, *appearance*	Lächeln, *smile, smiling*	Rauchen, *smoking*
Benehmen, *behaviour*	Lachen, *laugh(ing), laughter*	Reisen, *travelling*
Erstaunen, *astonishment*	Leben, *life, living*	Schweigen, *silence*
Essen, *eating, food*	Lesen, *reading*	Versprechen, *promise*
		Vertrauen, *confidence*

(ii) Declined like **Kloster(⁻⁻)**, i.e. plural modified:
Kloster, *monastery*.

(*d*) **Group IIIA (Mixed)**, declined like **Bett(-(e)s, -en)**:

Auge,[1] *eye*	Hemd, *shirt*	Interesse,[1] *interest*
Bett, *bed*	Insekt, *insect*	Ohr, *ear*
Ende,[1] *end*		

(*e*) **Group IIIB (Mixed)**, declined like **Herz(-ens, -en)**:

Herz, *heart*.

(*f*) **Neuter Nouns normally used only in the Singular:**

Alter, *age*	Glück, *happiness, luck*	Obst, *fruit*
Ausland, *abroad*	Gold, *gold*	Pfund, *pound*
Blut, *blood*	Kilo, *kilo*	Radio, *wireless*
Eis, *ice*	Leder, *leather*	Silber, *silver*
Eisen, *iron*	Liter,[2] *litre*	Unrecht, *injustice*
Fleisch, *meat, flesh*	Lob, *praise*	Vergnügen, *pleasure*
Gepäck, *luggage*	Meter,[2] *metre, yard*	Wetter, *weather*

20. Irregular Plurals

(*a*) das Auto(-s), *car*   das Hotel(-s), *hotel*   das Restaurant(-s),
   das Büro(s), *office*   das Kino(-s), *cinema*   *restaurant*
   das Café(-s), *café*   das Sofa(-s), *sofa*
(*b*) der Schutzmann (Schutzleute), *policeman*.
(*c*) der Rat (Ratschläge), *advice*.
(*d*) der Tod (Todesfälle), *death, casualty*.
(*e*) der Stock (Stockwerke), *story (of house), floor*

21. Nouns used normally only in the Plural

Eltern, *parents*	Kopfschmerzen,	Pfingsten,[3] *Whitsun*
Ferien, *holidays*	*headache*	Sommerferien,
Großeltern, *grand-*	Kosten, *costs*	*summer holidays*
parents	Leute, *people*	Weihnachten,[3]
Hosen, *trousers*	Ostern,[3] *Easter*	*Christmas*
Kleider, *clothes*		

---

[1] These nouns add only -*s*, -*n*.   [2] Colloquially: *der Liter, der Meter*.
[3] These nouns, when followed by a verb, are treated as singular, e.g.

Weihnachten **kommt** bald.   *Christmas is coming soon.*
But Fröhliche Weihnachten.   *Merry Christmas.*

22. Geographical Names

Continent, Country	Meaning	Inhabitant (fem. form given in brackets).	Adjective
Afrika	*Africa*	Afrikaner[1](-in)	afrikanisch
Amerika	*America*	Amerikaner[1] (-in)	amerikanisch
Asien	*Asia*	Asiat[2](-in)	asiatisch
Australien	*Australia*	Australier[1](-in)	australisch
Europa	*Europe*	Europäer[1](-in)	europäisch
Belgien	*Belgium*	Belgier[1](-in)	belgisch
China	*China*	Chines-e[2](-in)	chinesisch
Deutschland	*Germany*	der Deutsche[3]	deutsch
England	*England*	Engländer[1](-in)	englisch
Frankreich	*France*	Franz-ose[2] (-ösin)	französisch
Irland	*Ireland*	Irländer[1](-in)	irisch
Italien	*Italy*	Italiener[1](-in)	italienisch
Österreich	*Austria*	Österreicher[1] (-in)	österreichisch
Preußen	*Prussia*	Preuß-e[2](-in)	preußisch
Rußland	*Russia*	Russ-e[2](-in)	russisch
Schottland	*Scotland*	Schott-e[2](-in)	schottisch
die Schweiz [4]	*Switzerland*	Schweizer[1](-in)	schweizerisch
Spanien	*Spain*	Spanier[1](-in)	spanisch
die Vereinigten Staaten[4] (m. pl.)	*U.S.A.*	Amerikaner[1] (-in)	amerikanisch
Wales	*Wales*	Waliser[1](-in)	walisisch

Notes. (1) Die BRD (= Bundesrepublik Deutschland), *German Federal Republic (W. Germany)*; die DDR (= Deutsche Demokratische Republik), *German Democratic Republic (E. Germany)*.

(2) Names of continents and countries, unless otherwise indicated, are neuter.

THE CASES

23. The Nominative

The nominative is used to denote:

(a) The **subject** of the sentence:

Der König wurde krank.   *The king fell ill.*

[1] Declined like *Onkel* (§ 15, Group IC).
[2] Declined like *Mensch* (§ 17 (*d*) and note).
[3] Declined like an adjective, see § 31.
[4] Cf. § 13 (*h*).

(b) The **complement** of the verbs *sein, werden* and *bleiben*:

Er ist **ein berühmter Arzt.**	*He is a famous doctor.*
Er ist **ein Mann** geworden.	*He has become a man.*
Ich bleibe **dein Freund.**	*I remain your friend.*

24. The Accusative

The accusative is used:

(a) To denote the **direct object** of a transitive verb:

Ich gab ihm **den Bleistift.**	*I gave him the pencil.*

(b) To denote **duration of time** and **distance covered:**

Sie blieb **einen Monat.**	*She stayed for a month.*
Den ganzen Tag arbeitete er.	*He worked all day long.*
Er ging **einen Schritt** weiter.	*He went one step farther.*

(c) To denote **definite time when** unless *an* or *in* are used:

Er kam **jeden Tag** (**letzten Freitag**).	*He came every day (last Friday).*

(d) To denote **direction:**

Er ging **die Straße** hinunter.	*He went down the street.*

(e) In **absolute** constructions:

Er stand da, **den Hut** auf dem Kopf.	*He stood there with his hat on his head.*

(f) In certain phrases:

Vielen Dank; guten Tag!	*Many thanks; good day.*

(g) After certain prepositions, see §§ 79, 82.

25. The Genitive

The genitive is used:

(a) To denote **possession:**

Das Haus **meines Vaters.**	*My father's house.*

(b) To denote **indefinite time when:**

Eines Tages besuchte er mich.	*One day he visited me.*
Des Nachts konnte er nicht schlafen.	*He could not sleep at night.*

(c) To denote **manner:**

Er fährt nur **erster Klasse.**	*He only travels first class.*

(d) With certain adjectives:

Ich bin mir **dessen** bewußt.	*I am aware of it.*
Des Wartens müde.	*Tired of waiting.*
Des Erfolgs sicher.	*Sure of success.*

(e) In certain expressions:

Ich bin **der Meinung.**	*I am of the opinion.*

(f) After certain prepositions, see § 80.

(g) After certain verbs, see § 110.

26. The Dative

The dative is used:

(a) To denote the **indirect object:**

Er gab **mir** das Buch.	*He gave me the book.*

(b) To denote **interest** or **advantage:**

Du mußt es **mir** kaufen.	*You must buy it for me.*

(c) To denote **possession:**

Ich wusch **mir** die Hände.	*I washed **my** hands.*

(d) With certain adjectives:

Seiner Mutter ähnlich.	*Like his mother.*
Mir (un)bekannt.	*(Un)familiar to me.*
Seinen Eltern dankbar.	*Grateful to his parents.*
Mir nützlich (schädlich).	*Useful (harmful) to me.*
Es ist **mir** ganz gleich.	*It is all the same to me.*
Es ist **mir** klar, daß . . .	*It is clear to me that . . .*

(e) In certain idioms:

Mir ist kalt (warm).	*I feel cold (warm).*
Mir ist, als ob . . .	*I feel (it seems to me) as if . . .*

(f) After certain prepositions, see §§ 81, 82.

(g) After certain verbs, see §§ 108, 109.

27. Apposition

(a) The noun in apposition is always in the same case as the noun to which it stands in apposition:

N. **Mein Freund, der Arzt,** kommt nicht.	*My friend the doctor is not coming.*
A. Kennst du **meinen Freund, den Arzt?**	*Do you know my friend, the doctor?*

G. Das ist das Haus **meines** **Freundes, des Arztes.**	*That is the house of my friend, the doctor.*
D. Ich sprach mit **meinem** **Freund, dem Arzt.**	*I spoke to my friend, the doctor.*

(*b*) In measurements the noun denoting the object measured is usually in apposition to (and therefore in the same case as) the noun denoting the measure (cf. § 46). " Of " is then not translated:

Ein Glas Wasser.	*A glass of water.*
Ein Glas voll Wasser.	*A glass full of water.*
Er kam mit vier Dutzend Eier**n**.	*He came with four dozen eggs.*
Ein Glas heiß**es** Wasser.	*A glass of hot water.*
Er trank ein Glas süß**en** Wein.	*He drank a glass of sweet wine.*

Note. Die Stadt Berlin.	*The town of Berlin.*
Der Monat Mai.	*The month of May.*

ADJECTIVES

28. The Predicative Adjective

The adjective used predicatively, i.e. after the verb (usually *sein, werden* or *bleiben*) is indeclinable:

    Das Papier ist **weiß**.   Der Junge ist **krank**.

29. The Attributive Adjective

(*a*) The adjective used attributively, i.e. before the noun, may be declined either weak or strong:

	Weak Declension				**Strong Declension**			
	sing.			pl.	sing.			pl.
	m.	f.	n.	m.f.n.	m.	f.	n.	m.f.n.
N.	-e	-e	-e	-en	-er	-e	-es	-e
A.	-en	-e	-e	-en	-en	-e	-es	-e
G.	-en	-en	-en	-en	-en	-er	-en	-er
D.	-en	-en	-en	-en	-em	-er	-em	-en

Notes. (1) The attributive adjective is declined **WEAK** if preceded by the definite article or any other word similarly declined. Otherwise the adjective is declined **STRONG**.

      (2) Two or more adjectives preceding the noun have each the same endings.

(*b*) The adjective is declined **weak** after:

der	*the*		solcher	*such*
dieser	*this*		jeder (sing.)	*each, every*
jener	*that*		alle (plur.)	*all*
welcher	*which*			

sing.

	m.		f.		n.	
N.	der gute	Junge	die gute	Frau	das gute	Kind
A.	den guten	Jungen	die gute	Frau	das gute	Kind
G.	des guten	Jungen	der guten	Frau	des guten	Kindes
D.	dem guten	Jungen	der guten	Frau	dem guten	Kind

pl.
m.f.n.

N.	die	guten	Jungen,	Frauen,	Kinder
A.	die	guten	Jungen,	Frauen,	Kinder
G.	der	guten	Jungen,	Frauen,	Kinder
D.	den	guten	Jungen,	Frauen,	Kindern

(*c*) The adjective is declined **strong** if it stands alone before a noun, after numbers except 1 (but no genitive), and after *ein paar* (a few, one or two):

sing.

	m.		f.		n.	
N.	guter	Wein	frische	Milch	frisches	Obst
A.	guten	Wein	frische	Milch	frisches	Obst
G.	guten	Weines	frischer	Milch	frischen	Obstes
D.	gutem	Wein	frischer	Milch	frischem	Obst

pl.
m.f.n.

reife Äpfel
reife Apfel
reifer Äpfel
reifen Äpfeln

(*d*) The adjective is declined partly **weak** and partly **strong** after:

ein	*a*		ihr	*her, its, their*
kein	*not a, no*		unser	*our*
mein	*my*		euer	*your* (pl. of *dein*)
dein	*your, thy*		Ihr	*your* (polite form)
sein	*his, its*			

sing.

	m.		f.		n.	
N.	unser	alter Dom	unsere	alte Kuh	unser	altes Rad
A.	unseren	alten Dom	unsere	alte Kuh	unser	altes Rad
G.	unseres	alten Domes	unserer	alten Kuh	unseres	alten Rades
D.	unserem	alten Dom	unserer	alten Kuh	unserem	alten Rad

pl.

m.f.n.

N.	unsere	alten	Dome,	Kühe,	Räder
A	unsere	alten	Dome,	Kühe,	Räder
G.	unserer	alten	Dome,	Kühe,	Räder
D.	unseren	alten	Domen,	Kühen,	Rädern

Note. Above the line the adjective is declined strong ; below it, weak.

(e) The adjective is declined **strong** after the following indefinite numerals (plural):

einige	*some, a few*	viele	*many*
mehrere	*several*	wenige	*few*

N.	viele	reiche	Leute
A.	viele	reiche	Leute
G.	vieler	reicher	Leute
D.	vielen	reichen	Leuten

(f) The demonstrative or possessive adjective following **alle** has the same endings as **alle.** The adjective following the demonstrative or possessive adjective is declined weak:

N.	alle	diese	(jene)	reichen Leute
A.	alle	diese	(jene)	reichen Leute
G.	aller	dieser	(jener)	reichen Leute
D.	allen	diesen	(jenen)	reichen Leuten

N.	alle	meine	schönen Bücher
A.	alle	meine	schönen Bücher
G.	aller	meiner	schönen Bücher
D.	allen	meinen	schönen Büchern

30. Some Very Common Adjectives [1]

(a)

allein, *alone*	entfernt, *distant*	lieb, *dear, beloved, kind*
alt, *old*	erfolgreich, *successful*	link, *left*
ander, *other, different*	ernst, *serious, grave*	meist, *most*
angenehm, *pleasant*	erstaunt, *surprised*	modern, *modern*
ängstlich, *anxious*	fleißig, *diligent*	müde, *tired*
arm, *poor*	froh,[2] *glad, pleased*	mutig, *brave*
aufgeregt, *excited*	ganz, *whole, entire*	nächst, *next, nearest*
bedeckt, *covered*	gelb, *grey*	nötig, *necessary*
bedeutend, *important*	glücklich, *lucky, happy*	recht, *right*
bekannt, *well-known*	grau, *grey*	reich, *rich*
bequem, *comfortable*	halb, *half*	ruhig, *quiet*
bereit, *prepared, ready*	heiß, *hot*	schlecht, *bad, wicked*
beschäftigt, *busy*	hungrig, *hungry*	schlimm, *bad*
besonder, *special*	interessant, *interesting*	schmutzig, *dirty*
braun, *brown*	jung, *young*	stolz,[2] *proud*
durstig, *thirsty*	laut, *loud*	tot, *dead*
eigen, *own*	leise, *soft, gentle*	wach, *awake*
einzig, *sole, only*	letzt, *last*	zornig, *angry*

(b) Adjectives from which feminine abstract **nouns** are formed:

(i) By adding **-e** and modifying the vowel if possible (see § 18 (c) (iii) (α)):

blaß,[4] *pale*	fremd, *strange, foreign*	kurz, *short*
blau, *blue*	frisch, *fresh*	lang, *long*
breit, *wide, broad*	früh, *early*	leer, *empty*
dicht, *thick, dense*	groß, *big, great, tall*	nah, *near*
dick, *thick, fat*	gut, *good*	naß,[4] *wet*
dünn, *thin*	hart, *hard*	reif, *ripe, mature*
eng, *narrow, tight*	hell, *bright, light*	rot,[4] *red*
fern, *distant*	hoch,[3] *high*	sauer, *sour*
fest, *firm*	kalt, *cold*	scharf, *sharp*
flach,[2] *flat, shallow*	kühl, *cool*	schnell, *fast*

[1] In German the prefix **un-** added to the adjective corresponds to the English prefixes *un-, im-, in-* and *dis-*:

unbekannt, *unknown;* unmöglich, *impossible;* unfähig, *incapable;* unehrlich, *dishonest.*

[2] Does not modify in the comparative and superlative (see § 35 (b) note).

[3] Forms the noun *Höhe* (height), and attributive adjective *hohe*, etc.

[4] With or without modification in the comparative and superlative.

schwach, *weak*   still, *still*   treu, *loyal, faithful*
schwarz, *black*   streng, *severe*   warm, *warm*
schwer, *heavy; difficult* süß, *sweet*   weiß, *white*
stark, *strong*   tief, *deep, profound*   weit, *far, wide*

(ii) By adding **-heit** (see § 18 (*c*) (iii) (β)):

berühmt, *famous*   hübsch, *pretty*   sicher, *safe, certain*
blind, *blind*   klar,[3] *clear*   trocken, *dry*
böse,[1] *bad, evil; angry* klein, *small, little*   verschieden, *different,*
dumm, *stupid*   klug, *clever, wise*   *various*
dunkel, *dark*   krank, *ill, sick*   voll,[3] *full*
einfach, *simple*   leicht, *easy; light*   vollkommen, *perfect*
einzeln,[2] *single*   neu, *new*   wahr,[3] *true*
falsch,[3] *false, wrong* offen, *open*   weich, *soft*
faul, *lazy; rotten*   rund,[3] *round*   wild, *wild*
frei, *free*   schmal,[6] *narrow*   zahm,[3] *tame*
gerade,[4] *straight*   schön, *beautiful, lovely,* zufrieden, *content,*
gesund,[5] *healthy, well*   *fine, handsome*   *satisfied*
gewiß, *certain, sure*   selten, *rare*

(iii) By adding **-keit** (see § 18 (*c*) (iii) (γ)):

ähnlich, *similar*   herrlich, *magnificent*   sauber, *clean*
aufmerksam, *attentive*   herzlich, *cordial*   schläfrig, *sleepy*
billig, *cheap*   höflich, *polite*   schrecklich, *terrible*
bitter, *bitter*   langsam, *slow*   schuldig, *guilty, due*
dankbar, *grateful*   lustig, *merry*   schwierig, *difficult*
deutlich, *clear, distinct* menschlich, *human*   sonderbar, *peculiar,*
ehrlich, *honest*   möglich, *possible*   *strange*
einsam, *lonely*   natürlich, *natural*   teuer, *dear, expensive*
fähig, *able, capable*   niedrig, *low*   traurig, *sad*
fertig, *ready, finished*   nützlich, *useful*   wahrscheinlich,
freundlich, *friendly*   öffentlich, *public*   *probable*
gefährlich, *dangerous*   ordentlich, *respect-*   wichtig, *important*
genau,[7] *accurate, exact*   *able, tidy*   wirklich, *real*
gewöhnlich, *ordinary*   plötzlich, *sudden*   wunderbar, *wonder-*
häßlich, *ugly*   richtig, *right, correct*   *ful, marvellous*

---

[1] Forms the noun *Bosheit* (malice, naughtiness).
[2] Forms the noun *Einzelheit* (detail).
[3] Does not modify in the comparative and superlative (see § 35 (*b*)
note).
[4] Omits final *-e* before adding suffix.
[5] Modifies in the comparative and superlative (see § 35 (*b*) note).
[6] With or without modification in the comparative and superlative.
[7] Forms the noun *Genauigkeit*.

31. The Adjective used as a Noun

When adjectives are used as nouns they are declined like ordinary adjectives as in § 29. They are nearly always written with a capital.

sing.

	m.			f.			n.
N.	der Alte	ein	Alter	die Alte	eine Alte	das	Neue
A.	den Alten	einen	Alten	die Alte	eine Alte	das	Neue
G.	des Alten	eines	Alten	der Alten	einer Alten	des	Neuen
D.	dem Alten	einem	Alten	der Alten	einer Alten	dem	Neuen

pl.   sing.

	m.			f.			n.
N.	die Alten	Alte		die Alten	Alte	sein	Bestes
A.	die Alten	Alte		die Alten	Alte	sein	Bestes
G.	der Alten	Alter		der Alten	Alter	seines	Besten
D.	den Alten	Alten		den Alten	Alten	seinem	Besten

The most common nouns of this type are:

der Alte	*old man*	der Kranke	*patient*
der Arbeitslose	*unemployed man*	der Reiche	*rich man*
der Arme	*poor man*	der Reisende	*traveller*
der Beamte[1]	*official*	der Verwandte	*relative*
der Bekannte	*acquaintance*	die Elektrische	*tram*
der Blinde	*blind man*	mein Lieber	*my dear chap*
der Deutsche	*German*	meine Liebe	*my dear*
der Fremde	*stranger*	sein Bestes	*his best*
der Gefangene	*prisoner*		

32. The Adjective after *etwas, viel, wenig, nichts, allerlei* and after *alles*.

After *etwas, viel, wenig, nichts* and *allerlei* the adjective is declined like a strong neuter adjective, after *alles*, like a weak neuter adjective. The adjective is, with few exceptions, written with a capital.

N.	nichts Neues (*nothing new*)	alles	Gute (*all the best*)
A.	nichts Neues	alles	Gute
G.	nichts Neuen[2]	alles	Guten
D.	nichts Neuem	allem	Guten

[1]Feminine equivalent: *die Beamtin*. Rarely used.

Er sagte viel Liebes von dir.	He said a lot of nice things about you.
Er sah sich nach etwas Neuem um.	He looked round for something new.
Allerlei Interessantes.	All sorts of interesting things.

Note. Etwas **a**nderes. *Something else.*
Etwas ganz **a**nderes. *Something quite different.*
Alles **m**ögliche. *Everything possible.*

33. Adjectives derived from Place-names

Such adjectives are formed by the addition of *-er* to the place-name, are invariable and are written with a capital.

Der Köln**er** Dom.	Cologne Cathedral.
Im Köln**er** Dom.	In Cologne Cathedral.
Die Berlin**er** Schutzleute.	The Berlin policemen.

34. Adjective in Titles

Adjectives in titles are attributive, although they follow the noun; they are declined weak and are written with a capital.

N.	Karl	der	Groß**e**	(Erste)
A.	Karl	den	Groß**en**	(Ersten)
G.	Karl**s**	des	Groß**en**	(Ersten)
D.	Karl	dem	Groß**en**	(Ersten)

35. Comparison of Adjectives

(a) Predicative.

| warm | wärmer | am wärmsten |
| breit | breiter | am breit**e**sten[1] |

Der Fluß ist breit.	The river is wide.
Dieser Fluß ist breiter.	This river is wider.
Hier ist der Fluß am breitesten.	Here the river is widest.
Im Sommer sind die Tage am wärmsten.	The days are warmest in summer.

(b) Attributive.

| der warme | der wärmere | der wärmste |
| der breite | der breitere | der breiteste |

| Das ist ein breiter Fluß. | That is a wide river. |
| Das ist ein breiterer Fluß. | That is a wider river. |

[1] Adjectives ending in -*d*, -*s*, *sch*-, *t*-, *tz*- *x*-, *z*- add -*est* in the superlative.

Das ist der breiteste Fluß.   *That is the widest river.*
Dieser Fluß ist der breiteste.   *This river is the widest (one).*
Die wärmsten Tage des Jahres   *The warmest days of the*
    sind im Juli.   *year are in July.*

Note. Adjectives of **one** syllable usually modify the vowel **a, o** or **u** (but not **au**) in the comparative and superlative. (Cf. lists, § 30, in which exceptions are indicated.)

(c) Irregular Comparisons:

groß	größer	am größten	(der größte)	*big*
gut	besser	am besten	(der beste)	*good*
hoch	höher	am höchsten	(der höchste)	*high*
nah	näher	am nächsten	(der nächste)	*near*
viel	mehr	am meisten	(das meiste)	*much, many*

(d) Examples of Comparison of Adjectives:

  (i) Er ist so alt wie ich.   *He is as old as I (am).*
      Er ist ebenso alt wie ich.   *He is just as old as I.*
      Er ist nicht so alt wie ich.   *He is not so old as I.*
      Wir sind gleich alt.   *We are both the same age.*

  (ii) Er ist älter als ich.   *He is older than I (am).*
      Er ist weniger reich als ich.   *He is less rich than I.*
      Er ist zwei Jahre älter als   *He is two years older than I.*
        ich.
      Er ist noch reicher als ich.   *He is even richer than I.*
      Er wird immer dicker.   *He is getting fatter and fatter.*
      Da er älter ist als ich, hat   *As he is older than I (am) he*
        er . . . (Word order!)   *has . . .*
      Um so besser.   *All the better.*

(iii) Er ist der klügste von allen.   *He is the cleverest of all.*
      Das schönste aller Kleider.   *The prettiest of all the dresses.*

(iv) Es ist höchst interessant.   *It is most interesting.*

Note. Ein älterer Herr.   *A fairly old (elderly) gentleman.*
      Die meiste Zeit.   *Most of the time.*
      Die meisten Leute.   *Most people.*
      Die meisten von uns.   *Most of us*
      Er ist wie ich.   *He is like me.*
      Er ist als Dichter berühmt.   *He is famous as a poet.*

ADVERBS

36. Formation of Adverbs

(a) The predicative adjective may generally be used as an adverb:

Sie singt schön.   *She sings beautifully.*

(b) Some adverbs are formed from adjectives and other parts of speech by the addition of certain endings, e.g. *-erweise*, *-lings*, *-s*, *-e*, *-ns*, *-weise*, *-wärts*, *-lang*.

glücklicherweise, *fortunately*   namens, *by name, called*
blindlings, *blindly*   teilweise, *partly*
abends, *of an evening*   vorwärts, *forwards*
lange, *for a long time*   stundenlang, *for hours*

37. Comparison of Adverbs

(a) Adverbs have the same comparison as predicative adjectives (cf. § 35 (a)). Note, however, the following irregular comparisons:

bald	früher	am frühesten	*soon*
gern	lieber	am liebsten	*willingly*
gut	besser	am besten	*well*
viel (sehr)	mehr	am meisten	*much*

(b) Adverbs have in addition an absolute superlative.

aufs wärmste   aufs beste   aufs schönste

Compare:

Sie empfing uns am herzlichsten.   *She welcomed us most cordially (of all the guests).*

Sie empfing uns aufs herzlichste.   *She welcomed us most (= exceedingly) cordially.*

(c) Notice the following forms of the superlative:

(i) erstens   *in the first place*
frühestens   *at the earliest*
meistens   *mostly*
spätestens   *at the latest*
wenigstens   *at least*

(ii) höchst amüsant   *most amusing*
äußerst klug   *exceedingly, extremely clever*
möglichst schnell (bald)   *as quickly (soon) as possible*

38. Adverbs of Time (cf. § 50)

ab und zu	now and again	nachher	after(-wards)
bald (darauf)	soon (afterwards)	neulich	the other day
bisher	hitherto, till now	nicht mehr	no longer, no more
damals	then, at that time	nie	never
dann	then, next	noch	still
eben	just	noch einmal	once again
einmal	once; some day	noch nicht	not yet
einstweilen	for the time being	nun	now, well, then, why
endlich	finally, at last		
erst	only (§ 114), not until	von nun an	henceforth, from now on
früher	formerly	oft	often
heutzutage	nowadays	schon	already
immer	always	seitdem	since then
immer wieder	again and again	sofort	immediately
je	ever	unterdessen	meanwhile
jetzt	now (§ 114)	vorher	before
lange	for a long time	wieder	again
längst	long ago, long since	zuerst	(at) first
		zugleich	at the same time
manchmal	sometimes		

39. Adverbs of Manner and Degree

anders (als)	differently (from)	kaum	scarcely, hardly
		leider	unfortunately
besonders	especially	natürlich	of course
(ebenso) wie	(just) like, as	nein	no
eigentlich	really	nicht	not
fast	almost, nearly	nicht einmal	not even
ganz	quite, right, all	nur	only (§ 114)
gar nicht	not at all	sehr	very (much)
genug	enough	so	so, such, like this, like that
gerade	just		
gewiß	certainly	sogar	even
gleich	equally	umsonst	in vain; useless
glücklicher- weise	fortunately	ungefähr	about
		vielleicht	perhaps
gut	well	ziemlich	rather, fairly
hoffentlich	I (etc.) hope so	zu	too
ja	yes		

40. Adverbs of Place

(a) Definite:

(i)

hier	Er ist hier.	*He is here.*
hierher	Kommen Sie hierher!	*Come here.*
von hier	Er geht von hier.	*He goes from here.*
dort (da)	Er ist dort.	*He is there.*
dorthin (dahin)	Er geht dorthin.	*He goes there.*
dorther (von da)	Er kommt dorther.	*He comes from there.*
draußen.	Er ist draußen.	*He is outside.*
nach draußen (hinaus)	Er geht hinaus.	*He goes outside.*
von draußen	Er kommt von draußen.	*He comes from outside.*

Likewise:

drinnen (*inside*)	nach drinnen (hinein)	von drinnen
oben (*up*(-*stairs*))	nach oben (hinauf)	von oben
unten (*down* (-*stairs*), *below*)	nach unten (hinunter)	von unten
rechts (*on the right*)	nach rechts (*to the right*)	von rechts
links (*on the left*)	nach links (*to the left*)	von links
drüben (*over there*)	nach drüben (hinüber)	von drüben

(ii) **hin** (*away from the speaker*)   **her** (*towards the speaker*)

Ich gehe hin.	*I go there.*	Er kommt her.	*He comes here.*
Ich gehe hinaus.	*I go out.*	Er kommt heraus.	*He comes out.*
Ich gehe hinein.	*I go in.*	Er kommt herein.	*He comes in.*
Ich gehe hinauf.	*I go up.*	Er kommt herauf.	*He comes up.*
Ich gehe hinunter.	*I go down.*	Er kommt herunter.	*He comes down.*
Ich gehe hinüber.	*I go across.*	Er kommt herüber.	*He comes across.*

Note also the following examples:

Ich gehe die Treppe **hinunter**.	*I go downstairs, down the stairs.*
Er kommt den Berg **herauf**.	*He comes up the mountain.*
Er ging **hin** und **her**.	*He walked to and fro.*
Er ging **in** das Haus **hinein**.	*He went into the house.*
Er sah **vor** sich (A) **hin**.	*He looked straight in front of him.*
Herein!	*Come in!*

(iii) Cf. § 95 (b)

ab	off, down	Er geht ab (goes off).
		Er steigt ab (gets down).
an	on	Er zieht an (puts on).
auf	up, open	Er steht auf (gets up).
		Er macht auf (opens).
aus	out, off	Er geht aus (goes out).
		Er zieht aus (takes off).
ein	in	Er steigt ein (gets in).
fort	away, off, on	Er geht fort (goes away, off).
		Er lebt fort (lives on).
heim	home	Er geht heim (goes home).
nieder	down	Er fällt nieder (falls down).
vor	forward	Er tritt vor (steps forward).
vorbei	past	Er geht vorbei (goes past).
zu	to, shut	Er nickt mir zu (nods to me).
		Er macht zu (shuts).
zurück	back	Er geht zurück (goes back).

Note. Bergauf. *Uphill.* Auf und ab. *Up and down.*
Bergab. *Downhill.*

(b) Indefinite:

(i) überall — *everywhere* — Sie sind überall.
überallhin — *(to) everywhere* — Sie gehen überallhin.
überallher — *from everywhere* — Sie kommen überallher.

Likewise:

irgendwo (*somewhere*) — irgendwohin — (von) irgendwoher
nirgendwo (*nowhere*) — nirgendwohin — (von) nirgendwoher
anderswo (*elsewhere*) — anderswohin — (von) anderswoher

(ii) zusammen — *together* — Wir spielen zusammen.
unterwegs — *on the way* — Er ist unterwegs, *he is on his way.*
herum — *round, about (= around)* — Er lief um den Tisch herum, *he ran round the table.*
Sie lagen überall herum, *they lay about everywhere.*
umher — *about (=hither and thither)* — Er irrte in der Stadt umher, *he wandered about the town.*

41. Interrogative Adverbs

wann	*when*	wo	*where*
wie	*how, what . . . like*	wohin	*where (to)*
wieviel	*how much, how many*	woher	*where from*
wie viele	*how many*	womit	*with what*
wie lange	*how long*	worin	*in what*
wie oft	*how often*	wovon	*about what*
warum	*why*		etc., cf. § 58 (b)

Wo bist du?	*Where are you?*
Wo gehst du hin? (Wohin gehst du?)	*Where are you going (to)?*
Wo kommst du her? (Woher kommst du?)	*Where do you come from?*
Wovon spricht er?	*What is he talking about?*
Wie heißen Sie?	*What is your name?*

Note.   Wie schön ist dás!   (Wie schön das ist!)   *How lovely it is!*

NUMERALS, DATES, ETC.

42. Cardinals

0	null	40	vierzig
1	ein(s)	43	dreiundvierzig
2	zwei	50	fünfzig
3	drei	54	vierundfünfzig
4	vier	60	**sechzig**
5	fünf	65	fünfundsechzig
6	sechs	70	**siebzig**
7	sieben	76	sechsundsiebzig
8	acht	80	achtzig
9	neun	87	siebenundachtzig
10	zehn	90	neunzig
11	elf	98	achtundneunzig
12	zwölf	100	**hundert** (= one *or* a hundred)
13	dreizehn	101	hundert(und)ein(s)
14	vierzehn	200	zweihundert
16	**sechzehn**	202	zweihundert(und)zwei
17	**siebzehn**	1 000	**tausend** (=one *or* a thousand)
20	zwanzig	1 001	tausend(und)ein(s)
21	einundzwanzig	1 100	tausendeinhundert
30	**dreißig**	1 000 000	eine Million
32	zweiunddreißig		

1 654 937 eine Million sechshundertvierundfünfzigtausendneun-
hundertsiebenunddreißig.

43. Notes on the Cardinals

(a) In counting, the forms **eins, hunderteins,** etc., are used.

(b) **Ein** preceding a noun is declined like the indefinite article (§ 12).

(c) **Ein** is not inflected in certain expressions:

Um ein Uhr.	*At one o'clock.*
Vor ein oder zwei Tagen.	*One or two days ago.*
Mit ein paar Freunden.	*With one or two friends.*

(d) **Noch** preceding a numeral means *more, another*:

Noch ein (zwei) Glas Bier.	*Another glass (two glasses) of beer.*

(e) Notice the use of **beide:**

Meine beiden Brüder.	*My two brothers.*
Welcher von beiden?	*Which of the two?*
Keiner von beiden.	*Neither (of the two).*
Wir beide.	*Both of us.*
Sie sind beide alt.	*They are both old.*

44. Ordinals

1st	der, die, das **erste**	20th	der zwanzig**ste**
2nd	der, die, das zwei**te**	21st	der einundzwanzig**ste**
3rd	der, die, das **dritte**	100th	der hundert**ste**
4th	der, die, das vier**te**	101st	der hundert**erste**
8th	der, die, das **achte**	1000th	der tausend**ste**
19th	der, die, das neunzehn**te**		

Notes. (1) The ordinal numbers are declined like ordinary adjectives (§ 29).

       (2) After names of kings, etc., they are written with capital letters, e.g. *Friedrich der Zweite.*

45. Fractions, etc.

(a)
$\frac{1}{2}$ = halb/ein halb		$1\frac{1}{2}$ = anderthalb	
$\frac{1}{3}$ = ein Drittel		$2\frac{1}{2}$ = zweieinhalb	
$\frac{1}{4}$ = ein Viertel		$3\frac{1}{2}$ = dreieinhalb	
$\frac{1}{5}$ = ein Fünftel, etc.		etc.	

Note.
Eine Viertelstunde.	*A quarter of an hour.*
Eine Viertelmeile.	*A quarter of a mile.*
Eine halbe Stunde.	*Half an hour.*
Halb Berlin, halb Deutschland.	*Half Berlin, half Germany.*
Anderthalb Stunden.	*An hour and a half.*

(b) Einmal, zweimal, dreimal, etc.   *Once, twice, three times, etc.*

(c) Einfach, zweifach, dreifach, etc.   *Onefold (simple), twofold, threefold, etc.*
Doppelt so viel.   *Double as much.*

(d) Einerlei, zweierlei, dreierlei.   *Of one, two, three kinds.*
Vielerlei Schiffe.   *Many kinds of ships.*
Allerlei Leute.   *All sorts of people.*

(e) Einzig, einzeln, einsam.   *Single, separate(ly), lonely.*
Sein einziges Kind.   *His only child.*
Sie werden einzeln verkauft.   *They are sold separately.*
Ein einsamer Mensch   *A lonely person.*

(f) Erstens, zweitens, drittens, etc.   *In the first, second, third place, etc.*

46. Measurements

Masculine and neuter nouns denoting measurements remain uninflected; feminine nouns, however, usually inflect.

Zehn Pfund.   *Ten pounds.*
Zehn Schilling.   *Ten shillings.*
Fünf Pfennig.   *Five pfennigs.*
Der Tisch ist 4 Fuß lang.   *The table is 4 feet long.*
Drei Paar Handschuhe.   *Three pairs of gloves.*
Mit drei Paar Handschuhen.   *With 3 pairs of gloves.*
Zwei Tassen Tee.   *Two cups of tea.*

But Zwanzig Mark.   *Twenty marks.*

47. Time of Day

Wieviel Uhr ist es?   } *What is the time?*
Wie spät ist es?

1.0   Es ist ein Uhr (es ist eins).
1.5   Es ist fünf Minuten nach eins.
1.15   Es ist Viertel **zwei,** Viertel nach eins.
1.30   Es ist halb **zwei.**
1.40   Es ist zwanzig Minuten vor zwei.
1.45   Es ist dreiviertel **zwei,** Viertel vor zwei.

2.0 p.m.   Es ist zwei Uhr nachmittags (nachm.).

8.0 a.m.   Es ist acht Uhr vormittags (vorm.).

12.0   Es ist Mittag (*noon*); es ist Mitternacht (*midnight*).

But 11.30   Es ist halb **zwölf.**

Um wieviel Uhr stehen Sie auf?	*At what time do you get up?*
Ich stehe um 7 (Uhr) auf.	*I get up at 7 (o'clock).*
Der Zug fährt um 14.30 ab.	*The train leaves at 2.30 p.m.*
Der Film beginnt Punkt 5 Uhr.	*The film begins punctually at 5.*
Um Mittag; um Mitternacht.	*At about noon; at about midnight.*

Notes.	(1) Die Uhr geht vor.	*The clock is fast.*
	Die Uhr geht nach.	*The clock is slow.*
	Die Uhr geht richtig.	*The clock is right.*
	(2) Ein Uhr.	*One o'clock.*
	Eine Uhr.	*A* (or *one*) *clock.*
	Eine Stunde.	*An* (or *one*) *hour.*

48. Dates, Days

Der Januar, der Februar, der März, der April, der Mai, der Juni, der Juli, der August, der September, der Oktober, der November, der Dezember.

Der Sonntag, der Montag, der Dienstag, der Mittwoch, der Donnerstag, der Freitag, der Sonnabend (*or* der Samstag).

Der wievielte ist heute?	*What is the date to-day?*
Heute ist der erste Januar.	*It is January 1st to-day.*
Am zweiten März.	*On March 2nd.*
Am Dienstag, dem 8. Mai.	*On Tuesday, May 8th.*
(Im Jahre) 1939 brach der Krieg aus.	*War broke out* **in** *1939.*
Berlin, den 2. März 1954.	*Berlin, 2/3/54* (date at beginning of letter).
Am Sonntagmorgen.	*On Sunday morning.*

49. Age

Wie alt bist du?	*What is your age?*
Ich bin vierzehn Jahre alt.	*I am fourteen years of age.*
Wann bist du geboren?	*When were you born?*
Ich bin 1940 geboren.	*I was born in 1940.*

50. Useful Expressions of Time (cf. § 38)

heute	to-day	diesen Sommer	this summer
heute morgen	this morning	acht Tage	a week
heute nach-mittag	this afternoon	vierzehn Tage	a fortnight
heute abend	to-night (before bedtime).	vor acht Tagen	a week ago
heute nacht	to-night (after bed-time)	heute in 8 Tagen	to-day week
morgen	to-morrow	heute vor 14 Tagen	a fortnight ago to-day
morgen früh	to-morrow morning	morgens	in the morning
morgen abend	to-morrow evening	vormittags	in the forenoon
gestern	yesterday	nachmittags	in the afternoon
gestern morgen	yesterday morning	abends	in the evening
		nachts	at night
gestern abend	yesterday evening, last night (before bedtime)	voriges Jahr	last year
		nächstes Jahr	next year
übermorgen	the day after to-morrow	am Donners-tag	on Thursday
		an demselben Tage	(on) the same day
vorgestern	the day before yes-terday	am nächsten Morgen	(on) the next morning
letzten Dienstag	last Tuesday	am vorigen Abend	the night (i.e. evening) before
im Frühling	in spring		

PRONOUNS

PERSONAL PRONOUNS, ETC.

51. Declension of Personal Pronouns, Possessive Adjectives and Pronouns

Pers. Pron.	Possessive Adj. (Declension, see § 29 (d))	Possessive Pronoun ((a) Declined strong (b) Declined weak))
N. ich (I)	mein, meine, mein	(a) meiner, meine, meines
A. mich	(my)	(b) der, die, das mein(ig)e
G. meiner		(mine)
D. mir		

Pers. Pron.	Possessive Adj.	Possessive Pronoun
N. du (*thou, you*)	dein, deine, dein	(*a*) deiner, deine, deines
A. dich	(*thy, your*)	(*b*) der, die, das dein(ig)e
G. deiner		(*thine*)
D. dir		
N. er (*he, it*)	sein, seine, sein	(*a*) seiner, seine, seines
A. ihn	(*his, its*)	(*b*) der, die, das sein(ig)e
G. seiner		(*his, its*)
D. ihm		
N. sie (*she, it*)	ihr, ihre, ihr	(*a*) ihrer, ihre, ihres
A. sie	(*her, its*)	(*b*) der, die, das ihr(ig)e
G. ihrer		(*her, its*)
D. ihr		
N. es (*it*)	sein, seine, sein	(*a*) seiner, seine, seines
A. es	(*its*)	(*b*) der, die, das sein(ig)e
G. seiner		(*its*)
D. ihm		
N. wir (*we*)	unser, unsere,	(*a*) unserer, unsere,
A. uns	unser	unseres
G. unser	(*our*)	(*b*) der, die, das unsr(ig)e
D. uns		(*ours*)
N. ihr (*you*)	euer, eure, euer	(*a*) eurer, euere, eures
A. euch	(*your*)	(*b*) der, die, das eur(ig)e
G. euer		(*yours*)
D. euch		
N. sie (*they*)	ihr, ihre, ihr	(*a*) ihrer, ihre, ihres
A. sie	(*their*)	(*b*) der, die, das ihr(ig)e
G. ihrer		(*theirs*)
D. ihnen		
N. Sie (*you*)	Ihr, Ihre, Ihr	(*a*) Ihrer, Ihre, Ihres
A. Sie	(*your*)	(*b*) der, die, das Ihr(ig)e
G. Ihrer		(*yours*)
D. Ihnen		

Notes.   (1) All three forms are used though the forms of type (b)—*der mein(ig)e*, etc.—are now mainly restricted to the written language.

         (2) The possessive pronoun agrees in **gender** and **number** with the noun to which it refers:

             Dein Hund ist schöner als.   *Your dog is finer than mine.*
             meiner/der mein(ig)e.

         (3) Ein Freund von mir, von uns.   *A friend of mine, of ours.*

52. Notes on the Personal Pronouns

(a) **Du** (sing.) and **ihr** (pl.) are the familiar forms of address, i.e. used in addressing relatives, close friends, children and animals. **Sie** (sing. and pl.) is the polite form of address.

Note. Du, ihr, dein, euer, etc. are always written with capitals in letters.

(b) **Er** (der Apfel) war reif; ich aß **ihn.**

It (*the apple*) *was ripe*; *I ate* **it.**

Sie (die Tinte) ist blau.   **It** (*the ink*) *is blue.*
Es (das Obst) ist reif.   **It** (*the fruit*) *is ripe.*

(c) The words **dessen** (m. and n. sing.) and **deren** (f. sing. and m.f.n. pl.) usually replace *seiner* and *ihrer*, i.e. the genitive of *er, es* and *sie*, when **things** are referred to.

    Ich schäme mich **seiner.**   *I am ashamed* **of him.**
But Er schämt sich **dessen.**   *He is ashamed* **of it.**

(d) With most prepositions **da-** (**dar-** before a vowel) is usually used instead of the accusative and dative of the personal pronoun when referring to **things.** Compare:

    Er interessiert sich **für ihn.** *He is interested* **in him.**
    Er interessiert sich **dafür.** *He is interested* **in it, in that, in them** (= things).

Note. Such compounds are not possible with the prepositions außer, außerhalb, entlang, gegenüber, ohne and seit.

(e) Note the following uses of **es:**

Es regnet, es schneit.	*It is raining, it is snowing.*
Ich bin es; war er es?	*It is I; was it he?*
Es war einmal ein König.	*There was once* (*upon a time*) *a king.*
Es gibt viel zu tun.	*There is a lot to do.*
Was gibt's?	*What's the matter?*
Es gibt **einen** Gott. (A)	*There is* (= *exists*) *a God.*
Es ist **kein** Mensch da. (N)	*There is nobody there.*
But Kein Mensch ist da.	
Es sind keine Menschen da.	*There are no people there.*
But Da keine Menschen da sind,	*As no people are there . . .*

53. Reflexive Pronouns

	sing.	pl.	Polite Form (sing. and pl.)

1st Person:

   A. mich (*myself*)   uns (*ourselves*)
   D. mir   uns

2nd Person:

   A. dich (*yourself*)   euch (*yourselves*) sich (*yourself, yourselves*)
   D. dir   euch   sich

3rd Person:

   A. sich (*him-, her-,* sich (*themselves*)
   D. sich *it-self*)   sich

Ich wasche mich.	*I wash myself.*
Ich wasche mir die Hände.	*I wash my hands.*
Ich sah unter mir das Meer.	*I saw the sea beneath me.*
Er sah unter **sich** das Meer.	*He saw the sea beneath him.*

54. Reciprocal Pronouns

Wir lieben uns.	*We love one another.*
Sie kennen sich.	*They know one another.*
Sie sprechen miteinander.	*They speak to one another.*
Sie schieden voneinander.	*They separated from one another.*

INTERROGATIVE ADJECTIVES AND PRONOUNS

55. Welcher, welche, welches

	sing.		pl.
	m.	f.	n.	m.f.n.
N.	welcher	welche	welches	welche
A.	welchen	welche	welches	welche
G.	welches	welcher	welches	welcher
D.	welchem	welcher	welchem	welchen

Welches Gedicht ist das beste?	*Which poem is the best?*
Von welcher Frau sprechen Sie?	*Which woman are you speaking of?*

Note. Welch ein guter Mann!   *What a good man!*

56. Was für (ein) (adj.)

Declined like the indefinite article (§ 12), *ein* being omitted in the plural.

Was für ein Mann ist er?	*What sort of a man is he?*
Was für Männer sind das?	*What sort of men are those?*
Mit was für einem Bleistift?	*With what sort of a pencil?*

Note. Was für schlechtes Wetter!   *What bad weather!*
        Was für schöne Bilder!   *What lovely pictures!*

57. Wer, was

m.f.	n.
N. wer	was
A. wen	was (durch was, wodurch)
G. wessen	wessen
D. wem	— (womit, woran, etc.)

Wer ist da? Was ist das?	*Who is there? What is that?*
Wen liebt er?	*Whom does he love?*
Wessen Hund ist das?	*Whose dog is that?*
Wem schreibst du?	*To whom are you writing?*
Woran denkst du?	*What are you thinking of?*
Womit schreiben Sie?	*What are you writing with?*

RELATIVE PRONOUNS AND ADVERBS

58. Der, die, das (welcher, welche, welches)

	sing.		pl.
m.	f.	n.	m.f.n.
N. der (welcher)	die (welche)	das (welches)	die (welche)
A. den (welchen)	die (welche)	das (welches)	die (welche)
G. dessen	deren	dessen	deren
D. dem (welchem)	der (welcher)	dem (welchem)	denen
			(welchen)

(a)   (i) The relative pronoun agrees with its antecedent in **gender** and **number** but its case depends on the part it plays in its own clause.

      (ii) The finite verb has **final** position in a relative clause.

    (iii) The relative must **never** be omitted in German.

    (iv) **Welcher,** etc., is rarely used in spoken German.

Die Frau, **die** vor mir stand,   *The woman who stood in*
war alt.   *front of me was old.*

Der Mann, **den** ich vor mir sah, war jung.	*The man I saw in front of me was young.*
Das Mädchen, **dessen** Vater krank war, mußte schwer arbeiten.	*The girl whose father was ill had to work hard.*
Die Leute, **denen** wir geholfen haben, sind dankbar.	*The people we helped are grateful.*
Die Kinder, mit **denen** wir spielten, waren sehr jung.	*The children we were playing with were very young.*
Die Jungen, mit **deren** Lehrer ich sprach, arbeiteten fleißig.	*The boys with whose master I spoke were working hard.*

(*b*) The forms compounded with **wo(r)-** and a preposition are used with indefinite antecedents, but never when the antecedent is a person or animal and rarely now when it is a thing.

Das einzige, **wovon** er sprach, . . .	*of which he spoke*
Der Tisch, **an dem** (*rather than* woran) er saß, . . .	*at which he sat*

59. Was

The relative pronoun is **was** when its antecedent is:

(*a*) A singular indefinite pronoun :

Das ist alles, **was** ich weiß.	*That is all I know.*

(*b*) A superlative adjective or equivalent used as a neuter noun :

Das Beste, **was** er tun kann, . . .	*The best thing he can do . . .*

(*c*) A whole clause:

Er arbeitet nicht, **was** ich nicht verstehe.	*He does not work, a fact which I don't understand.*

(*d*) Equivalent to **that which:**

Tue (das), **was** du kannst.	*Do what (= that which) you can.*
Trotz dessen, **was** er sagt.	*In spite of what he says.*

60. Wer

Declension: see § 57.

Wer sucht, der findet.	*He who seeks shall find.*

61. Wo

Die Stadt, **wo** ich jetzt wohne, *The town where (in which) I*
. . .   *now live* . . .
Überall, **wo** man hingeht, . . .   *Wherever one goes* . . .

DEMONSTRATIVE ADJECTIVES AND PRONOUNS

62. Dieser, jener

Declined like *welcher* (§ 55).

Dieses Buch kostet mehr als jenes   *This book costs more than that*
(= das dort).   *one.*
K. und H. sind Brüder; **dieser**   *K. and H. are brothers;* **the**
ist groß, **jener** ist klein.   **latter** *is tall,* **the former**
                                                        is short.

63. Solcher

Declined like *welcher* (§ 55), except when preceded by *ein*, when
it is declined as in § 29 (*d*). It is uninflected when followed by
ein, and may remain uninflected when followed by an adjective:

Ich habe solchen Hunger.   *I am so hungry.*
Ich habe solche Schmerzen.   *I have such pain(s).*
Ein solcher Mensch.⎫
Solch ein Mensch. ⎭   *Such a man.*
Solch junge Menschen. ⎫
Solche jungen Menschen.⎭   *Such young people.*

64. Der, die, das

Declension: see § 58, but note that the genitive pl. is **derer**
when followed by a **relative pronoun.** (Cf. also § 52 (*c*).)

War es **der** Mann?—Nein, nicht   *Was it* **that** *man? No, not*
der.   **that one.**
Die kenne ich nicht.   *I don't know* **her.**
Er schämt sich dessen, was er   *He is ashamed of what he has*
gemacht hat.   *done.*
Der, der das sagt, lügt.   *He who says that lies.*
Viele **derer, die** . . .   *Many of those who* . . .
Unter denen, die . . .   *Amongst those who* . . .
Ihr Hut ist schöner als der ihrer   *Her hat is prettier than her*
Freundin.   *friend's.*

Note. **Das (dies)** ist mein Buch   *That (this) is my book.*
        Das (dies) sind meine Bücher.   *Those (these) are my books.*

65. Derselbe, dieselbe, dasselbe

	sing.		pl.
	m.	f.	n.	m.f.n.
N.	derselbe	dieselbe	dasselbe	dieselben
A.	denselben	dieselbe	dasselbe	dieselben
G.	desselben	derselben	desselben	derselben
D.	demselben	derselben	demselben	denselben

Sie hatte denselben Hut auf.	*She had the same hat on.*
An demselben Tage.	*(On) the same day.*
Das ist dasselbe.	*That is the same thing.*

66. Derjenige, diejenige, dasjenige

	sing.		pl.
	m.	f.	n.	m.f.n.
N.	derjenige	diejenige	dasjenige	diejenigen
A.	denjenigen	diejenige	dasjenige	diejenigen
G.	desjenigen	derjenigen	desjenigen	derjenigen
D.	demjenigen	derjenigen	demjenigen	denjenigen

Derjenige, der . . .	*He who . . .*
Diejenige, die . . .	*She who . . .*
Diejenigen Leute, die . . .	*Those people who . . .*
Mit allen denjenigen, deren . . .	*With all those whose . . .*

67. Selbst

Indeclinable.

Ich selbst, wir selbst.	*I myself, we ourselves.*
Gott selbst.	*God Himself.*
Von selbst.	*Of its own accord.*

INDEFINITE ADJECTIVES AND PRONOUNS

68. Man

Man ißt.	*One eats, you eat, people eat.*
Man sagt, daß . . .	*It is said (they say) that . . .*
Man klopft, klingelt.	*There is a knock, a ring.*

69. Einer, eine, ein(e)s

Declined like *welcher* (§ 55).

Eine(r) von euch hat es getan.	*One (f. or m.) of you has done it.*

Eines der Bücher.	*One* (n.) *of the books.*
Ich zeigte es einem von euch.	*I showed it to one* (m.) *of you.*
Irgendeiner.	*Someone or other.*

Notes.   (1) *Einer*, etc., agrees in gender with the noun for which it stands.

           (2) **One** is not translated when it occurs after an adjective :

Das ist das schönste.	*That is the finest* **one.**
Ein großer und zwei kleine.	*A* big **one** *and two small* **ones.**

70. **Keiner, keine, kein(e)s**

Declined like *welcher* (§ 55).

Keiner will es ihm sagen.	*Nobody will tell him.*
Keines der Bücher.	*None of the books.*

Note. Keiner, etc., agrees in gender with the noun for which it stands.

71. **Jemand**

Jemand ist gekommen.	*Somebody has come.*
Kennen Sie jemand, der . . .?	*Do you know anybody who . . .?*
Das muß jemand(e)s Hut sein.	*This must be somebody's hat.*
Er spricht mit jemand, der . . .	*He speaks to somebody who . . .*
Irgend jemand.	*Somebody or other.*
Sonst (noch) jemand.	*Anyone else* (*i.e. in addition*).

72. **Niemand**

Niemand hat Sie gesehen.	*Nobody saw you.*
Ich habe niemand gesehen.	*I haven't seen anybody.*
Das ist niemand(e)s Sache.	*That is nobody's business.*
Das gehört niemand.	*That belongs to nobody.*
Niemand sonst ist gekommen.	*Nobody else came.*

73. **Jeder**

Declined like *welcher* (§ 55).   There is no plural.

Jeder junge Mann weiß das.	*Every young man knows that.*
Er sitzt jeden Tag zu Hause.	*He stays at home every day.*
Jeder, der es weiß.	*Everybody who knows it.*
Das ist jedem bekannt.	*That is known to everybody.*

74. **Alles, alle**

Declined like *welcher* (§ 55), but usually contracted to *all* before the definite article, the demonstrative and possessive adjective.

Alles ist umsonst.	*Everything is in vain.*
Das alles war sehr traurig.	*All that was very sad.*
Er kann alles tun.	*He can do anything.*
Sonst alles.	*Anything else (otherwise).*
All mein Geld.	*All my money.*
Alles in allem.	*Taking all in all.*
Mit aller Kraft.	*With all one's strength.*
Trotz **all** dieser Arbeit.	*Despite all this work.*
Alle waren eingeladen.	*All were invited.*
All die Gäste kamen.⎫	
Alle Gäste kamen. ⎬	*All the guests came.*
Sie alle.	*All of you.*
Wir waren alle da.	*We were all there.*
Alle waren da.	*Everybody was there.*

75. **Etwas, was**

Indeclinable.

Ich will dir (et)was sagen.	*I will tell you something.*
Etwas Neues.	*Something new.*
So etwas ist unmöglich.	*That sort of thing is impossible.*
Etwas anderes.	*Something else.*
Irgend etwas.	*Something or other.*

76. **Nichts**

Indeclinable.

Er macht nichts.	*He doesn't do anything.*
Gar nichts.	*Nothing at all.*
Sonst nichts.	*Nothing else.*

77. **Welcher, welche, welches**

Declension, see § 55.

Er hat keinen **Tee;** gib ihm welch**en**!	*He hasn't any tea; give him some.*
Er hat keine **Blumen;** hast du welch**e**?	*He hasn't any flowers; have you any?*

Note. Welcher, etc., agrees in gender and number with the noun for which it stands.

78. Indefinite Numeral Adjectives and Pronouns

Those in group (*a*) are indeclinable; those in group (*b*) are all plural and declined like *welcher* (§ 55) ; and those in group (*c*) are declined weak or like *welcher* (§ 55) or not at all.

(*a*) **Etwas** Zucker, **genug** Wasser. *Some sugar, enough water.*
    Mehr Tee, **weniger** Milch. *More tea, less milk.*
    Ein bißchen Brot, **ein paar** *A little bread, one or two*
    Leute. *people.*

(*b*) **Viele** Leute, **mehrere** Leute. *Many people, several people.*
    (Nur) **wenige** Leute, **einige** *(Only a) few people, a few*
    Leute. *(some) people.*

(*c*) Den **ganzen** Monat. *The whole of the month.*
    Ganz Deutschland. *The whole of Germany.*
    Ich nehme nur **wenig** *I only take a little sugar.*
    Zucker.
    Ich nahm (**zu**) **viel** Milch. *I took (too) much milk.*
    Viel Vergnügen. *Much (a lot of) pleasure.*
But **Vielen** Dank. *Many thanks.*

(*d*) **Die einen . . . die anderen.** *Some . . . others.*

PREPOSITIONS

79. Prepositions governing the Accusative

bis, *till, as far as, by, to*   gegen, *against, towards, compared to*
durch, *through, by*
entlang, *along*   ohne, *without*
für, *for*   um, *round, at, for*

Notes. (1) Durchs = durch das; fürs = für das; ums = um das.
      (2) *Entlang* follows the noun it governs.

(*a*) **bis:**
    Er bleibt bis Ostern. *He is staying till Easter.*
    Er fuhr bis Berlin. *He went as far as Berlin.*

(*b*) **durch:**
    Er ging durchs Zimmer. *He went through the room.*
    Er wurde durch Gift getötet. *He was killed by poison.*

(*c*) **entlang:**
    Er ging die Straße entlang. *He walked along the street.*

(d) **für:**

| Er tat es für mich. | *He did it for me.* |

(e) **gegen:**

Er tat es gegen meinen Willen.	*He did it against my will.*
Gegen Ende des Monats.	*Towards the end of the month.*
Gegen Osten.	*Towards the east.*
Gegen 4 Uhr.	*About 4 o'clock.*

(f) **ohne:**

| Ich bin ganz ohne Mittel. | *I am entirely without any means.* |

(g) **um:**

Wir saßen um den Tisch.	*We were sitting round the table.*
Er ging um die Stadt herum.	*He went right round the town.*
Um 4 Uhr.	*At four o'clock.*

80. Prepositions governing the Genitive

(an)statt, *instead of*
außerhalb, *outside*
inmitten, *in the midst of*
innerhalb, *inside, within*
jenseits, *beyond*

trotz, *in spite of*
um . . . willen, *for the sake of*
während, *during*
wegen, *because of*

(An)statt des Weins.	*Instead of the wine.*
Inmitten dieser Leute.	*In the midst of these people.*
Innerhalb der Stadt.	*Inside the town.*
Trotz des schönen Wetters.	*In spite of the fine weather.*
Um Gottes willen.	*For Heaven's sake.*
Wegen des schlechten Wetters.	*Because of the bad weather.*

81. Prepositions governing the Dative

aus, *out of, from*
außer, *except (for), besides*
bei, *at, near, with*
entgegen, *towards*
gegenüber, *opposite*
mit, *with*

nach, *to(-wards), after, according to*
seit, *since*
von, *from, of, by (agent in passive)*
zu, *to*

Notes. (1) Beim = bei dem; vom = von dem; zum = zu dem; zur = zu der.

(2) *Entgegen* and *gegenüber* follow the nouns they govern, as does *nach* usually when it means " according to ".

(a) **aus:**

Er lief aus dem Hause.	*He ran out of the house.*
Aus Holz, Eisen (gemacht).	*(Made) of wood, iron.*
Aus welchem Grunde?	*For what reason?*
Ich weiß es aus Erfahrung.	*I know it from experience.*

(b) **außer:**

Außer dir habe ich niemand.	*I have nobody but (except) you.*

(c) **bei:**

Er wohnt bei seinem Onkel.	*He lives at his uncle's (with his uncle).*
Bei meiner Ankunft.	*On my arrival.*
Er hat kein Geld bei sich.	*He has no money on him.*
Bei schlechtem Wetter.	*In bad weather.*

(d) **entgegen:**

Er kam mir entgegen.	*He was coming towards me.*

(e) **gegenüber:**

Er wohnt dem Bahnhof gegenüber.	*He lives opposite the station.*

(f) **mit:**

Er kam mit seinem Vater.	*He came with his father.*
Mit dem Auto, mit dem Schiff.	*By car, by boat.*
Mit leiser, lauter Stimme.	*In a quiet, loud voice.*
Mit zehn Jahren.	*At the age of ten.*

(g) **nach:**

Nach der Stadt, nach Paris.	*To the town, to Paris.*
Nach Süden, nach England.	*To the south, to England.*
Er geht nach Hause.	*He is going home.*
Nach der Stunde.	*After the lesson.*
Meiner Meinung nach.	*In my opinion.*
In der Richtung nach London.	*In the direction of London.*
Der Reihe nach.	*In turn.*

(h) **seit:**

Seit dem Krieg habe ich ihn nicht gesehen.	*Since the war I haven't seen him.*
Seit 2 Jahren lerne ich Deutsch.	*I have been learning German for 2 years (cf. § 89 (b)).*

(*i*) **von:**

Der Zug kommt von Berlin.	*The train comes from Berlin.*
Die Königin von England.	*The Queen of England.*
Ein Bild von Dürer.	*A picture of Dürer.*
Von mir geschlagen.	*Beaten by me.*
Es war keine Spur von ihm zu sehen.	*There was no sign of him.*

(*j*) **zu:**

Er geht zum Bahnhof.	*He goes to the station.*
Er geht zur Schule, zur Kirche.	*He goes to school, to church.*
Er geht zum Arzt.	*He goes to the doctor's.*
Er geht zu Bett.	*He goes to bed.*
Er bleibt, ist zu Hause.	*He stays, is at home.*
Zu Fuß, zu Pferde.	*On foot, on horseback.*
Zu Mittag, zu Abend essen.	*To have lunch, dinner.*
Zu Weihnachten, zu Ostern.	*At Christmas, at Easter.*
Nötig zur Reise.	*Necessary for the journey.*
Zur Arbeit bereit.	*Ready for work.*

82. Prepositions governing the Accusative or Dative

(*a*) After the following nine prepositions the **accusative** is used to show movement **to** a place, the **dative** to show rest or movement **at** a place.

an, *on, at, to, by*	über, *over, across*
auf, *on (horizontal surface only)*	unter, *under, among*
hinter, *behind*	vor, *in front of, before*
in, *in, into*	zwischen, *between*
neben, *near, next to, beside*	

Note. Ans = an das; am = an dem; aufs = auf das; ins = in das; im = in dem; übers = über das; überm = über dem; vors = vor das; vorm = vor dem.

Er setzte sich an **den** Tisch.	*He sat down at the table.*
Er saß an **dem** Tisch.	*He was sitting at the table.*
Er setzt sich auf **den** Stuhl.	*He sits down on the chair.*
Er saß auf **dem** Stuhl.	*He was sitting on the chair.*
Er stellte sich hinter **mich.**	*He came and stood behind me.*
Er stand hinter **mir.**	*He was standing behind me.*

Er trat in **das** Zimmer.	*He came into the room.*
Er arbeitete in **dem** Zimmer.	*He was working in the room.*
Er ging **im** Zimmer auf und ab.	*He walked up and down (in) the room.*
Er setzte sich neben **mich.**	*He sat down beside me.*
Er saß neben **mir.**	*He was sitting beside me.*
Er hängt das Bild über **das** Sofa.	*He hangs the picture over the sofa.*
Das Bild hängt über **dem** Sofa.	*The picture hangs over the sofa.*
Er sank unter **den** Tisch.	*He sank down under the table.*
Er lag unter **dem** Tisch.	*He was lying under the table.*
Er legte es vor **mich** hin.	*He put it down in front of me.*
Es lag vor **mir.**	*It lay in front of me.*
Er setzt sich zwischen **sie** und **mich.**	*He sits down between her and me.*
Er saß zwischen **ihr** und **mir.**	*He was sitting between her and me.*

(b) Idiomatic expressions involving these prepositions:

(i) **an + accusative:**

Wir fahren ans Meer.	*We are going to the seaside.*
Es ist ein Brief an Sie da.	*There is a letter for you here.*
Er setzte sich ans Feuer.	*He sat down by the fire.*

(ii) **an + dative:**

Am Meer, am Strand.	*At the seaside, on the beach.*
Die Reihe ist an ihm.	*It is his turn.*
Er saß am Feuer.	*He was sitting by the fire.*
Am Tage, am Morgen.	*In the day-time, in (on) the morning(s).*
Am Nachmittag.	*In the afternoon.*
Am Abend.	*In the evening, at night.*
Am Tage vor, nach seiner Ankunft.	*The day before, after his arrival.*
Er kommt einmal am Tage.	*He comes once a day.*
An Ihrer Stelle.	*In your place, if I were you.*
Die Sterne am Himmel.	*The stars in the sky.*
Er hat keinen Mangel an Mut.	*He has no lack of courage.*
Er zitterte an allen Gliedern.	*He was trembling in every limb.*

(iii) **auf + accusative:**

Er ging auf die Post, die Bank.	*He went to the post, to the bank.*
Er ging auf den Markt.	*He went to the market.*
Eine Antwort auf die Frage.	*An answer to the question.*
Er fuhr aufs Land.	*He went into the country.*
Auf diese Weise.	*In this way.*
Auf jeden Fall (auf alle Fälle).	*In any case, anyhow.*
Sage es auf deutsch!	*Say it in German.*
Ich bin stolz auf ihn.	*I am proud of him.*
Auf Wiedersehen!	*Good-bye!*

(iv) **auf + dative:**

Er war auf dem Markt.	*He was in (at) the market.*
Er war auf der Straße.	*He was in the street.*
Er ist auf dem Bahnhof.	*He is at the station.*
Er wohnt auf dem Lande.	*He lives in the country.*
Auf dem Bild sehen wir . . .	*In the picture we see . . .*
Wann waren Sie auf der Schule?	*When were you at school?*

(v) **in + accusative:**

Er fuhr in die Schweiz.	*He went to Switzerland.*
Er kam in die Nähe.	*He came near.*
Er ging ins Freie.	*He went into the open.*
Er reiste ins Ausland.	*He went abroad.*
Er ging ins Theater, ins Kino.	*He went to the theatre, cinema.*
Er ging ins Büro.	*He went to the office.*

(vi) **in + dative:**

Er wohnt ganz in der Nähe.	*He lives quite near.*
Wir sind jetzt im Freien.	*We are now in the open.*
Die Leute im Ausland.	*People abroad.*
Er lernt nichts in der Schule.	*He learns nothing at school.*
In der Nacht.	*At night (after bed-time).*
In **dem** Augenblick.	*At that moment.*
In dem Fall.	*In that case.*
50 km in der Stunde.	*50 km. an hour.*
Er verdient 800 DM im Monat.	*He earns 800 marks a month.*
Einmal in der Woche.	*Once a week.*
Im Gegenteil.	*On the contrary.*
Im Radio.	*On the wireless/radio.*

(vii) **über + accusative:**

Er fuhr über Ostende nach B.   *He went to B. via Ostend.*
Er ist über 90 Jahre alt.   *He is over 90 years old.*
Ich bin erstaunt darüber.   *I am surprised at it (this).*

(viii) **unter + dative:**

Unter den Leuten.   *Among the people.*
Unter anderm.   *Among other things.*
Unter seiner Regierung.   *In his reign.*

(ix) **vor + dative:**

Vor vielen Jahren.   *Many years ago.*
Vor allem (vor allen Dingen).   *Above all.*
Vor Freude, Schmerz.   *For (with) joy, pain.*

VERBS

83. **Conjugation of the Auxiliary Verbs:** *haben, sein* **and**
    werden.

Infinitive

haben (*to have*)   sein (*to be*)   werden (*to become*)

Participles

Present	habend	seiend	werdend
Past	gehabt	gewesen	geworden

Imperative

2nd Sing.	habe!	sei!	werde!
2nd Plur.	habt!	seid!	werdet!
Polite form	haben Sie!	seien Sie!	werden Sie!

Present

	Ind.	Subj.	Ind.	Subj.	Ind.	Subj.
ich	habe	habe	bin	sei	werde	werde
du	hast	habest	bist	seiest	wirst	werdest
er, sie, es	hat	habe[1]	ist	sei	wird	werde[1]
wir	haben	haben	sind	seien	werden	werden
ihr	habt	habet	seid	seiet	werdet	werdet
sie (Sie)	haben	haben	sind	seien	werden	werden

[1] Only the third person singular is now used.

Imperfect

	Ind.	Subj.	Ind.	Subj.	Ind.	Subj.
ich	hatte	hätte	war	wäre	wurde	würde
du	hattest	hättest	warst	wärest	wurdest	würdest
er, sie, es	hatte	hätte	war	wäre	wurde	würde
wir	hatten	hätten	waren	wären	wurden	würden
ihr	hattet	hättet	waret	wäret	wurdet	würdet
sie (Sie)	hatten	hätten	waren	wären	wurden	würden

Perfect

Ind.	Subj.
ich habe gehabt, bin gewesen, bin geworden, etc.	er habe gehabt, sei gewesen, sei geworden, etc.

Pluperfect

ich hatte gehabt, war gewesen, war geworden, etc.	ich hätte gehabt, wäre gewesen, wäre geworden, etc.

Future

ich werde haben, werde sein, werde werden, etc.	er werde haben, werde sein, werde werden, etc.

Future Perfect

Ich werde gehabt haben, werde gewesen, sein, werde geworden sein, etc.	er werde gehabt haben, werde gewesen sein, werde geworden sein, etc.

Conditional

ich würde haben, würde sein, würde werden, etc.

Conditional Perfect (replaced often by Plpf. Subj.)

ich würde gehabt haben, würde gewesen sein, würde geworden sein, etc.

84. **Notes on** *haben, sein* **and** *werden.*

(a) **Haben** is used to form the perfect tenses of **all transitive** and **reflexive** verbs and modal auxiliaries, and of those intransitive verbs which do **not** describe a change of place or state.

Ich habe es gekauft.   *I have bought it.*
Ich hatte mich gesetzt.   *I had sat down.*

Er hat gemußt.   *He has had to.*
Er hat kommen müssen.   *He has had to come.*
Es hat geregnet.   *It has rained.*
Er hat mir gedient.   *He has served me.*

(*b*) **Sein** is used to form the perfect tenses of those **intransitive** verbs which **do** describe a change of place or state.

Er **ist** gegangen.   *He has gone.*
Er **war** eingeschlafen.   *He had fallen asleep.*

Note. Common exceptions to the rule are: **bleiben** (*stay*); **sein** (*be*); **geschehen** (*happen*); **gelingen** (*succeed*). These are all conjugated with **sein**.

(*c*) **Werden** is used with the **infinitive** of verbs to form the **future** tenses, and with the **past participle** of verbs to form the **passive voice**. (Cf. § 103.)

Er wird tragen.   *He will carry.* (Future)
Er **würde** tragen.   *He would carry.* (Conditional)

Er wird getragen.   *He is being carried.* (Pres. passive)
Er **wurde** getragen.   *He was carried.* (Impf. passive)

85. Conjugation of Regular Verbs

	WEAK		STRONG	
Infinitive	sag-**en** (*to say*)		trag-**en** (*to carry*)	
Participles				
Present	sag-**end**		trag-**end**	
Past	**ge**-sag-**t**		**ge**-trag-**en**	
Imperative				
2nd Sing.	sag-**e**!		trag-**e**!	
2nd Plur.	sag-**t**!		trag-**t**!	
Polite form	sag-**en** Sie!		trag-**en** Sie!	

Present

	Ind.	Subj.	Ind.	Subj.
ich	sag-**e**	sag-**e**	trag-**e**	trag-**e**
du	sag-**st**	sag-**est**	träg-**st**	trag-**est**
er, sie, es	sag-**t**	sag-**e**[1]	träg-**t**	trag-**e**[1]
wir	sag-**en**	sag-**en**	trag-**en**	trag-**en**
ihr	sag-**t**	sag-**et**	trag-**t**	trag-**et**
sie (Sie)	sag-**en**	sag-**en**	trag-**en**	trag-**en**

[1] Only the third person singular is now used.

	WEAK		STRONG	

Imperfect

	Ind.	Subj.	Ind.	Subj.
ich	sag-**te**	sag-**te**	trug	trüg-**e**
du	sag-**test**	sag-**test**	trug-**st**	trüg-**est**
er, sie, es	sag-**te**	sag-**te**	trug	trüg-**e**
wir	sag-**ten**	sag-**ten**	trug-**en**	trüg-**en**
ihr	sag-**tet**	sag-**tet**	trug-**t**	trüg-**et**
sie (Sie)	sag-**ten**	sag-**ten**	trug-**en**	trüg-**en**

Perfect

Ind.	Subj.[1]	Ind.	Subj.[1]
ich habe gesagt	habe gesagt	habe getragen	habe getragen
du hast gesagt	habest gesagt	hast getragen	habest getragen
etc.	etc.	etc.	etc.

Pluperfect

Ind.	Subj.	Ind.	Subj.
ich hatte gesagt	hätte gesagt	hatte getragen	hätte getragen
etc.	etc.	etc.	etc.

Future

Ind.	Subj.[1]	Ind.	Subj.[1]
ich werde sagen	werde sagen	werde tragen	werde tragen
du wirst sagen	werdest sagen	wirst tragen	werdest tragen
etc.	etc.	etc.	etc.

Future Perfect

Ind.	Subj.[1]	Ind.	Subj.[1]
ich werde gesagt haben, etc.	werde gesagt haben, etc.	werde getragen haben, etc.	werde getragen haben, etc.

Conditional

ich	würde sagen etc.	würde tragen etc.

Conditional Perfect (replaced often by Plpf. Subj.)

ich	würde gesagt haben, etc.	würde getragen haben, etc.

[1] Only the third person singular is now used.

86. Notes on the Conjugation of Verbs

(a) STRONG verbs (see §§ 88 and 115) change their stem vowel, and the past participle ends in **-en.**

  tragen: trägt   trug   getrag-**en.**

(b) In **regular** strong verbs, if the infinitive has as its stem vowel **a, e, o,** or **au,** these usually change in the 2nd and 3rd pers. sing. pres. ind. to **ä, i** or **ie, ö,** and **äu** respectively.

  tragen: trägt;   geben; gibt;   lesen: liest;
  stoßen: stößt;   laufen: läuft.

(c) WEAK verbs (see § 87) do not change their stem vowel, and the past participle ends in **-t:**

  sagen: sagt   sagte   gesag-**t.**

(d) Verbs ending in **-ern** and **-eln** (all weak) are conjugated in the pres. ind. as follows:

  ich zitt-(e)re   wir zitt-ern   ich samm-(e)le   wir samm-eln
  du zitt-erst   ihr zitt-ert   du samm-elst   ihr samm-elt
  er zitt-ert   sie zitt-ern   er samm-elt   sie samm-eln

(e) Verbs whose stem ends in **-t** or **-d, -chn, -ckn, -dn, -fn, -gn** or **-tm** retain the **e** of the 1st pers. sing. pres. throughout the conjugation:

  wartest; badet; rechnete; ordnet; öffnetet; geregnet.

(f) Verbs ending in **-ieren** and **-eien** (all weak) and verbs compounded with inseparable prefixes (see § 95 (a)) have no **ge-** in the past participle:

  er hat studiert; sie hat prophezeit; wir haben versucht.

(g) The impf. subj. of weak verbs is the same as the impf. ind.

(h) A few verbs—**brennen** (*burn*), **bringen** (*bring*), **denken** (*think*), **kennen** (*know*), **nennen** (*name*), **rennen** (*run*), **senden** (*send*), **wenden** (*turn*), and their compounds—are of mixed conjugation, i.e. though the stem vowel changes the past participle ends in **-t:**

  brennen: brennt   brann-**te**   gebrann-**t.**

(i) There are very few irregular verbs (weak and strong). The most common of these are shown in § 88 (l) and others are given in the list of strong verbs (§ 115).

87. Some Very Common Weak Verbs

(a)

amüsieren, *amuse*
arbeiten, *work*
baden, *bathe*
bauen, *build*
blicken, *glance, look*
blühen, *bloom, flourish*
borgen, *borrow; lend*
brauchen, *need, want*
enden, *end*
fürchten, *fear*
glauben, *believe*
grüßen, *greet*
heiraten, *marry*
holen, *fetch, get*
hören, *hear; listen*
interessieren, *interest*

kämpfen, *fight*
kaufen, *buy*
*klettern, *climb*
klopfen, *knock*
kochen, *cook, boil*
kosten, *cost*
lächeln, *smile*
lachen, *laugh*
leben, *live*
legen, *lay, put*
lernen, *learn*
machen, *make, do*
nähen, *sew*
rauchen, *smoke*
reparieren, *mend*
schütteln, *shake*

setzen, *set, put*
spielen, *play*
stecken, *set, put*
studieren, *study*
tanzen, *dance*
töten, *kill*
träumen, *dream*
wagen, *dare, venture*
wählen, *choose*
warten, *to wait*
wecken, *wake up*
(*tr.*)
weinen, *weep*
wissen, *know* (§ 115)
zählen, *count*
zittern, *tremble*

(b) Verbs from which feminine **nouns** are derived by the omission of the last letter of the infinitive (see § 18 (c) (v) (α)):

dauern, *last*
decken, *lay* (*table*)
*eilen, *hurry*
fragen, *ask, question*
füllen, *fill*

klingeln, *ring*
lieben, *love, like*
pflanzen, *plant*
regeln, *regulate, settle*
*reisen, *travel*

ruhen, *rest*
stellen, *place, put*
stimmen, *be correct*
strafen, *punish*
suchen, *seek, look for*

(c) Verbs from which feminine **nouns** are derived by the addition of -ung to the stem (see § 18 (c) (v) (β)):

ändern, *alter, change*
bilden, *form, cultivate*
 (*mind*)
fühlen, *feel*
führen, *lead*
handeln,[1] *act;*
 bargain
hoffen,[2] *hope*
meinen, *opine, say*

öffnen, *open*
ordnen, *put in order*
packen, *seize; pack*
prüfen, *examine*
rechnen, *count*
regieren, *govern*
retten, *save, rescue*
richten, *judge; direct*
sammeln,[1] *collect*

stören, *disturb*
teilen, *share, divide*
üben, *practise*
*wandern, *wander, hike*
wirken, *effect*
wohnen, *dwell, live*
zahlen, *pay* (*for*)
zeichnen, *draw*
zögern, *hesitate*

[1] The ' e ' of the stem is omitted before -ung is added.
[2] Adds -nung to the stem.

88. Some Very Common Strong Verbs

(a) Group I (**ie—o—o**, e.g. (b**ie**gt, b**o**g, geb**o**gen):

(*)biegen, *bend, turn*   gießen, *pour*   schließen, *shut, con-*
(*)fliegen, *fly*   riechen, *smell*   *clude*
(*)fliehen, *flee, shun*   schieben, *shove, push*   wiegen, *weigh (intr.)*
 *fließen, *flow*   schießen, *shoot*   (*)ziehen,[1] *pull, move*
(*)frieren, *be cold,*
     freeze

(b) Group II (a) (**ei—i—i**, e.g. b**ei**ßt, b**i**ß, geb**i**ssen):

beißen, *bite*   leiden,[1] *suffer*   (*)reiten,[1] *ride (horse)*
gleichen, *resemble*   pfeifen,[1] *whistle*   schneiden,[1] *cut*
greifen,[1] *seize, grab*   (*)reißen, *tear*

(c) Group II (b) (**ei—ie—ie**, e.g. bl**ei**bt, bl**ie**b, gebl**ie**ben):

 *bleiben, *remain*   scheinen, *seem; shine*   (*)treiben, *drive, do;*
  leihen, *lend*   schreiben, *write*   *drift*
  reiben, *rub*   schreien, *shout*
(*)scheiden, *part;*   schweigen, *be silent*
     separate   *steigen, *rise, climb*

(d) Group III (a) (**i—a—o**, e.g. br**i**cht, br**a**ch, gebr**o**chen):

  beginnen, *begin*   helfen, *help*   stechen, *sting, stab*
(*)brechen, *break*   nehmen,[1] *take*   *sterben, *die*
  gelten,[1] *be worth,*   (*)schwimmen, *swim*   treffen,[1] *hit; meet*
     valid   sprechen, *speak*   werfen, *throw*

(e) Group III (b) (**ie—a—o**, e.g. st**ie**hlt, st**a**hl, gest**o**hlen):

befehlen, *order*   stehlen, *steal.*

(f) Group IV (**i—a—u**, e.g. b**i**ndet, b**a**nd, geb**u**nden):

binden, *bind, tie*   *sinken, *sink*   trinken, *drink*
finden, *find*   *springen, *jump*   zwingen, *compel*
singen, *sing*

(g) Group V (a) (**i—a—e**, e.g. g**i**bt, g**a**b, geg**e**ben):

bitten,[1] *ask, request*   geben, *give*   (*)treten,[1] *step, walk;*
essen,[1] *eat*   messen, *measure*   *tread*
fressen, *eat (of animals)*

[1] Somewhat irregular, see § 115.

(*h*) Group V (*b*) (**ie—a—e,** e.g. liest, las, gelesen):
*geschehen, *happen*   liegen, *lie*   sehen, *see*
lesen, *read*

(*i*) Group VI (*a*) (**ä—i—a,** e.g. fängt, fing, gefangen):
fangen, *catch, capture*   hängen, *hang (intr.)*

(*j*) Group VI (*b*) (**ä—ie—a,** e.g. hält, hielt, gehalten):
blasen, *blow*   lassen, *let, leave*   schlafen, *sleep*
*fallen, *fall*   *laufen, *run*
halten, *hold, stop*   raten,[1] *advise*

(*k*) Group VII (**ä—u—a,** e.g. fährt, fuhr, gefahren):
(*)fahren, *ride, drive,*   laden, *load, invite*   *wachsen, *grow*
      go   schlagen, *strike, beat*   waschen, *wash*
   graben, *dig*   tragen, *carry, bear, wear*

(*l*) Group VIII (Irregular, see § 115):
*gehen, *go, walk*   *kommen, *come*   stehen, *stand*
heben, *lift, raise*   rufen, *call, shout*   tun, *do*
heißen, *be called, bid*   sitzen, *sit*

NOTES ON THE TENSES

89. The Present

(*a*) Ich schreibe jeden Tag einen   *I* **write** *a letter every day.*
     Brief.
     Ich schreibe jetzt einen Brief.   *I* **am writing** *a letter now.*

(*b*) The present with *seit* or *schon* expresses what has been going
     on and is still going on:
        Er **wohnt** seit zwei Jahren   *He* **has been living** *here*
        hier.   *for two years.*
        Er **wartet** schon lange (seit   *He* **has been waiting** *for*
        langem) auf Sie.   *you for a long time now.*

(*c*) The present is often used to express a single future action
     especially when the idea of futurity is already indicated by
     an adverb or by the sense:
        Morgen reise ich nach Deutsch-   *I am going to Germany to-*
        land.   *morrow.*

---

[1] Somewhat irregular, see § 115.

90. The Imperfect

(a) Er schrieb jeden Tag einen Brief.   *He* **wrote** (**used to, would write**) *a letter every day.*

Er schrieb einen Brief, als ...   *He* **was writing** *a letter when* ...

(b) The imperfect is the tense of narrative:

Er setzte sich an den Tisch, nahm eine Feder in die Hand und schrieb ein paar Seiten.

He sat down at the table, took a pen in his hand and wrote a few pages.

(c) The imperfect with *seit* or *schon* expresses what had been going on and was still going on:

Er **wohnte** seit zwei Jahren (schon zwei Jahre) dort.   *He* **had been living** *there for two years.*

Seit wann **wartete** er auf mich?   *How long* **had** *he* **been waiting** *for me?*

91. The Perfect

(a) The perfect is used for isolated acts in the past.

Sie haben uns geschlagen.   *They beat us.*

Er hat es mir gesagt.   *He told me so.*

Sind Sie je in Berlin gewesen?   *Have you ever been to Berlin?*

(b) The perfect expresses what took place before an event in the present or future:

Nachdem ich gegessen habe, lese ich die Zeitung.   *After I have eaten I read the paper.*

92. The Pluperfect

The pluperfect expresses what took place before a past event:

Nachdem ich gegessen hatte, las ich die Zeitung.   *After I had eaten I read the paper.*

93. The Future

(a) The future is used of an action that is to take place at some time yet to come (cf. however, § 89 (c)):

Er wird arbeiten müssen.   *He will have to work.*

(*b*) The future is often used to indicate probability:

Er wird schon da sein.   *I expect he is there already.*

Note. When **will** expresses determination or desire the present of **wollen** is used:

Er will nicht kommen.   He **won't** (= *refuses to*) *come.*
Wollen Sie kommen?   **Will** *you come?*

94. The Conditional (Future in the Past):

(*a*) The future in the past is used of an action that was to take place at some future time:

Ich wußte, daß er kommen würde.   *I knew he would come.*

(*b*) The conditional is used in the main clause of a conditional sentence (cf. § 106 (*b*)):

Ich würde es machen, wenn . . .   *I should do it if . . .*

Note. When **would** expresses determination, the imperfect of **wollen** is used:

Er wollte nicht kommen.   He **would** not (= *refused to*) *come.*

95. Compound Verbs [1]

(*a*) INSEPARABLE verbs are compounded with the prefixes **be-, emp-, ent-, er-, miß-, ver-** and **zer-**. These prefixes are **never** stressed.

Er besucht uns nicht. (*Present*)   *He doesn't visit us.*
Er besuchte uns nicht. (*Imperfect*)   *He didn't visit us.*
Er hat uns nicht **besucht.** (*Perfect*)   *He hasn't visited us.*
Er wünscht uns zu besuchen.   *He wishes to visit us.*
  (*Infinitive with* zu)
Obgleich er uns nicht besucht,   *Although he doesn't visit*
  . . . (*Subordinate clause*)   *us . . .*

Note. There is **no** *ge-* in the past participle.

WEAK	STRONG (see § 115)
bedeuten, *mean, signify*	beginnen, *begin*
begleiten, *accompany*	bekommen, *get, obtain, receive*
bemerken, *notice, remark*	beschließen, *decide, resolve*
bereiten, *prepare*	besitzen, *possess*

[1] Cf. § 18 (*c*) (v) (*β*).

WEAK	STRONG (see § 115)
bestellen, *order (e.g. food)*	besteigen, *climb, mount, board*
besuchen, *visit*	empfangen, *receive, welcome*
bewegen, *move (tr.)*	enthalten, *contain*
entschuldigen, *excuse, pardon*	erhalten, *get, receive; preserve*
entwickeln, *develop, evolve (tr.)*	*erscheinen, *appear*
erkennen, *recognize (§ 86 (h))*	*erschrecken, *be frightened*
erreichen, *reach, catch (train)*	genießen, *enjoy*
erschrecken, *frighten*	gewinnen, *win, gain*
*erwachen, *awake, wake up (intr.)*	verbergen, *conceal*
erwarten, *expect*	verbinden, *connect, unite*
gebrauchen, *use*	(*)verderben, *spoil, go bad*
verbringen, *spend (time) (§ 86 (h))*	*vergehen, *pass, elapse*
verdienen, *deserve, earn*	vergessen, *forget*
verhindern, *prevent*	verlassen, *leave, forsake, quit*
verkaufen, *sell*	verlieren, *lose*
verlangen, *ask, want, demand*	vermeiden, *avoid*
verpassen, *miss, lose (train)*	*verschwinden, *disappear*
versuchen, *try, attempt; tempt*	verstehen, *understand*
zerstören, *destroy*	(*)zerbrechen, *smash, break*

(b) SEPARABLE verbs are compounded with the following
prefixes (cf. § 40 (a) (iii)): **ab-, an-, auf-, aus-, bei-,
daher-, dahin-, dar-, ein-, empor-, entgegen-,
entzwei-, fort-, her-** and **hin-** and their compounds (see
§ 40 (a) (ii)), **inne-, los-, mit-, nach-, nieder-, statt-,
teil-, vor-, voran-, voraus-, vorbei-, vorüber-, weg-,
zu-, zurück-** and **zusammen-.** These prefixes, unlike
the inseparable ones, all have an independent meaning
and are **always** stressed.

Er macht die Tür **zu.** (*Present*)   *He shuts the door.*
Er machte die Tür **zu.** (*Imperfect*)   *He shut the door.*
Er hat die Tür **zu**gemacht. (*Perfect*)   *He has shut the door.*
Er versuchte, die Tür **zuzu**machen.   *He tried to shut the door.*
(*Infinite with zu*).
Als er die Tür **zu**machte, . . .   *When he shut the door . . .*
(*Subordinate clause*).

Notes. (1) *Ge-* is retained in the past participle.
      (2) *Zu* is inserted between the prefix and the verb.
      (3) The prefix rejoins its verb in subordinate clauses in the
          present and imperfect.

WEAK	STRONG (see § 115)
abholen, *fetch, meet*	*abfahren, *set off, start*
ablehnen, *decline, refuse*	anfangen, *begin*
*abreisen, *leave* (*intr.*), *set off*	*ankommen, *arrive*
andrehen, *turn on* (*e.g. light*)	annehmen, *accept; suppose*
anzünden, *light, kindle*	anziehen, *put on* (*clothes*)
aufhören, *cease, stop*	aufgeben, *give up; post*
aufmachen, *open* (*tr.*)	*aufgehen, *rise* (*sun*); *open* (*intr.*)
aufsetzen, *put on* (*hat*)	*aufstehen, *get up, stand up*
ausdrücken, *express*	ausgeben, *spend* (*money*)
ausführen, *carry out, execute*	*ausgehen, *go out*
einholen, *catch up* (*with*)	*aussteigen, *get out, get off*
einstecken, *pocket; post*	ausziehen, *take off* (*clothes*)
fortsetzen, *continue* (*tr.*)	einladen, *invite*
hinzufügen, *add*	*einschlafen, *fall asleep, go to sleep*
niederlegen, *lay down*	*einsteigen, *get in, get on*
vorbereiten, *prepare* (*in advance*)	(*)fortfahren, *drive away; continue*
zuhören, *listen*	(*intr.*)
zumachen, *shut*	stattfinden, *take place*
*zurückkehren, *return* (*intr.*)	*vorkommen, *happen*
	vorlesen, *read aloud*
	vorschlagen, *suggest*
	vorziehen, *prefer*

(*c*) Verbs with the prefixes **durch-, hinter-, über-, um-, unter-, voll-, wider-** and **wieder-** may be either SEPAR-ABLE or INSEPARABLE or, usually with different meanings, both.

Er setzte ihn über.	*He ferried him across.*
Er übersetzte das Buch.	*He translated the book.*

Notes. (1) Verbs compounded with these prefixes are usually separ-able if they can be translated literally.

(2) When separable the prefix is stressed; when inseparable the stem of the verb is stressed.

SEPARABLE	INSEPARABLE
(i) WEAK	
(*)über-setzen, *ferry across; jump across*	übersetzen, *translate*
	überraschen, *surprise*
	überreden, *persuade*
	überzeugen, *convince*

SEPARABLE	INSEPARABLE
*um-kehren, turn (back)	
	umarmen, embrace
	untersuchen, investigate, examine
wieder-holen, fetch (bring) back, retrieve	wiederholen, repeat
(ii) STRONG (see § 115)	
*über-fahren, pass over (intr.)	überfahren, run over (s.b.)
	übertreiben, exaggerate
*um-steigen, change (trains, etc.)	
*um-ziehen, move (residence)	
	umgeben, surround
unter-halten, hold (s.th.) under	unterhalten, entertain, maintain, keep going (s.th.)
	unterbrechen, interrupt
	unterscheiden, distinguish
*unter-gehen, set (of sun), sink	

96. Reflexive Verbs

Pres.	ich	wasche	mich	wasche	mir	die Hände
	du	wäschst	dich	wäschst	dir	die Hände
	er, sie, es	wäscht	sich	wäscht	sich	die Hände
	wir	waschen	uns	waschen	uns	die Hände
	ihr	wascht	euch	wascht	euch	die Hände
	sie (Sie)	waschen	sich	waschen	sich	die Hände
	(I wash myself, etc.)			(I wash my (lit. to myself the) hands, etc.)		

Impf.	ich	wusch	mich	wusch	mir	die Hände

Pf.   ich **habe** mich gewaschen | ich **habe** mir die Hände gewaschen

Fut.   ich werde mich waschen | ich werde mir die Hände waschen

Imper.   wasch(e) dich! | wasch(e) dir die Hände!
      wascht euch! | wascht euch die Hände!
      waschen Sie sich! | waschen Sie sich die Hände!

97. Some Common Reflexive Verbs (cf. also §§ 108-112)

WEAK	STRONG (see § 115)
sich amüsieren, *enjoy o.s.*	sich anziehen, *dress (intr.)*
sich ändern, *change, alter (intr.)*	sich aufhalten, *stay, sojourn*
sich begegnen, *meet (intr., fig.)*	sich ausziehen, *undress (intr.)*
sich bewegen, *move (intr.)*	sich befinden, *be (situated), feel*
sich erholen, *recover (health)*	sich benehmen, *behave*
sich erkälten, *catch cold*	sich entschließen, *resolve*
sich fragen, *wonder*	sich schließen, *shut, close (intr.)*
sich fühlen, *feel*	sich treffen, *meet (intr.)*
sich niederlegen, *lie down*	sich um-ziehen, *change (clothes)*
sich öffnen, *open (intr.)*	sich unterhalten, *converse*
sich setzen, *sit down*	sich verbergen, *hide (intr.)*
sich um-wenden, *turn round*	sich waschen, *wash (intr.)*
(§ 86 (h))	

98. Impersonal Verbs

(a)

blitzen, *lighten*	frieren, *freeze*
dämmern, *dawn, grow dark*	regnen, *rain*
donnern, *thunder*	schneien, *snow*

    Es regnet heute.   *It is raining to-day.*

(b) Verbs used impersonally:

Es freut mich, daß . . .	*I am glad that . . .*
Es geht (nicht).	*It will (won't) do.*
Wie geht's Ihnen?	*How are you?*
Es geht mir gut, schlecht.	*I am well, unwell.*
Es gelingt mir, das zu tun.	*I succeed in doing it.*
Es schadet nichts.	*It does not matter.*
Es tut mir leid.	*I am sorry.*

Note. **Er** tut mir leid.   *I am sorry for* **him.**

99. The Infinitive with and without *zu*

(a) The simple infinitive stands after *werden* and the modal auxiliaries (cf. § 102):

Er wird schreiben.	*He is going to write.*
Er will kommen.	*He wants to come.*

(b) The simple infinitive stands after *sehen, hören* and *lassen:*

Ich sah ihn kommen.	*I saw him come.*
Ich hörte ihn sprechen.	*I heard him speak.*
Ich lasse ihn sprechen.	*I let him talk.*

(c) After most other verbs and verbal expressions the dependent infinitive must be immediately preceded by **zu**:

Er wünschte zu gehen. *He wished to go.*

Er hat die Absicht, morgen zu kommen. *He intends to come to-morrow.*

(d) To express purpose **um . . . zu** with the infinitive is required:

Er kam, um mich zu sehen. *He came (in order) to see me.*

(e) Note the use of **um . . . zu** with the infinitive after *genug* or *zu* followed by an adjective:

Er ist alt genug, um das zu wissen. *He is old enough to know that.*

Er ist zu alt, um noch zu lernen. *He is too old to learn.*

100. The Imperative

(a) The 2nd person singular of the imperative of most verbs is either the stem alone or with **-e** added:

sag(e)!   mach(e)!   lauf(e)!   geh(e)!

(b) Those strong verbs that change the **e** of the stem to **ie** or **i** in the 2nd and 3rd person singular present form the 2nd person singular of the imperative by dropping the ending **-(s)t** from the 2nd person singular present:

du gibst > gib!   du nimmst > nimm!   du liest > lies!

(c) The 2nd person plural of the imperative of **all** strong and weak verbs corresponds to the 2nd person plural of the present indicative, but there is **no** pronoun:

sagt!   lauft!   gebt!   nehmt!

(d) The polite form (cf. § 52 (a)) of the imperative is simply an inversion of the corresponding person of the present subjunctive; there is no hyphen:

sagen Sie!   laufen Sie!   geben Sie!

(e) The 1st person plural of the imperative is expressed in any one of the following ways:

Gehen wir!
Wir wollen gehen!
Laß (laßt, *or* lassen Sie) uns gehen! } *Let us go.*

(*f*) For the imperative of *haben*, *sein* and *werden*, see § 83.

For the imperative of reflexive verbs, see § 96.

For the passive imperative, see § 103 (*a*).

For the imperative of the 3rd person singular and plural, see § 107 (*a*).

For position of *nicht* in the negative imperative, see § 5 (*c*) (i)

Note. The imperative is usually followed by an exclamation mark.

101. The Interrogative

In questions **not** introduced by an interrogative adverb (§ 41) or interrogative pronoun (or adjective) (§§ 55-57) the interrogative is shown by inversion of the verb and subject **and** by the question mark:

Siehst du ihn?	*Do you see him?*
Hast du ihn nicht gesehen?	*Haven't you seen him?*
Wollen wir ins Theater gehen?	*Shall we go to the theatre?*
Kommen Sie?	*Are you coming?*

Note the form of the question with **ja/nicht wahr** and **doch:**

Du hast ihn gesehen, ja/nicht wahr?	*You've seen him,* **haven't you?**
Du kennst ihn, ja/nicht wahr?	*You know him,* **don't you?**
Du bist müde, ja/nicht wahr?	*You are tired,* **aren't you?**
Du wirst kommen, nicht wahr?	*You will come,* **won't you?**
Er hat es doch nicht gemacht?	*He didn't do it,* **did he?**
—Doch.	**Yes, he did.**

102. Auxiliary Verbs of Mood and *lassen*

(*a*) Conjugation:

Pres. Ind.	**dürfen**	**können**	**mögen**	**müssen**	**sollen**	**wollen**
ich	darf	kann	mag	muß	soll	will
du	darfst	kannst	magst	mußt	sollst	willst
er, sie, es	darf	kann	mag	muß	soll	will
wir	dürfen	können	mögen	müssen	sollen	wollen
ihr	dürft	könnt	mögt	müßt	sollt	wollt
sie (Sie)	dürfen	können	mögen	müssen	sollen	wollen

Pres. Subj.

ich	dürfe	könne	möge	müsse	solle	wolle

Impf. Ind.

| ich | durfte | konnte | mochte | mußte | sollte | wollte |

Impf. Subj.

| ich | dürfte | könnte | möchte | müßte | sollte | wollte |

Pf. Ind.

| ich habe | gedurft | gekonnt | gemocht | gemußt | gesollt | gewollt |

Plpf. Ind.

| ich hatte | gedurft | gekonnt | gemocht | gemußt | gesollt | gewollt |

Plpf. Subj.

| ich hätte | gedurft | gekonnt | gemocht | gemußt | gesollt | gewollt |

Fut

| ich werde | dürfen | können | mögen | müssen | sollen | wollen |

Note. The modal auxiliaries and *lassen* have two past participles: preceded by the infinitive of another verb, **dürfen** is used for **gedurft, können** for **gekonnt, lassen** for **gelassen,** etc.

| Ich habe nicht kommen **können.** | *I have not been able to come.* |
| Er hatte es fallen **lassen.** | *He had let it fall (dropped it).* |

(b) Examples of use:

(i) **dürfen:**

Er darf es tun.	*He may, is allowed to, do it.*
Er darf es nicht tun.	*He must not do it.*
Er durfte es tun.	*He was allowed to do it.*
Er dürfte es tun.	*He would be allowed to do it.*
Er hat (hatte) es tun dürfen.	*He has (had) been allowed to do it.*
Er hat es gedurft.	*He has been allowed to.*
Er hätte es (nicht) tun dürfen.	*He would (not) have been allowed to do it.*
Er wird es tun dürfen.	*He will be allowed to do it.*

(ii) **können:**

Er kann es tun.	*He may, can do it.*
Er konnte es tun.	*He could (=was able to) do it.*
Er könnte es tun.	*He might, could (= would be able to) do it.*

Er hat (hatte) es tun können.	*He has (had) been able to do it.*
Er hat es gekonnt.	*He has been able to.*
Er hätte es (nicht) tun können.	*He might, could (not) have done it (= would (not) have been able to do it).*
Er wird (würde) es tun können.	*He will (would) be able to do it.*
Er hofft es tun zu können.	*He hopes to be able to do it.*
Das kann sein.	*That may be.*
Er kann nichts dafür.	*He cannot help it.*
Er kann es getan haben.	*He may have done it.*

(iii) **mögen:**

Er mag es (tun).	*He likes it (he may possibly do it).*
Er mag es nicht (tun).	*He does not like (doing) it.*
Er mochte es nicht (tun).	*He did not like (doing) it.*
Er möchte es (tun).	*He would like (to do) it.*
Er hat es nicht tun mögen.	*He did not like to do it.*
Er hat es gemocht.	*He has liked it.*
Er hätte es (nicht) tun mögen.	*He would (not) have liked to do it.*
Er wird es tun mögen.	*He will like to do it.*

(iv) **müssen:**

Er muß es tun.	*He must, has to, do it, cannot help doing it.*
Er muß es nicht tun.	*He does not have to do it.*
Er mußte es tun.	*He had to do it.*
Er müßte es tun.	*He would have to do it.*
Er hat (hatte) es tun müssen.	*He has (had) had to do it.*
Er hat es gemußt.	*He has had to.*
Er hätte es (nicht) tun müssen.	*He would (not) have had to do it.*
Er wird (würde) es tun müssen.	*He will (would) have to do it.*
Er muß (mußte) lachen.	*He cannot (could not) help laughing.*
Er muß es getan haben.	*He must have done it.*

(v) sollen:

Er soll es tun.	*He is, is said, to do it.*
Er sollte (ind.) es tun.	*He was, was destined, was said, was due, to do it.*
Er sollte (subj.) es tun.	*He should, ought to, do it.*
Er hat (hatte) es tun sollen.	*He has (had) been called upon to do it.*
Er hätte es (nicht) tun sollen.	*He ought, should (not) have done it.*
Er wird es tun sollen.	*He will be called upon to do it.*
Er soll(te) reich sein.	*He is (was) supposed to be rich.*
Du sollst nicht stehlen.	*Thou shalt not steal.*
Er wußte nicht, was er tun sollte.	*He did not know what to do.*

(vi) wollen:

Er will es tun.	*He will do it, intends to do it.*
Er wollte es tun.	*He wanted, intended to, do it.*
Er wollte es nicht tun.	*He would not, refused to, do it.*
Er hat (hatte) es tun wollen.	*He has (had) been willing to do it.*
Er hätte es (nicht) tun wollen.	*He would (not) have been willing to do it.*
Er wird es tun wollen.	*He will want to do it.*
Er würde es tun wollen.	*He would be willing to do it.*
Wollen Sie bitte warten?	*Will you please wait?*
Wollen wir ins Theater gehen?	*Shall we go to the theatre?*
Wir wollen gehen!	*Let us go.*
Wir wollen eben ausgehen.	*We are just about to go out.*
Wir wollten eben sprechen.	*We were just going to speak.*
Er will, daß ich es tue.	*He wants me to do it.*

(vii) lassen[1]:

Er läßt mich das machen.	*He lets me do that.*
Er läßt mich warten.	*He keeps me waiting.*
Er ließ den Arzt kommen.	*He sent for the doctor.*
Er ließ es fallen.	*He dropped it (let it fall).*
Ich habe mir die Haare schneiden lassen.	*I have had my hair cut.*
Er läßt herzlich grüßen.	*He sends his kindest regards.*

[1] *Lassen*, though not an auxiliary verb of mood, tends to be used like one.

103. **Passive Voice**

(a) Conjugation (subjunctive forms given in brackets):

Pres.	Es wird (werde) getragen.	*It is (= is being) carried.*
Impf.	Es wurde (würde) getragen.	*It was (=was being) carried.*
Pf.	Es **ist** (sei) getragen **worden.**	*It has been carried.*
Plpf.	Es **war** (wäre) getragen **worden.**	*It had been carried.*
Fut.	Es wird (werde) getragen werden.	*It will be carried.*
Cond.	Es würde getragen werden.	*It would be carried.*
Fut. Pf.	Es wird (werde) getragen **worden sein.**	*It will have been carried.*
Pf. Cond.	Es würde getragen **worden sein.**	*It would have been carried.*
Imper.	**Sei** gegrüßt!¹	*Greetings!*

(b) With a **modal** verb:

Es muß gemacht werden.	*It must be done.*
Es mußte gemacht werden.	*It had to be done.*
Es müßte gemacht werden.	*It would have to be done.*
Es hat gemacht werden müssen.	*It has had to be done.*
Es hätte gemacht werden müssen.	*It would have had to be done.*
Es wird gemacht werden müssen.	*It will have to be done.*
Es hätte gemacht werden sollen (können).	*It should (could, might) have been done.*

(c) All **transitive** verbs (except reflexives) can be used **passively.** The direct object of the active verb becomes the subject of the passive verb; the subject of the active verb becomes the agent:

Er tötete den Löwen.	*He killed the lion.*
Der Löwe wurde von ihm getötet.	*The lion was killed by him.*

(d) The **agent** is expressed by:

   (i) **von** + dative, if animate or actively responsible for the action.

   (ii) **durch** + accusative, if inanimate, particularly when not **actively** responsible for the action.

¹ The passive imperative is limited to one or two verbs.

Er wurde **von** seiner Mutter geweckt.　*He was woken up by his mother.*

Er wurde **durch** den Lärm geweckt.　*He was woken up by the noise.*

(e) The **instrument** is expressed by **mit** + dative:

Der Brief wurde von ihm **mit** diesem Bleistift geschrieben.　*The letter was written by him with this pencil.*

(f) The **infinitive** in German often has **passive** meaning:

Es war niemand zu sehen.　*There was nobody to be seen.*

Nichts war zu machen.　*There was nothing to be done.*

(g) If the auxiliary **sein** is used instead of **werden** a state, not an action, is expressed. The past participle then has adjectival force:

Der Tisch **ist** (**war**) gedeckt.　*The table **is** (**was**) laid. (= state.)*

Der Tisch **wird** (**wurde**) gedeckt.　*The table **is** (**was**) **being** laid. (= action.)*

(h) When a verb has two objects, one dative and the other accusative, the dative object **remains** in the dative case in the passive construction, while the accusative object becomes the subject of the passive construction:

Man gab mir einen Bleistift.　*They gave me a pencil.*

Mir wurde **ein** Bleistift gegeben.　**I** *was given a pencil.*

(i) With verbs governing the **dative** or followed by a **preposition** it is simpler to use an active construction with *man*:

Man hat ihm nicht geholfen.　*He has not been helped.*

Man hat nicht an ihn gedacht.　*He has not been thought of.*

THE SUBJUNCTIVE

104. Formation of the Subjunctive

(a) The **endings** of the present and imperfect subjunctive are the same for **all** verbs (except *sein*, see § 83):

-e, -est, -e, -en, -et, -en

(b) The **present subjunctive**[1] is formed by adding these endings to the stem of the verb:

er **sag-e**   wir **sei-en**   ich **könn-e**

(c) The **imperfect subjunctive** of **weak verbs** is, with few exceptions (see (e) below) the same as the imperfect indicative:

er **mach-te**   du **wart-etest**   sie **sag-ten.**

(d) The **imperfect subjunctive** of **strong verbs** is formed by adding the subjunctive endings to the first person singular imperfect indicative; the vowel is modified if possible:

trug: trüg-e; gab: gäb-e; schlief: schlief-e.

(e) **Irregular** forms of the imperfect subjunctive:

befehlen	beföhle[2]	rennen	rennte
beginnen	begönne[2]	schwimmen	schwömme[2]
brennen	brennte	senden	sendete
bringen	brächte	stehen	stünde[2]
denken	dächte	sterben	stürbe
empfehlen	empföhle[2]	verderben	verdürbe
helfen	hülfe[2]	wenden	wendete
kennen	kennte	werfen	würfe
nennen	nennte	wissen	wüßte

105. The Subjunctive in Indirect Speech

In turning direct speech—statements and questions—into indirect speech the following changes in the mood and tense of the verbs take place:

Direct Speech		Indirect Speech
Present Indicative	becomes	Present Subjunctive
Imperfect Indicative ⎫ Perfect Indicative ⎬ Pluperfect Indicative ⎭	(= Past) become	Perfect Subjunctive
Future Indicative ⎫ Conditional ⎭	(= Future) become	Future Subjunctive

[1] Except with very few verbs, only the 3rd person singular is now used.
[2] Has also the regular form.

(*a*) **Statements:**

Direct Speech	Indirect Speech
Er sagte zu mir:	Er sagte mir,
„ Ich **bin** krank."	daß er krank **sei.**
„ Ich **war** beim Arzt."	daß er beim Arzt **gewesen sei.**
„ Ich **werde** bald **abreisen**."	daß er bald **abreisen werde.**

Notes. (1) If in indirect speech the present, perfect or future subjunctive are indistinguishable from the corresponding indicative tenses, the imperfect subjunctive, pluperfect subjunctive or conditional must be used instead:

> Er sagte mir, daß sie nicht **arbeiteten** (*not* arbeiten).
> Er sagte mir, daß sie uns nicht gesehen **hätten** (*not* haben).
> Er sagte mir, daß sie morgen kommen **würden** (*not* werden).

(2) If *daß* is omitted the finite verb is the **second** idea in the dependent clause:

> Er sagte mir, er **werde** bald abreisen.

(3) The indicative is generally used after verbs like *wissen* and *erfahren* which imply greater certainty:

> Wir wußten, daß er gekommen **war.**

(*b*) **Questions:**

If in the direct question there is an interrogative adjective, adverb or pronoun (e.g. *welcher, wann, wer*) this is retained in the indirect question. If there is no such interrogative word, **ob** (*whether, if*) must introduce the indirect question:

Direct Speech	Indirect Speech
Er fragte ihn:	Er fragte ihn,
„ **Sind** Sie Herr Schmidt? "	ob er Herr Schmidt **sei.**
„ Wann **sind** Sie **gekommen?** "	wann er **gekommen sei.**
„ Wie lange **werden** Sie **bleiben?** "	wie lange er **bleiben werde.**

(*c*) **Commands:**

The present subjunctive of **sollen** is used to render indirect commands (but see § 105 (*a*), note 1):

Direct Speech	Indirect Speech
Er sagte zu ihm:	Er sagte ihm:
„Stehen Sie auf!"	daß er aufstehen **solle.**
	(*He told him to get up.*)

106. The Subjunctive in Conditional Sentences

(*a*) In the present and future the **indicative** is used in both clauses:

Er **hilft** mir, / Er **wird** mir **helfen,** } wenn er **kann.** *He helps (will help) me if he can.*

(*b*) In the first past tense the **conditional** is normally used in the main clause and the **imperfect subjunctive** in the subordinate clause:

Er **würde** mir **helfen,** wenn er **könnte.** *He would help me if he could.*

(*c*) In the second past tense the **pluperfect subjunctive** is normally used in both clauses:

Er **hätte** mir **geholfen,** wenn er **gekonnt hätte.** *He would have helped me if he had been able to.*

(*d*) When the *wenn*-clause precedes the main clause the word *so* or *dann* is often inserted between the two clauses:

Wenn er kann, (so/dann) hilft er mir.
Wenn er könnte, (so/dann) würde er mir helfen.
Wenn er gekonnt hätte, (so/dann) hätte er mir geholfen.

107. Other Uses of the Subjunctive

(*a*) To express the imperative 3rd person singular and plural:

Es lebe die Königin! *Long live the Queen!*
Er komme sofort. *Let him come at once.*

(b) In clauses dependent on *als ob*:

Er sieht aus, als ob er krank wäre.   *He looks as if he is ill.*

Er sah aus, als ob er krank wäre.   *He looked as if he were ill.*

Er tat (so), als ob er nicht verstanden hätte.   *He pretended he had not understood.*

Note. If *ob* is omitted, the verb immediately follows *als*:
Er sieht aus, als **wäre** er krank.

GOVERNMENT OF VERBS

108. Verbs Governing the Dative

WEAK	STRONG (see § 115)
antworten, *answer (s.b.)*	gefallen, *please, like*
*begegnen, *meet*	*gelingen, *succeed* (§ 98)
danken, *thank*	*geschehen, *happen*
dienen, *serve*	gleichen, *resemble*
(*)folgen, *follow; obey*	helfen, *help*
gehorchen, *obey*	leid tun, *be sorry (for)* (§ 98)
gehören, *belong to (s.b.)*	*vorkommen, *seem to*
glauben, *believe (s.b.)*	weh tun, *hurt, ache*
sich nähern, *approach*	zusehen, *watch*
schmecken, *taste (intr.),*	
enjoy	
vertrauen, *trust*	
zuhören, *listen*	

Er kommt mir ganz alt vor.   *He seems quite old to me.*

Der Finger tut mir weh.   *My finger aches, hurts.*

109. Verbs Governing the Accusative and Dative
(cf. § 5 (a))

WEAK	STRONG (see § 115)
bringen, *bring, take* (§ 86 (h))	anbieten, *offer*
erklären, *explain, declare*	befehlen, *order, command*
erlauben, *allow, permit*	beschreiben, *describe*
erzählen, *tell (e.g. story)*	empfehlen, *recommend*
reichen, *reach, hand, pass*	geben, *give*

WEAK	STRONG (see § 115)
sagen, *say, tell*	leihen, *lend*
schenken, *give, present*	raten, *advise*
schicken, *send*	schreiben, *write*
verkaufen, *sell*	stehlen, *steal from*
vorstellen, *introduce*	verbieten, *forbid*
wünschen, *wish*	vergeben, *forgive*
zahlen, *pay*	versprechen, *promise*
zeigen, *show, point out*	verzeihen, *pardon*
	vorlesen, *read aloud*
	zurückgeben, *give back, return*
	zurufen, *call out to*

Er verbot es mir.   *He forbade me to (do so).*

110. Verbs Governing the Genitive

WEAK   STRONG (see § 115)

sich schämen, *be ashamed of*

Er schämt sich seines Sohnes.   *He is ashamed of his son.*

111. Verbs Governing Two Accusatives

WEAK   STRONG (see § 115)

kosten, *cost*
lehren, *teach*
nennen, *call* (§ 86 (*h*))

Er lehrt mich Deutsch.   *He teaches me German.*

112. Verbs followed by a Prepositional Object

WEAK   STRONG (see § 115)

(*a*) **an + accusative:**

denken, *think of* (§ 86 (*h*))   binden, *tie to*
erinnern, *remind of*   schreiben, *write to*
sich erinnern, *remember*

Er erinnert sich an ihn.   *He remembers him.*

(*b*) **an + dative:**

zweifeln, *doubt*   *vorbeigehen, *go past*

Er ging an mir vorbei.   *He went past me.*

WEAK	STRONG (see § 115)

(c) auf + accusative:

antworten, *answer* (*e.g. a question*)
sich freuen, *look forward to*
warten, *wait for*
zeigen, *point to*

*zugehen, *go up to*
*zukommen, *come up to*

    Er kam auf mich zu. *He came up to me.*

(d) auf + dative:

bestehen, *insist on*

    Ich bestehe auf einer Antwort. *I insist on an answer.*

(e) aus + dative:

übersetzen, *translate from*

bestehen, *consist of*
*werden, *become of*

    Aus dem Englischen übersetzt. *Translated from English.*

(f) bei + dative:

wohnen, *live with*

helfen, *help with*

    Er half mir bei der Arbeit. *He helped me with my work.*

(g) für + accusative:

sich interessieren, *be interested in*

halten, *consider, think to be*

    Er hielt ihn für einen Arzt. *He thought he was a doctor.*
    Er hält ihn für dumm. *He thinks he is stupid.*

(h) in + accusative:

übersetzen, *translate into*

*ausbrechen, *break (burst) out (into)*
*treten, *enter*

    Sie brach in Tränen aus. *She burst out into tears.*

(i) in + dative:

*ankommen, *arrive at, in*

    Er kam in dem Dorf an. *He arrived at the village.*

WEAK   STRONG (see § 115)

(*j*) **mit + dative:**

nicken, *nod*   sprechen, *speak, talk to*

Er nickte mit dem Kopf. *He nodded his head.*

(*k*) **nach + dative:**

fragen, *ask about, after, for*   sehen, *look after*
schicken, *send for*

Er schickte nach dem Arzt. *He sent for the doctor.*

(*l*) **über + accusative:**

sich freuen, *be glad, pleased about* schreiben, *write about*
lachen, *laugh at*   sich unterhalten, *converse about*

Er lachte über mich. *He laughed at me.*

(*m*) **um + accusative:**

sich handeln, *be a question*   bitten, *ask for*
  (*matter*) *of, concern*

Er bat uns um Hilfe. *He asked us for help.*

(*n*) **von + dative:**

erzählen, *relate, tell about*   halten, *think* (*e.g. well*) *of*
wissen, *know about* (§ 114)   sprechen, *speak of, about*

Was halten Sie von ihm? *What do you think of him?*

(*o*) **vor + dative:**

Angst haben⎰ *be afraid of*
sich fürchten⎱

Sie fürchtet sich vor ihm. *She is afraid of him.*

(*p*) **zu + dative:**

wählen, *elect*   einladen, *invite to*
sich wenden, *turn (round) to*
  (§ 86 (*h*))

Er lud mich zum Tee ein. *He invited me to tea.*

113. Translation of English Verbal Forms in -ing

These forms may be rendered by:

(*a*) The present participle when used adjectivally:

Ein unterhaltendes Buch.	*An entertaining book.*
„Ja", antwortete er lächelnd.	*" Yes," he replied smiling.*

(*b*) The infinitive used as a noun:

Das Rauchen ist verboten.	*Smoking is prohibited.*
Beim Lesen schlief er ein.	*He fell asleep while reading.*

(*c*) The simple infinitive after *sehen, hören, fühlen* and *bleiben*:

Ich sah ihn kommen.	*I saw him coming.*
Ich hörte sie singen.	*I heard her singing.*
Ich fühlte mein Herz schlagen.	*I felt my heart beating.*
Er blieb dort stehen.	*He remained standing there.*

(*d*) The infinitive with *zu* when there is no change of subject:

Es ist angenehm, hier zu sitzen.	*It is pleasant sitting here.*
Es gelang mir, es zu tun.	*I succeeded in doing it.*
Ich liebe **es** (hasse **es,** ziehe **es** vor), nichts zu tun.	*I love (hate, prefer) doing nothing.*
Er kam ins Zimmer, ohne mich zu sehen.	*He came into the room without seeing me.*
Anstatt mir zu helfen, tut er nichts.	*Instead of helping me he does nothing.*

(*e*) A dependent clause introduced by *indem* (= by -ing), *ohne daß* or *anstatt daß*:

Man lernt, indem man Fehler macht.	*One learns by making mistakes.*
Er kam ins Zimmer, ohne daß ich ihn sah.	*He came into the room without my seeing him.*
Anstatt daß er mir hilft, muß ich ihm helfen.	*Instead of helping me I have to help him.*

(*f*) A dependent clause introduced by *da, nachdem, ehe* or *indem*:

Da er müde war, ging er zu Bett.	*Being tired he went to bed.*

Nachdem er sich umgezogen hatte, ging er aus.	*Having changed* (or *after changing*) *he went out.*
Ehe er zu Bett ging, las er die Zeitung.	*Before going to bed he read the paper.*
Indem er das sagte, starb er.	*Saying this, he died.*

(g) A relative clause:

Der Mann, der den Wagen fuhr, schlief ein.	*The man driving the car fell asleep.*

(h) The finite verb together with *gern, lieber, am liebsten*:

Ich spiele gern Tennis.	*I like playing tennis.*
Ich spiele lieber Fußball.	*I prefer playing football.*
Ich spiele am liebsten Golf.	*I like playing golf best.*

114. Translation of certain English Words

ask:

Er bat mich zu kommen.	*He asked me to come.*
Er bat mich um Feuer.	*He asked me for a light.*
Er lud mich zum Tee ein.	*He asked me to tea.*
Er fragte mich nach dem Weg.	*He asked me the way.*
Er fragte mich, wo ich wohnte.	*He asked me where I lived.*
Er stellte mir dieselbe Frage.	*He asked me the same question.*
Er verlangte zehn Pfund.	*He asked for £10.*

Note. Bitten = to request; *fragen* = to make an enquiry; *verlangen* = demand.

call:

Er heißt Robert.	*He is called* (= *his name is*) *Robert.*
Wir nennen ihn Bob.	*We call him Bob.*
Er rief ihn.	*He called* (= *summoned*) *him.*
Er besuchte mich.	*He called on me* (= *visited me*).

enjoy:

Hat dir das Konzert gefallen?	*Did you enjoy the concert?*
Hast du dich gut amüsiert?	*Did you enjoy yourself?*
Er weiß, das Leben zu genießen.	*He knows how to enjoy life.*

Er erfreut sich guter Gesundheit.	*He enjoys good health.*
Das Essen hat uns gut geschmeckt.	*We enjoyed the food.*

get:

Er hat den Brief eben bekommen, erhalten.	*He has just got (= received) the letter.*
Ich bin alt geworden.	*I have got (= become) old.*
Wann ist er nach Hause gekommen?	*When did he get (= come) home?*
Wir erreichten die Insel.	*We got to (= reached) the island.*
Wir stiegen aus (dem Schiff).	*We got out (off the boat).*
Wir stiegen auf (in) die Elektrische/Straßenbahn.	*We got on (in) the tram.*
Willst du mir den Brief holen?	*Will you get (= fetch) me the letter?*
Er macht alles fertig.	*He is getting everything ready.*

go:

Er geht zur Schule.	*He goes to school (on foot).*
Er fährt mit dem Auto zur Schule.	*He goes to school by car.*
Er macht einen Spaziergang.	*He goes for a walk.*
Er macht einen Ausflug, eine Reise.	*He goes on an excursion, a journey.*
Wann fährt der Zug ab?	*When does the train go (off)?*

know:

Ich kenne ihn.	*I know him.*
Ich kenne Berlin.	*I know Berlin.*
Ich weiß alles.	*I know everything.*
Ich weiß den Weg.	*I know the way.*
Ich weiß, daß er nichts weiß.	*I know that he knows nothing.*
Ich weiß, wie er heißt.	*I know what his name is.*
Ich kann Deutsch.	*I know German.*

Note. *Kennen* = to be acquainted with personally. (*Kennen* cannot be followed by a clause, or the equivalent of a clause.)

Wissen = to know through having learnt, to know facts.

late:

Er **kommt** immer **zu** spät.	*He is always late.*

Es ist spät.	*It is late.*
Der Zug hat (5 Minuten) Verspätung.	*The train is (5 minutes) late.*

learn:

Er hat das Gedicht gelernt.	*He has learnt the poem.*
Er hatte die Wahrheit erfahren.	*He had learnt (= found out) the truth.*

leave:

Ich ließ den Schirm zu Hause.	*I left my umbrella at home.*
Ich verließ das Haus um 8 Uhr.	*I left (= quitted) home at 8.*
Sein Zug fährt um neun Uhr ab.	*His train leaves at 9.*

lie:

Er legte sich auf das Bett.	*He lay down on the bed.*
Er liegt auf dem Bett.	*He is lying on the bed.*

look:

Er sieht gesund aus.	*He looks well.*
Er sah ihn genau an.	*He looked at him closely.*
Er sah sich um.	*He looked round (= about him).*
Er suchte es überall.	*He looked (= searched) for it everywhere.*

now:

Ich wohne jetzt in Hamburg.	*I now live in Hamburg.*
Wir kamen nun in die Stadt.	*We now (= then) came to the town.*

only:

Es ist erst 8 Uhr.	*It is only 8 o'clock.*
Er kam erst um 8 Uhr an.	*He only arrived at 8. (He did not arrive till 8.)*
Er ist erst zehn Jahre alt.	*He is only ten years old.*
Es kostet nur 8 Mark.	*It only costs 8 marks.*
Es war nur ein Traum.	*It was only a dream.*

Note. Erst always refers to **time,** *nur* to **manner, degree** or **quantity.**

put:

Stell die Lampe auf den Tisch!	*Put the lamp on the table.*
Leg das Buch auf den Tisch!	*Put the book on the table.*
Setz das Kind auf den Stuhl!	*Put the child on the chair.*
Steck das Geld in deine Tasche!	*Put the money in your pocket.*
Tue Wasser in die Flasche!	*Put some water in the bottle.*

Note. *Stellen* = put in an upright position; *legen* = put in a lying position; *setzen* = put in a sitting position; *stecken* = poke or stuff into; *tun* = put in a general and vague sense.

sit:

Er setzte sich auf den Stuhl.	*He sat down on the chair.*
Er saß auf dem Stuhl.	*He was sitting on the chair.*

stop:

Der Regen hat aufgehört.	*The rain has stopped (= ceased).*
Hör auf zu weinen!	*Stop crying.*
Der Zug hat gehalten.	*The train has stopped.*
Meine Uhr ist stehengeblieben.	*My watch has stopped.*
Er blieb plötzlich stehen.	*He suddenly stopped.*
Er hat den Wagen angehalten.	*He stopped the car.*

take:

Bringen Sie ihm das Buch!	*Take the book to him.*
Er brachte mich nach Hause.	*He took me home.*
Trag das Paket auf die Post!	*Take the parcel to the post-office.*
Nimm es aus dem Schrank!	*Take it out of the cupboard.*
Nimm es (ihn) mit!	*Take it (him) with you!*
Er holte es aus der Tasche.	*He took it out of his pocket.*
Führe ihn über die Straße!	*Take him across the road.*
Er nahm den Zug, das Schiff.	*He took the train, the boat.*
Er folgte meinem Rat.	*He took my advice.*
Es dauerte lange, bis wir dahin kamen.	*It took us a long time to get there.*

Note. *Bringen* = to carry **from** as well as **to** the speaker.

then:

Damals wohnte ich in B.	*Then (= at that time) I lived in B.*
Dann zog ich nach F. um.	*Then (= subsequently) I moved to F.*

Dann kann man nichts machen.	*Then (= in that case) nothing can be done.*

thing:

Wir haben andere Dinge zu tun.	*We have other things to do.*
Sind meine Sachen schon da?	*Have my things come?*

time:

Mit der Zeit.	*In time (= in course of time).*
Zur rechten Zeit.	*In time (= punctually).*
Zur selben Zeit.	*At the same time.*
Eine Zeitlang.	*For some time (= past).*
Zu dieser Zeit.	*At this (or that) time.*
Zu allen Zeiten.	*At all times.*
Vor langer Zeit.	*A long time ago.*
Nach einer Weile.	*After a time.*
Das erste Mal.	*The first time.*
Das nächste Mal.	*The next time.*
Mehrere Male.	*Several times.*
Zum erstenmal (letztenmal).	*(For) the first (last) time.*
Um wieviel Uhr?	*At what time?*
Wie spät ist es?	*What is the time?*

wake:

Er hat ihn geweckt.	*He woke him.*
Er ist spät erwacht.	*He woke (intr.) late.*

115. List of Strong and Irregular Verbs

Infinitive	3rd Pers. Sing. Pres.	3rd Pers. Sing. Impf.	Past Part.	Meaning
backen	backt	backte	gebacken	*bake*
befehlen	befiehlt	befahl [1]	befohlen	*order*
beginnen	beginnt	begann [1]	begonnen	*begin*
beißen	beißt	biß	gebissen	*bite*
betrügen	betrügt	betrog	betrogen	*deceive, cheat*
(*)biegen	biegt	bog	gebogen	*bend, turn*
bieten	bietet	bot	geboten	*offer, bid*
binden	bindet	band	gebunden	*tie*
bitten	bittet	bat	gebeten	*ask, request*
blasen	bläst	blies	geblasen	*blow, sound*
*bleiben	bleibt	blieb	geblieben	*remain, stay*

[1] See § 104(e).

Infinitive	3rd Pers. Sing. Pres.	3rd Pers. Sing. Impf.	Past Part.	Meaning
braten	brät	briet	gebraten	*roast*
(*)brechen	bricht	brach	gebrochen	*break*
brennen	brennt	brannte[1]	gebrannt	*burn*
bringen	bringt	brachte[1]	gebracht	*bring, take*
denken	denkt	dachte[1]	gedacht	*think*
dürfen[2]	darf	durfte	gedurft	*be allowed to*
empfehlen	empfiehlt	empfahl[1]	empfohlen	*recommend*
*erschrecken[3]	erschrickt	erschrak	erschrocken	*be frightened*
essen	ißt	aß	gegessen	*eat*
(*)fahren	fährt	fuhr	gefahren	*go (not on foot) ; drive*
*fallen	fällt	fiel	gefallen	*fall*
fangen	fängt	fing	gefangen	*catch*
finden	findet	fand	gefunden	*find*
(*)fliegen	fliegt	flog	geflogen	*fly*
(*)fliehen	flieht	floh	geflohen	*flee, shun*
*fließen	fließt	floß	geflossen	*flow*
fressen	frißt	fraß	gefressen	*eat (of animals)*
(*)frieren	friert	fror	gefroren	*freeze, be cold*
geben	gibt	gab	gegeben	*give*
*gehen	geht	ging	gegangen	*go, walk*
*gelingen[4]	gelingt	gelang	gelungen	*succeed*
gelten	gilt	galt	gegolten	*be valid, worth*
genießen	genießt	genoß	genossen	*enjoy*
*geschehen	geschieht	geschah	geschehen	*happen*
gewinnen	gewinnt	gewann	gewonnen	*win, gain*
gießen	gießt	goß	gegossen	*pour*
gleichen	gleicht	glich	geglichen	*resemble*
*gleiten	gleitet	glitt	geglitten	*glide, slide*
graben	gräbt	grub	gegraben	*dig*
greifen	greift	griff	gegriffen	*grasp*
haben[5]	hat	hatte	gehabt	*have*
halten	hält	hielt	gehalten	*hold, stop (intr.)*
hängen[6]	hängt	hing	gehangen	*hang (intr.)*
heben	hebt	hob	gehoben	*raise, lift*
heißen	heißt	hieß	geheißen	*be called; bid*
helfen	hilft	half[1]	geholfen	*help*
kennen	kennt	kannte[1]	gekannt	*be acquainted with*
klingen	klingt	klang	geklungen	*sound*
*kommen	kommt	kam	gekommen	*come*
können[2]	kann	konnte	gekonnt	*can, be able to*
*kriechen	kriecht	kroch	gekrochen	*crawl*

[1] See § 104 (*e*).
[2] See § 102 (*a*).
[3] Weak = frighten.

[4] See § 98 (*b*).
[5] See § 83.
[6] Weak = hang (tr.).

Infinitive	3rd Pers. Sing. Pres.	3rd Pers. Sing. Impf.	Past Part.	Meaning
laden	lädt	lud	geladen	*load; invite*
lassen	läßt	ließ	gelassen	*let, leave (behind)*
*laufen	läuft	lief	gelaufen	*run*
leiden	leidet	litt	gelitten	*suffer, bear*
leihen	leiht	lieh	geliehen	*lend*
lesen	liest	las	gelesen	*read*
liegen	liegt	lag	gelegen	*lie*
lügen	lügt	log	gelogen	*tell lies*
messen	mißt	maß	gemessen	*measure*
mögen[1]	mag	mochte	gemocht	*may; like*
müssen[1]	muß	mußte	gemußt	*must, have to*
nehmen	nimmt	nahm	genommen	*take*
nennen	nennt	nannte[2]	genannt	*name, call*
pfeifen	pfeift	pfiff	gepfiffen	*whistle; pipe*
raten	rät	riet	geraten	*advise; guess*
reiben	reibt	rieb	gerieben	*rub*
(*)reißen	reißt	riß	gerissen	*tear*
(*)reiten	reitet	ritt	geritten	*ride (on animal)*
*rennen	rennt	rannte[2]	gerannt	*run*
riechen	riecht	roch	gerochen	*smell*
rufen	ruft	rief	gerufen	*call*
(*)scheiden	scheidet	schied	geschieden	*separate*
scheinen	scheint	schien	geschienen	*seem; shine*
schieben	schiebt	schob	geschoben	*shove, push*
schießen	schießt	schoß	geschossen	*shoot*
schlafen	schläft	schlief	geschlafen	*sleep*
schlagen	schlägt	schlug	geschlagen	*beat, strike*
schließen	schließt	schloß	geschlossen	*shut, conclude*
schneiden	schneidet	schnitt	geschnitten	*cut*
schreiben	schreibt	schrieb	geschrieben	*write*
schreien	schreit	schrie	geschrie(e)n	*shout, shriek*
schweigen	schweigt	schwieg	geschwiegen	*be(come) silent*
*schwellen[3]	schwillt	schwoll	geschwollen	*swell (intr.)*
(*)schwim- men	schwimmt	schwamm[2]	geschwom- men	*swim*
schwingen	schwingt	schwang	geschwun- gen	*swing*
schwören	schwört	schwur	geschworen	*swear (on oath)*
sehen	sieht	sah	gesehen	*see*
*sein[4]	ist	war	gewesen	*be*
senden	sendet	sandte[2]	gesandt	*send*
singen	singt	sang	gesungen	*sing*
*sinken	sinkt	sank	gesunken	*sink (intr.)*

[1] See § 102 (a).   [3] Weak = swell (tr.).
[2] See § 104 (e).   [4] See § 83.

Infinitive	3rd Pers. Sing. Pres.	3rd Pers. Sing. Impf.	Past Part.	Meaning
sitzen	sitzt	saß	gesessen	*be sitting, sit*
sollen[1]	soll	sollte	gesollt	*be obliged to*
sprechen	spricht	sprach	gesprochen	*speak*
*springen	springt	sprang	gesprungen	*jump, spring*
stechen	sticht	stach	gestochen	*prick, sting; trump*
stehen	steht	stand	gestanden	*stand*
stehlen	stiehlt	stahl	gestohlen	*steal*
*steigen	steigt	stieg	gestiegen	*mount, rise*
*sterben	stirbt	starb[2]	gestorben	*die*
(*)stoßen	stößt	stieß	gestoßen	*push; stumble on*
tragen	trägt	trug	getragen	*carry, bear; wear*
treffen	trifft	traf	getroffen	*meet; hit*
(*)treiben	treibt	trieb	getrieben	*drive; do; drift*
(*)treten	tritt	trat	getreten	*step, go; kick*
trinken	trinkt	trank	getrunken	*drink*
tun	tut	tat	getan	*do*
verbergen	verbirgt	verbarg[2]	verborgen	*hide, conceal*
(*)verderben	verdirbt	verdarb[2]	verdorben	*spoil, ruin*
vergessen	vergißt	vergaß	vergessen	*forget*
verlieren	verliert	verlor	verloren	*lose*
vermeiden	vermeidet	vermied	vermieden	*avoid*
*verschwinden	verschwindet	verschwand	verschwunden	*disappear*
verzeihen	verzeiht	verzieh	verziehen	*pardon*
*wachsen	wächst	wuchs	gewachsen	*grow (intr.)*
waschen	wäscht	wusch	gewaschen	*wash (tr.)*
wenden	wendet	wandte[2]	gewandt	*turn (tr.)*
*werden[3]	wird	wurde	geworden	*become*
werfen	wirft	warf[2]	geworfen	*throw*
wiegen[4]	wiegt	wog	gewogen	*weigh (intr.)*
wissen	weiß[5]	wußte	gewußt	*know (as a fact)*
wollen[1]	will	wollte	gewollt	*want to*
(*)ziehen	zieht	zog	gezogen	*draw, pull; grow (tr.); go, move*
zwingen	zwingt	zwang	gezwungen	*compel, force*

[1] See § 102 (a).   [2] See § 104 (e).   [3] See § 83.   [4] Weak = rock.
[5] Present tense irregular: *weiß, weißt, weiß, wissen, wißt, wissen.*

SECTION II

SENTENCES AND PHRASES ON GRAMMATICAL POINTS

The numbers in brackets at the head of each exercise refer to the paragraphs of the Grammar Section.

Words enclosed in round brackets either (1) give the German equivalent for the preceding English word(s), or (2) give an alternative form of wording for literal translation into German, or (3) refer to a particular paragraph of the Grammar. Words enclosed in square brackets are to be omitted for purposes of translation into German.

1. WORD ORDER
(§§ 1-4)

1. He writes a letter. 2. Every day he writes a letter. 3. When has he written the letter? 4. When will he write the letter? 5. Has he written the letter? 6. He wrote the letter and then he read the book. 7. He sat down and read the book. 8. He sat down, for he was tired. 9. " He is tired," she said. 10. They sit down when they come home. 11. When I come home I sit down. 12. Since they are tired they sit down. 13. Read the paper every day. 14. When he reads the paper I say nothing. 15. He sat down but said nothing.

2. WORD ORDER (*cont.*)
(§ 5)

1. He wrote me the letter. 2. He will bring it to you to-morrow. 3. Have you given your brother the money? 4. He gave it to us. 5. He gave them to your mother. 6. We gave the book to her. 7. You sent it to me. 8. I sent the book to you. 9. He read the letter out to us. 10. I have given the book to my friend. 11. I go to school every day. 12. I go to school by train. 13. I did not go to school yesterday. 14. We enjoyed ourselves yesterday. 15. I haven't seen her. 16. It is not very warm to-day.

17. If he does not do it I cannot come. 18. That is not **her** book. 19. I gave her the book yesterday. 20. He gave it to her yesterday. 21. She sat down on the chair. 22. No, he didn't sit down. 23. If you sit down I [will] bring it to you. 24. If it is not cold to-morrow I shall work outside. 25. He did not look round.

3. CONJUNCTIONS
(§§ **6-8**)

1. Although he is old he still works. 2. As soon as I saw him I recognized him. 3. Despite the fact that it is cold it is very warm here. 4. I don't know when I can come. 5. You can do it, for it is quite simple. 6. Since it is quite simple you can do it alone. 7. While he was talking I was reading a book. 8. He never rests but always works. 9. When he came we were not there. 10. Wait until I come. 11. As you know, she is still very young. 12. He was tired because he had worked hard. 13. Since he left us nobody has seen him. 14. I don't know who your father is. 15. After he had spoken we went home. 16. Before I forget it I must give you back your pencil. 17. When I see her I always speak with her. 18. I don't know if I have your pencil. 19. He is not clever but stupid. 20. Scarcely had he left the house when they knocked. 21. He was younger than we thought. 22. I speak clearly so that they can understand. 23. I had an umbrella, so that I didn't get wet. 24. I shall never forget it as long as I live. 25. We always go out except when it rains.

4. CONJUNCTIONS (*cont.*)
(§§ **9-10**)

1. She is neither young nor pretty. 2. Either it is cold or it is wet. 3. I have not read it either. 4. Anyhow it is not true. 5. Now she laughs, now she cries. 6. Both he and I have read it. 7. They are not only dear but also badly made. 8. In spite of that I cannot come. 9. Meanwhile his son had left school. 10. The more I see them the more I love them. 11. We must hurry or else it will be too late. 12. He has neither courage nor pride.

13. You can have either a book or a picture.   14. He can neither read nor write.   15. He was very poor, so I gave him some money.

5. The Articles
(§§ 11-14)

1. They live in Switzerland, not in Germany.   2. As soon as he woke up he jumped out of bed.   3. He was very thirsty but not hungry.   4. He goes to school every day, but his sister works in an office in town.   5. Since I haven't any tea will you drink coffee?   6. It's a pity, we have visitors and so we cannot come.   7. In England the summer holidays are in August and September.   8. The Rhine flows through Switzerland, Germany and Holland.   9. He never drinks any milk.   10. " You are right," he said. " I was in a great hurry."   11. She didn't feel inclined to read after breakfast as she had a headache.   12. He wants to be a soldier although his father is a famous doctor.   13. In autumn the days begin to get shorter.   14. The apples cost two marks a pound or fifty pfennigs each.   15. At night it is now very dark.   16. In fact you are wrong; he is very rarely in a bad mood.   17. He is in bed, for he is very ill.   18. As a rule they go to church on Sundays.   19. If you know the answer raise your hand.   20. He learns nothing at school.

6. Nouns
(§ 17)

A. (§ 17 (a) (i)):

1. The evenings are now getting cool.   2. He had many friends and few enemies.   3. The moon and the stars were shining brightly.   4. His birthday is in the spring.   5. The war lasted three months.   6. The mountains there are very high.   7. She was wearing red shoes and white gloves. 8. What are the advantages and disadvantages of this step?   9. The circle of the king's friends had little success. 10. I bought this material in the autumn.   11. We have five senses.   12. He never carries out my orders.   13. The stones of these rings are very beautiful.   14. Since we had a visitor we could not see the film.   15. Have you read these parts of the letter?   16. The landlord brought us

wine.   17. This place has no buses.   18. The cathedral was empty but it made no difference.   19. What is the price of this umbrella?   20. The dogs ran past like (the) lightning.

B. (§ 17 (a) (ii) and (b) (i) and (ii)):

1. She made several purchases there.   2. She was wearing neither hat nor stockings.   3. These rivers flow very slowly.   4. The farm had many fruit-trees.   5. He always carries his head high.   6. These men had at last given up their plans.   7. The guests took their seats (took seat) in the hall and waited.   8. He cannot see the wood for (vor + D) the trees.   9. The struggle lasted [a] long [time].   10. If it is possible we shall accept your suggestion.   11. For (aus + D) this reason he did not come.   12. Because of (wegen + G) the gale the train was late (§ 114).   13. That had always been her wish.   14. The suit is still too tight.   15. When the doctor goes (§ 114) for a walk he always takes a stick.   16. (The) wealth is not everything.   17. Her sons have very big feet.   18. Have you any envelopes?   19. These sentences are not very difficult.   20. The cupboards were empty.

C. (§ 17 (c)):

1. The workmen only work here in winter.   2. The emperor has many loyal servants.   3. How many grandsons have you?   4. Why do schoolboys make so many mistakes?   5. The morning was quite fine, but since it was cold I put on my coat.   6. The birds begin to sing very early in summer.   7. We have no lack of (an + D) shops here.   8. The speaker spoke very fast.   9. The plates are not warm and you have forgotten the spoons.   10. My uncle is a judge and my father is a teacher.   11. The postman has not come yet.   12. My brother knows (§ 114) several writers and one poet.   13. Many foreigners come every summer (§ 24 (c)).   14. The tradesmen here are very friendly.   15. He was lying on (auf + D) his back.   16. I have lost my keys in the garden.   17. These apples are sweet.   18. Grandfather gave us some cakes.   19. The porter will carry the suit-cases.   20. We were sitting in the shade of the rocks.

D. (§ 17 (d)-(g)):

1. I am very hungry. 2. The traffic makes a lot of (much) noise. 3. He is a nephew of the prince. 4. I have forgotten the name of the scoundrel. 5. We don't drink coffee, we only drink tea. 6. The rain comes from (*von* + D) the west. 7. I have two cousins. 8. He accepted the tobacco with thanks. 9. (The) men need peace. 10. These states are too small. 11. He had some very good ideas. 12. The soldiers and sailors were very thirsty. 13. We had snow in the north but they had sunshine in the south. 14. This beach is very flat. 15. Yes, I always take sugar. 16. His comrades are now dead. 17. We cannot all be heroes. 18. When our neighbours heard the thunder they came back immediately. 19. (The) farmers work very hard. 20. The boys have a very good appetite.

E. (§ 17 (a)-(g)):

1. The shop assistants showed us suits, hats, gloves, shoes and stockings. 2. The enemy made many attempts to get (§ 114) to the top of the hill but without success. 3. In summer my nephew spent two months in Germany. 4. My friend planted several fruit-trees in the autumn. 5. The hall contains many tables and chairs. 6. We handed the porter our suit-cases, baskets, umbrellas and sticks. 7. All the platforms of the station were full [of] soldiers who were making a lot of noise. 8. Her brother had great pain(s). 9. Every day we have either rain or snow; but perhaps to-morrow we shall have sunshine. 10. The branches of the trees cast (threw) long shadows. 11. My cousin has three sons; they are all teachers. 12. His brothers are all successful tradesmen. 13. In Germany there are many rivers, forests, mountains and lakes. 14. In the (*am*) sky the moon and the stars were shining brightly. 15. I must visit the dentist on Monday; he wants to examine my teeth. 16. The names of the workmen are very unusual. 17. My grandson is very fond of (loves very) dogs. 18. Many foreigners came to England in the spring. 19. I saw two films last Tuesday. 20. We have our writers, poets and artists too. 21. He did it without [any] reason. 22. We have only plates and spoons.

23. Many objects lay on (*auf* + D) the table—pencils, balls, mirrors and banknotes.   24. Nobody wants (the) war; everybody wants (the) peace.   25. Our neighbours are farmers; they have two or three farms.   26. There (*es*) is no lack of (*an* + D) sugar, tea and coffee in the shops.   27. The sailor was the hero of the day.   28. The postman brings us letters every morning.   29. I had to give up my plans since guests were staying with (*bei* + D) us.   30. "Take [a] seat," he said.   "The chair is comfortable and the stove is still quite warm."

7. NOUNS (*cont.*)
(§ **18**)

A. (§ 18 (*a*)-(*c*) (i) (α)):

1. Her daughter had little white hands.   2. (The) half (of) the class was ill.   3. I have no desire to come into danger.   4. The cat was playing with the mouse.   5. You need a ticket to work in the library.   6. Their grandmother came by rail but lost her ticket.   7. The family was sitting on the bench in front of (*vor* + D) the cottage.   8. We have only had two meals to-day.   9. I need help with (*bei* + D) this work.   10. The lamp was burning in the kitchen.   11. There was a crowd [of] women on the island.   12. He wanted to see his home again.   13. The nights are very long now.   14. There (*es*) were flowers of (*von* + D) every colour.   15. He took his pen and began to write.   16. The town has a beautiful situation.   17. He told us a story about (*von* + D) the bridge.   18. He has good knowledge(s) of the (in the) arts.   19. As it was very hot he took off his jacket.   20. The bottle was standing in the corner.

B. (§ 18 (*c*) (i) (β) and (*c*) (ii)):

1. It is my duty.   2. It is a fact that he smokes cigarettes.   3. The streets were quite empty.   4. He asked (§ 114) the waitress for the newspaper.   5. His granddaughter is now learning languages.   6. We have read fifty pages already.   7. The schoolmistress was standing in front of (*vor* + D) the blackboard.   8. The queen's niece had no choice.   9. Is [there any] post for me (there)?—

Only two postcards.   10. I cannot read your aunt's writing.
11. After a while he opened the door and went down the
stairs (§40 (a) (ii)).   12. The drawers were empty.   13. I
am in your debt.   14. Her neighbour had trouble in explaining (to explain) the matter.   15. My sister has had
no news of (von + D) her friend.   16. We are proud of
(auf + A) our past.   17. The peasant-women were working
in (auf + D) the meadow.   18. He went (became) red with
(vor + D) shame.   19. The girl-students stayed several
weeks with (bei + D) us.   20. The princess loves (the)
music.

C. (§ 18 (c) (iii)-(v)):
    1. These (§ 64, note) are his weaknesses, but that is his
strength.   2. They gave him back his freedom.   3. She
accepted the invitation with gratitude.   4. The translation
of his speech was not very accurate.   5. The development
of the movement had unpleasant consequences.   6. What is
the meaning of this remark?   7. The mood of the company
was wonderful.   8. What is the explanation of this hurry?
9. She has had various illnesses.   10. The government
made (treffen) all preparations.   11. He has his examina-
tions now behind him (§ 53).   12. In the darkness he had
great difficulty in finding (to find) their flat.   13. His de-
scriptions of the scenery (landscape) are very beautiful.
14. I have a cold and I am not in a good mood.   15. In
(bei + D) this cold it is impossible to work.   16. I made
his acquaintance yesterday.   17. I have a request [to make]
to (an + A) you.   18. That is my concern.   19. He has only
good qualities.   20. Truth for him is a passion.

D. (§ 18 (a)-(c)):
    1. I know from (aus + D) experience that the journey
is quite pleasant.   2. I had no opportunity to read the
newspaper.   3. The door of the library was open.   4. The
cat was sitting on the wall.   5. Have you heard the news?
The danger is past.   6. My wife had bought butter, milk,
cigarettes and flowers.   7. We had the joy of seeing (to see)
your nieces again.   8. The cause of the illness is unknown.
9. The future belongs to the youth of the nation.   10. My

aunt had no choice, for the situation was serious.   11. He has sold his collection of (*von* + D) drawings.   12. It is his duty not to give up hope.   13. The police found in the drawer a watch, a bottle full [of] ink, two forks, a pipe and a rose.   14. I am going to (*auf* + A) the bank if I have time.   15. Our flat has a very modern kitchen.   16. He is always in a bad mood when he has a cold.   17. We received an invitation for next week.   18. His speech had no effect.   19. Don't give yourself the trouble; it is only an hour by rail.   20. He has learnt two or three languages, but he has no desire to travel.   21. She became red with (*vor* + D) shame and wanted to sink into (*in* + A) the ground.   22. He has got (the) permission to buy the island.   23. I have the honour of introducing (to introduce) to you my daughters.   24. We had the intention of showing (to show) you our gratitude in (*auf* + A) another way.   25. The formation of the clouds was quite strange.   26. My grandmother has a beautiful handwriting.   27. He had got together (collected) all sorts of (*allerlei*) knowledge(s).   28. Some women have great fear of (*vor* + D) cows and mice.   29. He had great strength in his hands.   30. He seems to bear all the cares of the world on his shoulders.

8. Nouns (*cont.*)

(§ 19-21)

A. (§ 19 (*a*) (i) and (ii)):

1. Animals have four legs.   2. I have no feeling in my legs.   3. " That is a secret," she said.   4. I have told you that many times.   5. He always travels (flies) by aeroplane. 6. We haven't yet had breakfast.   7. This compartment is empty.   8. He was carrying many parcels.   9. They have learnt these poems at last.   10. He is spending two years there.   11. He has at last reached his aim.   12. He spoke only a few words.   13. People experience (have) strange fates.   14. There were several rafts on the sea.   15. They want to go to (*in* + A) the concert.   16. They came by boat (ship).   17. Business is business.   18. These couples dance well.   19. While we were in London we saw three plays.   20. I have not read his works.

B. (§ 19 (*b*) and (*c*)):

1. The valleys contain only a few villages. 2. In front of each picture there were two lights. 3. The grass and the leaves were no longer green. 4. Behind (*hinter* + D) the castle are several fields. 5. "Have you [a] light (fire)?"—"No, I have no matches." 6. He was not without means, though he did not spend much money. 7. The children always lose their handkerchiefs. 8. He gave me a sign to come into the room. 9. (The) smoking is forbidden in this theatre. 10. The girls were wearing beautiful frocks. 11. The roofs of the houses in this village are red. 12. The maid's bedroom is quite big. 13. Great buildings stand on (*an* + D) this bank. 14. Travelling costs a lot of money. 15. His face showed that he had confidence in (*zu* + D) him. 16. All the windows were without glass. 17. He trembled in (*an* + D) all [his] limbs. 18. The behaviour of the children was very good. 19. His supper consisted of (*aus* + D) vegetables. 20. The monastery was right in (*auf* + D) the country.

C. (§§ 19 (*d*)-(*f*), 20 and 21):

1. She bought a pound [of] meat. 2. He goes (§ 114) to (*in* + A) the office by car. 3. His parents do not often go to (*in* + A) the cinema. 4. People abroad (§ 82 (*b*) (vi)) do not understand (it). 5. Shirts were lying on the bed. 6. The wireless gives (makes) him much pleasure. 7. During the holidays the weather was very bad. 8. They wished us a merry Christmas. 9. The policemen were always ready to help us. 10. The fruit was very cheap. 11. These hotels have many floors. 12. As I had a headache I went to bed early. 13. In the (*am*) end I carried my luggage myself. 14. Those (§ 64, *note*) are people after my heart. 15. She has no interest in (*für* + A) clothes. 16. He has had more luck than he deserves. 17. His trousers were [made] of (*aus* + D) leather. 18. That is no age! 19. These insects do not sting. 20. You must keep your ears and eyes open.

D. (§§ 19–21):

1. The girls all had very long hair (*plural*) and blue

eyes.   2. She bought three loaves and a dozen eggs.   3. His works consist of fairy-tales and poems.   4. In the room [there] were two beds.   5. Blood is thicker than water.   6. The desks were [made] of wood and iron.   7. The buildings in this quarter are all very old.   8. These people have other interests.   9. He told us of (*von* + D) the fate of their victims.   10. The weights and measures of this country are difficult to learn.   11. Books, exercise-books and papers lay on the desk.   12. It is no wonder that sheep and horses are dear.   13. Meat is dear, but fruit and vegetables are cheap.   14. He had many presents, a bicycle, several toys, a knife and six handkerchiefs.   15. As I had no money I could not buy an ice.   16. As soon as he gave the sign the aeroplane stopped (§114).   17. They have the right to (*auf* + A) happiness.   18. (The) pleasure is the aim of her life.   19. The weather is usually fine at (*zu* + D) Easter.   20. That is no problem nowadays.   21. He followed his parents' advice.   22. During the summer holidays the restaurants here are full.   23. The reading of plays gives (makes) him much pleasure.   24. At last he broke the silence and burst into (§ 112 (*h*)) laughter.   25. One must obey the laws of one's country.   26. These knives are very sharp.   27. He will keep his promise.   28. I should like (§ 102 (*b*) (iii)) a glass of water, please.   29. The law-courts are closed now. 30. He wanted to become a member but he hadn't enough money.

9. Nouns (*cont.*)

(§§ 16-22)

1. The buildings in some cities of the United States often have ten or more floors.   2. My mother is a French-woman and my father is an Englishman and I was born in Austria.   3. Many people spend their holidays in Switzer-land or in France nowadays.   4. My parents never go to the (*in* + A) cinema, but they sometimes go to the (*in* + A) theatre.   5. In front of the hotel stood a row [of] cars.   6. The inhabitants of Switzerland speak French, German or Italian.   7. The four seasons of the year are spring, summer, autumn and winter.   8. The church has a high tower.

9. We have a fortnight['s] (§ 50) holiday(s) at Christmas, three weeks' holiday(s) at Easter, and a month['s] holiday(s) in summer. 10. He gave me good advice (*plural*); but I was still in doubt. 11. The village is three miles away; (the) night will come before we reach it. 12. The bank of the river was very low. 13. I am of the opinion that the difficulty is too great. 14. The countess had blue rings round her (the) eyes. 15. This is a work according to all the rules of art. 16. What is the meaning of this dream? 17. German is a difficult language, and many Germans make mistakes. 18. The difference between the brother and the sister is very great. 19. The bird's wings were white but its body was grey. 20. In (*unter* + D) the reign of this queen the people were content. 21. Every nation has the government (which) it deserves. 22. We don't want any disturbance of the peace. 23. In London one sees Frenchmen, Italians, Germans and Americans everywhere. 24. I wish you health and wealth. 25. The walls of the room were yellow, the ceiling was white and the windows and door were red. 26. He is an artist of the first class. 27. We must pay the bill immediately; there (*es*) is no time to lose. 28. She had tears of joy in her eyes. 29. This wind always brings rain. 30. He spoke of (*von* + D) the advantages and disadvantages of this step.

10. THE CASES

(§§ 23-27)

1. He remained a year. 2. She comes every morning. 3. One day he received a letter from his uncle. 4. He was very grateful to his teachers. 5. He always travels third class. 6. They were going down the street. 7. He is a young artist. 8. He gave it to Mr. Brown, my uncle's friend. 9. I am sure of success. 10. She feels cold. 11. Do you know my friend, the judge? 12. I feel as if I have forgotten something. 13. It is all the same to him. 14. " Give me a glass of fresh water, please." 15. " Many thanks," he said. 16. As he had worked the whole day long he was very tired. 17. She is very like her mother. 18. He brought her two dozen eggs. 19. That is the picture of my friend, the poet. 20. He was aware of it.

11. DECLENSION OF ADJECTIVES

(§§ 28-34)

A. (§§ 29 (a)–(d); 30 (a)). Translate and decline in the singular and plural where possible:

1. This comfortable chair. 2. Her rich neighbour. 3. Dirty water (*sing.*). 4. Which well-known town? 5. A modern library. 6. Hot milk (*sing.*). 7. Her dear child. 8. A tired face. 9. Old iron (*sing.*). 10. Every diligent schoolboy. 11. Not a pleasant [bit of] news. 12. Another maid. 13. That serious book. 14. An interesting person. 15. Every successful artist. 16. Her brave daughter. 17. This proud queen. 18. Our poor dog. 19. The dead soldier. 20. A happy thought.

B. (§§ 29 (a)–(d); 30 (b) (i)):

1. The wide streets of the great city were empty. 2. He wrote us a short, cool letter. 3. She had a severe face, cold eyes, a hard mouth and long thin hands. 4. The fat man drank a glass of fresh milk. 5. She sold us sour apples but we wanted sweet ripe [ones]. 6. I drink weak tea and strong coffee. 7. The high mountains were covered with deep snow. 8. We live in the narrow circle of our faithful friends. 9. We have had a cold wet summer. 10. In the (am) early morning the distant mountains looked (§ 114) quite blue.

C. (§§ 29 (a)–(d); 30 (b) (ii)):

1. He is a famous poet and has written lovely but simple poems. 2. She has a healthy colour and clear eyes. 3. There (*es*) were little dark narrow clouds in the sky. 4. I have various reasons for thinking (to think) that that is not a true story. 5. This lazy man must eat dry bread. 6. I am only a stupid girl and I don't understand your clever speeches. 7. It is his free will; he has perfect freedom of choice. 8. We sleep with (*bei* + D) open windows, although it is not quite safe. 9. We have wild animals and rare birds in that big forest. 10. This satisfied person has a soft heart.

D. (§§ 29 (e)–(f); 30 (b) (iii)):

1. It was natural that he received many grateful letters.

2. All his usual toys no longer pleased the sad child. 3. The name of the real painter of all these magnificent pictures is unknown. 4. She shared the terrible fate of many lonely people. 5. All our important public buildings are in the vicinity. 6. The friendly policeman asked (§ 114) only a few necessary questions. 7. I am tired of all your impossible requests. 8. All these wonderful ready[made] clothes were quite cheap. 9. We need several capable workmen. 10. Several dear friends are in a difficult if not dangerous situation.

E. (§§ 31–34):

1. I haven't any acquaintances in the town. 2. We have many relatives abroad. 3. The official examined all [the] suit-cases of the travellers. 4. The London policemen are very friendly. 5. I will do everything possible. 6. The reign of Charlemagne lasted forty-six years. 7. There are (*es gibt*) few unemployed men in England. 8. I have just read something quite interesting. 9. A stranger asked (§ 114) me the way to the station. 10. Our friends came by tram as they haven't a car.

12. COMPARISON OF ADJECTIVES
(§ 35)

1. I have two younger sisters and one elder brother. 2. My sister is younger than I am. 3. In winter the days are much shorter than in summer. 4. It is just as warm to-day as yesterday. 5. He is even cleverer than you think. 6. The Zugspitze (*f.*) is the highest mountain in Germany. 7. Here the street is narrowest. 8. The nearest letter-box is a hundred yards away. 9. It is best if we walk. 10. This is the best of all possible worlds. 11. Most people take their holidays in summer. 12. This hotel is biggest. 13. She was most excited. 14. Berlin is the biggest town in Germany. 15. She is less beautiful than her elder sister. 16. She is three years younger than her brother. 17. Most of us spend most of the time at home. 18. One gets older and older. 19. Since it is later than I thought I must go immediately. 20. Although it is brighter than yesterday it will soon rain.

13. ADVERBS

(§§ 36-38)

1. First I came, then you came and finally your sister came.   2. I used to like dancing formerly (I danced formerly willingly).   3. I prefer now playing cards (I play now more willingly cards).   4. His son prefers most of all going (goes most willingly) to the cinema.   5. Come at the latest at ten o'clock.   6. He came immediately and stayed for hours.   7. Come again soon, the oftener the better.   8. Have you ever been in Germany?—No, not yet, but I hope to go there (*dorthin*) one day.   9. Fortunately he can only come afterwards.   10. That happens mostly of an evening. 11. The other day I saw him in town and we spoke with one another for a long time.   12. Soon afterwards he disappeared, at least we didn't see him again.   13. Come as quickly as possible; I have long since had the wish to speak with you.   14. I see her now and again but not often, not as often as formerly.   15. In the first place he is most unwise, and then he is exceedingly lazy.   16. You will understand it some day although you sometimes doubt it (*daran*).   17. Since then a boy called George comes every day.   18. From now on I have the intention of working (to work) much harder than ever before.   19. At the same time he knew that hitherto he had again and again used a false expression. 20. Nowadays young people do not like staying at home of an evening.

14. ADVERBS (*cont.*)

(§§ 39-41)

1. It is almost noon.   We must go back immediately. 2. She is still fairly young and loves (it) to go everywhere. 3. Where are you going?—I am going nowhere especially. 4. He may be somewhere else; perhaps he is upstairs.   5. Max has become quite different.   He is quite friendly now. 6. He walked up and down for about ten minutes and then went into the house.   7. On the left he could see the cathedral, on the right the river.   8. You must do it like this, otherwise your work is in vain.   9. Unfortunately I have only a little money, not enough to buy you some

flowers. 10. I hope the postman hasn't gone past already. 11. The three sisters were all equally beautiful. 12. " Come in," he said. I opened the door and he got up. " Come here," he said. 13. He speaks just like his father. 14. I am not at all ill, I am not even tired. 15. That is well possible, for they are playing together. 16. Why are they dancing round him like that? 17. First she put on her glove, then she took it off. 18. Even he thinks differently from us. 19. Yes, of course you must come up; it is much too early to go home. 20. The doctor is certainly already on the way.

15. NUMERALS, DATES, ETC.
(§§ 42-50)

1. He is sixteen years old. 2. Goethe, the famous German poet, died in 1832. 3. Bring us another two glasses of beer, please. 4. He has more than a thousand books in his library. 5. My two brothers have already left school. 6. In (*unter* + D) the reign of Frederick II Prussia became a very important country in Europe. 7. We live two and a half miles away from the station, but a bus goes there two or three times an (in the) hour. 8. How much money have you?—I have only thirty marks. 9. Is your watch right?—No, it's fast. It's only half-past ten. 10. What is the date to-day?—I think it is January 3rd. 11. When did the second World War break out?—In 1939. 12. What did you do the day before yesterday?—On Wednesday? I went to the cinema. 13. A fortnight ago to-day my son came home. He had been a prisoner in Russia for several years. 14. I worked for an hour and a half yesterday morning and half an hour yesterday afternoon. I must work much harder to-morrow morning. 15. When does the train leave?—It leaves punctually at 3.55 p.m. 16. When were you born?—I was born in 1939. 17. How high is this mountain?—It is three thousand three hundred feet high. 18. All sorts of people were standing in front of the little church. 19. A week ago her only child died and now she is very lonely. 20. We have one clock in the sitting-room and a second [one] in the bedroom. Both our clocks are always slow.

16. Personal and Reflexive Pronouns, etc.

(§§ 51-54)

1. My hat is prettier than hers. 2. Your kitchen is bigger than mine. 3. Their village is even smaller than ours. 4. Our teachers are much more friendly than theirs. 5. I received an interesting letter to-day; it came by (with) the first post. 6. He was not aware of it. 7. He is ashamed of you (*3 forms*). 8. We are interested in her. 9. They are interested in it. 10. We don't speak to (with) one another. 11. They left the town behind them. 12. Is it you?—Yes, it is I. 13. There was once upon a time a young prince. 14. There was nobody in the room. 15. There are such people. 16. He is a friend of ours. 17. Have you seen your cousins (*3 forms*). 18. You write nothing about (*von*) yourself (*3 forms*). 19. You wash your hands (*3 forms*). 20. It is not raining, it is snowing.

17. Interrogative and Relative Pronouns

(§§ 55-61)

1. Which table shall (*wollen*) we choose? 2. By (with) which train are you coming? 3. What a beautiful woman! 4. In what sort of village do you live? 5. What sort of poems does he write? 6. Whose bicycle is that? 7. Who were you speaking with? 8. The trouble we gave ourselves! 9. The man whose wife was ill looked grave. 10. The woman with whose son he was playing is very lazy. 11. The children he was helping were very grateful to him. 12. The river on whose banks this great city stands (*liegt*) is very narrow. 13. The mountains on the top of which deep snow was lying are very high. 14. The teacher they were most grateful to has just died. 15. The man who got (§ 114) out of the car seemed to be in a great hurry. 16. The girl whose mother was in bed was working in the kitchen. 17. The table we were sitting at was round. 18. The chairs we were sitting on were most uncomfortable. 19. I did what I could, that's all I can say. 20. Everywhere I went I saw sad faces, a fact which I could not understand.

18. Demonstrative Adjectives and Pronouns
(§§ **62-67**)

1. This pencil is better than that one. 2. I am so thirsty and I have such a headache. 3. Such a child is quite impossible. 4. Those are our exercise-books, not yours. 5. His car is much bigger and much newer than the doctor's. 6. Amongst those who came the same day were his two cousins. 7. He who said that was mistaken. 8. Him I don't know, but I know his wife very well. 9. He is no longer (he) himself. 10. They must come of their own accord. 11. I write better with this pen than with that. 12. He is ashamed of those who behave like that. 13. My family is smaller than my brother's. 14. Were you aware of it? 15. Anne and Mary are sisters; the former is very clever but the latter is rather stupid.

19. Indefinite Adjectives and Pronouns
(§§ **68-78**)

1. There was a knock [at the door] and then there was a ring. 2. One of the pictures was quite unusual; some liked it (it pleased some), others didn't (it did not please others). 3. I take less milk and more sugar, please. 4. All were invited but only a few guests came. 5. You (one) cannot do that sort of thing in England. 6. Do you know anybody who has visited Berlin?—No, I don't know anybody. 7. That is something quite new. 8. I only take a little milk, and that is enough sugar. 9. If you don't try with all your strength everything is in vain. 10. He wished all of us much pleasure. 11. That is nobody's business. 12. He has lost all his money. Have you any on (*bei* + D.) you? 13. One must try to do something or other. 14. Nobody else came, for they were all too tired. 15. You must read something else, something more interesting. 16. The whole of Germany was deeply moved. 17. There were many people there already; some had flowers in their hands, others had brought presents. 18. Are the children here already?—There are some here. 19. Was there nothing else in the cupboard? 20. He didn't show it to any of us (he showed it to none of us).

20. Prepositions

(§§ **79-81**)

1. He came home about seven o'clock after he had gone right round the town.   2. They all sat round the long table till nine o'clock.   3. In spite of the great difficulties since the last war the Germans haven't lost (the) courage.   4. He lives at his uncle's opposite the white house.   5. On our arrival we went immediately to bed.   6. In my opinion he did it against his will.   7. We have lunch every day at home.   8. They were walking in the direction of London. 9. In this weather it is quite impossible to work in the garden.   10. He is not entirely without means, for he has been working now (already) for two years.   11. For what reason did you come along this street?   12. He went to school at the age of six.   13. Because of the cold weather they stayed at home.   14. They came by boat towards the end of the month.   15. During the last war many people lived outside the bigger towns.   16. As he hadn't any money on him he couldn't go by train.   17. He said in a quiet voice: " Yes, it is a picture by Dürer."   18. Although I live in the midst of all these people, except for you I hardly see anybody (I see almost nobody).   19. The judge was a man of sixty.   20. What are you doing at Christmas? We are going to Paris.

21. Prepositions *(cont.)*

(§ **82**)

A. (§ 82 (*a*)):

1. Put (§ 114) the book on the table.   2. He went to the window.   3. He walked across the street.   4. He sat down between me and my friend.   5. He was standing in front of the picture.   6. Among my papers I found this letter.   7. He lay down under a tree.   8. We are sitting at the table.   9. He came and stood behind them.   10. There were many beautiful pictures on the walls.   11. The hotel stands between the station and the church.   12. A friend of mine was sitting behind me.   13. He came into the room. 14. In the theatre he was sitting next to me.   15. He was lying on the bed.   16. He was walking up and down in the

room.   17. He was lying under a tree.   18. The bird flew across the sky.   19. A lamp hung over the table.   20. He sat down in the corner.

B. (§ 82 (*b*)):

1. They come once a day in summer but only twice a week in winter.   2. People abroad go more often to the theatre and less often to the cinema.   3. At that moment there was a knock.   " There is a letter for you here," said the postman.   4. In your place I should go to the seaside and not to the country.   5. Among other things I must go to the bank.   6. A long time ago he lived quite near but since he went abroad we haven't seen him.   7. On the contrary, in the evening one can hear a lot of music on the wireless.   8. It is now your turn, but don't drive more than 50 km. an hour.   9. As a rule he goes to the office in the morning.   10. There are many people in the street but almost nobody at the station.   11. Above all I am waiting for (*auf* + A) an answer to my question.   12. In any case you will be able to spend the day in the open.   13. In this way he could earn almost two hundred marks a month.   14. Their youngest son has not learned anything at school yet, and he is already fifteen years old.   15. The day after our arrival our friends who are now living in the country visited us.

22 Conjugation of Verbs

(§§ **83-94**)

A. (§ 83):

1. Have (*3 forms*).   2. You have (*3 forms*).   3. You had (*3 forms*).   4. He has had.   5. She had had.   6. Be (*3 forms*).   7. You are (*3 forms*).   8. You were (*3 forms*).   9. He has been.   10. She had been.   11. Become (*3 forms*).   12. You become (*3 forms*).   13. He has become.   14. She has become.   15. She had become.   16. We have done.   17. We should have.   18. They would have been.   19. Pres. subj. of *sein*; the 3rd person sing. pres. subj. of *häben*, *werden*, *sagen*, *tragen*.   20. Impf. subj. of *haben*, *sein*, *werden*.

B. Weak Verbs (§§ 84–87; 89–94):

1. He has answered. 2. They smiled. 3. He is bathing. 4. It lasts. 5. We fear. 6. I have hurried. 7. You count (*3 forms*). 8. There is a ring [at the door]. 9. Work (*3 forms*). 10. They had chosen. 11. She rests every day. 12. He is disturbing us. 13. I have been saying that for months. 14. To-morrow he is travelling to Switzerland. 15. He used to practise for two hours every day. 16. The children were playing in the corner of the room while their parents were working at the table. 17. They had been waiting for hours. 18. He shook his head and said: " I don't smoke, thank you." 19. After she had laid the table she filled all the glasses with water. 20. I hoped that he would act immediately.

C. Strong Verbs (§§ 84–86; 88–94):

1. He has fled. 2. She is dying. 3. Read (*3 forms*). 4. Don't sleep (*3 forms*). 5. We helped. 6. They have not written. 7. I was silent. 8. She steals. 9. They would have found. 10. Give (*3 forms*). 11. He reads a book every day. 12. The sun is now shining. 13. We have been flying against the wind for three hours. 14. After he had eaten he read. 15. I expect he will compel you. 16. He wouldn't speak. 17. The water was rising. 18. He had been riding for half an hour. 19. Will you remain here? 20. He ate some bread and cheese, drank a glass of beer and then went to the cinema.

23. Compound Verbs

(§ 95)

A. Inseparable (§ 95 (*a*)):

(*a*) Weak:

1. What does this word mean? 2. His sister only woke up at half-past nine. 3. Our family spent the holidays in Austria this summer. 4. This workman has earned 150 marks this week. 5. My brother hasn't yet developed the film. 6. I knew that your grandfather would miss the train. 7. You must excuse the child; he is rather stupid.

8. What do they want for this hat? 9. He tried to see his grandson but without success. 10. The young man accompanied us to the station. 11. We were expecting the doctor yesterday. 12. Did you catch the train? 13. His appearance quite frightened his mother. 14. Our teacher didn't notice us in the crowd. 15. He couldn't move the drawer at all.

(b) Strong:

1. What does this bottle contain? 2. Father has forgotten the key again. 3. Her face appeared at (+ D) the window and then immediately afterwards disappeared. 4. Our neighbour possesses a very big house. 5. Time goes very quickly. 6. I am beginning to understand why she left her parents. 7. It is rare that he loses his head in this way. 8. They had resolved to win the match (game). 9. You must avoid this mistake in future. 10. The sailor got a letter this morning, which is very unusual. 11. His wife stood at the door of the sitting-room and welcomed the guests. 12. We shall get different weather soon. 13. I was frightened when I saw him. 14. We haven't received any news from him. 15. The maid broke several plates and cups.

B. Separable (§ 95 (b)):

(a) Weak:

1. He has declined our invitation. 2. When did your aunt return? 3. He continued the story last night just before the children went to bed. 4. He is preparing the boy for an examination. 5. He shut the door and turned on the light. 6. If you walk quickly you [will] catch him up. 7. Fortunately it has stopped raining (to rain). 8. "But," he added, "I have no desire to visit her." 9. "When do you leave?" he asked me. 10. He met his friend at the (from the) station. 11. The speaker could not express his thoughts clearly. 12. His nephew in the end did not carry out his plan. 13. Don't light the lamp yet; it is still quite light. 14. You don't need to hurry; she hasn't put on her hat yet. 15. He pocketed the money and said nothing.

(*b*) Strong:

1. It was impossible to accept the invitation. 2. When do you get up in the morning?—As late as possible. 3. The train starts at 6.35 p.m. We must hurry if we want to catch it. 4. The little girl has spent all her money. 5. " And," he went on, " I expect something better of (from) you." 6. The friends who live opposite us have invited us to supper. 7. " When does the concert take place? " he asked his young friend. 8. " When do I get out? " she asked the official. 9. The sun rises very early in June. 10. The student never seems to go out; he prefers to read his books. 11. He took off his clothes, went to bed and fell asleep almost immediately. 12. That sort of thing often happens. 13. She has given up hope of seeing (to see) her son again. 14. He hasn't yet begun his work. 15. As soon as the king arrived everybody stood up.

C. Separable or inseparable (§ 95 (*c*)):

1. We changed at (in) Cologne. 2. We cannot distinguish between the colours. 3. Has he already translated this book? 4. They moved [house] shortly before Christmas. 5. The sun sets very early in December. 6. He ran over the child only last week but it is now playing in the street again. 7. The dog always retrieves the ball. 8. Hold your hand under so that you can catch it if it falls. 9. He convinced everybody that he had not stolen the knife. 10. Water surrounds the city on three sides.

24. REFLEXIVE AND IMPERSONAL VERBS
(§§ 96-98)

1. Sit down (*3 forms*). 2. The earth moves round the sun and the moon moves round the earth. 3. After he had dressed he came downstairs. 4. He catches cold very easily but he soon recovers again. 5. Don't turn round (*3 forms*). 6. The door opened and Fred came in. " Don't forget," he said. " We'll meet (§ 89 (*c*)) at the station to-night." 7. We undressed and lay down, but although we felt very tired we couldn't fall asleep. 8. Before they went to the theatre they washed and changed. 9. It was

already getting dark and so it was easy to hide in the wood.
10. He succeeded in getting (§ 114) home before it began
to snow.   11. How are you?—I am very well, thank you.
12. I believe it is freezing already.   13. We conversed for
a long time before we went to bed.   14. " I am sorry, and
I am very sorry for you," he said.   15. " It doesn't matter,"
she answered.

25. The Infinitive
(§ 99)

1. He does not intend to work hard.   2. He is unfortunately not able to come.   3. It is quite impossible to distinguish between them.   4. In order to catch the train he
had to run as quickly as possible.   5. I saw them come up
the stairs.   6. He is not yet old enough to understand this.
7. He wished to stay there.   8. He lets them do all they
want.   9. It is too good (beautiful) to be true.   10. He
did not dare to say a word.   11. It is too cold (to be able)
to go out.   12. He is going to stay with us in summer.   13.
It is easy to say that.   14. To understand properly (cor-
rectly) you have to read every page two or three times.
15. I heard her knock but I didn't want to open the door
because she talks too much and I was in a great hurry.

26. The Imperative and Interrogative
(§§ 100-1; 41; 55-57)

(Where possible give the three forms of the imperative.)

1. Throw the ball.   2. Take [a] seat.   3. Write soon.
4. Let us go to the cinema to-night.   5. Look at me.   6.
Amuse yourself (well).   7. Translate that.   8. Take it, it's
your book.   9. Be serious.   10. Have the goodness to do
it immediately.   11. Don't get angry.   12. Shall we go to
the theatre or to the cinema?   13. You haven't seen him,
have you?—Yes, I have.   14. Hasn't he come home yet?
15. He will meet us at the station, won't he?   16. Which
German towns do you know?   17. What is your name?
18. Why did she go there?   19. When do you get up in

the morning?   20. Whom did you go to the cinema with last night?

27. Auxiliary Verbs of Mood

(§ 102)

1. He cannot swim.   2. I should like to sleep.   3. He was not allowed to whistle.   4. You ought to drink less. 5. He has not been allowed to come.   6. He had to be silent.   7. He refused to speak.   8. Thou shalt not steal.   9. He is to speak first.   10. He wanted to dig. 11. He might fall.   12. They ought to have seen him.   13. He could have written the letter.   14. He should not have swum.   15. He has to remain.   16. He will be able to ride again soon.   17. He has had to.   18. He would not have liked to [have] come.   19. I should have to walk.   20. Let us go there.   21. May I open the window, please?   22. Their youngest son was said to be very clever. 23. The sun was just about to set.   24. I can't help it.   25. He dropped the glass.   26. We couldn't help laughing.   27. Mother sends her kindest regards.   28. I may have done it, in fact I must have done it.   29. You must have your hair cut to-morrow   30. I simply don't know what to say.

28. Passive Voice

(§ 103)

A.

1. This most interesting book was bought by your brother.   2. Whom were you woken up by this morning? 3. The letter hasn't yet been written.   4. Sugar and tea are sold in the shop opposite the station.   5. The papers unfortunately had been stolen.   6. He will never be recognized in that hat.   7. The newspaper is now being read by your father.   8. All the money has been spent in vain.   9. We had been warned by your example.   10. He has been cut with a knife.   11. There was not a single person to be seen.   12. I am sorry, there is nothing to be done.   13. The table was not yet laid.   14. The table was being laid by the servant when I came into the room.   15. All the shops are shut already.   16. I was given a glass of milk.

17. The postman has been given a new suit.   18. They had been sent an invitation but they had forgotten to accept it.   19. We were not helped at all.   20. That had not yet been thought of (*avoid passive*).

B. Passive with modal verbs (§ 103 (*b*)):

1. The drawer of the table in the kitchen cannot be opened.   2. This mistake must not be made again by you. 3. The window of the bedroom ought not to be shut at night.   4. In that case the house should have been built already.   5. The house ought not to have cost so much money.   6. The letter to the schoolmistress will have to be written later.   7. Her husband has never had to be woken up in the morning.   8. The letter to your granddaughter could not have been written earlier.   9. This German sentence must be repeated again and again till you can say it without a mistake.   10. Since the book is very easy it can be read quickly.

29. INDIRECT SPEECH
(§§ 104-105)

(Translate both with *daß* and without *daß* wherever possible.)

1. He said he did not want to come.   2. They said they would come to-morrow.   3. She said she was not ill. 4. The doctor asked me if I had been ill.   5. The farmer told the boys to go home at once.   6. The official asked the traveller why he hadn't a ticket.   7. I thought you had no time.   8. The teacher told us to sit down.   9. Uncle wrote to us [saying] that he was coming in the afternoon.   10. Her father asked me if I was sleeping.   11. He said he had tried to come earlier.   12. I knew that he was still ill, but my friend thought that he had recovered.   13. The policeman asked the man what he was carrying in his suit-case. 14. The patient said he was dying, but the doctor knew that he was not very ill.   15. I was told he spoke German quite well (quite well German).   16. My mother told the other

children to play in the garden. 17. The maid said that
the family was not at home. 18. Our friends wrote [to
say] that they intended to spend a fortnight at the seaside
at Easter. 19. The old man wanted to know why (the)
times had changed so [much]. 20. The doctor said that he
would visit the patient the next morning.

30. CONDITIONAL SENTENCES
(§§ 104, 106)

1. If he works hard he will earn a lot of money. 2. If
he worked harder he would earn more money. 3. If he had
worked hard he would have earned a lot of money. 4. I
shall go abroad next summer if I have enough money.
5. I should go abroad next summer if I had the money.
6. I should have gone abroad in the summer if I had had
the opportunity. 7. If the book had been more interesting
she would have read it with pleasure. 8. If the boy had
been more attentive he would not have made so many
mistakes. 9. If I had my own aeroplane I should always
fly everywhere. 10. If German were easier I should now
be able to speak it. 11. If you had tried you could have
done it. 12. He would not have noticed us if we had not
spoken. 13. They would have missed the train if they had
not taken a bus. 14. He won't recover if he doesn't eat.
15. If I were in your place I should send for the doctor
immediately. 16. If I knew that I should not ask. 17.
They would all be very poor if he died. 18. If he ate less
he would not be so fat. 19. We should have stayed at
home by the fire if it had been too cold (to be able) to go
out. 20. If he read more German he would speak better.

31. OTHER USES OF THE SUBJUNCTIVE
(§§ 104, 107)

1. Long live (the) freedom! 2. May he rest in peace!
3. Long live the King! 4. Peace be with you! 5. She
looks as if she is tired. 6. They looked as if they had eaten
nothing. 7. She behaves as if she is very rich. 8. I feel
as if (§ 26 (e)) I couldn't go (tun) one step further. 9. They
pretended to be tired. 10. He made himself (did as if he
were) at home.

32. GOVERNMENT OF VERBS

(§§ **108-11**)

A. (§ 108):

1. We all listened to him attentively. 2. He said he could not help me. 3. The dog would not obey its master. 4. She had served the family faithfully all her life. 5. We had met him in the street. 6. They were approaching a big town. 7. Whom do these books belong to? 8. He had at last succeeded in selling both his houses. 9. The child resembles its father more than [it does] its mother. 10. After they had watched the game they went home. 11. Why won't you answer me? 12. We had to follow the crowd. 13. I am sorry you don't believe me, but it is true. 14. It seemed very strange to me that my arm should hurt (me) so [much]. 15. I am very sorry for him, for nobody trusts him. 16. I forgot to thank you. 17. He trusted his friends blindly. 18. Nothing serious [will] happen to the children. 19. It is impossible to please everybody. 20. I don't like these pictures at all.

B. (§§ 5 (*a*), 109)):

1. Pass me the milk and sugar, please. 2. He wished me [a] good journey. 3. I can warmly recommend you this hotel. 4. The old soldier told my young brother a sad but interesting story. 5. The policeman showed the stranger the way to the station. 6. He promised the old sailor a large sum of money. 7. She will never be able to forgive him [for] it. 8. My friend gave me a pair of gloves as a present for (to) Christmas. 9. I introduced my new acquaintance to my wife. 10. I intend to write a very long letter to you. 11. I cannot describe to you my gratitude. 12. My father has forbidden him the house. 13. The doctor sent me a bill for (*über* + A) ten pounds. 14. After you have read the book don't forget to return it to me. 15. He did not do what I advised him. 16. Can you explain this sentence to me? 17. We believed that the boy had stolen the money from his mother. 18. He always offers his guests wine. 19. Do what I tell (order) you. 20. We took him the newspaper which he then read out to us.

C. (§§ 110–111):

1. It cost me a lot of trouble.   2. He was ashamed of his handwriting.   3. He taught us French and history.   4. God called the light Day and the darkness He called Night. 5. She is not ashamed of what (§ 59 (d)) she has said.

33. Verbs Followed by a Prepositional Object

(§ 112)

A. (§ 112 (a)-(i)):

1. She suddenly burst into tears of gratitude.   2. The book consists of three hundred or more pages.   3. " What will become of her ? " he asked me.   4. He tied the horse to the tree.   5. We are not looking forward very [much] to her visit.   6. You do not need to answer my question. 7. The book has been translated from German into English. 8. He remembered his promise to come back.   9. I thought she was a teacher.   10. He rang the bell and entered the house.   11. When did you write to him?   12. Although I am not interested in stamps a friend of mine gives me some as a present (presents some to me) every Christmas.   13. He arrived at the village before me and ordered a meal at the inn.   14. I reminded him of his promise to help me with the work.   15. I have never doubted his good intention, but that is not enough.   16. The foreigner went up to the policeman and asked him where the nearest post-office was. 17. He insists on an explanation, but what can I say to him? 18. He walked past the cathedral and did not look at it. 19. My brother thinks of everything.   20. He had been waiting for this opportunity for years.

B. (§ 112 (j)-(p)):

1. I knew that it was a matter of life or death.   2. He was talking to his wife about the children.   3. Why do you laugh at me? Have I said something quite impossible? 4. You need not be afraid of the consequences; everything is in order.   5. We were invited to supper but unfortunately we could not accept the invitation.   6. We finally decided to send for the doctor.   7. He knows nothing at all about

the matter.   8. Charles the Fifth was elected Emperor in 1519.   9. He came up to me and asked me for some money as he hadn't any on him.   10. We were very pleased about the news of (*von*) his success.   11. I forgot to ask after her health when I saw her this morning.   12. He told us all sorts of interesting [things] about his life in the Far East. 13. He nodded his head and said that he too was of the same opinion.   14. They conversed with one another the whole evening about their past as old people do (it).   15. " I must look after my patients," said the doctor.   16. What do you think of his mother?   17. He turned round to me and asked after my cousin.   18. They have written nothing about it in the paper yet.   19. It concerns your future, your happiness.   20. He asked me the way to the station.

34. Translation of English Verbal Forms in -ing

(§ 113)

1. Having dressed he went downstairs.   2. He likes dancing but he prefers playing cards.   3. Instead of waiting for us he went home immediately.   4. Saying this he smiled. 5. In German theatres smoking is generally forbidden.   6. The weather is not very inviting.   7. Without saying a word he put on his hat and went out.   8. Having a lot to do he got up early.   9. One learns by being diligent and attentive.   10. He succeeded in finding a comfortable room in the village.   11. The man reading the paper in the corner of the compartment suddenly got up and opened the window. 12. By doing that he shows that he has courage.   13. One ought not to read while eating but I do (it) sometimes.   14. Before leaving the house he wrote several letters to his acquaintances and friends.   15. The new play has been a surprising success.   16. He had come into the room without our hearing him.   17. By saying that he hopes to get the job.   18. He saw them going past the church in the direction of Castle Street.   19. I know from experience that such films are most entertaining.   20. " I prefer going to the theatre in the afternoon instead of in the evening," she said smiling.

35. TRANSLATION OF CERTAIN ENGLISH WORDS

(§ 114)

A. (" ask "-" lie "):

1. I leave the house at half-past eight and go to school by bus. 2. I got home at seven o'clock to-night because the train was an hour late. 3. There are certain people who always ask stupid questions. 4. He called the waiter and asked him for a light. 5. She knew that I wanted to go for a walk. 6. They got into the car and went to Hamburg. 7. He asked me if I had enjoyed the film. 8. When does your train leave?—I don't know, I'll ask a porter. 9. We enjoyed ourselves last night and we particularly enjoyed the food. 10. I don't know your friend but I know where he lives. 11. He was late because he left his umbrella at home and had to go back to get it. 12. When he learnt the truth he had to lie down on the bed. 13. I asked for my money but he said he had lost it. 14. They have got very old but they still enjoy good health. 15. He was lying on his bed learning German poems when we called on him. 16. I was asked to lunch but I had to refuse the invitation because I was about to go on a journey. 17. It is late. Do you think he got my letter? 18. I don't know what his name is. 19. His name is Robert but they call him Bob. 20. " Do you know the way? " he asked.

B. (" look "-" time "):

1. I looked at him closely; he certainly did not look very well. 2. What is the time? My watch has stopped, not for the first time. 3. Will you please take these letters and parcels to the post-office?—I have already said " No " several times; I have other things to do. 4. Fortunately it had now stopped raining. 5. He suddenly stopped the car and asked me the way to the nearest post-office. 6. He took my advice, went to the station and found his things there. 7. After a time he woke up; and then he knew that it had only been a dream. 8. We looked about us but could see nobody. 9. He said that he had been looking for the book that he had put on the table. 10. He turned to me and said: " I can only come at seven." 11. He was

sitting on a chair because he was tired.   12. He put the money in his pocket, went out and took the next train.   13. He woke me in time and took me home.   14. " Will you take me with you? " he asked smiling.   15. It took a long time before he succeeded in waking up the landlord.   16. He took the book out of the cupboard and put it in his pocket.   17. When the train stopped the next time he got out and bought himself a cup of coffee.   18. When he entered the room I asked him to sit down.   19. I am sure you will understand it in time.   20. I took him the book and at the same time some flowers.

SECTION III

ENGLISH PROSE PASSAGES
FOR TRANSLATION

1. *My brother and I*

My name[1] is Jack.   I have a little brother whose name[1] is Fred.   He is much younger than I am[2].   He is only[3] five years old.   I am nearly[4] eight.   I go to school every morning[5], except of course[4] on Saturdays[6] and Sundays[6], but my little brother does not go to school yet[7].   He is still[7] too[4] young.   He stays at[8] home all day[9]; but when[10] the weather is fine he plays in[11] the garden most[12] of the time. School[13] begins at a quarter past nine[14], so[15] I leave[3] home about[16] five to nine[14].   Mother no longer[7] takes[3] me to school.   "You[17] are old enough[4] to[18] be able[19] to walk there[20] alone," she says.[21]   School[13] is not far away and I usually play outside[20] with the other children for a few minutes[9] before[22] school[13] begins.   But when[10] it rains[23] I leave[3] home later because I then[3] go[3] to school by[24] bus in order not to[25] get[3] wet.

1. §114: "call".   2. §35 (*d*) (ii).   3. §114.   4. §39.   5. §5 (*b*) (i).
6. §13 (*e*).   7. §38.   8. §81 (*j*).   9. §24 (*b*).   10. §8.   11. §82 (*a*).
12. §35 (*d*) (iv), note.   13. §13 (*a*).   14. §47.   15. §9.   16. §79 (*e*).
17. §52 (*a*).   18. §99 (*e*).   19. §102 (*b*) (ii).   20. §40 (*a*) (i).
21. §4 (*b*).   22. Preposition or conjunction?   23. §98 (*a*).   24. §81 (*f*).
25. §99 (*d*).

2. *My friend Richard*

When[1] I go to school in the morning[2] I always[3] meet my friend Richard at[4] the corner of our street.   He lives quite[5] near[6].   He is a year older than I am[7] but I am as tall as he is[7].   He is in[4] the same[8] class as I am although he is older.   Last year[9] he was ill for a very long time[3].   I am sometimes[3] ill but never[3] for very long[3].   When[1] I am ill I

am never[3] absent from school[10] for[11] more than a week[2] or a
fortnight[2]. My friend and I always[3] go[12] to school together[13],
except when[14] it rains[15]. Then[12] I go[12] to school by[16] bus
and he goes[12] there[17] by[16] car. His father has a very big
car and drives past[18] the school every morning[9, 13]; but he
usually leaves[12] home at least[19] half an hour[20] after[21] Richard
has gone to school.

1. § 8.   2. § 50.   3. § 38.   4. § 82 (a).   5. § 39.   6. § 82 (b) (vi).
7. § 35 (d).   8. § 65.   9. § 24 (c).   10. § 13 (a).   11. § 24 (b).   12.
§ 114.   13. § 5 (b) (i).   14. § 7 (a).   15. § 98 (a).   16. § 81 (f).   17.
§§ 40 (a) (i).   18. § 112 (b).   19. § 37 (c) (i).   20. § 45 (a), note.
21. Preposition or conjunction?

3. *My two[1] sisters*

Besides[2] my younger brother I have two sisters. They
are both[1] older than I am. One[3] of them still[4] goes to
school. Her name is Mary and she is nearly[5] fourteen
years old. She is very clever and my parents hope that
she will study at[6] the university when she leaves[7] school.
She sometimes[4] helps me with[8] my homework, but unfortunately[5] not as[9] often as[9] I should like[10]. My other sister
Anne has just[4] left[7] school. She is now[7] seventeen and
goes[7] every day to[11] the office. She has to[12] get up[13] fairly[5]
early in order to[14] catch[15] the train at 8.20[16]. She has to[12]
be in[17] the office at half-past nine[16]. If[18] she misses[15] this
train she arrives late at[19] the office; but that happens very
rarely, for[20] she is always in time[7] at[21] the station. But
quite[5] often[4] the train is late[7], especially[5] when it snows[22],
and then[7] she has to[12] wait sometimes[4] more than a quarter
of an hour[23].

1. § 43 (e).   2. § 81.   3. § 69.   4. § 38.   5. § 39.   6. § 82 (b) (ii).
7. § 114.   8. § 112 (f).   9. § 35 (d) (i).   10. § 102 (b) (iii) and add
"it".   11. § 82 (b) (v).   12. §102 (b) (iv).   13. § 95 (b).   14. § 99 (d).
15. § 95 (a).   16. § 47.   17. § 82 (a).   18. § 106 (a).   19. § 112 (i).
20. § 2 and § 6.   21. § 82 (b) (iv).   22. § 98 (a).   23. § 45 (a), note.

4. *Getting up[1]*

Every morning I get up[2] at a quarter to eight[3]. Mother
wakes[4] me usually at half-past seven[3]. In the morning[5] I

am always very sleepy. I don't like[6] getting up[2], especially[7] when it is cold. Do you like[6] getting up[2]? I love[8] lying[4] in bed[9] after[10] I have woken[4] up. Mother often[11] has to call[4] me again.[11] I rub my[12] eyes and then[4] jump out of bed[9] and go into[13] the bathroom where[14] I take a cold bath. Then[4] I go back[15] into[13] my bedroom and dress[16] quickly. As soon as[17] I am ready I hurry downstairs[18], go into[13] the dining-room, greet my parents who are already sitting[4] at the table and sit[4] down on[13] my chair. I always have a[19] good appetite and breakfast[20] is the meal[21] I prefer[2]. Father usually reads the newspaper during breakfast[20]; sometimes he gets letters or postcards which[21] he then[4] reads instead[22] of the newspaper. I never[11] get[4] any[23] letters. I am still[11] too[7] young.

1. § 113 (*b*). 2. § 95 (*b*). 3. § 47. 4. § 114. 5. § 82 (*b*) (ii) or § 50. 6. § 113 (*h*). 7. § 39. 8. § 113 (*d*). 9. § 13 (*i*). 10. Preposition or conjunction? 11. § 38. 12. § 13 (*g*) and § 96. 13. § 82 (*a*). 14. § 58 (*a*) (ii). 15. § 40 (*a*) (iii) and § 95 (*b*). 16. § 97. 17. § 7 (*a*). 18. § 40 (*a*) (ii). 19. § 14 (*c*). 20. § 13 (*e*). 21. § 58 (*a*). 22. § 80. 23. § 14 (*b*).

5. *Fred goes shopping*[1]

While I am at[2] school my little brother Fred plays in the garden if it is fine or in the house if it is raining. When[3] mother goes shopping[1] he likes[4] going with her[5]. He is very pleased when he is allowed[6] to carry a little parcel. There[7] are some shops quite near[2]; and when[3] mother has forgotten[8] the bread or the meat and is very busy in the house she sends Fred to[9] the shop with money and tells[10] him what[11] he has to say. It is not dangerous, for[12] it is not necessary to go across[13] the road in order to get[14] to the shops; and Fred never loses[8] the money or forgets[8] what[11] he has to buy. But when[3] Fred doesn't come back[15] immediately[16] mother begins to get[14] anxious and goes again and again[16] to[13] the window to[17] see if[3] he is coming. How[18] glad she is when[3] she hears his voice or sees his face.

1. Say "makes purchases". 2. § 82 (*b*) (vi). 3. § 8. 4. § 113 (*h*). 5. Omit. 6. § 102 (*b*) (i). 7. § 52 (*e*). 8. § 95 (*a*). 9. § 81 (*j*). 10. § 109. 11. § 58 (*a*) (ii) and § 59 (*d*). 12. § 2 and § 6. 13. § 82 (*a*). 14. § 114. 15. § 95 (*b*). 16. § 38. 17. § 99 (*d*). 18. § 41, note.

6. *Lunch*[1]

In[2] the morning school finishes[3] at a quarter to one[4] and begins again in[2] the afternoon at two o'clock[4]. Since[5] I do not live far from school I have lunch[6] at[6] home. Neither[7] my father nor[7] my sisters come home[8] to lunch[1]. Father and my elder sister work in an office in town[9]—but not in the same[10] office; they only[11] get[11] home at half-past five[4], and so they have to lunch[6] in a restaurant. My other sister has lunch[6] at school, for her school is half an hour by bus from our house[12]. I prefer[13] having lunch[6] at[6] home, though many other[14] boys who do not live far from school seem to prefer[13] having lunch[6] at school. After lunch I go back[15] to school and have three more[16] lessons, except on Wednesdays[1], when we have a free afternoon. I am sometimes very sleepy in[2] the afternoon, especially in summer[1], and do not always listen[15] attentively. Then[11] I cannot answer[17] my teacher's questions and he gets[11] very dissatisfied with me.

1. § 13 (*e*).   2. § 82 (*b*) (ii).   3. § 14 (*c*).   4. § 47.   5. § 8.   6. § 81 (*j*).   7. § 10 (*b*).   8. § 81 (*g*).   9. § 13 (*i*).   10. § 65.   11. § 114.   12. Add "distant".   13. § 113 (*d*).   14. § 29 (*e*).   15. § 95 (*b*).   16. § 43 (*d*).   17. § 112 (*c*).

7. *The holidays*

I am very much[1] looking forward to[2] the holidays. The whole family is going to[3] the seaside by car. A friend of ours[4] has a small house there which he is lending[5] us this year[6] again for the summer holidays. It stands all[1] alone by[7] the sea and it has a big garden with several old fruit-trees and many magnificent flowers. Behind[8] the garden is a large meadow where we often see cows and horses belonging[9] to a farmer who lives quite near. We have been there once[10] already. Last year[6] we went there at[11] Easter. The weather was bright, we had little[12] rain and a lot[12] of sunshine, but a cold wind was usually blowing and the sea was very cold too[13]. I only[1] bathed once[10] but father used[14] to bathe every morning[6] before breakfast. When[15] he came back his face and hands were blue, although he always said he[16] was[17] quite warm. I intend[18] to bathe every day[6] in summer. I can't[19] swim yet[20], but I hope to be able[19] to swim this summer[6]. I hope[1] the weather will be fine.

1. § 39.   2. § 112 (c).   3. § 82 (b) (i).   4. § 51, note (2).   5. § 109. 6. § 24 (c).   7. § 82 (b) (ii).   8. § 82 (a).   9. § 108 and § 113 (g). 10. § 38.   11. § 81 (j).   12. § 78 (c).   13. § 9.   14. § 90 (a).   15. § 8. 16. § 26 (e).   17. § 105 (a).   18. § 99 (c).   19. § 102 (b) (ii).   20. § 38.

8. *Preparations for the holidays*

At last[1] the holidays have begun and to-morrow[2] we are all[3] going to the seaside. To-day[2] everybody[3] has been very busy, but mother of course[4] most[5] of all. She has had[6] to get[7] all our[8] things[7] ready and pack the bags. Anne packed her own bag but we children are still much too young to[9] do this.[10]. We should[11] probably forget our shirts or our handkerchiefs or even[4] our shoes if we packed our own bags. But we help[12] mother by[13] bringing[14] her all our[8] things[7] and putting[7] them on[15] the bed. We stand near[15] her while she packs and when she asks[7] us to fetch something[16] she has forgotten my brother and I run immediately[1] to[17] look[7] for it. Father is getting[7] the car ready, and as soon as mother has packed a bag Mary and I sit[7] on it[18] and shut[19] it[20]; and then[21] we take[7] the bag to father and he puts[7] it in[15] the car. We are setting off[19] about[22] ten o'clock to-morrow morning[2], and as[23] the drive takes[7] five or six hours we have to take[7] our lunch with us.

1. § 38.   2. § 50.   3. § 74.   4. § 39.   5. § 37 (a) ; omit " of all ". 6. § 102, note.   7. § 114.   8. § 29 (f).   9. § 99 (e).   10. § 64, note. 11. § 106 (b).   12. § 108.   13. § 113 (e).   14. § 109.   15. § 82 (a). 16. § 59 (a).   17. § 99 (d).   18. § 52 (d).   19. § 95 (b).   20. § 52 (b). 21. § 2.   22. § 79 (e).   23. § 8.

9. *Journey to the seaside*

I woke[1] up very early this morning[2] because I was so excited. I jumped out of bed, ran to the window and looked out[3]. It was not raining, but there[4] were big black clouds in[5] the sky and no[6] sun. It was, however[7], still very early and perhaps[8] the sun had not yet risen[9]. I went to[10] bed again and slept till half-past eight. The sky was still covered when[11] I got up but after breakfast the sun was shining and the clouds had all[12] disappeared[13]. We all[12] got[1] into the car. There[4] was not very much room in it[14], but it was all the same to[15] us. As soon as we had left[16] London behind us father drove very fast. We stopped[1] in the New Forest and had our lunch in[17] the open. It had become very hot in the car and we were glad to be able to lie[1] in the shade of the trees. But soon afterwards[18] we had to set off[9] again; and two hours later we were in our friend's house by the sea.

1. § 114. 2. § 50. 3. § 40 (a) (ii). 4. § 52 (e). 5. § 82 (b) (ii). 6. § 12. 7. § 9. 8. § 39. 9. § 95 (b). 10. § 81 (j). 11. § 8. 12. § 74. 13. § 95 (a). 14. § 52 (d). 15. § 26 (d). 16. Omit. 17 § 82 (b) (vi). 18. § 38.

10. *At the seaside*

We sometimes spend[1] our holidays in[2] the country, but I prefer spending[1] them by the sea. This year the weather was magnificent. We had sunshine every day except on the first Sunday morning[3]; but it didn't matter[4], for we went to church[5]. The sea was very warm and we often bathed three times a[6] day; and I learnt at last to swim. Father taught[7] me. I was very proud of[8] it. After bathing[9] we usually played all sorts of[10] games on the sand or we simply lay[11] in the sun. We all[12] got[11] very brown except mother who is afraid of[13] the sun. Sometimes we made excursions along[14] the sea-shore and found strange fishes and plants everywhere. Once we were[15] cut off by[16] the sea and had to climb up[17] on to the rocks and wait at least[18] two or three hours. Fortunately[19] mother was not with us and knew nothing of[20] the danger till we were back. It could[21] easily have been very dangerous if we had lost our heads[22].

1. § 95 (a). 2. § 82 (b) (iv). 3. § 48. 4. § 98 (b). 5. § 13 (i). 6. § 82 (b) (ii). 7. § 111; add " it ". 8. § 82 (b) (iii). 9. § 113 (f). 10. § 45 (d). 11. § 114. 12. § 74. 13. § 112 (o). 14. § 79 (c). 15. § 103 (g). 16. § 103 (d). 17. § 40 (a) (ii). 18. § 37 (c) (i). 19. § 39. 20. § 112 (n). 21. § 102 (b) (ii) and § 106 (c). 22. Singular : § 13 (f).

11. *Our house*

We lived then[1] in a small town in the south in a big house made of[2] wood, which[3] my father had bought, as[4] I learnt[1] later, for two hundred[5] pounds[6]. From the windows of the two rooms in which[3] I lived with my little sister we could see our garden which[3] was not very beautiful, although it was fairly[7] big. Here and there were a few small fruit-trees, but there were only a few[8] flowers and not a single[9] big tree and no shade. But this garden gave[10] us great joy, especially to my little sister, who had seen neither[11] mountains nor[11] fields nor[11] forests, whereas[12] I had travelled more than five hundred[5] miles and had seen the beauty of nature[13]. I was never tired of telling[14] my little sister about[15] this journey. She always listened[16] to me most[17] attentively, but the expression in her eyes seemed to say very clearly: I really[7] don't understand[18] a single[9] word. It was indeed[19] no wonder, for I was only[1] five years old and she was not more than three.

1. §114. 2. §81 (a). 3. §58 (a). 4. §8. 5. §42. 6. §46. 7. §39. 8. §78 (b). 9. §45 (e). 10. Say "made". 11. §10 (b). 12. §7 (a). 13. §13 (a). 14. §113 (d). 15. §112 (n). 16. §108. 17. §35 (d) (iv). 18. §95 (a). 19. §13 (i).

12. *Fear of[1] the future*

Soon afterwards[2] she came one day[3] into the room where we children were all working and she sat[4] down opposite[5] me, not in[6] her usual place, but[7] as if[8] she wanted to see my work. I was mending some shirts, and after a while she began to talk to[9] me. "You[10] foolish child," she said[11], "you[10] are always crying" (for I was crying at[12] that moment); "why are you[10] crying?" "Because they[13] will[14] take me away[15]," I said[11], "and force me to do housework, which[16] I can't do." "Well[2], child," she said[11], "but though you can't do housework you will learn[4] it[17] in time[4] and you won't have to do anything[18] hard[19] at first[2]." "Yes[20] I shall[20]," I said[11], "and if I can't do it they[13] will beat me, and I am only[4] a little girl, and I can't do it "; and then I burst into[21] tears again so that[7] I could not speak any more [2] to[9] her.

1. § 112 (o). 2. § 38. 3. § 25 (b). 4. § 114. 5. § 81 (e). 6. § 82 (b) (ii). 7. § 8. 8. § 107 (b). 9. § 112 (j). 10. § 52 (a). 11. § 4 (b). 12. § 82 (b) (vi). 13. § 68. 14. § 102 (b) (vi). 15. § 40 (a) (iii). 16. § 59 (c). 17. § 52 (b). 18. § 76. 19. § 32. 20. § 101. 21. § 112 (h).

13. *The farmer is afraid*

Many years ago[1], in a little cottage between the village and the mountain, a farmer lived with his wife and their little son. The farmer spent his days—and at certain times[2] of the year his nights too—alone in[3] the open. But the little boy, when he wasn't helping[4] his mother, and often too when he was helping[4] her, was always reading the big books he borrowed[5] from the doctor. His parents were very fond of him, and rather proud of[6] him too, so he was allowed[7] to read as[8] much as[8] he liked[9]; for they knew[2] that it was sometimes useful to be able to read books, in spite of what[10] their neighbours said. What the boy liked[11] best of all to read was natural history[12] and fairy-tales.

One evening[13] the farmer, who for[14] some days had been behaving[15] rather strangely, came home quite excited. He was trembling in[16] every limb. He sat[2] down at the table where his wife and son were working and said: " It is impossible, Mary. I can never go up[17] that mountain again."

1. § 82 (b) (ix). 2. § 114. 3. § 82 (b) (vi). 4. § 108. 5. Add " for himself ", § 26 (b). 6. § 82 (b) (iii). 7. § 102 (b) (i). 8. § 35 (d) (ii). 9. § 102 (b) (iii). 10. § 59 (d). 11. § 113 (h). 12. Say " nature-history ". 13. § 25 (b). 14. § 90 (c). 15. § 97. 16. § 82 (b) (ii). 17. § 40 (a) (ii).

14. *The professor*

A well-known Berlin[1] professor had spent the evening in the house of an old friend. The conversation had been most[2] interesting and the wine very good. It was getting late, however, and the professor said he must[3] go home. When he was just about to[4] leave the house it was raining hard[5]. His friend's young wife persuaded[6] him to spend the night in their house since the rain would probably not stop[7] till[8] the next morning[9]. The professor accepted[10] the invitation with pleasure.

But suddenly the guest had disappeared without their knowing[11] where[12] he had gone. They were just about to[4] go to bed when the professor came into the room again. He was wet through[13].

" But, my dear chap[14]," his friend asked[7] him, " where have you been? I thought you were intending[4] to spend the night here in order not to get wet."

" Certainly[15], my dear friend," the professor answered. " I only[15] went home quickly to fetch my nightshirt."

1. § 33.   2. § 35 (d) (iv).   3. § 105 (a).   4. § 102 (b) (vi).   5. Say "strong".   6. § 95 (c) (i).   7. § 114.   8. § 114 ; "only".   9. § 50.   10. § 95 (b).   11. § 113 (e).   12. § 41.   13. Say " quite wet ".   14. § 31.   15. § 39.

15.   *The youth hostel*

We had been hiking all day. Now[1] it was getting late and we had just come into a beautiful old town. We asked for[2] the Youth Hostel. It was outside[3] the town and we had to walk another[4] ten minutes. At last we saw the Youth Hostel. How[5] pretty the house was, and how[5] beautifully it was situated on the edge of the wood!

We asked[1] the warden if[6] there[7] was[8] still room for two. He said that we could[9] still have beds although many hikers had come[9]. He took[1] us upstairs[10] and showed[11] us our beds. How[5] glad we were to be able to take off[12] our clothes and wash[13]!

After washing[14] we went downstairs[10] again. As[6] there[7] were tables and benches in front of the house we decided[15] to have our supper outside[10] in the open, for it was a warm evening and still quite light; so we took[1] out of one[16] of the rucksacks the bread, sausage and cheese we had brought with us[17] and began to eat.

1. § 114.   2. § 112 (k).   3. § 80.   4. § 43 (d).   5. § 41, note.   6. § 8.   7. § 52 (e).   8. § 105 (b).   9. § 105 (a).   10. § 40 (a) (i).   11. § 5 (a) and § 109.   12. § 95 (b).   13. § 97.   14. § 113 (f).   15. § 95 (a).   16. § 69.   17. Omit.

16. *The excursion*

"Don't forget[1]," I said to him again. "At five o'clock.
At the corner of the street. And you mustn't[2] tell[3] anybody[4]. It's a secret, a secret between you and me, and
nobody[4] knows[5] it except[6] ourselves."

He promised to say nothing and said he would come[7]
back as soon as he had[7] had[8] tea. He kept his word. I
had been waiting for[9] him for[10] five minutes, but I had
arrived early. I said only two words: "Follow[11] me,"
and went off[12] quickly without looking[5,13] round. But I
knew[5] he was behind me. We did not[14] say a[14] word till
we came to the bank of the river. "There it is," I said,
and pointed to[9] a long, narrow boat. "Everything[15] is
ready. I hope[16] you can swim. But it is not dangerous
really[16]. You aren't afraid, are you[17]?" It seemed to me
as if[18] he was trembling, but perhaps not.

"No," he answered, "I'm not afraid; and I can swim
like[19] a fish."

"Good," I said, "jump in[20]. We must hurry. We
have no time to lose. It will soon be dark."

1. § 100 (*b*). 2. § 102 (*b*) (i). 3. Add "it". 4. § 72. 5. § 114.
6. § 81 (*b*). 7. § 105 (*a*). 8. Say "drunk". 9. § 112 (*c*). 10. § 90
(*c*). 11. § 108. 12. § 40 (*a*) (iii). 13. § 113 (*d*). 14. § 12. 15. § 74.
16. § 39. 17. § 101. 18. § 26 (*e*) and § 107 (*b*). 19. § 35 (*d*) (iv), note.
20. § 40 (*a*) (ii).

17. *Poor[1] Peter*

Peter lived in a big dark forest. He didn't love his
parents, but that was quite natural, for they didn't love
him either[2]. They were very poor and worked very hard
all day, and Peter had to work hard too, although he was
still very young; and nobody had time to smile, and they
were all very unhappy.

One day Peter was alone. He had for a moment
stopped[3] working and was thinking. How lovely it would
be if he could[4] lie the whole summer in the sun with only
a few sheep around[5] him, instead of having[6] to work all day
long in this dark forest where he only saw the sun sometimes at noon[7]. And suddenly he knew that he was no

longer alone. He looked up[8] and saw in front of him[9] a little old man. " I've been watching[10] you for a long time," he said, " and it seems to me[11] as if you don't like[12] working here."

" No," replied the boy, " I should like[13] to go[14] where the sun shines all day long and where people are happy and smile."

1. § 13 (b).   2. § 9.   3. § 114.   4. § 106 (b).   5. § 40 (b) (ii). 6. § 113 (d).   7. § 47.   8. § 40 (a) (iii).   9. § 53.   10. § 89 (b) and § 108.   11. § 26 (e).   12. § 113 (h).   13. § 102 (b) (iii).   14. Add " there ", § 40 (a) (i).

18. *A late visit*

At last the clock struck eleven, and all[1] was silent in the house. Dorothy got up and went slowly to the door of the library, where she waited a moment. Then she knocked, and then she waited again. Her father had answered[2] her, but she had not the courage to open[3] the door. She heard him move[4] inside[5], and he came and opened[3] the door for[6] her.

" What is the matter[7]? " asked the doctor. " You are standing there like[8] a ghost."

She went into the room, but at first she could not say a word. Her father, who looked[9] very grave, had been busy at his desk, and after looking[9] at her for some moments he went back and sat[9] down at his desk again. She could only see his back—she began to hear him writing[10]. She remained standing[10] near the door. She could feel her heart beating[10]. At last she began to speak in[11] a very quiet voice.

1. § 74.   2. § 108.   3. § 95 (b).   4. § 97 and § 99 (b).   5. § 40 (a) (i). 6. § 26 (a).   7. § 52 (e).   8. § 39.   9. § 114.   10. § 113 (c).   11. § 81 (f).

19. *A conversation*

" I don't understand why you have seen[1] him. I don't think[2] it was right," Margaret said.

" I was so sorry[3] for him—it seemed to me as if some-one ought[4] to see him."

" No one but[5] I," said Margaret.

" But you wouldn't[6], my dear[7]," Aunt Mary said, " and somebody had to see[1] him, otherwise[8] I don't know what might[9] have become of[10] him."

" I have not seen[1] him, because my father has forbidden[11] me to do so," Margaret said very simply.

" If your father were to[4] forbid[11] you to go to sleep[12]," replied her aunt, " you would, I suppose[13], remain awake."

Margaret looked[14] at her. " I don't understand you. You seem[15] very strange to me."

" Well[16], my dear[7], you will understand me one day! " And Mrs. Graham, who was reading the evening paper, pretended[17] the news interested her very much[18]. But Margaret was silent for so long that she almost lost hope; and she was just going to[19] say to her that she had no heart when the girl at last spoke.

" What did he say? " she asked.

1. Say "visited". 2. § 112 (g). 3. § 98 (b), note. 4. § 102 (b) (v). 5. § 81 (b). 6. § 94 (b), note. 7. § 31. 8. § 9. 9. § 102 (b) (ii). 10. § 112 (e). 11. § 109. 12. § 95 (b). 13. Invert; § 95 (b). 14. § 114. 15. § 108. 16. § 38. 17. § 107 (b). 18. § 39. 19. § 102 (b) (vi).

20.   *Mother and son*

At the edge of a big wood stood a little cottage. In this cottage a woman had been living for nine or ten years alone with her little son. Her husband had died shortly before the boy was born; and if[1] the child had not been there she too would have died, for she had loved her husband very much. However the child had given her hope and courage, and she had done all[2] she could for the child, although she had only very little[3] money. He was a wild child and would[4] sometimes disappear all day in the wood and would[4] not come home till supper-time[5], his[6] pockets filled with insects, lovely round white stones, and feathers of rare birds. His mother had been of course at first very anxious, but now she knew that it really wasn't dangerous and that he would finally[7] come home. But one day it had got very dark and there was still no sign of[8] the boy and she was already[7] beginning[4] to feel[9] very restless. She was standing[4] at the open door and didn't know what to[10] do, when suddenly she heard voices.

1. § 106 (c).   2. § 59 (a).   3. § 78 (c).   4. § 90 (a).   5. Say "only to supper", § 13 (e) and § 114: "only".   6. § 13 (f) and § 24 (e). 7. § 38.   8. § 81 (i).   9. § 97.   10. § 102 (b) (v).

21.   *Our garden*

On Saturday afternoon[1] my wife and I decided that we ought to do something in the garden. It was looking very untidy. The grass was growing in[2] the wrong places. There were no flowers to be seen[3]. Spring would[4] soon come and we should[5] not be able to sit in the garden as[6] we had done[7] last year on fine days. Why not? Simply because we should be ashamed of it[8]. For we have neighbours who are very friendly but who are very proud of their own garden. They work in it every Saturday afternoon[1] and most[9] Sundays, and of course it always looks very beautiful. They succeed[10] in having flowers all the year round[11]; and everything is always tidy. And although they never say anything[12] it seems to me always as if they thought[13] we were very lazy. We aren't lazy really, we work very hard; but not in the garden. We are not especially interested in[13] the garden, though we do like looking at flowers. But something had to be done[14]. So last Saturday afternoon[1] we worked in the garden instead of doing[15] something interesting[16].

1. § 48.   2. § 82 (b) (ii).   3. § 103 (f).   4. § 94.   5. § 102 (b) (ii). 6. § 8.   7. Add "it".   8. § 52 (c).   9. Say "on most Sundays", § 35 (d) (iv), note.   10. § 98 (b).   11. Omit.   12. § 76.   13. § 112 (g). 14. § 103 (b).   15. § 113 (d).   16. § 32.

22.   *Our village*

Our village is quite small. It consists of[1] a few big houses and twenty or thirty fairly small ones[2]; and not far

away there are three or four farms. The church is very
old and has a tall tower. One[3] has to go across[4] two
meadows to get[5] there. There are always cows in these
meadows, and when some old ladies from the town were
staying in our village last year they asked us if the cows
were[6] dangerous. They did not seem to believe[7] us when
we said that they needn't be afraid of [8] them. They preferred
not to go to church on Sunday only because they were not
quite sure. There is a school in the village too, but only
for young children; we are too old now and go by bus
every day to the school in the next town. But in the
holidays we don't go to the town very often. We amuse
ourselves usually down[9] by the little river where we catch
fish[10] or swim or lie in the sun on the little raft which we
made this year. It isn't very firm and we often fall into
the river.

1. § 112 (e).   2. § 69, note 2.   3. § 68.   4. § 82 (a).   5. § 114.
6. § 105 (b).   7. § 108.   8. § 112 (o).   9. § 40 (a) (i).   10. Plural.

23. *A Friend in need*

It was useless[1]. Nothing could be[2] done now. He
could not get home in time if he went back to the town;
and yet he couldn't come home without the present.
Elizabeth would never forgive[3] him. So he turned[4] and
ran back wildly, blindly. He was very tired but he ran
on[5]. He had only one thought in his head—to arrive at[6]
the shop before it was shut. When he was about to give
up[7] all hope he heard a car behind him[8]. He looked round
and recognized William. " Why are you running like[1]
that[1] ? " he asked; " and you're going in the wrong direction. They are waiting for[9] you at home." Richard
explained with some[10] trouble what had happened and
William said: " Well, jump in. I'll[11] drive you there and
we'll[11] be home again in ten minutes." Robert got in
without saying another word and after a few minutes they
were already in the town. Meanwhile[12] Robert had
recovered[13] sufficiently to[14] be able to tell William where[15]
to[16] go. As[17] they approached[18] the shop the woman was

waiting at the door with the parcel. How glad Robert
was!

1. § 39.   2. § 103 (b).   3. Add " it "; § 109 and § 5 (a) (ii).   4.
§ 95 (c) (i).   5. Say " further ".   6. § 112 (i).   7. § 95 (b).   8. § 53.
9. § 112 (c).   10. § 14 (b).   11. § 89 (c).   12. § 9.   13. § 97.   14.
§ 99 (e).   15. § 41.   16. § 102 (b) (v).   17. § 8.   18. § 108.

24. *Arrival at[1] the station*

We had both[2] wanted to meet[3] Diana at[4] the station,
but as we had gone[5] for a long walk in the afternoon my
wife felt[6] fairly tired, and so I had come alone. We had
not seen Diana for[7] more than six months and we were very
much looking forward to[8] her visit. Her parents died
some years ago and since then[9] she has spent her holidays
several times[5] with[10] us; and perhaps because we have no
children of our own[11] we are very fond of the girl. The
train arrived at eight o'clock and Diana got[5] out of the
compartment opposite me; but I only noticed it when I
felt her arms round my neck. " How sweet of you[12] to
come[13] and[13] meet[3] me! " she said. " How is[14] Pauline? I
hope you[12] are[14] both[2] well." " Yes," I answered, " we're[14]
very well, though Pauline is a little tired, otherwise she
would have come too. You look very well, as usual. Is
this all your luggage? Let me carry the bag. We can
walk home past[15] the cathedral."

1. § 82 (b) (iv).   2. § 43 (e).   3. § 95 (b).   4. Say " from ".   5.
§ 114.   6. § 97.   7. § 81 (h).   8. § 112 (c).   9. § 38.   10. § 81 (c).
11. Say " no own children ".   12. § 52 (a).   13. Omit.   14. § 98 (b).
15. § 112 (b).

25. *The flesh is weak*

I had intended[1] to work hard this morning[2]. I had got
up early and as soon as I had eaten my breakfast I stopped[3]
reading the newspaper and went upstairs to my room. I
sat down at my desk, opened[4] the drawer, took out[5] my
papers and began to write. I noticed that the weather
was magnificent and thought how wonderful it would be
to spend the day in the open. During the last weeks

we had had rain, snow and gales, but to-day the weather had changed[6] quite suddenly. My work of course is very interesting and it rarely happens[4] that I have such a[7] good opportunity of working[8]. What was that? Was that somebody ringing[9]? Who could that be? I recognized neither[10] the voice nor[10] the step. There was a knock[9] at my door. " Come in[5]," I cried. The door opened[6]. " Oh, it's you[11]! " I said, getting up[12] and going[12] up to[13] my friend whom I hadn't seen since[14] last Christmas. " Yes," he said, " we decided to visit you. We are on our way[15] to[16] Swinemünde. We thought perhaps you might like[17] to spend the day with us."

1. § 99 (c). 2. § 50. 3. § 114. 4. § 95 (b). 5. § 40 (a) (ii). 6. § 97. 7. Say "a such good", § 39 or § 63. 8. § 113 (d). 9. § 68. 10. § 10 (b). 11. § 52 (e). 12. § 113 (f). 13. § 112 (c). 14. § 81 (h). 15. § 40 (b) (ii). 16. § 81 (g). 17. § 102 (b) (iii).

26. *A disturbed night*

A few days ago we had gone to bed very late. Shortly after midnight I woke up. Why was the dog making so much noise? He is usually very quiet at[1] night. I listened[2]. " Are you awake? " I heard my wife say quietly. " Yes, the dog woke me up. What can[3] have disturbed him? It's probably only the neighbour's cat." I got[4] out of bed, turned on[2] the light, put on[2] my shoes and went downstairs. There was nothing unusual[5] in the kitchen, but the dog was behaving[6] very strangely. Now[7] he would[8] run to the door that led into the garden, now[7] he would[8] run back to me, as if he wanted to tell me that there was[9] something or somebody outside. I put on[2] a coat, took a torch out of the cupboard and opened the door. The dog ran immediately into the garden and disappeared in the darkness. I followed[10] him as quickly as possible[11] to[12] the end of the garden. There, right[13] in the corner stood the dog in front of[12] a big suit-case. How had it got[4] there? Had somebody thrown it over[12] the wall?

1. § 82 (b) (vi). 2. § 95 (b). 3. § 102 (b) (ii). 4. § 114. 5. § 32. 6. § 97. 7. § 10 (a). 8. § 90 (a). 9. § 105 (a). 10. § 108. 11. § 37 (c) (ii). 12. § 82 (a). 13. § 39.

27. *A letter*

Oxford, 20th April, 1954[1]

Dear Joan,

I must thank[2] you both very much for the wonderful week[3] I spent with you. I was sorry[4] I had to leave[5] so early in the morning. I could have prepared my own breakfast and then you needn't have[6] got up so early. But it was sweet of you nevertheless to prepare my breakfast for me. It was a pity[7] it was raining. However, I had a raincoat and an umbrella and so I didn't get very wet. I caught[8] the train but I should have missed[8] it if it hadn't been a few minutes late[9]. I arrived in Oxford at a quarter to ten, and I was in the office before ten—only half an hour late[9].

I did so[10] enjoy[9] my visit. What[11] lovely walks we had[12]! I shall never forget the magnificent scenery, the blue hills, the birds singing[13] in the woods, the sheep in the meadows, all the fruit-trees in blossom[14], the beautiful little villages in the valleys. And then the evenings by[15] the fire in your house! I don't often have the opportunity of meeting[2] such[16] pleasant people and listening[2] to such[16] interesting conversations.

Mary sends her kindest regards[17].

Once again[18] many thanks[19].

Yours affectionately[20],
DIANA.

1. § 48. 2. § 108. 3. § 58 (a) (iii). 4. § 98 (b). 5. § 95 (b). 6. § 102 (b) (iv). 7. § 14 (c). 8. § 95 (a). 9. § 114. 10. Add " very ". 11. § 56, note. 12. Say " we have made ". 13. § 113 (g). 14. Say " blooming fruit-trees ". 15. § 82 (b) (ii). 16. § 63. 17. § 102 (b) (vii). 18. § 38. 19. § 78 (c). 20. Say " very cordially your Diana ".

28. *An unknown cousin*

The young man, with his hat in his hand[1], still looked at her, smiling[2]. It was very strange.

" Will[3] you please tell me," said the stranger[4] at last, " whether I have the honour of speaking to Miss Latham? "

"My name is Margaret Latham," replied the young woman.

"In that case[5] I have the honour, the pleasure, of being your cousin."

"What[6] cousin? Who are you?" asked Margaret.

He laughed. "I see it must seem[7] to you very strange," he said. Margaret looked at him from head to[8] foot. Yes, he looked extremely handsome. "It is very still," he continued[7], coming nearer[9] again. And as she only looked at him instead of replying he added[7], "Are you all alone?"

"Everybody[10] has gone to church," said Margaret.

"I feared that!" the young man said. "But I hope you are not afraid of me."

"You ought to tell me who you are," Margaret answered.

"I am afraid of you!" said the young man. "I had a different[11] plan. I expected that a servant would take my card and that you would let me come in only after you had learnt[12] who I was."

1. §24 (e). 2. §113 (a). 3. §102 (b) (vi). 4. §31. 5. §82 (b) (vi). 6. §55. 7. §95 (b). 8. Say "till". 9. Say "approaching", §108 and §113 (f). 10. §74. 11. §30 (a). 12. §114.

29. *A visit to the theatre*[1]

We decided at[2] the last moment to go to the theatre. We had our supper quickly, got[3] on a bus and, five minutes before the play was due to[4] begin, we were at the theatre. Yes, there were still some seats, I learnt. Not particularly cheap, but not too expensive. I had just[5] enough money on[6] me. Soon after we had sat down the play began. We enjoyed[3] the play very much. We laughed almost the whole time. We were very glad we had come. If we hadn't come to-night we should probably never have seen it, for I was very busy during the next weeks, and my wife never goes to the theatre alone.[7]

When we were about to leave the theatre it was raining hard. Of course I had forgotten my umbrella and if we had had to wait for a bus we should have got very wet.

Fortunately[5], however, while we were wondering[8] what to do[4], a bus stopped[3] just[5] in front of us and we succeeded[9] in getting home without getting too wet. My wife says that the rain has spoiled her hat, but I don't believe it. I think she simply wants[10] me to buy her a new one[11].

1. Say "a theatre-visit". 2. §82 (b) (vi). 3. §114. 4. §102 (b) (v). 5. § 39. 6. § 81 (c). 7. § 5 (b) (i). 8. § 97. 9. § 98 (b). 10. § 102 (b) (vi). 11. § 69, note 2.

30. *The patient*[1]

When Julia awoke she saw her old bed at home and her old room. It seemed to her at first as if all that[2] had taken place[3] since the days when[4] these objects were familiar to her[5] was only a dream; but after a few minutes she began to remember[6] everything again.

She could scarcely[7] move her head for[8] pain and she was very weak. For some time[9] she didn't seem to notice the presence of her little sister in the room. Even after their eyes had met[10], and her sister had approached[11] her bed, Julia lay there for some minutes and looked at her without saying a word before she asked:

" When was[12] I brought into this room? "

" Last night[13], Julia."

" Who brought me here[14]? "

" Elsie, I believe."

" Why do you believe it? "

"Because I found her here this morning. She didn't come to my bed to wake me, as[4] she always does[15]; and I went to look[9] for her. She was not in her own room either[16]; and I continued[3] to look[9] for her everywhere in the house, until I found her here. Will you see father? Elsie said I was to tell him as soon as you woke."

1. §31. 2. §59 (a). 3. §95 (b). 4. §8. 5. §26 (d). 6. §112 (a). 7. §39. 8. §82 (b) (ix). 9. §114. 10. §97. 11. §108. 12. §103 (a). 13. §50. 14. §40 (a) (i). 15. Add "it". 16. §9.

31. *In Switzerland*[1]

Berne is the capital of Switzerland[1]. It is a very old and beautiful town, and so I always go there when I spend

my holidays in Switzerland[1]. I like it especially because
they play very good music at[2] the concerts in the Town
Hall. When I went to a concert there for the first time[3]
they played our National Anthem[4] at the end of the concert.
I was very surprised at[5] this and stood up of course, although
all[6] the other people remained sitting. Afterwards my
neighbour who was Swiss[7] turned to[8] me and said: " It
was very polite of you to stand up while our National
Anthem[4] was being[9] played." " Oh! " I said, " I thought
it was our National Anthem[4]." " No," he replied, " but
we have borrowed the music from you and added[10] our
own words." " What are the words? " I asked him.
" Well," he replied, " the words are different[11] in the different[11] parts of the country. Sometimes they are French[7],
sometimes Italian[7], sometimes German[7]. In Berne of
course they are German[7]." And then he said the words in[12]
German. But I can't say what they were, because I don't
understand the German language very well yet.

1. § 13 (h). 2. Say " in ". 3. § 114. 4. *Nationalhymne, f.* 5.
§ 82 (b) (vii). 6. § 74. 7. § 22. 8. § 112 (p). 9. § 103 (a). 10.
§ 95 (b). 11. § 30 (b) (ii). 12. § 82 (b) (iii).

32. *Unhappy abroad*[1]

It is terrible to speak of[2] it, yet I must tell[3] you everything. My father took me away[4]. I thought we were only
going[5] on a little journey; and I was pleased. There was a
bag with all my little things in it. But we went on board[6]
a ship and got[5] farther and farther[7] away[4] from the land.
Then I got[5] ill; and I thought it would never end. But
at last we reached[6] the harbour. I knew nothing then[5],
and believed everything my father said. He told me I
should go back to my mother. But it was America[8] we
had reached[6], and long years passed[6] before we came back
to Europe[8]. At first I often asked my father when we
should go back; and I soon learnt[5] to write, because I
wanted to write to[9] my mother. But one day when he
saw me writing[10] to[9] my mother he put[5] me on his knee

and told me that my mother and brother were dead and that was the reason why we did not go back.

1. § 82 (*b*) (vi).   2. § 112 (*n*).   3. § 109.   4. § 40 (*a*) (iii).   5. § 114.   6. § 95 (*a*).   7. § 35 (*d*) (ii).   8. § 22.   9. § 112 (*a*).   10. § 113 (*c*).

33. *Uncle and niece*

When Susan came down to tea she learned that her uncle wished to see her in the dining-room. He put down[1] the paper when she came into the room and greeted her with his usual kindness. As his wife had said, she always meant a good deal to him, and now that[2] she had become so rich, more than ever[3]. " My dear," he said, holding her hand, " I want to speak to you about[4] something very important[5]. Of course, I do not know exactly what the subject of your conversation with Mr[6]. Raven has been, but it is clear to me[7] that he wishes to marry you."

Susan did not speak immediately, and her uncle said: " Do you doubt that[8] yourself[9], my dear ? "

" Yes, perhaps. I don't know. But he may perhaps think quite differently[10] to-morrow," said Susan.

" Why to-morrow ? Did[11] he ask for[12] your hand, and did[11] you say no ? "

" Well, I didn't[11] say yes. I talked about[4] something else[5]."

" And will you tell[13] me your reasons ? "

" I am not certain that I had any[14] reasons, uncle."

" No reasons ! But it concerns[12] your happiness, your future, your whole life ! "

1. § 95 (*b*).   2. § 61.   3. § 38.   4. § 112 (*n*).   5. § 32.   6. § 17 (*d*). 7. § 26 (*d*).   8. § 52 (*d*) and § 112 (*b*).   9. § 67.   10. § 39.   11. § 91 (*a*). 12. § 112 (*m*).   13. § 109.   14. § 14 (*b*).

34. *Stephen in danger*

Joan got up and looked[1] about her. The landscape, so beautiful in its stillness a few moments ago, now seemed to her empty and unfriendly. There was nobody to be[2] seen. " Gertrude, we must not lose a moment. We must run in different[3] directions. Go back the way we have come, and I will go on[4] farther. Tell every one[5] you see what has happened. Think of[6] Stephen! "

She knew that Gertrude would do all she could. And after standing for a moment to see her running she turned[7]. Then she tied her handkerchief to[6] a tree so that[8] she should recognize the spot again and ran as she had never run before[9].

At last she came to a bridge where two men were sleeping in the shade. Only with some trouble did she succeed in waking them; but as soon as she had told them what had brought her there they got up quickly and ran with her. Then a horse was found. She told one of the men to ride[10] to the nearest town to fetch a doctor. With the other she at last came to a village where in a quarter of an hour they had collected everything necessary[11] for[12] the rescue.

1. § 114.   2. § 103 (f).   3. § 30 (b) (ii).   4. Omit.   5. § 73.   6. § 112 (a).   7. § 97.   8. § 8.   9. § 38.   10. § 88 (b) and § 105 (c).   11. § 32.   12. § 81 (j).

35. *A hard life*

Mrs. Crowther is an Englishwoman[1]. She is a farmer's wife. She is about[2] fifty years old. The farm is small and the buildings are dirty and untidy, for the farmer tries to do everything[3] only with the help of his own family. They are, however, not at all[2] poor. Mrs. Crowther works extremely hard. She does all[3] her housework, washes and mends all[3] the clothes, looks after[4] the cows and chickens, and writes all[3] the letters, for her husband can neither read nor write. Usually she works a hundred[5] hours a[6] week, and even[7] more in summer when she helps her husband and sons in the fields. She loves her two[8] sons and is ready to do anything[3] for them. She goes to church about[2] once a[6] month and has one free day a[6] year when she goes[9] on an excursion to the seaside in a bus. She has never ridden in a train and has never spent a night anywhere else but[10] at home. She doesn't smoke and only rarely drinks a glass of[11] beer. In spite of all[3] this work she is a very happy woman and wouldn't like[12] to lead a different[13] life.

1. §22. 2. §39. 3. §74. 4. §112 (k). 5. §42. 6. §82 (b) (vi). 7. §35 (d) (ii). 8. §43 (e). 9. §114. 10. Say "not elsewhere (§40 (b) (i)) than". 11. §27 (b). 12. §102 (b) (iii). 13. §30 (a).

36. *Her shadow*

He was not alone, but had a young lady on[1] his arm. She was beautifully dressed[2], and I looked at her with great interest. Her face was sad and quite pale, but she was very pretty. He introduced[3] her to me as[4] his niece, Miss Lowe.

" Will you come with us, Mr. Kitson? "

" With pleasure."

The young lady walked between us, and we walked along the beach in the direction of[5] Filey.

" There have been wheels here," said Mr. Lawton. " Margaret, your shadow without doubt! "

" Miss Lowe's shadow? " I repeated[6], looking at it on the ground.

" Not that one[7]," Mr. Lawton replied laughing[8]. " Margaret, tell[9] Mr. Kitson."

" Indeed[10]," said the young lady, turning to[11] me, " there[12] is nothing further to tell—only that I see the same old gentleman at all times[13] everywhere. I have told[9] my uncle, and he calls[14] the gentleman my shadow."

" Does he live in Scarborough? "

" He is staying[15] here."

" Do you live in Scarborough? "

" No, I am staying[15] here too—with a family, for the sake of my health."

" And your shadow? " I said smiling[8].

" My shadow," she answered smiling[8] too, " is like[4] me —not very well, I fear."

1. §82 (b) (ii). 2. §95 (b). 3. §109. 4. §35 (d) (iv), note. 5. §81 (g). 6. §95 (c) (i). 7. §64. 8. §113 (a). 9. Add "it". 10. §13 (i). 11. §112 (p). 12. §52 (e). 13. §114. 14. §111. 15. §97.

37. *Saved*

How Manfred had succeeded in getting to the island he never knew. After the ship had sunk he swam about[1] in the sea till night came; and then he gave up hope. But when he thought his last moment had come[2] he found to his astonishment that he could stand. Wearily he walked a few more steps until he found himself on[3] the beach; and here he lay down[4] and fell asleep immediately. It must[5] have been almost midday when he woke, for the sun was high up[6] in[3] the sky. He was extremely hungry and thirsty. He got up and looked[7] about him. His first concern was to find some[8] fresh water. It didn't take[7] long before he found a little river where he could drink and where he bathed his[6] face, hands and legs. He felt better now, but he was still just as[9] hungry as[9] before. He did not know whether the island had any inhabitants. Nor[10] did he know what sort of[11] men might[12] live there. It might[12] be that they would kill him as soon as they saw him. He would have to[5] run the danger, for he would die any-how[13] if he didn't eat.

1. § 40 (*b*) (ii).   2. § 105 (*a*).   3. § 82 (*b*) (ii).   4. § 97.   5. § 102 (*b*) (iv).   6. Omit.   7. § 114.   8. § 14 (*b*).   9. § 35 (*d*) (i). 10. § 9.   11. § 56.   12. § 102 (*b*) (ii).   13. § 82 (*b*) (iii).

38. *Unpleasant news*

" Oh, poor mother, poor father! " said Mary, her eyes full of[1] tears. She looked straight before[2] her. She had forgotten Fred. She was only aware[3] of the consequences at home. He too remained silent for some moments, feeling more unhappy than ever.

" You can never forgive me? "

" What does it help whether I forgive you or not? " said Mary angrily. " Would that make it easier for my mother? She has been earning[4] the money for four years by giving[5] lessons, so that[6] she might[7] send Robert abroad[8]. Would you think[9] all[10] that pleasant if I forgave you? "

" Say what you like[11], Mary. I deserve it all[10]."

" I don't want to say anything," said Mary, more

calmly. It is silly to be angry." She got up, went to the window and looked out. Fred followed her with his eyes, in the hope that she would turn round[12] and that their eyes would meet[12]. But no! He saw only her back.

" I am so unhappy, Mary—if you knew how unhappy I am, you would be sorry[13] for me."

1. § 27 (b). 2. § 40 (a) (ii). 3. § 25 (d). 4. § 89 (b) and § 95 (a). 5. § 113 (e). 6. § 8. 7. § 102 (b) (ii). 8. § 82 (b) (v). 9. § 112 (g). 10. § 74. 11. § 108. 12. § 97. 13. § 98 (b), note.

39. *A town wakes up*

Early on the seventh morning after he had left home Ernest arrived in the little town. All the shops were[1] shut; the streets were empty; nobody had yet woken up. The sun was just about to rise[2]; but the light only showed[3] the boy even[4] more clearly how lonely he was as he sat tired and hungry on the steps in front of the door of a tall building. After about half an hour he saw signs of[5] life. Windows were[1] shut or opened; people began to go to and fro[6] past him. A few stopped[7] to look at him for a moment; but no one gave himself the trouble to ask him how he had come there; and he hadn't the courage to ask somebody for[8] bread or money.

While he sat there he noticed that a boy who had gone past him some minutes before had returned[2] and now stood opposite him and was watching[9] him. At first Ernest showed no interest; but the boy remained standing there so long that Ernest raised his head and their eyes met.

1. § 103 (g). 2. § 95 (b). 3. § 109. 4. § 35 (d) (ii). 5. § 81 (i). 6. § 40 (a) (ii). 7. § 114. 8. § 112 (m). 9. § 108.

40. *In vain*

" Mary," he began, " take the money—the notes and the gold—you shall have it all—do as I tell you."

He tried to hand[1] her the key, but Mary went back a step[2].

" I will not take your key or your money. Don't ask[3] me again to do it. If you do[4] I must call[3] your brother."

He let[5] his hand fall, and for the first time[3] in her life Mary saw the old man[6] cry like[7] a child. She said in a very soft voice, " Please put[3] your money in your box," and then[8] went to her seat by the fire, in the hope that this[9] at least would convince[10] him. Soon he recovered and said:

" Call[3] the young man. Call[3] my nephew."

Mary's heart began to beat more quickly. Various thoughts went one[11] after the other through her[12] head. At last she said:

" I will call[3] him, if you will allow[1] me to call[3] your brother and your other relatives[6]."

" Nobody else[13], I say. Only the young man."

" No, I will not do it. I will do anything else[14]."

" Anything else[14]! " the old man[6] said angrily. " I want nothing else[15]."

1. §109.   2. §24 (b).   3. §114.   4. Add "it".   5. §102 (b) (vii).
6. §31.   7. §35 (d) (iv), note.   8. §2.   9. §64, note.   10. §95 (c) (i).
11. §69.   12. §13 (g).   13. §72.   14. §74.   15. §76.

41. *The future*

After waiting[1] for an answer and getting[1] none[2], Henry suddenly looked up and asked:

" Have you gone to sleep, Julia? "

" No, Henry. I am looking at the fire."

" You seem to find a lot of interesting pictures in it," said Henry. " I have never found any[3]."

" Henry," asked his sister slowly, as if she were reading in the fire what she asked and as if it were not quite clearly written there, " do you look forward to your new job? "

" I shall at least not have to live any longer at home," replied Henry, getting up from his chair and going to the window.

" Yes, that is at least something," said Julia after a while.

They were both silent for a few minutes. Then Henry turned round and said: " I don't of course like leaving you, Julia. We shall both feel very lonely. But I must go, you know, whether I like it or not. But why do you look at the fire like that[4]? What do you see in it? "

" I don't see anything special in it, Henry. I'm only thinking—of[5] us, of[5] the future. Will it be as unhappy as the present, as the past? "

1. § 113 (f).   2. § 70, note.   3. § 77.   4. § 39.   5. § 112 (a).

42. *The Russian*[1]

The Russian[1] soldier must have been fifty years old, but he himself[2] did not know how old he was. But his white strong teeth which showed[3] when he laughed—as he often did—were all good, he hadn't a single[4] grey hair on[5] his head, and his body was healthy and strong. In spite of his age his face had an expression of innocence and youth; his voice was pleasant and friendly. He was the only[4] prisoner[6] who was never tired or ill. As soon as he lay down[7] he fell asleep like a stone; and after he had shaken himself he was ready immediately for[8] work, just as[9] children are ready for[8] play as soon as they awake. He could do everything, not very well, but not badly. He baked, cooked, sewed, and mended boots. He was always busy, and only at night[10] allowed[11] himself conversation—of which he was fond—and songs. He did not sing like some one who knows he is[12] listened to, but like the birds, without thinking of the effect, and his face at such times was very serious.

1. § 22.   2. § 67.   3. Add " themselves ", § 53.   4. § 45 (e).   5. § 82 (b) (iv).   6. § 31.   7. § 97.   8. § 81 (j).   9. § 39.   10. § 82 (b) (ii). 11. § 109.   12. § 103 (i).

43. *War*

" May[1] I ask you," said Laurence, " what[2] the name of that village is that lies in front of us? "

" Reichshoffen, isn't it[3]? " said the officer, turning to a companion.

"No, Morsbronn," the other replied.

The officer, who was glad to have an opportunity to talk, came up to[4] Laurence.

"Are those[5] our men there?" Laurence asked.

"Yes, and there farther on[6] are the French[7]!" said the officer. "There they are, there, you can see them."

"Where? Where?" asked Laurence.

"One can see them quite clearly . . . over there[8]!"

The officer pointed with his hand to[4] the smoke on the left[8] beyond the river, and the same stern and serious expression that Laurence had noticed on many of the faces he had met[9] came into his face too.

"Ah, so those[5] are the French[7]! And over there[8]?" . . . Laurence pointed to[4] a little hill on the right[8] not far from which many more[10] soldiers were to be seen.

"Those[5] are ours[11]."

"Ah, ours[11]! And there?" . . . Laurence pointed to[4] another hill with a big tree on it, near a village that lay in a valley where some fires were smoking too.

"That belongs[9] to the enemy again," said the officer. "It was ours[11] yesterday, but now it is his[11]."

1. §102 (b) (i).   2. §41.   3. §101.   4. §112 (c).   5. §64, note. 6. Omit.   7. §22.   8. §40 (a) (i).   9. §108.   10. §43 (d).   11. §51 and note (1).

44. Truants[1]

That night I slept badly. In the morning I arrived before the others at[2] the bridge, as I lived nearest[3]. I hid my books in the long grass at the end of the garden where[4] nobody came, and hurried along the bank of the river. It was a bright warm morning in the first week of June. I sat down on the bridge. People went to and fro. All the branches of the tall trees with their little light-green leaves were dancing merrily in the air, and the sun shone through them[5] on to the water. The stone of the bridge was already beginning to get warm. I was very happy.

After I had been sitting there for five or ten minutes I saw Michael's grey suit approaching. He came down[6] the hill, smiled and sat down beside me. While we were

waiting for John he drew a knife out of his pocket. He
said it was a present and that his elder brother had given it
to him for[7] his birthday. We waited for another quarter
of an hour, but still there was no sign of John. Michael at
last jumped down and said:

"Let's[8] go. I knew John wouldn't have the courage."

1. *Schulschwänzer, m.* 2. § 82 (b) (ii). 3. § 35 (a) and (c). 4.
§ 41. 5. Add *hindurch*. 6. § 24 (d). 7. Say "to". 8. § 102 (b)
(vi).

45. *The ride in the tram*[1]

Mary wanted to take[2] something special to John's
father and mother, something that they would certainly
like, and so she went into a very good shop and bought a
cake for which she paid a large sum of[3] money. Then she
got into the tram. She thought she would have to stand
in the tram because none[4] of the young men seemed to
notice her, but an elderly[5] gentleman made room for her.
He was a stout gentleman and he wore a brown hat and
yellow gloves; he had a red face and friendly blue eyes.
Mary thought[6] he was an officer and said to herself how
much more polite he was than the young men who simply
looked straight before them[7]. The gentleman began to
speak to her about the bad weather and about all sorts of
interesting things[8]. He was very nice with her, and when
she got out of the tram she thanked him, and he smiled
pleasantly; and while she was going up the street she
thought how easy it was to recognize a gentleman even
when[9] he has drunk a glass too many[10].

1. § 31. 2. § 114. 3. § 27 (b). 4. § 70. 5. § 35 (d) (iv), note.
6. § 112 (g). 7. § 40 (a) (ii). 8. § 32. 9. § 7 (a). 10. Say "much".

46. *Strange behaviour*

One night[1], after the family had gone to bed, I heard
him go downstairs, open the door and go out. I did not
hear him come in again, and in the morning I learnt that
he was still away[2]. It was in April: the weather was warm
and bright, the grass as green as rain and sun could make

it and the two little fruit-trees by the wall at the end of the garden looked magnificent. After breakfast Catherine suggested that I should bring a chair into the garden and sit under the trees. I took[3] her advice and was sitting there quite comfortably when Catherine, who had gone into the wood behind the house to get[3] some flowers for the table, came back after a few minutes and told me that Mr. Holman was coming in. "And he spoke to me," she added. I noticed that her face was very pale.

" What did he say? " I asked.

" He told me to go away[2] as quickly as possible[4]," she answered. " But he looked so completely different[5] that I stopped[3] a moment to look at him more closely."

" How? " I asked.

" Why, almost joyful—very excited, and wild, and glad."

1. § 25 (*b*).   2. § 40 (*a*) (iii).   3. § 114.   4. § 37 (*c*) (ii).   5. § 39.

47. *A strange house*

While leading me upstairs she told me to hide the light and not to make a noise; for her master would[1] never let anybody spend[2] the night there if he could[3] prevent it. I asked[4] the reason. She did not know[5], she answered; she had only been living[5] there a year or two[6]; and so many strange things[7] had happened[5] since her arrival that it was[5] all the same to[8] her now.

When the old woman had left me I shut the door quietly, put[9] a chair firmly against it so that it could not be opened and looked about me. It was a large room with very little furniture in it. A bed stood in one corner not far from the window. Besides the chair in front of the door there were two other small ones[10] and in the middle of the room stood a big round table. That was all, except some old books lying on the table. I took one in my hand and opened it. To my great astonishment I saw on the first page my own name. I must have written it at least twenty years ago. How had the book got[9] here?

1. § 94, note.   2. § 99 (*b*).   3. " Was able to " or " would be able to "?   4. § 112 (*k*).   5. Indirect speech, § 105.   6. § 43 (*c*).   7. § 32. 8. § 26 (*d*).   9. § 114.   10. § 69, note (2).

48. *A sad moment*

He counted his money and found that he had exactly
ten shillings[1]; he had also a knife which he might sell for
two or three shillings[1] and the watch his Aunt Elizabeth
had given him shortly before she died. The carriage must
have started[2] a full quarter of an hour ago, but he would
do his best[3] to catch it up[2]. He left the house at once and
soon he could see the carriage, which now looked very
small, perhaps a mile and a half[4] in front of him. To run
six or seven miles across fields was nothing unusual for him;
and as he knew[5] a much shorter way than the road Henry
did not give up hope of seeing Helen at the station before
the train left[5]. But he probably would not have caught up[2]
the carriage if John, who was driving it, had not turned
round and seen him making signs to him to stop[5]. When
Henry reached them he offered[6] Helen his watch, his knife
and all the money he possessed. Helen at first would not
take anything, but at last she accepted them. Then Henry
said good-bye[7] to her, and the two parted from one another[8]
amid[9] many tears.

1. § 46.   2. § 95 (*b*).   3. § 31.   4. § 45 (*a*).   5. § 114.   6. § 109.
7. § 82 (*b*) (iii).   8. § 54.   9. § 82 (*b*) (viii).

49. *The secret*

" You're not alone. I want to speak to you alone."
Neumann looked at the doctor, and the doctor looked at
the other three men.   " Alone—for five minutes," Paul repeated.   " Please leave us."   The doctor went out and the
others followed him. Neumann shut the door behind them
and came back to Paul, who had watched every movement
attentively.

" It's very bad, it's very bad," he said after Neumann
had seated himself next to him.   " The[1] more I think of it,
the[1] worse it is."

" Oh, don't think of it," said Neumann.

" Even if[2] they change their opinion the shame is still
there."

" Oh, they won't change their opinion."

" Well, you can force them to do it."

" Force them? "

" I can tell you something—a great secret.   You can use it against them—frighten them with it."

" A secret? " Neumann repeated.

" Something happened[3] to my father in Oberstdorf.   I don't know what.   I've been ashamed, afraid.   I haven't dared to know.   My mother knows—my brother knows."

" Something happened[3] to your father? " Neumann allowed himself to ask.

" Yes, he didn't[4] recover.   They didn't[4] let[5] him recover."

1. § 10 (a).   2. § 7 (a).   3. § 108 and § 91 (a).   4. § 91 (a).   5. § 102 (a), note.

50. John and the children

" You must see the children," said Mrs. Smith, who was very proud of her three small daughters.   " They should have been in bed long ago[1], but whenever you visit us they are allowed to stay up for a while in the bedroom.   They would like very much to hear one of your fairy-tales." John smiled sadly and nodded[2] his head, for he never went away without telling the children a story.   Really he did not like children at all, especially the young Smiths, but once he had had to tell them about Hansel[3] and Gretel in order to entertain[4] them for half an hour when their parents were not there and of course they had never forgotten it. He now always had to pretend[5] to like telling fairy-tales, so instead of saying that he did not know any more stories he went slowly upstairs.   " Well, children," he was saying a few minutes later, " there[6] was once upon a time a little girl called[7] Little Red Riding Hood[8].   Do you know why? Listen attentively. . . ."

1. § 38.   2. § 112 (j).   3. Hänsel.   4. § 95 (c) (ii).   5. § 107 (b). 6. § 52 (e).   7. § 36 (b).   8. Rotkäppchen.

SECTION IV

FREE COMPOSITION

HINTS ON WRITING FREE COMPOSITION

Your compositions should run to about 150 words. You should aim at simplicity and accuracy. If you attempt anything complicated you will almost certainly be inaccurate. Do not therefore write out or think out your composition first in English and then translate it into German, for that will only make your task far harder since your English composition, though it may seem simple to you, will certainly be far more difficult than the German you can be expected to write at this stage.

Simplicity will make for accuracy, but it does not necessarily follow that your German will in fact be accurate merely because it is simple. It is also essential to have at your command a vocabulary which, though quite small, is yet thoroughly known. You must, therefore, for German free composition, have much the same sort of intimate knowledge of German as is required for translating into German. But there is one great difference: in free composition you have a chance to show what you know, since you can decide what you are going to write. Do not therefore use words or expressions which you are not quite certain of, but replace them by others that you really know.

When given a subject it is perhaps a good plan to write down first a number of the simplest, barest statements which will form, as it were, the skeleton of your composition. When this has been done you can begin to elaborate. Adjectives can be added to nouns, adverbs can be inserted into clauses and some of the simple statements can be welded into compound or complex sentences. This process can best be shown by an example.

Subject:

Zwei Jungen verirren sich in den Bergen. Sie kommen an ein Bauernhaus und fragen nach dem Wege.

	Conjunctions	Relative Pronouns	Adjectives	Adverbs and Adverbial Phrases
1. Fritz und Hans waren auf einen Berg gestiegen.			hoch (hohen)	im Schwarzwald
2. Sie ruhten sich aus.				eine halbe Stunde auf dem Gipfel
	nachdem			
3. Sie standen auf.				
	denn			
4. Es war spät.				schon
5. Sie mußten zu Hause sein.	und			wieder
	bevor			
6. Es wurde dunkel.				
7. Sie gingen den Berg hinunter.			steil(en)	
	während			
8. Sie sprachen miteinander.				
	und			
9. Sie paßten nicht auf.				gut
10. Fritz blieb stehen.				plötzlich
	und			
11. Er sah sich um.				
12. Er sagte.				
13. „ Wir haben uns verirrt."				
14. „ Wir müssen zurückkehren."				sofort
	und			
15. „ Wir müssen den Weg finden."			richtig(en)	
16. Hans erblickte ein Bauernhaus.			klein(es)	in dem Augenblick
		das		
17. Es stand nicht weit entfernt.				
18. Sie kamen ans Bauernhaus.				
	als			
19. Sie klopften an die Tür.				
20. Eine Frau machte die Tür auf.		die	alt(e)	
21. Fritz sagte.				
22. „ Guten Tag! "				
23. Er fragte.				
24. „ Wie kommen wir nach Badenweiler ? "				bitte
25. Die Frau sagte ihnen den Weg				
	und			
26. Sie verließen das Bauernhaus.	nachdem			
27. Sie dankten der Frau.				höflich
28. Die Sonne wollte untergehen.				eben
	als			
29. Sie erreichten Badenweiler.				endlich

Note that in a narrative you should, unless you are told otherwise, normally use the imperfect tense and not the perfect. (Cf. §§ 90, 91.) The first column gives the barest outline of the narrative in the form of short simple statements. If your composition were left in this state it would certainly be simple and, as far as it goes, it would be accurate. But it would sound very jerky and bare. To make it run more smoothly the conjunctions and relative pronouns suggested in the second and third columns could be used to link up clauses with one another, the brackets indicating which clauses could be so linked up. Great care must be taken with the word order, which will be affected by the subordinating conjunctions and relative pronouns, but not by the co-ordinating conjunctions. Sometimes too the tense of the verb will have to be altered. The fourth column suggests possible adjectives which would serve to make the narrative less bare. See that these adjectives have the right endings. In the fifth column there are given a number of adverbs and adverbial phrases which could be usefully employed to give further details as to the time, manner and place of the various actions. Remember that an adverb or adverbial phrase coming at the head of a main clause must be followed by the finite verb.

Applying all these modifications to our first draft we shall get something like this:

Fritz und Hans waren auf einen hohen Berg im Schwarzwald gestiegen. Nachdem sie sich eine halbe Stunde auf dem Gipfel ausgeruht **hatten**, standen sie auf, denn es war schon spät, und sie mußten wieder zu Hause sein, bevor es dunkel **wurde**. Während sie den steilen Berg **hinuntergingen**, sprachen sie miteinander und paßten nicht gut auf. Plötzlich blieb Fritz stehen und sah sich um. „ Wir haben uns verirrt", sagte er. „ Wir müssen sofort zurückgehen und den richtigen Weg finden." In dem Augenblick erblickte Hans ein kleines Bauernhaus, das nicht weit entfernt **stand**. Als sie ans Bauernhaus **kamen**, klopften sie an die Tür, die eine alte Frau **aufmachte**. „ Guten Tag! " sagte Fritz. „ Wie kommen wir nach Badenweiler, bitte? " fragte er. Die Frau sagte ihnen den Weg, und sie verließen das Bauernhaus, nachdem sie ihr höflich gedankt **hatten**. Die Sonne wollte eben untergehen, als sie Badenweiler endlich **erreichten**.

Now this is simple, straightforward and correct German, and you are not expected at your stage to be able to write anything more ambitious. It is obvious that you could have written something much more exciting in English—but you simply do not yet command the vocabulary, phrases and syntax that would enable you to write something comparable in German. Be content therefore, at first, with a plain simple narrative of the kind shown in the example above.

I

Erzählen Sie, was Sie gestern gemacht haben. *Use the perfect tense.*

*auf-stehen, *get up.*
Toilette machen, *wash and dress.*
mein Frühstück essen, *have breakfast.*
zur Schule *gehen, *go to school.*
am Morgen, *in the morning.*
die Stunde, *lesson.*
die Geschichte, *history.*
die Mathematik, *mathematics.*
Französisch, *n., French.*
Deutsch, *n., German.*
zu Mittag essen, *have lunch.*
am Nachmittag, *in the afternoon.*
die Erdkunde, *geography.*
Latein, *n., Latin.*

Englisch, *n., English.*
nach Hause *gehen, *go home.*
Tee trinken, *have tea.*
die Schularbeit machen, *do homework.*
einen Aufsatz schreiben, *write an essay.*
starke Verben lernen, *learn strong verbs.*
mein Abendbrot essen, *have supper.*
ein Konzert hören, *listen to a concert.*
im Radio, *on the wireless/radio.*
zu Bett *gehen, *go to bed.*

2

Erzählen Sie, wie man einen Brief schreibt.

das Briefpapier, *note paper.*
der Bogen, *sheet.*
die Tinte, *ink.*
die Feder, *pen.*
oben rechts, *in the top right hand corner.*
die Stadt, *town.*
das Datum, *date.*
der Anfang, *beginning.*
Lieber Hans! *Dear Jack.*

Liebe Paula! *Dear Pauline.*
Dein Freund Fritz, *yours sincerely, Fred.*
Deine Freundin Vera, *yours sincerely, Vera.*
der Schluß, *conclusion.*
mit vielen Grüßen, *with kind regards.*
durch-lesen, *read through.*
noch einmal, *once again.*

falten, *fold.*
stecken in (A), *put into.*
der Briefumschlag, *envelope.*
der Name, *name.*

die Adresse, *address.*
zu-kleben, *stick down.*
die Briefmarke, *stamp.*
kleben, *stick.*

3

Sie sind gestern mit dem Zug nach N. gefahren. Beschreiben Sie genau, was Sie gemacht haben.

früh *auf-stehen, *get up early.*
zum Bahnhof *gehen, *go to the station.*
der Schalter, *booking-office.*
eine Fahrkarte lösen, *book a ticket.*
eine Rückfahrkarte zweiter Klasse, *a second class return ticket.*
die Sperre, *barrier.*
seine Fahrkarte vor-zeigen, *show one's ticket.*
der Beamte, *official.*
untersuchen, *examine.*
das Datum, *date.*
knipsen, *clip, punch (ticket).*
der Bahnsteig, *platform.*

warten auf (A), *wait for.*
der Zug, *train.*
halten, *stop.*
*ein-steigen, *get in.*
der Eckplatz, *corner seat.*
das Abteil, *compartment.*
sich in Bewegung setzen, *start moving.*
die Fahrt, *journey.*
dauern, *last.*
*an-kommen, *arrive.*
pünktlich, *punctually.*
*aus-steigen, *get out.*
seine Fahrkarte ab-geben, *give up one's ticket.*

4

Sie sehen, wie jemand ins Wasser fällt und gerettet wird. Beschreiben Sie, was geschah.

Mein Freund und ich—Spaziergang am Kanal entlang —Mädchen sitzen auf Geländer—scherzen—ein Mädchen fällt ins Wasser—kann nicht schwimmen—mein Freund guter Schwimmer—zieht Jacke aus—springt ins Wasser— erreicht Mädchen—sie klammert sich an—Gefahr—taucht Kopf des Mädchens unter—wehrt sich nicht mehr—kommen an die Treppe—Leute helfen—kommt ins Leben zurück— Ende gut, alles gut.

einen Spaziergang machen, *go for a walk.*
der Kanal, *canal.*
das Geländer, *railing.*
scherzen, *joke.*
das Gleichgewicht verlieren, *lose one's balance.*
zögern, *hesitate.*
die Jacke, *coat.*
aus-ziehen, *take off.*
aufregend, *exciting.*
aus-sehen, als ob . . . *look as if.*

sich an-klammern an (A), *cling to.*
die Gefahr, *danger.*
*ertrinken, *drown.*
unter-tauchen, *push under.*
sich wehren, *resist.*
die Menge, *crowd.*
das Ufer, *bank.*
heraus-ziehen, *pull out.*
ins Leben zurück-bringen, *revive.*
die Sache, *affair.*
gut *ab-gehen, *end well.*

5

Sie gingen mit Ihrer Mutter auf den Markt. Beschreiben Sie, was Ihre Mutter dort machte, und was Sie erlebten.

Mutter geht auf den Markt—ich gehe mit—kauft immer in denselben Läden—wir sind beim Fleischer—eine Frau vor uns will bezahlen—ein Hund kommt—stiehlt Wurst—eine lange Reihe von Würsten—andere Hunde kommen—Würste verschwinden—Frau hat kein Geld— Fleischer gibt neue Würste.

ein-kaufen, *do shopping.*
manchmal, *sometimes.*
der Bäcker, *baker.*
der Gemüsehändler, *greengrocer.*
bestellen, *order.*
die Waren schicken, *send the goods.*
der Korb, *basket.*
auf den Boden setzen, *put down on the ground.*

hinter sich her-ziehen, *pull along after one.*
sich zanken, *quarrel.*
auf-fressen, *eat up (of animals).*
komisch anzusehen, *funny to look at.*
arm, *poor.*
großmütig, *generous.*

6

Sie müssen unerwartet verreisen. Sie erreichen gerade noch den Zug, aber verlieren in der Eile Ihre Fahrkarte. Beschreiben Sie, was Sie machten.

Ich bekomme Nachricht—ich muß verreisen—gehe zum Bahnhof—löse Fahrkarte—gehe durch Sperre—setze mich auf Bank—will etwas in Koffer tun—Zug kommt sofort— steige ein—Zugführer will Fahrkarte sehen—nicht da—bitte Stationsvorsteher auf nächster Haltestelle zurückzutelefonieren—komme am Ziel an—gebe Namen und Adresse —man glaubt mir—komme am Abend zurück—Fahrkarte war auf der Bank gefunden worden.

das Telegramm, *telegram.*
erfahren, *learn.*
das Krankenhaus, *hospital.*
unerwartet, *unexpected(ly).*
zur rechten Zeit, *just in time.*
keine Zeit haben, *have no time.*
*eilen, *hurry.*
*ein-steigen, *get in (train).*
*ab-fahren, *move off.*

vermissen, *miss.*
verlieren, *lose.*
telefonieren (D), *telephone.*
der Vorfall, *incident.*
warten auf (A), *wait for.*
glücklich, *happy.*
danken (D) für, *thank for.*

7

Beschreiben Sie, was ein Briefträger im Dienst tut.

Briefträger geht früh zur Post—muß Postsachen nach Straßen und Hausnummern aussortieren—packt in Tasche ein—oft wird Tasche schwer—Weihnachtszeit und Neujahr —im Sommer—im Winter—muß auf Runde gehen—Leute erwarten Post—keine Post am Sonntag—zweimal am Tag —man erwartet den Briefträger—Briefträger tut nur seine Pflicht.

das Paket, *parcel.*
sorgfältig, *careful(ly).*
die Adressenänderung, *change of address.*
die falsche Adresse, *wrong address.*
ledern, *leather (adj.).*
zu Fuß *gehen, *walk.*
mit dem Fahrrad *fahren, *cycle.*
im Freien *sein, *be in the open.*
er hat es gut, *he is lucky.*

bei schlechtem Wetter, *in bad weather.*
zur bestimmten Stunde, *at a definite time.*
sonntags, *on Sundays.*
wochentags, *on weekdays.*
ungeduldig, *impatient(ly).*
furchtsam, *apprehensive(ly).*
er kann nichts dafür, *he cannot help it.*

8

Am Sonntag nahm Onkel Sie mit in den Zoo. Beschreiben Sie, wie Sie den Tag verbrachten.

Onkel nimmt mich mit in den Zoo—ich wache früh auf —Wetter ist schön—zu früh im Eßzimmer—esse Frühstück —bald verlassen wir das Haus—wir nehmen Autobus—wir sehen viele Kinder—wir sind am Zoo—es gibt viel zu sehen—sehr heiß—wir laufen viel—müde—Konzert— abends gehen wir wieder nach Hause.

letzten Sonntag, *last Sunday.*
aufgeregt, *excited.*
zum Glück, *fortunately.*
das Frühstück auf-tragen, *serve breakfast.*
endlich, *at last.*
der Appetit, *appetite.*
fertig *sein, *be ready.*
in derselben Richtung, *in the same direction.*
*an-kommen, *arrive.*

das Billett lösen, *buy a ticket.*
der Vogelkäfig, *birdcage.*
das Affenhaus, *monkey-house.*
das Raubtier, *beast of prey.*
der Lärm, *din.*
die Eiswaffel, *ice.*
die Limonade, *lemonade.*
sich aus-ruhen, *rest.*
die Militärkapelle, *military band.*
zufrieden, *contented.*

9

Auf Bahnhöfen werden Handkoffer gestohlen. Man
kann die Diebe nicht finden. Ein kleiner Junge sieht einen
Diebstahl. Erzählen Sie den Vorgang.

Reisenden werden Handkoffer gestohlen—Bahnhofspersonal paßt auf—kein Dieb wird gefangen—Reisende
werden nervös—viele Leute warten auf Bahnsteig—Koffer
gestohlen—kleiner Junge sieht es—großer Koffer mit offe-
nem Boden über kleinen Koffer gestellt—wieder schließen
—Koffer ohne viel Bewegung verschwunden—Dieb wird
verhaftet.

seit einiger Zeit, *for some time.*
der Vorfall, *incident.*
sich mehren, *increase in number.*
trotz, *in spite of.*
das Bahnhofspersonal, *station staff.*
das Rätsel, *puzzle.*
die Wachsamkeit, *vigilance.*
der Diebstahl, *theft.*
unerwartet, *unexpected(ly).*
das Reisegepäck, *luggage.*

versichern, *insure.*
einmal, *one day, once.*
geduldig, *patient(ly).*
Verspätung haben, *be late (of train).*
spurlos, *without a trace.*
beobachten, *observe.*
ein Knöpfchen drücken, *press a button.*
verhaften, *arrest.*

10

Sie haben von Ihrem Onkel einen Zwanzigmarkschein
zum Geburtstag bekommen. Bedanken Sie sich in einem
Brief dafür.

Brief mit Zwanzigmarkschein auf Geburtstagstisch—
was damit getan werden soll—möchte Flöte spielen—will
Geld sparen—zwanzig Mark haben noch gefehlt—Summe
ist jetzt vollzählig—gehe morgen Flöte kaufen.

das Geburtstagsgeschenk, *birthday present.*
sich schrecklich freuen, *be terribly pleased.*
wissen wollen, *want to know.*
erzählen, *tell.*
seit langer Zeit, *for a long time.*
in Erfüllung *gehen, *be fulfilled.*
es ist mir ernst damit, *I really mean it.*

die Sparbüchse, *money-box.*
das Sparkassenbuch, *savings-book.*
das Taschengeld, *pocket-money.*
nichts aus-geben, *spend nothing.*
sparen, *save.*
die Belohnung, *reward.*
es möglich machen, *make (it) possible.*
das Schaufenster, *shop-window.*

11

Drei Kinder spielen bei regnerischem Wetter auf dem Boden (*attic*).   Sie entdecken einen Koffer.   Es sind Kleider darin.   Sie ziehen sie an.   Beschreiben Sie den Vorgang.

Es regnet—Kinder spielen im Zimmer—alle Spiele gespielt—fragen Mutter—dürfen auf Boden gehen—finden Koffer—öffnen—Kleider—Schwester findet Kleid—es paßt ihr—gehen zur Mutter ins Wohnzimmer—Gemälde von Großmutter an der Wand—Schwester sieht genau so aus—dasselbe Kleid.

seit einigen Tagen, *for some days.*
es regnet Bindfaden, *it's raining cats and dogs.*
das Gewitter, *thunder-storm.*
sich langweilen, *be bored.*
die Erlaubnis geben, *give permission.*
in einer dunklen Ecke versteckt, *hidden in a dark corner.*
ans Licht ziehen, *bring to the light.*

altmodisch, *old-fashioned.*
aus-packen, *unpack.*
an-probieren, *try on.*
die Treppe *herunter-laufen, *run downstairs.*
das Gemälde, *painting.*
das Porträt, *portrait.*
aufs Haar gleichen, *be as like as two peas.*

12

Beschreiben Sie die Stadt, in der Sie wohnen.

Provinzstadt—alte Straßen immer schön, sogar wenn es regnet—zum Einkaufen muß man zur Hauptstraße gehen—kann Freund im Café treffen—für Fremde gibt es Hotels—für Unterhaltung sorgen Kinos und Sportplätze—für Konzerte geht man in den Dom—vor der Stadt fließt Fluß.

das Gebäude, *building.*
der Erker, *bow-window.*
hervor-ragen, *jut out.*
der Eingang, *entrance.*
modern, *modern.*
der Laden, *shop.*
eine große Auswahl, *a great choice.*
das Café, *café.*
die Teestube, *tea room.*
die Sehenswürdigkeiten (pl.), *the " sights ".*
berühmt, *famous.*

die Stadtmauer, *city wall.*
der Dom, *cathedral.*
das Rathaus, *town hall.*
das Theater, *theatre.*
der Schauspieler, *actor.*
das Fußballspiel, *football match.*
das Tennis, *tennis.*
das Orchester, *orchestra.*
das Ufer, *bank (of river).*
die Brücke, *bridge.*
das Ruderboot, *rowing-boat.*

13

Sie sind eingeladen, die Osterferien in Deutschland zu verbringen. Was für Vorbereitungen treffen Sie?

Man braucht Paß—deutsches Geld—Deutsche lieben englischen Tee—wieviel darf man ausführen?—man muß Briefe schreiben—Geschenk für den (die) Freund (-in)—man muß Wahl treffen—Fahrplan studieren—Fahrkarten bestellen—Liste machen—wichtig, daß Koffer auch Schlüssel haben.

rechtzeitig, *in time.*
erneuern, *renew.*
sich erkundigen (nach), *inquire (about).*
die Formalitäten, *formalities.*
das Kleingeld, *small change.*
der Reisescheck, *traveller's cheque.*
mit-bringen, *take with one.*

die Platzreservierung, *seat reservation.*
das Toilettenzeug, *toilet articles.*
die Kleider, *clothes.*
der Schuh, *shoe.*
der Regenmantel, *waterproof.*
das Schloß, *lock.*
in Ordnung *sein, be in order.*

14

Sie wollen einen Kuchen selbst backen. Erzählen Sie, was Sie tun.

Mutter hat Geburtstag—beschließen, Kuchen selbst zu backen—Einkäufe—Zutaten abwiegen—Dotter vom Eiweiß trennen—Butter zu Sahne rühren—Zutaten hinzugeben—zuletzt Eierschnee darunter ziehen—Teig in Form tun—im Ofen backen.

selbstgemacht, *home-made.*
das Rezept, *recipe.*
studieren, *study.*
die Zutat, *ingredient.*
die Waage, *scales.*
ab-wiegen, *weigh* (tr.).
das richtige Gewicht, *right weight.*
sorgfältig, *careful(ly).*
das Ei, *egg.*
das Dotter, *yoke.*
das Eiweiß, *white of egg.*
der Eierschnee, *whipped white of eggs.*
die Sahne, *cream.*
schlagen, *beat, whip.*

steif, *stiff.*
das Mehl, *flour.*
sieben, *sift.*
das Backpulver, *baking-powder.*
der Zucker, *sugar.*
die Rosine, *raisin.*
die Mandel, *almond.*
die Milch, *milk.*
leicht, *light.*
der Teig, *dough.*
mit Papier aus-legen, *line with paper.*
bei gelinder Hitze, *in a moderate oven.*

15

Schreiben Sie einen Brief an Ihre(n) Freundin (Freund), in dem Sie Ihre gute Ankunft zu Hause berichten und für die schönen Ferien danken, die Sie bei ihr (ihm) haben verbringen dürfen.

Datum und Überschrift—schöne Ferien vorbei—Reise verläuft gut—sehe zum Fenster hinaus—esse Äpfel—Zeit kommt nicht lang vor—Mutter auf dem Bahnhof—sie freut sich—braun und gesund—muß viel erzählen—lachen viel—Alltag fängt wieder an—danke vielmals—Grüße an alle—Unterschrift.

der Zwischenfall, *incident.*
10 Minuten Verspätung haben, *be 10 minutes late.*
guten Anschluß haben, *have a good connection.*
*um-steigen, *change trains.*
die Landschaft, *scenery.*
das Kornfeld, *corn-field.*
die Ernte, *harvest.*
köstlich, *delicious.*
gut schmecken, *taste good.*

schneller als gedacht, *quicker than one had thought.*
*vergehen, *pass (of time).*
vom Bahnhof ab-holen, *meet at station.*
aus-sehen, *look (e.g. well).*
einen Ausflug machen, *to go on an excursion.*
der Stier, *bull.*
*hinterher-laufen, *run along behind.*
grüßen lassen, *send one's kind regards.*

16

Sie fahren ins Seebad. Ihr Koffer ist noch nicht angekommen. Beschreiben Sie den ersten Tag Ihres Aufenthaltes an der See.

Kommen im Hotel an—erzählen Wirt von verlorenem Koffer—verspricht zu telefonieren—Wetter sehr schön —kein Badeanzug—gehen einkaufen—Morgen vergeht schnell—Mittagessen im Garten—nachmittags in Sonne liegen—in See baden—sich von der Sonne bräunen lassen— manche Leute sehr rot von Sonne—Koffer im Hotel vor Abendbrot—umziehen—nach Abendbrot Konzert—schöner Tag zu Ende.

17

Eine Szene im Autobus. Der Schaffner wurde zornig.

Ich gehe zum Tee—fahre mit Autobus—es ist schneller als zu Fuß gehen—zu dieser Tageszeit Autobus oft besetzt

—besonders bei schlechtem Wetter—lange Schlangen an Haltestellen—Schaffner hat Mühe, Fahrgeld einzusammeln —kommt nicht schnell genug durch Wagen—Leute steigen ohne Fahrschein wieder aus—ein Mann will das auch tun —Schaffner sagt: „ das Fahrgeld, bitte."—Mann bietet Zwanzigmarkschein an—Schaffner hat nicht genug Kleingeld—Autobus hat schon Verspätung—Schaffner sehr ärgerlich—läßt Mann ohne Fahrschein aussteigen—Schaffner schimpft.

18

Sie kommen zu spät zur Schule. Erzählen Sie, wie Sie sich entschuldigt haben.

Um Entschuldigung bitten—vergessen Wecker aufzuziehen—spät aufgewacht—keine Elektrizität zum Kochen— schnell kaltes Frühstück gegessen—gerade noch zur rechten Zeit Haus verlassen—Hund ins Fahrrad gelaufen—gefallen —Fahrrad verbogen—muß zu Fuß gehen—dauert viel länger—deshalb zu spät gekommen.

19

Sie schreiben einen Brief an eine(n) deutsche(n) Freundin (Freund) und laden sie (ihn) ein, die nächsten Ferien bei Ihnen zu verbringen.

Datum und Überschrift—Dank für letzten Brief— immer erfreut, Nachricht zu bekommen—Beschreibung von Erlebnissen sehr interessant—wären gern dabei gewesen— Mutter erlaubt, für nächste Ferien nach England einzuladen —vielleicht in dem deutschen Theaterstück mitspielen— wann beginnen Ferien?—ungeduldig auf Antwort warten —Grüße und Unterschrift.

20

Ihr Onkel fährt mit Ihnen in einem Taxi. Als Sie ankommen, entdeckt Ihr Onkel, daß er kein Geld zum Bezahlen hat.

Mit Onkel im Taxi fahren—kommen am Ziel an—
Onkel will bezahlen—hat Zwanzigmarkschein im Taxi
verloren—Taxifahrer hört das—fährt sehr eilig davon—
Onkel sehr erstaunt—findet Zwanzigmarkschein in Tasche—
unehrlicher Taxifahrer ist bestraft.

21

Setzen Sie " A strange employment " fort (Nr. 7, S. 186).

Mann verspricht, alles zu tun—Frau gibt ihm einen
Beutel voll Geld—sie besprechen den Weg, den er nehmen
soll—er tritt die Reise an—tut, wie sie ihm befohlen hat—
Kästchen—besonderes Zimmer—Tür zuschließen—lebt für
sich allein—nach ein paar Tagen langweilt sich—lebt in
Gesellschaft—verliert Geld beim Spiel—geht auf sein
Zimmer—hört Bewegung im verschlossenen Zimmer—will
aufschließen—Tür springt von selbst auf—Frau tritt ihm
entgegen—er gesteht ihr seinen Fehler—sie gibt ihm noch
mehr Geld—warnt ihn vor Wein und Spiel.

22

Setzen Sie " A fire " fort (Nr. 18, S. 196).

Leontin läuft die Treppe hinauf—viel Rauch—tritt ins
Schlafzimmer—Julie schläft—Leontin weckt sie—wickelt
sie in Bettdecken—wollen Treppen hinuntersteigen—Treppe
hat Feuer gefangen—Julie will nicht weiter—Leontin trägt
sie durchs Feuer—setzt Mädchen auf den Hof—fällt bewußtlos auf den Boden hin—kommt wieder zu sich—Julie kniet
neben ihm—reicht ihm Wasser.

23

Setzen Sie " A lodging for the night " fort (Nr. 24, S. 201).

Friedrich zu aufgeregt, um schlafen zu können—setzt
sich ans Fenster—eine Stunde vergeht—Hund bellt—
Stimmen unten—wieder still—er steht auf—untersucht
seine Pistolen—legt sein Schwert auf den Tisch—Tür geht
auf—mehrere Männer treten ein—bleiben stehen—Müller

drückt eine Pistole ab—Schuß geht fehl—Kampf entsteht
—Mädchen kommt ihm zu Hilfe—zwei Männer verwundet
—andere laufen fort—Friedrich gerettet.

24

Setzen Sie " A deal " fort (Nr. 27, S. 204).

Schlemihl kommt wieder zu Sinnen—füllt Taschen mit
Gold—verbirgt Beutel—eilt nach der Stadt fort—alte Frau
ruft: ,, Sie haben Ihren Schatten verloren "—andere Leute
bemerken es auch—vermeidet es, in die Sonne zu treten—
muß über die Straße gehen—Jungen lachen über ihn—
springt in eine Droschke—fährt zum Hotel—läßt Sachen
holen—fährt zum besten Hotel—wirft einige Goldstücke
hin—bekommt bestes Zimmer—verschließt sich darin—
weint—so viel Geld aber keinen Schatten—was wird aus
ihm werden?

25

Setzen Sie " Trapped " fort (Nr. 29, S. 206).

Menschenstimmen nähern sich — vier Männer mit
Fackeln (*torches*)—Tor wird aufgemacht—Treppe—großes
Zimmer—feste Wände, hohe Fenster—Betten, Stühle—eine
Stunde allein gelassen—junger Mann kommt—stellt Fragen
—Wilhelm überreicht ihm Papiere—Erklärung: Diebe
benutzten den Weg, um junge Bäume zu stehlen; Falle
(*trap*) wurde eingerichtet—Wilhelm und Felix werden
freigelassen—finden Fritz wieder—kommen glücklich nach
Hause.

26

Setzen Sie " A near escape " fort (Nr. 30, S. 207).

Dankbarkeit der Fürstin—verspricht Honorio eine Belohnung—Honorio möchte die Welt sehen—Fürstin will
ihren Mann um die Erlaubnis bitten—Gespräch unterbrochen—Frau kommt auf sie zu—wirft sich vor den Tiger
hin—weint—ohne Not getötet—zahmes Tier.

27

Setzen Sie " The rescue " fort (Nr. 32, S. 209).

Arzt behandelt Knaben—wird ins Leben zurückge-
rufen—Kahn kommt—Hauptmann springt hinein—blickt
sich um—alle sind gerettet—geht nach Hause—zieht sich
um—kommt zurück—gibt Zeichen zum Beginn des Festes
—Feuerwerk—herrliches Schauspiel—dauert halbe Stunde
—alle gehen vergnügt nach Hause.

28

Setzen Sie " A mystery " fort (Nr. 41, S. 221).

Olivier folgt ihm weiter—Cardillac verschwindet—Einfahrt eines Hauses—Olivier drückt sich ans Haus—ein Mann
kommt—Cardillac stürzt sich auf ihn—Mann sinkt zu
Boden—Olivier schreit auf—Cardillac läuft fort—Olivier
kniet bei dem Mann nieder—will ihm helfen—tot—Polizei
—Olivier wird verhaftet (*arrested*).

29

Setzen Sie " The secret button " fort (Nr. 46, S. 227).

Vittoria weckt Bruder—er erzählt: er sei zurückgekommen; habe wichtige Papiere im Haus suchen wollen;
sei überrascht; er habe zufällig Knöpfchen gefunden;
habe unbemerkt dort bleiben können; habe wichtige
Unterredung gehört; habe nicht fortkommen können; sei
eingeschlafen—verläßt Zimmer—macht Wand wieder zu
—geht in den Garten—klettert über die Mauer—entkommt
—Vittoria kehrt in ihr Zimmer zurück—weiß jetzt, wo er
wohnt.

30

Setzen Sie " The flood " fort (Nr. 50, S. 233).

Hund bellt—sie blicken sich um—Elsbeths Hund an
einem oberen Fenster des Hauses—sie kehren zurück—
Hund springt ins Wasser—schwimmt zum Boot—wird

hereingezogen—Elsbeth weint vor Freude—alle jetzt bei-sammen—Wasser steigt immer noch—müssen einen Tag und eine Nacht im Boot zubringen—Wasser fällt wieder—kommen aufs Trockene (*dry land*).

31

Continue "The farmer is afraid" (No. 13, p. 131) explaining why the farmer is so agitated.

Every evening—sunset—stranger—old man—looks like his father—approaches slowly—sits down—says nothing—stares at him—ten minutes—gets up—goes away slowly—stops twice—looks round—disappears.

32

Continue "The excursion" (No. 16, p. 133).

We set off—say nothing—it gets dark—a quarter of an hour—small creek (*Bucht, f.*)—stop—light lamp—begin to fish (*angeln*)—half an hour—catch fish—return journey—hear footsteps—stop—footsteps go away—arrive at landing-stage (*Landungsplatz, m.*)—I give fish to friend—very poor.

33

Continue "Poor Peter" (No. 17, p. 133).

Man gives him advice—boy tells parents he wants to leave home—sets off early next day—walks all day—open country—comes to farm—farmer and wife—offer him meal and bed—happy and smiling—ask him what he wants to do—their son stolen from them when quite small—will he work with them?—boy gladly accepts—wife notices birth-mark (*Muttermal, n.*) on boy's leg—her son.

34

Continue "A late visit" (No. 18, p. 134).

Daughter is resolved to marry (*heiraten*) cousin—unable to obey father—she knows she will be poor—father will give her nothing—cousin without means—father listens in silence

—daughter stops talking—father says nothing—daughter goes out—goes to her room—packs bag—leaves home—goes to friend—marries cousin—wedding-present (*Hochzeitsgeschenk, n.*) from father.

35

Relate what the boy had been doing (No. 20, p. 135).

He shows mother small box—mother opens it—gold coins—boy explains—strange bird—white wings—he follows it—keeps stopping in front of him—on and on—tall tree—perches on branch—boy climbs tree—hole in trunk—puts his arm in—discovers box—bird flies off—boy comes down tree—gets home late.

36

Continue " A disturbed night " (No. 26, p. 139).

I carry suit-case to house—open it—gold watches and rings—telephone police—policeman comes—goods stolen from shop near by—police knew of it—looking for burglars (*Einbrecher*)—jeweller (*Juwelier*) delighted—gives reward—I buy wireless set with money—my wife has long wanted one.

37

Continue " Stephen in danger " (No. 34, p. 144).

Joan comes back to spot with four men and doctor—one man ties rope (*Seil, n.*) round him —is lowered (*hinuntergelassen*) in the pit (*Grube, f.*) by others—very deep—lantern—discovers Stephen—no sign of life—unties rope—ties rope round Stephen—Stephen hauled up (*heraufgezogen*)—doctor examines Stephen—no limbs broken—life not in danger—warmth and rest necessary—will soon recover.

38

Continue " Saved " (No. 37, p. 147).

Manfred decides to walk south—two hours—very hungry and thirsty—stream—drinks—goes on—smoke—

village—natives (*Eingeborene*)—no one understands—makes signs—they give him food—he falls asleep—is woken up by native—man speaks to him in English—Englishmen in camp (*Lager, n.*) near by—takes him there—Englishmen seeking uranium (*Uran, n.*).

39

Continue " Truants " (No. 44, p. 151).

We buy bread and cheese—set off through woods— come to lake—undress and bathe—lie in sun—eat lunch— pity (*bedauern*) school-comrades—" now doing Latin "— what shall we say to the master to-morrow?—head-ache? (*Kopfschmerzen*)—return home—Michael's mother angry— master has just called—sends Michael supperless to bed— goes to my mother—punishment.

40

Continue " A strange house " (No. 47, p. 153).

I undress and go to bed—fall asleep quickly—wake up at midnight—hear steps on stairs—somebody tries to open door—chair moves slightly—steps go downstairs again—I get up and dress—spend night seated in chair—listen anxiously—try to read—sunrise—leave house very quietly.

41

Sie sind vor ein paar Tagen umgezogen. Beschreiben Sie was geschah.

42

Beschreiben Sie das Haus, in dem Sie geboren sind.

43

Erzählen Sie, wie Sie gewöhnlich Weihnachten in Ihrer Familie feiern.

44

Was ist Ihre Lieblingsbeschäftigung? Erzählen Sie uns davon.

45

Wie würden Sie Ihre Ferien verbringen, wenn Sie 50 Pfund dazu geschenkt bekämen?

46

Schreiben Sie einen Dialog am Telefon.

47

Sie sind krank. Der Doktor muß kommen. Erzählen Sie uns von seinem Besuch.

48

In Ihrem Elternhaus ist eingebrochen worden. Erzählen Sie, wie es entdeckt wurde.

49

Erzählen Sie eine Anekdote, die zeigt, daß Tiere Verstand haben.

50

Ein Mann hat vergessen, einen Brief für seine Frau einzustecken. Beschreiben Sie die Unterhaltung zwischen den beiden, als es herauskommt.

SECTION V

GERMAN PROSE EXTRACTS

HINTS ON ANSWERING COMPREHENSION QUESTIONS

When a German passage is set for comprehension the German questions are, or should be, so framed as to make it impossible to give the appropriate answer by a mere reproduction of sentences taken from the passage or from the questions themselves; for this could obviously be done without any comprehension of either passage or questions. Such reproduction serves no purpose and scores no marks. It will usually be found that some change, particularly in word order or in tense, has to be made before the answer suits the question. The answers should be in the form of a complete sentence. Generally speaking, the questions are asked in a progressive order, the first questions being asked about the first part of the passage, the last about the last part; but there may be a question or two set in order to discover whether you have understood the passage as a whole.

Before attempting such an exercise you should read through the passage carefully several times. Only then can you hope to be in a position to answer the questions sensibly. This applies also to comprehension tests in which the questions are asked in English.

Examiners find only too often that candidates do not know what is the right form of answer to suit the form of the question. We are therefore showing, by means of an example, what it is that examiners do in fact require, and what they would reject.

An attempt at murder

Der Prinz ließ sich neulich spät in der Nacht aus dem Theater nach Hause tragen; zwei Diener, unter denen

Biondello war, begleiteten ihn. Da die Sänfte zerbrach, sah der Prinz sich gezwungen, den Rest des Weges zu Fuß zu machen. Biondello ging voran, der Weg führte durch einige dunkle abgelegene Straßen. Nach einer Viertelstunde machte Biondello die Entdeckung, daß er sich verirrt hatte. Die Ähnlichkeit der Brücken hatte ihn getäuscht, und anstatt in St. Markus befand man sich in einem unbekannten Viertel. Es war in einer der abgelegensten Straßen, und man sah nichts Lebendiges weit und breit; man mußte umkehren, um sich in einer Hauptstraße zu orientieren. Sie waren nur wenige Schritte gegangen, als sie nicht weit von sich in einer Straße ein lautes Geschrei hörten. Der Prinz riß einem Diener den Stock aus der Hand, und mit entschlossenem Mut eilte er nach der Stelle, woher diese Stimme kam. Drei Männer waren eben im Begriff, einen vierten niederzustoßen, der sich mit seinem Begleiter nur noch schwach verteidigte; der Prinz erschien noch eben zur rechten Zeit, um den tödlichen Stoß zu hindern. Sein Rufen erschreckte die Mörder, die sofort die Flucht ergriffen. Halb ohnmächtig sank der Verwundete dem Prinzen in die Arme; sein Begleiter sagte diesem, daß er den Neffen des Kardinals A. gerettet habe. Da der Verwundete viel Blut verlor, trug der Prinz dafür Sorge, daß er nach dem Palast seines Onkels gebracht wurde, wohin er ihn selbst begleitete. Hier verließ er ihn in der Stille und ohne seinen Namen genannt zu haben.

Nach Johann Christoph Friedrich von Schiller (1759-1805):
Der Geisterseher

3. Die Sänfte: *sedan chair*.

German Questions:

1. Wo war der Prinz an dem Abend gewesen?
2. Warum mußte der Prinz einen Teil des Weges zu Fuß machen?
3. Warum hatte man sich verirrt?
4. Woher wußte Biondello, daß er sich verirrt hatte?
5. Wen konnte man nach dem richtigen Weg fragen?
6. Zu welchem Zweck riß der Prinz einem Diener den Stock aus der Hand?

7. **Woraus** kann man schließen, daß der Prinz keine Angst hatte?

8. **Was** wäre geschehen, wenn der Prinz nicht erschienen wäre?

9. **Warum** ergriffen die Mörder die Flucht?

10. **Weshalb** durfte man nicht viel Zeit verlieren?

When German questions are asked German answers are expected. The following are the suggested answers to the German questions. Alternative answers are given in brackets. Answers that would be rejected are shown within square brackets, a brief reason being given in most cases for their rejection. We also give a few typical forms of answer to certain common forms of questions you may be set.

1. Der Prinz (*or* er) war an dem Abend im Theater gewesen.

   [*Not:* (*a*) Der Prinz . . . tragen. (Does not answer the question.)

   (*b*) Der Prinz war im Theater an dem Abend gewesen. (Wrong word-order.)]

2. Der Prinz (*or* er) mußte einen Teil des Weges zu Fuß machen, weil die Sänfte zerbrochen war.

   [*Not:* (*a*) Weil die Sänfte zerbrochen war. (Incomplete sentence.)

   (*b*) Er mußte . . . machen, da die Sänfte zerbrach. (Incorrect form of answer to a *warum* question.)

   (*c*) Er mußte . . . machen, weil die Sänfte zerbrach. (Wrong tense.)

   (*d*) Da die . . . zu machen. (Answer unsuited to form of question.)]

3. Man hatte sich verirrt, weil die Ähnlichkeit der Brücken Biondello getäuscht hatte (*or* weil B. die Brücken verwechselt hatte).

   [*Not:* (*a*) Weil die Ähnlichkeit der Brücken B. getäuscht hatte. (Incomplete sentence.)

   (*b*) Man . . . verirrt, weil . . . ihn getäuscht hatte. (B. is not mentioned in the question.)

   (*c*) Die Ähnlichkeit . . . ihn getäuscht. (B. is not mentioned in the question, and answer does not tie up closely enough with the question.)

(*d*) Man . . . verirrt, weil der Weg durch einige
dunkle abgesonderte Straßen führte.   (This is
not the real reason.)]

4. Biondello (*or* er) wußte, daß er sich verirrt hatte, weil **er** (*or*
man) sich in einem unbekannten Viertel (anstatt **in St.**
Markus) befand (*or* weil er in einem unbekannten
Viertel war.)

   [*Not:* (*a*) Anstatt in St. Markus . . . Viertel.   (Answer
does not tie up closely enough with the
question.)

   (*b*) Die Ähnlichkeit . . . getäuscht.   (Wrong answer.)]

5. Man konnte niemand (*or* keinen Menschen *or* keine Leute)
nach dem richtigen Weg fragen.

   [*Not:* (*a*) Es war . . . Straßen.   (Does not answer the
question.)

   (*b*) Man sah . . . breit.   (Does not answer the
question.)]

6. Der Prinz (*or* er) riß einem Diener den Stock aus der Hand,
um dem vierten Mann *or* dem Angegriffenen *or* den
Angegriffenen *or* dem Neffen des Kardinals) zu Hilfe
zu kommen (*or* zu helfen) (*or* um den vierten Mann,
den (die) Angegriffenen, den Neffen des Kardinals zu
verteidigen.)

   [*Not:* (*a*) . . . , um den tödlichen Stoß zu hindern.   (Suggests prince knew exactly what was going to
happen.)

   (*b*) . . . und mit . . . Stelle (woher . . . kam).
(Inept reproduction.)]

7. Das (*or* daß der Prinz (*or* er) keine Angst hatte,) kann man
daraus schließen, daß er (mit entschlossenem Mut) nach
der Stelle eilte (woher diese Stimme kam) (*or* daß er
sich mutig entschloß, nach der Stelle zu eilen) (*or* daß
er dem Angegriffen zu Hilfe kommen wollte.)

   [*Not:* (*a*) Er eilte (mit entschlossenem Mut) nach der
Stelle.   (Does not tie up closely enough with
the question.)

   (*b*) Er riß . . . aus der Hand.   (Does not answer
the question.)]

8. Wenn der Prinz nicht erschienen wäre, so wäre der vierte
Mann (der Neffe des Kardinals) niedergestoßen (getötet,
gemordet, ermordet) worden.

[*Not:* (a) Der Prinz erschien . . . zu hindern. (Does not
answer the question.)

    (b) Der vierte Mann etc. wäre niedergestoßen worden.
(Incomplete answer.)]

9. Die Mörder (*or* sie) ergriffen die Flucht, weil das Rufen des
Prinzen sie erschreckte (*or* erschreckt hatte).

[*Not:* (a) . . . , weil sein Rufen sie erschreckte. (Prince
not mentioned in the question.)

    (b) Der Prinz erschien . . . Zeit. (Not the specific
reason for the assailants' flight.)]

10. Man durfte nicht viel Zeit verlieren, weil der Verwundete
(Neffe des Kardinals) viel Blut verloren hatte (*or*
schwer verwundet war *or* halb ohnmächtig war).

[*Not:* (a) . . . , da der Verwundete viel Blut verlor.
(Incorrect form of answer to a *warum* question.)

    (b) Da . . . verlor. (Incomplete sentence.)

    (c) Weil . . . verlor. (Incomplete sentence.)

    (d) Da . . . geschafft wurde. (Wrong answer and
formally incorrect.)

    (e) Halb . . . die Arme. (Does not answer the
question.)]

Note the types of answer to the following forms of
question:

1. Warum, weshalb (a) why (*for what reason*).

                (b) why (*for what purpose*). Cf. zu wel-
chem Zweck.

  (a) Q. Warum (weshalb) konnte er nicht kommen?

     A. Er konnte nicht kommen, weil er krank war.

   or Er konnte wegen seiner Krankheit nicht kommen.

  (b) Q. Warum (weshalb, zu welchem Zweck) hat er das
gesagt?

     A. Er hat das gesagt, damit sie alles weiß.

     A. Er hat das gesagt, um ihr Freude zu machen.

  Note. Do not try to use *denn* (for) or *da* (since) in your answers
to questions beginning with *warum*.

2. Auf welche Weise, wie (*in what way*).

    Q. Auf welche Weise (wie) weckte er den Prinzen.

       Er weckte ihn, indem er seinen Namen nannte (*by
saying his name*).

3. Was für ein, mit was für einem, einer ((*with*) *what sort of a*).

    Q. Was für ein Mann war er?

    A. Er war ein alter Mann?

    Q. Mit was für einer Stimme sprach er?

    A. Er sprach mit lauter Stimme.

4. Woran, worauf, wodurch, woraus, wovor, etc.

    Q. Woran kann man erkennen, daß er krank ist?

    A. Daß er krank ist, kann man daran erkennen, daß er
        blaß aussieht.

    or Man kann das an seinem blassen Gesicht erkennen.

    Q. Worauf bestand er?

    A. Er bestand auf einer Antwort.

    or Er bestand darauf, daß sie ihm antwortete. (*He
        insisted on her answering him.*)

    Q. Wodurch gelang es ihm, das Examen zu bestehen?

    A. Es gelang ihm, das Examen dadurch zu bestehen,
        daß er fleißig arbeitete (*by working hard*).

    or Es gelang ihm, durch seinen Fleiß das Examen zu
        bestehen.

    Q. Woraus kann man schließen, daß er faul ist.

    A. Das (*or* daß er faul ist,) kann man daraus schließen,
        daß er immer spät aufsteht.

    or Man kann aus seinem späten Aufstehen schließen,
        daß er faul ist.

    Q. Wovor warnte sie ihn?

    A. Sie warnte ihn vor der Gefahr?

5. Woher.

    Q. Woher wissen Sie, daß er krank war? (*How do
        you know that he was ill?*)

    A. Ich weiß das (*or* daß er krank war), weil er blaß
        aussah (*because he looked pale*).

English Questions:

1. How was the prince expecting to get home?
2. Why couldn't this be done in this way?
3. Why did the prince and his servants retrace their steps?
4. What aroused their attention?
5. What was the prince able to avert?
6. What did the assailants do on hearing the prince?
7. Who had been in danger of being murdered?
8. Why did the victim of the attack sink into the prince's arms?
9. Where was the victim taken to?
10. What did the prince refrain from doing?

Where English questions are asked English answers are expected. Here again complete sentences are required and the answer must be strictly relevant to the question and as concise as possible. The following are the suggested answers to the English questions. Alternatives are given in brackets. Where translations are offered (as must often be the case) these should be as accurate as possible.

1. The prince was expecting to be carried home (in a sedan-chair).
2. This couldn't be done because the sedan-chair had broken.
3. They retraced their steps in order to get their bearings in a main thoroughfare (street, road).
4. A loud shout (clamour) aroused their attention.
5. The prince was able to avert the mortal (fatal) blow (being struck).
6. On hearing the prince the assailants took to flight (took to their heels, fled).
7. The cardinal's nephew had been in danger of being murdered.
8. The victim of the attack sank into the prince's arms owing to (because of) loss of blood (because he had become weak owing to loss of blood) (because he had been severely wounded) (because he was faint from loss of blood).
9. The victim was taken to his uncle's palace (to the Cardinal's palace).
10. The prince refrained from saying who he was (from revealing his name, from giving his name).

A. PASSAGES FOR TRANSLATION OR COMPREHENSION

1. *A sleepless night*

Den ganzen Abend konnte ich keine Gelegenheit finden, Biondello zu sprechen; ich mußte mich also mit meiner unbefriedigten Neugierde schlafen legen. Der Prinz hatte uns früh entlassen; aber tausend Gedanken, die mir durch den Kopf gingen, hielten mich wach. Lange hörte ich ihn über meinem Schlafzimmer auf und ab gehen; endlich überwältigte mich der Schlaf. Spät nach Mitternacht weckte mich eine Stimme—eine Hand fuhr über mein Gesicht; als ich aufsah, war es der Prinz, der, ein Licht in der Hand, vor meinem Bette stand. Er könne nicht einschlafen, sagte er und bat mich, ihm die Nacht verkürzen zu helfen. Ich wollte mich in meine Kleider werfen—er befahl mir, zu bleiben, und setzte sich zu mir vor das Bett.

Nach Johann Christoph Friedrich von Schiller (1759-1805):
Der Geisterseher

1. Was war dem Erzähler nicht gelungen?
2. Warum wollte er Biondello sprechen?
3. Warum schlief er nicht sofort ein?
4. Woher wußte er, daß der Prinz nicht früh zu Bett gegangen war?
5. Wie lange schlief er?
6. Auf welche Weise weckte ihn der Prinz?
7. Woher wußte er, daß der Prinz vor ihm stand?
8. Warum war der Prinz zu ihm gekommen?
9. Warum blieb der Erzähler im Bett liegen?
10. Womit war das Zimmer erleuchtet?

2. *The gipsy fortune-teller*

Mitten in dem Haufen bemerkte ich bald darauf ein altes Weib, das ich bei dem Widerscheine der Flamme nicht ohne Schreck für dieselbe Zigeunerin wiedererkannte, die mir als Kind so fürchterlich prophezeit hatte. Ich ging zu ihr hin, sie kannte mich nicht mehr.—Von unserem letzten Zusammentreffen in Rom wußte oder mochte sie nichts wissen.—Ich reichte ihr noch einmal die Hand hin. Sie betrachtete alle Linien sehr genau, dann sah sie mir scharf in die Augen und sagte, während sie ihre Worte mit seltsamen Gebärden begleitete: „ Es ist höchste Zeit, der Feind ist nicht mehr weit, hüte dich, hüte dich! " Darauf verschwand sie sofort unter dem Haufen, und ich sah sie nicht mehr wieder. Mir wurde dabei nicht wohl zumute, und ihre Worte gingen mir noch lange im Kopfe herum.

Nach Joseph von Eichendorff (1778-1857):
Ahnung und Gegenwart

1. Zu welcher Zeit des Tages traf der Erzähler die Zigeunerin?
2. Woher wissen Sie, daß er die Zigeunerin nicht zum erstenmal sah?
3. Warum erschrak der Erzähler, als er sie sah?
4. War er sicher, daß sie ihn nicht erkannte?
5. Warum reichte er ihr die Hand hin?
6. Was für Leute begleiten ihre Worte mit Gebärden?
7. Vor wem warnte die Zigeunerin den Erzähler?
8. Wie lange blieb sie noch bei ihm?
9. In was für einer Stimmung war er nachher?
10. Woher wissen Sie, daß er die Worte nicht vergessen konnte?

3. *New guests*

Als sich die beiden Reiter eine Viertelstunde später dem Hotel näherten, sahen sie deutlich, daß der letzte Zug viele Gäste gebracht haben mußte, denn der große Balkon war noch sehr belebt. Alles war hell erleuchtet, und in dem Lichte bewegten sich die Kellner hin und her. Einer trug eine große Teekanne, was zweifellos bedeutete, daß Engländer oder Holländer angekommen sein mußten. Gleich danach hielten die Reiter vor dem Hotel, hoben sich aus den Sätteln und traten in das Vestibül. Eine Welt von Koffern und Reisetaschen lag hier durcheinander, und als Cecile die Treppe hinaufstieg, tat ihr die Wärme wohl, die die Gasflammen ausstrahlten.

„ Ich denke, wir nehmen den Tee noch gemeinschaftlich auf dem Balkon. Nicht wahr, Herr von Gordon? "

Und wirklich saßen die Freunde nach einigen Minuten mit unter den Gästen, und zwar an demselben Tisch, an dem sie erst vor wenigen Tagen sich kennengelernt hatten.

Nach Theodor Fontane (1819-98): Cecile

1. Wieviel Gäste waren da, als die Reiter das Hotel verließen?
2. Zu welcher Zeit des Tages und des Jahres war es?
3. Woraus konnte man schließen, daß Engländer oder Holländer gekommen waren?
4. Worauf sitzt ein Reiter auf dem Pferd beim Reiten?
5. War der Balkon im Erdgeschoß oder im ersten Stock?
6. Wem gehörten die Koffer und Reisetaschen im Vestibül?

7. Woher wissen Sie, daß es Cecile kalt war?
8. Wozu dienten die Gasflammen?
9. Waren die beiden Freunde allein, als sie Tee tranken?
10. Waren die beiden alte Freunde?

4. *Aftermath of war*

So kam er an einem unfreundlichen, stürmischen Abend in einem abgelegenen Dorfe an. Die Gärten waren alle verwüstet, die Häuser niedergebrannt, die wenigen übriggebliebenen schienen von den Bewohnern verlassen; es war ein trauriges Denkmal des kaum beendigten Krieges, der an diesen Gegenden besonders seine Wut ausgelassen hatte. An dem anderen Ende des Dorfes fand Friedrich endlich einen Mann, der auf einem schwarzgebrannten Balken seines umgerissenen Hauses saß und ein Stück trockene Brotrinde aß. Friedrich fragte um Unterkommen für sich und sein Pferd. Der Mann lachte ihm ins Gesicht und zeigte auf das abgebrannte Dorf.

Ermüdet band Friedrich sein Pferd an und setzte sich zu dem Manne hin. Er fragte ihn, wie so großes Unglück dieses Dorf getroffen habe.—Der Mann sagte gleichgültig: „Wir haben uns den Feinden widersetzt, worauf unser Dorf abgebrannt und mancher von uns erschossen wurde."

Joseph von Eichendorff (1778-1857):
Ahnung und Gegenwart

1. Wie war das Wetter, als Friedrich im Dorfe ankam?
2. Wie reiste Friedrich?
3. Woher wissen Sie, daß nichts in den Gärten wuchs?
4. Warum standen nur wenige Häuser im Dorfe?
5. Wo waren die Bewohner des Dorfes?
6. Was mußte Friedrich zuerst tun, bevor er einen Mann traf?
7. Warum lachte der Mann ihm ins Gesicht?
8. Warum zeigte der Mann auf das abgebrannte Dorf, statt zu antworten?
9. Warum hatte der Feind das Dorf abgebrannt?
10. Woher wissen Sie, daß nicht alle übrigen Bewohner getötet worden waren.

5. *Old friends*

Korb. Ist hier Herr Bolz zu finden?

Bolz. Korb! lieber Korb! Willkommen, herzlich willkommen! Das ist sehr nett von Ihnen, daß Sie
mich nicht vergessen haben. Ich freue mich sehr,
Sie zu sehen.

Korb. Und erst ich!—Da sind wir in der Stadt! Das
ganze Dorf läßt grüßen! Von Anton, dem Pferde-
jungen—er ist jetzt Großknecht—bis zum alten
Nachtwächter, dem Sie das Horn damals auf die
Turmspitze gehängt haben. Nein, ist das eine
Freude!

Bolz. Wie geht es dem Fräulein? Erzählt, Alter!

Korb. Jetzt ganz vortrefflich. Aber es ist uns schlecht
gegangen. Vier Jahre war der General krank, das
war eine böse Zeit, Sie wissen, er war immer ein
ärgerlicher Herr.

Bolz. Ja, er war schwer zu behandeln.

Korb. Und besonders in seiner Krankheit. Aber das
Fräulein hat ihn liebevoll gepflegt. Jetzt, seit er
tot ist, führt das Fräulein allein die Wirtschaft,
jetzt ist wieder gute Zeit im Dorfe. Ich werde
Ihnen alles erzählen, aber erst heute abend, das
Fräulein wartet auf mich, ich bin nur schnell
hergesprungen, Ihnen zu sagen, daß wir hier sind.

Nach Gustav Freytag (1816-95): Die Journalisten

6. *A retired life*

Finsterer, als die Nacht um mich, eilte ich durch den
Garten. Ein Kahn stand unten am Ufer des Stromes
angebunden. Ich stieg hinein und ließ ihn den Strom
hinabfahren. Die Nacht verging, die Sonne ging auf und
wieder unter, ich saß und fuhr noch immerfort. Am anderen Morgen verlor sich der Strom zwischen wilden einsamen
Wäldern und Schluchten. Der Hunger trieb mich ans
Land. Es war diese Gegend hier. Ich fand nach einigem
Herumirren das Schloß. Ein alter Mann wohnte damals

ganz allein darin, von dessen früherer Lebensweise ich nie
etwas erfahren konnte. Es gefiel mir in dieser Wüste, und
ich blieb bei ihm. Kurze Zeit darauf starb der Alte und
hinterließ mir seine alten Bücher, sein verfallenes Schloß
und eine Menge Gold in den Kellern. Ich hätte nun mit
dem Schatz wieder in die Welt zurückkehren können. Aber
ich fühle mich nirgends mehr in der Welt zu Hause.

Nach Joseph von Eichendorff (1778-1857):
Ahnung und Gegenwart

1. In welcher Stimmung befand sich der Erzähler?
2. Was mußte der Erzähler zuerst machen, bevor er mit dem
   Kahn fahren konnte?
3. Wie lange fuhr der Erzähler auf dem Strom?
4. Warum ging der Erzähler endlich an Land?
5. Was mußte er tun, bevor er das Schloß fand?
6. Wie viele Leute wohnten im Schloß?
7. Was wollte der Erzähler entdecken?
8. Wie lange wohnte er bei dem Alten auf dem Schloß?
9. Warum wurde er plötzlich reich?
10. Warum zog er es vor, auf dem Schloß zu bleiben?

7. *A strange employment*

„Verlangen Sie, was Sie wollen!" rief ich aus, „aber
nehmen Sie mir nicht alle Hoffnung." Sie antwortete
lächelnd: „Wenn Sie mir dienen wollen, so hören Sie die
Bedingungen! Ich komme hierher, eine Freundin zu
besuchen, bei der ich mich einige Tage aufhalten will;
unterdessen wünsche ich, daß mein Wagen und dieses
Kästchen weiter gebracht werden. Wollen Sie es übernehmen?
Sie haben dabei nichts zu tun, als das Kästchen
vorsichtig hinein und aus dem Wagen zu heben, sich daneben
zu setzen, wenn es darin steht, und jede Sorge dafür zu
tragen. Wenn Sie in ein Wirtshaus kommen, so wird es
auf einen Tisch gestellt, in eine besondere Stube, in der Sie
weder wohnen noch schlafen dürfen. Sie verschließen das
Zimmer jedesmal mit diesem Schlüssel, der alle Schlösser
auf- und zuschließt und dem Schlosse die besondere Eigen-

schaft gibt, daß es niemand in der Zwischenzeit öffnen kann."

Nach Johann Wolfgang von Goethe (1749-1832):
Wilhelm Meisters Wanderjahre

1. Was hätte dem Erzähler alle Hoffnung genommen?
2. Woher wissen Sie, daß die Frau auf der Reise war?
3. Was hatte sie mitgebracht?
4. Wie lange Aufenthalt wollte sie dort machen?
5. Wie sollte der Erzähler reisen?
6. Was sollte er verhindern?
7. Wo sollte er auf der Reise die Nacht verbringen?
8. Was für einen Schlüssel gab die Frau dem Erzähler?
9. Was konnte nicht gemacht werden, wenn das Zimmer mit dem Schlüssel verschlossen wurde?
10. Was halten Sie von den Bedingungen der Frau?

Zum Fortsetzen (Umriß, S. 168).

8. *The song*

In diesem peinlichen Augenblick trat Asra aus dem Nebenzimmer an den Tisch heran und flüsterte der Mutter zu: „ Elisabeth will etwas singen. Darf sie? "

„ Gewiß darf sie. Aber wer wird sie begleiten? "

„ Ich. Es ist sehr leicht, und wir haben es eben durchgenommen. Ich denke, es wird gehen. Und wenn ich steckenbleibe, so ist es kein Unglück."

Und damit ging sie an den Flügel, während die große Mitteltür aufblieb. Das Notenblatt war schon aufgeschlagen, die Lichter brannten, und beide begannen. Aber das Gefürchtete geschah, Begleitung und Stimme gingen nicht zusammen, und nun lachten sie halb lustig und halb verlegen. Gleich danach aber versuchten sie es zum zweiten Male, und nun klang Elisabeths noch halb kindliche Stimme hell und klar durch beide Räume hin. Alle schwiegen und lauschten. Besonders die Gräfin schien gerührt, und als die letzte Strophe gesungen war, erhob sie sich und zog sich, ohne ein Wort zu sagen, aus der Gesellschaft zurück.

Nach Theodor Fontane (1819-98): Unwiederbringlich

1. Wie sprach Asra zu ihrer Mutter?
2. Was wollte sie wissen?
3. Auf welchem Instrument begleitete Asra Elisabeth?
4. Was fürchtete Asra?
5. Wie hatten die Mädchen das Gefürchtete vermeidan wollen?
6. Wo wurde gespielt?
7. Was hatte Asra vor sich?
8. Warum lachten die Mädchen verlegen?
9. Was für eine Wirkung hatte Elisabeths Stimme auf die Zuhörer?
10. Warum zog sich die Gräfin aus der Gesellschaft zurück?

9. *Safe arrival*

Aber keine der gefürchteten Gefahren traf ein. Die Nächte vergingen still und lautlos, die Tage waren heiter und jeder so schön und wolkenlos oder scheinbar noch schöner und klarer als sein Vorgänger. Die Mitglieder der Gesellschaft waren wohl, die kleine Ditha war gesund, und die freie Luft hatte schon ihre Wangen gerötet. Man hatte auf der Reise weder Menschen noch Tiere gesehen, manchen einsamen Adler ausgenommen, der zuweilen, wie sie weitergingen, hoch über ihnen in den leeren Lüften hing. Ein schönes Glück hatte sie geführt, als ob ein glänzender Engel sie begleitete.

Am frühen Morgen des neunundzwanzigsten Tages ihrer Reise, da sie einen sanften Hügel hinaufstiegen, änderte sich plötzlich die Farbe des Landes. Vor ihnen lag ein dunkelblauer, fast schwarzer Streifen. Uram riß die Augen auf.

„ Das ist das Mittelmeer ", sagte Abdias, „ jenseits dessen das Land Europa liegt, in welches wir ziehen."

Nach Adalbert Stifter (1805-1868): Abdias

1. Warum hatte man sich gefürchtet?
2. Was für Wetter hatte man?
3. Woran konnte man erkennen, daß Ditha die frische Luft gut bekam.
4. Durch welchen Erdteil reiste man?
5. Wie war die Landschaft?
6. Was sah man auf der Reise?
7. Wann erblickte man das Mittelmeer?

8. Wie sah das Meer aus?
9. Welches war das Reiseziel der Gesellschaft?
10. Aus wieviel Personen bestand die Gesellschaft?

10. *Hope deferred*

Piepenbrink. Gott sei Dank, daß wir aus diesem Gedränge heraus sind.

Frau Piepenbrink. Es war sehr heiß.

Kleinmichel. Und die Musik ist zu laut, es sind zu viel Trompeten im Orchester.

Piepenbrink. Hier ist ein ruhiger Ort, hier können wir uns setzen.

Fritz. Bertha möchte noch in dem Saal bleiben, könnte ich nicht mit ihr zurückgehen?

Piepenbrink. Ich habe nichts dagegen, daß ihr jungen Leute in den Saal zurückgeht, aber es ist mir lieber, wenn ihr bei uns bleibt.

Frau Piepenbrink. Bleibe bei deinen Eltern, mein Kind!

Piepenbrink. Setzt euch! Fritz kommt neben mich. Nehmt Bertha zwischen euch, Nachbarn, sie wird doch bald an euren Tisch kommen.

Fritz. Wann wird das sein, Herr Piepenbrink? Sie sagen das schon lange und schieben den Hochzeitstag immer wieder hinaus.

Piepenbrink. Das geht dich nichts an.

Fritz. Im Gegenteil, Herr Piepenbrink, ich bin's ja, der Bertha heiraten will.

Piepenbrink. Das kann jeder wollen. Aber ich soll sie dir geben, Junge, und das will mehr sagen, denn es wird mir schwer genug, die Kleine aus meinem Nest zu lassen. Darum warte. Du sollst sie haben, aber warte.

Nach Gustav Freytag (1816-95): Die Journalisten

11. *The quaint clock*

Die Uhr hatte aber auch wirklich ihren eigenen Kopf; sie war alt geworden und kümmerte sich nicht mehr viel um die neue Zeit; daher schlug sie oft sechs, wenn sie zwölf schlagen sollte, und ein andermal, um es wieder gutzumachen, wollte sie nicht aufhören zu schlagen, bis Marthe das Gewicht von der Kette nahm. Das Seltsamste war, daß die Uhr zuweilen gar nicht dazu kommen konnte; dann schnurrte und schnurrte es zwischen den Rädern, aber der Hammer wollte nicht schlagen; und das geschah meistens mitten in der Nacht. Marthe wurde jedesmal wach; und im kältesten Winter oder in der dunkelsten Nacht stand sie auf und ruhte nicht, bis sie die alte Uhr aus ihrer Not erlöst hatte. Dann ging sie wieder zu Bette und fragte sich, warum die Uhr sie wohl geweckt habe, ob sie in ihrem Tagewerk etwas vergessen oder ob sie vor dem Schlafengehen schlechte Gedanken gehabt habe.

Nach Theodor Storm (1817-88): Marthe und ihre Uhr

1. Warum sagt der Erzähler, daß die Uhr ihren eigenen Kopf hatte?
2. Warum konnte die Uhr nicht in Ordnung sein?
3. Warum mußte Martha manchmal das Gewicht von der Kette nehmen?
4. Warum schnurrten die Räder manchmal nur?
5. Woher wissen Sie, daß Martha nicht fest schlief?
6. Warum stand Martha auf?
7. Wie wußte Martha, daß die Uhr in Not war?
8. Schlief Martha sofort wieder ein?
9. Woher wissen Sie, daß Martha die Uhr als etwas Lebendes ansah?
10. Was für eine Frau war Martha?

12. *Indifference*

„Vieles", fing er an, „hat sich an dieser Stelle geändert, seit ich vor zehn Jahren hier war. Aber ich finde mich doch zurecht. Das Plateau dort oben, mit dem großen Gasthause, muß der Hexentanzplatz sein. Ich höre, man kann jetzt bequem hinauffahren."

„O gewiß kann man", sagte sie gleichgültig, während sie mit ihrem Auge den Balkon überflog.

„Hexentanzplatz", nahm sie nach einer Weile das Gespräch wieder auf. „Wahrscheinlich ein Felsen mit einer Sage, nicht wahr? Wir hatten auch in Schlesien so viele;

sie sind alle so kindisch.   Immer Prinzessinnen und Riesen.
Ich dachte, der Felsen, den man hier sähe, hieße die
Roßtrappe."
„Gewiß, Cecile.   Das ist der andre; gleich hier der
nächste."
„Müssen wir hinauf? "
„Nein, wir müssen nicht.   Aber ich dachte, du würdest
es wünschen. Der Blick ist schön, und man sieht meilen-
weit in die Ferne."
„Bis Berlin?   Aber nein, darin irre ich mich, das ist
nicht möglich."

Nach Theodor Fontane (1819-98): Cecile

4. Der Hexentanzplatz: *a flat rocky ledge in the Harz mountains.*
10. Schlesien: *Silesia.*
13. Die Roßtrappe: *another flat rocky ledge in the Harz mountains.*

1. Wann war der Erzähler zum letzten Mal da?
2. Was hätte man daher erwarten können?
3. War der Hexentanzplatz unbewohnt?
4. Wie mußte man früher auf den Hexentanzplatz steigen?
5. Woher wissen Sie, daß das Gespräch die Dame nicht sehr
   interessierte?
6. Woraus kann man schließen, daß ein Stillschweigen folgte?
7. Wo hatte die Dame eine Zeitlang verbracht?
8. Was für Personen spielen in Sagen eine Rolle?
9. Glauben Sie, daß die Dame auf die Roßtrappe steigen
   wollte?
10. Warum ist es nicht möglich, von der Roßtrappe bis Berlin
    zu sehen?

13. *Second sight*

In einer engen Straße, wo noch zwei Reihen der urältesten Gebäude der Stadt stehen, sieht man ein kleines,
schmales und spitzes Haus, die jetzige Werkstatt eines
Schuhmachers.   Im obersten Teile desselben soll aber
früher ein junger Mann allein gewohnt haben, dessen
Lebensweise niemandem näher bekannt gewesen war, der
sich auch niemals hatte blicken lassen, außer jedesmal vor

dem Ausbruche eines Feuers. Da sah man ihn mit tod-
blassem Gesicht, eine seltsame rote Mütze auf dem Kopf,
unruhig am kleinen Fenster auf und ab schreiten, zum
sichersten Vorzeichen, daß das Unglück nahe bevorstehe.
Ehe noch der erste Feuerlärm entstand, ehe ein Mensch
wußte, daß es irgendwo brenne, kam er auf seinem mageren
Pferd unten aus dem Stalle hervorgesprengt und war wie
der Satan davongejagt, unfehlbar nach dem Orte des Feuers
hin, als hätte er es im Geist gefühlt.

Nach Eduard Mörike (1804-75): Maler Nolten

1. In welchem Teil einer Stadt sind gewöhnlich die urältesten
   Gebäude?
2. Woher wissen Sie, daß das Haus mehrere Stockwerke hatte?
3. Bei wem wohnte der junge Mann?
4. Was wußte man von der Lebensweise des jungen Mannes?
5. Bei welcher Gelegenheit sah man den jungen Mann?
6. Wie sah der junge Mann aus?
7. Woher wußten die Nachbarn, daß ein Feuer bald ausbrechen
   würde?
8. Was macht man, wenn ein Feuer ausgebrochen ist?
9. Was war wahrscheinlich aus dem Stall geworden?
10. Wie ritt der junge Mann nach dem Orte des Feuers?

14. *The traveller and the pack-animals*

Tief in der Nacht war ich endlich in einem Gasthaus
angekommen, das sich weit unter dem Gipfel des Berges
befand. Schon vor Tagesanbruch aber wurde ich durch
ein lautes Glockengeläute aus tiefem Schlaf aufgeweckt.
Eine lange Reihe Saumtiere zog vorbei, ehe ich mich an-
kleiden und ihnen vorauseilen konnte. Als ich mich auf
den Weg machte, erfuhr ich bald, wie unangenehm solche
Gesellschaft sein kann. Das monotone Geläute betäubte
die Ohren; das Gepäck, das zu beiden Seiten der Tiere
abstand (sie trugen diesmal große Säcke Baumwolle),
streifte entweder an die Felsen, oder, wenn das Tier, um
dieses zu vermeiden, sich gegen die andere Seite zog,
schwebte es so über dem Abgrund, daß dem Zuschauer
schwindlig zumute wurde. Das Schlimmste war, daß man

in beiden Fällen gehindert war, an ihnen vorbeizuschleichen, um schneller vorwärts zu kommen.

Nach Johann Wolfgang von Goethe (1749-1832):
Wilhelm Meisters Wanderjahre

1. Woher wissen Sie, daß der Reisende einen langen Weg gemacht hatte?
2. Was bekommt man in einem Gasthaus?
3. Warum erwachte der Reisende?
4. Wozu hatte der Reisende nicht mehr Zeit?
5. Woher wissen Sie, daß dem Reisenden das Glockengeläute mißfiel?
6. Weshalb brauchten die Saumtiere viel Platz zum Gehen?
7. Was kann man aus Baumwolle machen?
8. Warum schwebte das Gepäck manchmal über dem Abgrund?
9. Warum konnte der Reisende nicht an den Saumtieren vorbeikommen?
10. Wann wird einem schwindlig zumute?

15. *The thesis*

Gottlieb. Soeben ist ein junger Mann angekommen und fragt—

Erna *erschreckt*. Nach mir?

Gottlieb. Nein, nach dem gnädigen Herrn.

Erna *erleichtert*. Ah, so!—wie sieht er denn aus?

Gottlieb. Ziemlich schlecht angezogen.

Erna. Er wird ein Bettler sein.

Gottlieb. Nein, er sagt, er sei Gelehrter.

Erna. So lassen Sie ihn eintreten. *Für sich.* Jedenfalls ein großer Mann.

Gottlieb. Sehr wohl.

Bruno *tritt ein*. O—verzeihen Sie—ich wollte nur—; ich dachte—Herr Kerner—

Erna. Herr Kerner wird bald erscheinen; ich bin seine Tochter. Mit wem habe ich die Ehre?

Bruno. Bruno Helbing, Student der Philologie und Literaturgeschichte. Erlauben Sie, daß ich Ihnen meine Karte—*Er sucht in allen Taschen.* Ich muß sie wohl vergessen haben—

Erna. Ich glaube Ihnen auch so, Herr Helbing. Wollen Sie nicht Platz nehmen?

Bruno. Sie sind sehr—aber ich störe doch nicht?

Erna. Nicht im mindesten. Womit können wir Ihnen dienen?

Bruno. Es ist sehr unbescheiden, daß ich mir diese Freiheit genommen habe—die Sache ist nämlich so: Ich stehe vor meinem Examen und muß eine Dissertation schreiben. Sie verzeihen schon, daß ich von mir spreche—

Erna. Bitte sehr. Erzählen Sie mir nur etwas von Ihrer Dissertation.

Bruno. Das kann ich nicht, da sie—noch nicht existiert.

Nach Ludwig Fulda (1862-1939): Das Recht der Frau

16. *The third man*

Fritz zog seinen Mantel wieder an, und Paul nahm den Hausschlüssel. Kaum hatten beide mit der Kerze den Saal verlassen, als Brachmann, der jedes Wort gehört hatte, sich aus seinem engen Kabinett vorsichtig herausschlich, die Tür wieder zumachte und den beiden mit leisen Schritten nachging. Der Saal stand offen, auf dem Gange folgte Brachmann dem Licht in der Ferne. Nun standen die beiden an der Tür des Hauses, und Paul steckte den großen Schlüssel ein, um zu öffnen. Die Tür tat sich leise und langsam auf, und Fritz schlüpfte auf die Gasse; im selben Moment aber blies Brachmann, der jetzt dicht hinter Paul stand, die Kerze aus, gab diesem einen kleinen Stoß und sprang aus dem Hause, sich nach der entgegengesetzten Seite wendend, als wo er Fritz im aufdämmernden Dunkel gehen sah. Paul wußte nicht, wie ihm geschehen war, zitternd und halb ohnmächtig verschloß er die Tür, begab sich in sein Zimmer und konnte sich lange von seinem Schreck nicht erholen.

Nach Johann Ludwig Tieck (1773-1853):
Vittoria Accorombona

1. Wie hieß der Hauswirt?
2. Was hatte Brachmann im Kabinett gemacht?

3. Warum verließ er das Kabinett?
4. Woher wissen Sie, daß er nicht entdeckt werden wollte?
5. Wo hatten Fritz und Paul sich unterhalten?
6. Wann blies Brachmann die Kerze aus?
7. Warum blies er die Kerze aus?
8. Um welche Tageszeit verließ Fritz das Haus?
9. Ging Brachmann in derselben Richtung wie Fritz?
10. Warum zitterte Paul?

17. *Under arrest*

Der Prinz und ich standen noch und überlegten, was wir tun sollten, als die Tür sich öffnete und einige Bediente der Staatsinquisition hereintraten. Sie zeigten uns einen Befehl der Regierung, worin uns beiden befohlen wurde, ihnen sofort zu folgen. Von einer starken Wache begleitet, gingen wir bis zum Kanal. Hier erwartete uns ein Boot, in das wir uns setzen mußten. Ehe wir ausstiegen, wurden uns die Augen verbunden. Man führte uns eine große steinerne Treppe hinauf und dann durch einen langen gewundenen Gang über Gewölbe, wie ich aus dem Echo schloß, das unter unsern Füßen hallte. Endlich erreichten wir eine andere Treppe, welche uns sechsundzwanzig Stufen in die Tiefe hinunterführte. Hier öffnete sich ein Saal, wo man uns die Binde wieder von den Augen nahm. Wir befanden uns in einem Kreise ehrwürdiger alter Männer, alle schwarz gekleidet, der ganze Saal mit schwarzen Tüchern behangen und kaum erleuchtet, eine Totenstille in der ganzen Versammlung, was einen schreckhaften Eindruck machte.

Nach Johann Christoph Friedrich von Schiller (1759-1805):
Der Geisterseher

1. Woher wissen Sie, daß der Prinz und sein Begleiter nicht wußten, was sie tun sollten?
2. Warum traten die Bedienten der Staatsinquisition herein?
3. Wer hatte den Befehl gegeben?
4. Woraus besteht gewöhnlich eine Wache?
5. Wo wurden den beiden Männern die Augen verbunden?
6. Woher wußte der Erzähler, daß sie über Gewölbe gingen?
7. Woher wissen Sie, daß der Erzähler sehr aufmerksam auf seinen Weg war?

8. Warum hatte man den beiden Männern die Augen verbunden?
9. Warum machte das Ganze einen schreckhaften Eindruck auf die beiden?
10. Zu welchem Zweck, glauben Sie, wurden sie in den Saal geführt?

18. *A fire*

„ Um Gottes willen, das ist Feuer im Schloß!" rief Viktor erblassend, und sie ruderten, ohne ein Wort zu sprechen, rasch auf das Ufer zu. Als sie ans Land kamen, sahen sie bereits rötlichen Rauch zum Dachfenster hervordringen. Alles im Hause und im Hofe schlief noch in tiefster Ruhe. Viktor machte Lärm an allen Türen und Fenstern. Leontin eilte in die Kirche und zog die Sturmglocke. Der Nachtwächter ging durch die Gassen des Dorfes und erfüllte die Luft mit den fürchterlichen Tönen seines Hornes. Und so wurden nach und nach alle lebendig und rannten mit blassen Gesichtern, gleich Gespenstern, bestürzt durcheinander. Schon schlug die helle Flamme oben aus dem Dache, das Hinterhaus aber stand noch ruhig, da das Feuer es noch nicht erreicht hatte. Niemandem fiel es im ersten Augenblick ein, daß Julie im Hinterhause schlief und daß sie ohne Rettung verloren sei, wenn die Flamme die einzige Treppe ergriffe, die dort hinaufführte. Leontin dachte daran und stürzte sich sogleich in das brennende Haus.

Nach Joseph von Eichendorff (1778-1857):
Ahnung und Gegenwart

1. Wo war man, als Viktor das Feuer bemerkte?
2. Was mußte man tun, um an das Ufer zu kommen?
3. Woher wissen Sie, daß die Schloßbewohner noch nichts vom Feuer wußten?
4. Auf welche Weise wurde man aufgeweckt?
5. Warum vergleicht der Erzähler die Leute mit Gespenstern?
6. Welcher Teil des Schlosses hatte Feuer gefangen?
7. Woraus schließen Sie, daß das Schloß sehr groß war?
8. Woran hatte man nicht gedacht?
9. Warum war Julie in großer Gefahr?
10. Warum stürzte sich Leontin in das brennende Haus?

Zum Fortsetzen (Umriß, S. 168).

19. *Seven-league boots*

Ich war in meine Gedanken sehr vertieft und sah kaum, wo ich den Fuß hinsetzte, denn ich dachte an das Bergwerk, wo ich an dem Abend noch anzukommen hoffte, und wo ich nicht recht wußte, wie ich mich anmelden sollte. Ich war noch keine zweihundert Schritte gegangen, als ich bemerkte, daß ich von dem Wege abgekommen war; ich sah mich danach um, ich befand mich in einem wüsten, uralten Tannenwalde, woran die Axt nie gelegt worden war. Ich drang noch einige Schritte vor, ich sah mich mitten unter Felsen, die nur mit Moos bewachsen waren und zwischen welchen Schnee- und Eisfelder lagen. Die Luft war sehr kalt, ich sah mich um, der Wald war hinter mir verschwunden. Ich machte einige Schritte—um mich herrschte die Stille des Todes, unabsehbar dehnte sich das Eis, worauf ich stand, und worauf ein dichter Nebel schwer ruhte; die Sonne stand blutig am Rande des Horizonts. Die Kälte war unerträglich.

Nach Adalbert von Chamisso (1781-1838): Peter Schlemihl

1. Warum sah der Erzähler kaum, wo er den Fuß hinsetzte?
2. Welches war sein Reiseziel?
3. Woraus kann man schließen, daß der Erzähler an seinem Reiseziel nicht erwartet wurde?
4. Woher wußte er, daß er vom Wege abgekommen war?
5. Was tat er, um den richtigen Weg zu finden?
6. Woraus kann man schließen, daß der Wald nicht bewohnt war?
7. Wie lange blieb der Erzähler im Wald?
8. Wo findet man Schnee- und Eisfelder?
9. Woher wissen Sie, daß das Wetter nicht mehr klar war?
10. Woher wissen Sie, daß der Erzähler nicht warm angezogen war?

20. *A false scent*

Bruno. Ich störe wohl?
Kerner. Im Gegenteil. Sie wünschen . . .?
Bruno. Ich wollte—mich verabschieden, da ich heute abreisen muß.

Kerner. Wie? Sie wollen uns schon verlassen?

Bruno. Mein Ziel ist hier erreicht, und ich gehe; aber
mein Herz wird—das heißt, meine Dankbarkeit soll—

Gottlieb *tritt ein.* Herr Kerner, der Verwalter ist draußen
und möchte Sie sprechen.

Kerner. Der Verwalter? Sie verzeihen, Herr Helbing.
Ich hoffe jedenfalls, Sie noch zu sehen. *Er geht ab.*

Bruno. Sie wissen wohl, Fräulein Kerner, warum ich
abreise?

Erna. Nein, eigentlich nicht. Übrigens muß ich Ihnen
noch für Ihre schönen Verse danken.

Bruno. Aber—bitte—; es war ja nur ein schwacher
Versuch, meine Gefühle—oder vielmehr eine kleine
Erinnerung an—

Erna. Und nun wollen Sie heute schon gehen?

Bruno *zieht das blaue Heft hervor.* Ich kam, um dieses Heft
zu suchen; jetzt da ich es gefunden habe, muß ich fort.

Erna. Dieses Heft werden Sie aber nicht mitnehmen
können.

Bruno. Wie? Nicht mitnehmen?

Erna. Weil es nicht das kürzlich entdeckte Stück von
Goethe ist.

Bruno. Es i s t von Goethe; das kann ich wissenschaftlich beweisen.

Erna. Und ich kann es wissenschaftlich widerlegen; denn
i c h habe es geschrieben.

Nach Ludwig Fulda (1862-1939): Das Recht der Frau

21. *Strange encounter*

Ich hatte mich schon durch den Rosengarten hin-
durchgeschlichen und befand mich auf einem freien Grasplatz, als ich aus Furcht, hier gefunden zu werden, einen
schnellen Blick um mich warf. Wie erschrak ich, als ich
den Mann im grauen Rock hinter mir her und auf mich
zukommen sah. Er nahm sogleich den Hut vor mir ab
und verbeugte sich so tief, wie es noch niemand vor mir
getan hatte. Es war kein Zweifel, er wollte mich anreden,
und ich konnte, ohne unhöflich zu sein, es nicht vermeiden.

Ich nahm den Hut auch ab, verbeugte mich auch und
stand bewegungslos in der Sonne mit bloßem Haupt wie
versteinert da. Ich starrte ihn voller Furcht an und war
wie ein Vogel in der Gegenwart einer Schlange. Er selber
schien sehr verlegen zu sein; er hob den Blick nicht auf,
verbeugte sich mehrmals, trat näher und redete mich an
mit leiser, unsicherer Stimme, ungefähr im Tone eines
Bettlers.

Nach Adalbert von Chamisso (1781-1838): Peter Schemihl

1. Warum warf der Erzähler einen schnellen Blick um sich?
2. Warum erschrak er?
3. Sah er den Mann jetzt zum erstenmal?
4. Wie zeigte der Mann seinen Respekt vor dem Erzähler?
5. Warum benahm sich der Mann so höflich?
6. Was hätte der Erzähler gern vermieden?
7. Wie war der Tag?
8. Was tut ein Vogel in der Gegenwart einer Schlange?
9. Wie zeigte der Mann seine Verlegenheit?
10. Was ist ein Bettler?

22. *A faithful slave*

„ Uram", sagte Abdias, „ wo sind denn die andern? "
„ Ich weiß es nicht", antwortete der Sklave.
„ Seid ihr denn nicht miteinander fortgelaufen? "
„ Ja, aber alle sind nach verschiedenen Richtungen
entkommen. Und als ich gehört habe, daß du zurück-
gekehrt bist, bin ich wiedergekommen und habe gemeint,
die andern werden auch schon da sein, weil du uns schützen
wirst."
„ Nein, sie sind nicht da", sagte Abdias, „ kein einziger
ist da—Uram", fuhr er dann sehr sanft fort, „ komme
näher und höre, was ich dir sagen werde."
Der Jüngling sprang empor und starrte Abdias an.
Dieser aber sprach: „ Du mußt, solange ich fort bin—denn
ich werde ein wenig weggehen—deine kranke Herrin und
dieses Kind bewachen. Setze dich hierher auf diesen
Erdhaufen—so—hier hast du eine Pistole—so mußt du sie
halten; und wenn nun einer hereinkommt und die schlum-
mernde Frau und das Kind anrühren will, so sag ihm, er

solle gehen, sonst wirst du ihn töten.　Wenn er nicht geht, so schieße ihn tot.　Verstehst du alles?"

Uram nickte und setzte sich auf den Boden.

Nach Adalbert Stifter (1805-1868): Abdias

1. Wer war Abdias?
2. Wo war Uram am Anfang des Gesprächs?
3. Warum wußte Uram nicht, wo die anderen Sklaven waren?
4. Warum war Uram zurückgekommen?
5. Warum sprang er empor?
6. Waren Abdias und Uram die einzigen dort?
7. Was beabsichtigte Abdias zu tun?
8. Warum gab Abdias dem Jüngling eine Pistole?
9. Wessen Frau und Kind sollte er bewachen?
10. Woher wissen Sie, daß Uram alles verstand?

23.　*A serious case*

Der Doktor schüttelte bedenklich den Kopf.　„ Wie", rief der Musiklehrer heftig, indem er vom Stuhle aufsprang, „ wie! so sollte Bettinas Katarrh wirklich böse Folgen haben?"　Der Doktor nahm die Tabaksdose heraus und steckte sie wieder ein, ohne zu schnupfen, richtete den Blick starr nach oben und hustete, ohne ein Wort zu reden. Das brachte den Musiklehrer außer sich, denn er wußte schon, solche Gebärden des Doktors bedeuteten in lebendigen Worten nichts anderes als: „ ein böser Fall—und ich weiß nicht, was ich raten soll."　„ Nun, so sagen Sie es denn nur geradezu heraus", rief der Musiklehrer ungeduldig, „das Leben wird es sie doch nicht kosten." „Nein, gar nicht", sprach der Doktor, indem er nochmals die Tabaksdose herausnahm, jetzt aber wirklich schnupfte, „ nein, aber höchst wahrscheinlich wird sie in ihrem ganzen Leben keine Note mehr singen!"　Da fuhr sich der Musiklehrer mit seinen beiden Händen in die Haare und rannte im Zimmer auf und ab und schrie wie besessen: „ Nicht mehr singen?—nicht mehr singen?—Bettina nicht mehr singen? —Gestorben all die herrlichen Lieder, die von ihren Lippen strömten?— Sie lügen, Doktor, Sie lügen!"

Nach Ernst Theodor Amadeus Hoffmann (1766-1822): Das Sanctus

1. Warum schüttelte der Doktor bedenklich den Kopf?
2. Warum sprang der Musiklehrer vom Stuhle auf?
3. Wo war die Tabaksdose, bevor der Doktor sie herausnahm?
4. Sah der Doktor den Musiklehrer an?
5. Warum war der Musiklehrer außer sich?
6. Woher wissen Sie, daß er den Arzt gut kannte?
7. Was würde wahrscheinlich die Folge des Katarrhs sein?
8. Warum hatte der Doktor nicht sagen wollen, was für eine
   Folge Bettinas Katarrh für sie haben könnte?
9. Warum rannte der Musiklehrer im Zimmer auf und ab?
10. Woher wissen Sie, daß er dem Doktor nicht glauben wollte?

24. *Lodging for the night*

Ein ungeheurer Hund empfing ihn in dem Hofe der
Mühle. Friedrich und sein Pferd waren zu ermattet, um
noch weiterzureisen. Er klopfte daher an die Haustür.
Eine rauhe Stimme antwortete von innen, bald darauf ging
die Tür auf, und ein langer, dünner Mann trat heraus. Er
sah Friedrich, der ihn um Unterkommen bat, von oben bis
unten an, nahm dann sein Pferd und führte es stillschweigend nach dem Stalle. Friedrich ging nun in die Stube
hinein. Ein Mädchen stand drinnen und wollte eben ein
Licht anzünden. Als sie das Licht angezündet hatte,
betrachtete sie den Grafen mit freudigem Erstaunen.
Darauf ergriff sie das Licht und führte ihn, ohne ein Wort
zu sagen, die Treppe hinauf in ein großes Zimmer mit
mehreren Betten. Als sie oben in der Stube waren, blieb
das Mädchen stehen und sah den Grafen furchtsam an.
„ Geh", sagte er gutmütig, „ geh schlafen, liebes Kind."
Sie sah sich nach der Tür um, dann wieder nach Friedrich.
„ Ach Gott! " sagte sie endlich, legte die Hand aufs Herz
und ging zögernd fort. Dem Grafen kam ihr Benehmen
sehr sonderbar vor, denn er hatte bemerkt, daß sie beim
Hinausgehen an allen Gliedern zitterte.

Nach Joseph von Eichendorff (1778-1857):
Ahnung und Gegenwart

1. Woher wissen Sie, daß Friedrich lange geritten war?
2. Wo bat Friedrich um Unterkommen?

3. Woraus können Sie schließen, daß er kein willkommener Gast war?
4. Um welche Tageszeit war er angekommen?
5. Woher wissen Sie, daß das Mädchen den Grafen kannte?
6. In welchem Stock waren die Schlafzimmer?
7. Warum sah das Mädchen den Grafen furchtsam an?
8. Woher wissen Sie, daß das Mädchen ihm nur ungern gehorchte?
9. Warum kam dem Grafen ihr Benehmen sonderbar vor?
10. Was für eine Nacht würde der Graf wahrscheinlich verbringen?

Zum Fortsetzen (Umriß, S. 168).

25. *Fate shall decide*

Stifter. Halt! Jetzt habe ich das rechte! Eins ist dir noch neu—der Ehestand!

Lips. Darüber habe ich schon zu viel gehört.

Stifter. Triff nur eine originelle Wahl!

Lips. Eine originelle Wahl? Wie ist das möglich? Wenn ich vernünftig wähle, so haben schon hundert so gewählt, und wenn ich dumm wähle, so haben schon Millionen Leute so gewählt. Am besten ist's, ich treffe eine Wahl, ohne zu wählen.

Diener *kommt herein.* Eine Frau Schleier wünscht Sie zu sprechen.

Lips. Schicksal, du handelst schnell!

Stifter. Wer ist sie denn?

Diener. Sie verbringt hier ihre Ferien.

Lips. Gut. Nur herein, sie ist willkommen.

Diener. Sehr wohl.

Lips. Halt! Du mußt erst fragen, ob sie Witwe ist.

Diener. Sehr wohl.

Lips. Verstanden! Nur wenn sie Witwe ist, will ich sie sehen.

Diener. Sehr wohl. *Er geht ab.*

Stifter. Erkläre, wie ist das zu verstehen?

Lips. Die erste Frau, die mir heute begegnet, will ich heiraten!

Stifter. Bist du toll?

Lips. Schön oder häßlich, gut oder böse, jung oder alt—
es ist alles eins—ich heirate sie sofort.

Stifter. Wenn aber—

Lips. Kein Wenn und kein Aber! Ich bin sehr gespannt
zu wissen, wer die erste sein wird.

Stifter. Die Sache wird ernst.

Lips. Wenn sie kommt, ist sie Witwe, und wenn sie Witwe
ist, kommt sie.

Nach Johann Nestroy (1801-1862): Der Zerrissene

SECTION B

PASSAGES FOR TRANSLATION, COMPREHENSION OR REPRODUCTION

26. *Divine inspiration*

Christ Church, eines der großen Colleges der Oxforder
Universität, hatte seit vielen Jahren einen Bankier, der in
gutem Ruf stand. Als College-Rentmeister[1] hatte der
Kanonikus von Christ Church, Dr. Bell, alles Finanzielle
mit ihm zu ordnen. Das Bankhaus galt als blühend, und
niemand zweifelte an seiner Solvenz. Einmal aber hatte
Dr. Bell den Bankier wieder zum Essen eingeladen, und da
fielen ihm die frommen und orthodoxen Redensarten des
Mannes auf.

Nun, dachte Bell, solche Redensarten hätte ich, der
Kanonikus, gut gebrauchen können, aber wohl nicht dieser
weltliche Londoner Bankier. Da ist wohl etwas nicht ganz
in Ordnung. Ohne Worte und klug fuhr der Kanonikus am
folgenden Morgen nach London und zog alles Geld und alle
Papiere des Colleges aus der Bank. Am folgenden Tage
große Aufregung in London: die Bank war bankrott, viele
Leute verloren ihr Geld, aber Christ Church hatte seines
durch göttliche Inspiration gerettet.

Nach Max Müller (1823–1900)

1. Was ist Christ Church?
2. Wie hieß der College-Rentmeister?

[1] Der College-Rentmeister: *college-bursar.*

3. Warum stand der Bankier in gutem Ruf?
4. Woher wissen Sie, daß der Bankier nicht zum erstenmal nach Oxford gekommen war?
5. Auf welche Weise benahm sich der Bankier anders als gewöhnlich?
6. Warum hätte Dr. Bell die frommen Redensarten gut gebrauchen können und nicht der Bankier?
7. Was schloß Dr. Bell aus dem Benehmen des Bankiers?
8. Zu welchem Zweck fuhr er am folgenden Morgen nach London?
9. Was erfuhr man am folgenden Tage?
10. Warum verloren viele Leute ihr Geld?

Zum Nacherzählen (Umriß, S. 234)

27. *A deal*

Er steckte die Hand in die Tasche und zog einen ziemlich großen Beutel, aus starkem Leder, an zwei kräftigen ledernen Schnüren heraus und händigte ihn mir ein. Ich griff hinein und zog zehn Goldstücke heraus und wieder zehn und wieder zehn und wieder zehn; ich hielt ihm schnell die Hand hin: „ Abgemacht! Für den Beutel haben Sie meinen Schatten." Er nahm meine Hand, kniete dann sogleich vor mir nieder, und mit einer bewundernswürdigen Geschicklichkeit sah ich ihn meinen Schatten, vom Kopf bis zu meinen Füßen, leise von dem Grase lösen, aufheben, zusammenrollen und falten und zuletzt in die Tasche stecken. Er stand auf, verbeugte sich vor mir und zog sich nach dem Rosengebüsche zurück. Mir war, als hörte ich ihn da leise für sich lachen. Ich aber hielt den Beutel bei den Schnüren fest, rund um mich her war die Erde sonnenhell, und ich wußte noch nicht, was ich getan hatte.

Nach Adalbert von Chamisso (1781–1838):
Peter Schlemihl

1. Warum hatte der Beutel Schnüre?
2. Was befand sich in dem Beutel?
3. Was wollte der Mann mit dem Beutel kaufen?
4. Woher wissen Sie, daß der Erzähler zu verkaufen bereit war?
5. Warum kniete der Mann vor ihm nieder?

6. Was machte der Mann mit dem Schatten, nachdem er ihn
   vom Gras gelöst hatte?
7. Wo verschwand der Schatten?
8. Woraus schließen Sie, daß der Mann höflich war?
9. War der Mann mit seinem Einkauf zufrieden?
10. Wann kann man seinen Schatten sehen?

Zum Nacherzählen (Umriß, S. 234)
Zum Fortsetzen (Umriß, S. 169)

28. *The Tsar*

Der Zar Iwan Basilowitz, mit dem Beinamen der Tyrann,
ließ einem fremden Gesandten, der, nach der damaligen
europäischen Etikette, mit bedecktem Haupt vor ihm
erschien, den Hut auf den Kopf nageln. Diese Grausamkeit
vermochte nicht den Botschafter der Königin Elisabeth von
England, Sir Jeremias Bowes, abzuschrecken. Er hatte die
Kühnheit, den Hut auf dem Kopf, vor dem Zaren zu erscheinen. Dieser fragte ihn, ob er nicht von der Strafe
gehört hatte, die einem anderen Gesandten widerfahren
wäre, welcher sich eine solche Freiheit erlaubt hätte?
„Ja, Herr ", erwiderte Bowes, „ aber ich bin der Botschafter
der Königin von England, die nie vor irgendeinem Fürsten
in der Welt anders wie mit bedecktem Haupt erschienen ist.
Ich bin ihr Repräsentant, und wenn mir die geringste
Beleidigung widerfährt, so wird sie mich zu rächen wissen."
—„ Das ist ein braver Mann ", sagte der Zar, indem er sich
zu seinen Hofleuten wandte, „ der für die Ehre seiner
Monarchin zu handeln und zu reden versteht: wer von euch
hätte das nämliche für mich getan? "

Heinrich von Kleist (1777–1811)

1. In welchem Jahrhundert fand dieser Vorfall statt?
2. Warum ließ der Zar dem Gesandten den Hut auf den Kopf
   nageln?
3. Was für ein Mann war der englische Botschafter?
4. Warum erstaunte der Zar?
5. Wen repräsentierte der englische Botschafter?
6. Warum bestand er darauf, vor dem Zaren mit bedecktem
   Kopf zu erscheinen?

7. Was würde geschehen, wenn der englische Botschafter beleidigt würde?
8. Fand die Audienz unter vier Augen statt?
9. Woran zweifelte der Zar?
10. Warum verdiente der Zar seinen Beinamen?

Zum Nacherzählen (Umriß, S. 234)

29. *Trapped*

„ Wir haben noch einen ziemlichen Umweg zu machen ", sagte Fritz, „ wenn wir die Straße, die in den Garten hineinführt, erreichen wollen. Doch weiß ich auch einen Eingang von dieser Seite. Wenn wir durch diesen gehen, ist der Weg viel kürzer. Die Gewölbe öffnen sich hier; sie sind hoch und breit genug, daß man bequem hindurch-kommen kann." Als Felix von Gewölben hörte, konnte er sich vor Neugierde nicht halten, diesen Eingang sofort zu betreten. Wilhelm folgte den Kindern, und sie stiegen zusammen die Stufen in die Gewölbe hinunter. Sie befanden sich bald im Hellen, bald im Dunkeln; aber endlich kamen sie an eine ziemlich ebene Stelle und schritten langsam vor, als auf einmal in ihrer Nähe ein Schuß fiel, zu gleicher Zeit sich zwei verborgene eiserne Tore schlossen und sie von beiden Seiten einsperrten. Zwar nicht die ganze Gesellschaft: nur Wilhelm und Felix waren gefangen. Denn Fritz, als der Schuß fiel, sprang sogleich rückwärts, und das zuschlagende Tor faßte nur seinen weiten Ärmel: er aber, sehr schnell das Jäckchen abwerfend, war entflohen, ohne sich einen Augenblick aufzuhalten.

Nach Johann Wolfgang von Goethe (1749–1832):
Wilhelm Meisters Wanderjahre

1. Aus wieviel Personen bestand die Gesellschaft?
2. Was wollten sie finden?
3. War der Umweg der einzige Weg zum Ziel?
4. Wie wurde Felix, als er das Wort „ Gewölbe " hörte?
5. Was mußten sie machen, um zu den Gewölben zu kommen?
6. Woraus schließen Sie, daß Öffnungen in den Gewölben waren?
7. Aus welchem Grund schritten sie langsam vor?

8. Was geschah in demselben Augenblick, wo sie einen Schuß
   hörten?
9. Wie hat Fritz es vermieden, eingeschlossen zu werden?
10. Warum mußte er das Jäckchen abwerfen?

Zum Nacherzählen (Umriß, S. 235)
Zum Fortsetzen (Umriß, S. 169)

30. *A near escape*

In das friedliche Tal einreitend, waren sie kaum einige
Schritte von der Quelle des Baches herabgekommen, als die
Fürstin ganz unten im Gebüsche des Tals etwas Seltsames
erblickte, das sie sogleich für den Tiger erkannte; heran-
springend kam er entgegen. „ Flieht! gnädige Frau ", rief
Honorio, „ flieht! " Sie wandte das Pferd um, dem steilen
Berg zu, wo sie herabgekommen waren. Der Jüngling aber
ging dem Tier entgegen, zog die Pistole und schoß, als er
sich nahe genug glaubte: leider jedoch fehlte er. Der Tiger
sprang seitwärts und verfolgte seinen Weg, aufwärts
unmittelbar der Fürstin nach. Sie sprengte, so schnell das
Pferd rennen konnte, den steilen, steinigen Pfad hinauf. Das
Pferd aber stieß an die kleinen Steine das Weges immer
wieder an und stürzte zuletzt kraftlos zu Boden. Der
Fürstin gelang es, sich auf ihre Füße zu stellen; auch das
Pferd richtete sich auf; aber der Tiger nahte schon, Honorio
unmittelbar hinter ihm her. Beide Renner erreichten
zugleich den Ort, wo die Fürstin am Pferd stand; der Ritter
beugte sich herab, schoß und traf mit der zweiten Pistole
den Tiger durch den Kopf, so daß er sogleich niederstürzte.

Nach Johann Wolfgang von Goethe (1749–1832):
Novelle

1. Wer bemerkte den Tiger zuerst?
2. In welcher Richtung ging er?
3. Was mußte die Fürstin zuerst tun, um dem Tiger zu
   entkommen?
4. Was hatte Honorio tun wollen?
5. Warum konnte der Tiger seinen Weg verfolgen?
6. Warum stürzte das Pferd zu Boden?
7. Wie weit war der Tiger von der Fürstin entfernt?

8. Was versuchte Honorio zu tun?
9. Woher wissen Sie, daß Honorio zu Pferde war?
10. Warum stürzte der Tiger nieder?

Zum Nacherzählen (Umriß, S. 235)
Zum Fortsetzen (Umriß, S. 169)

31. *Presence of mind*

Ein Badegast hielt sich in einem Seebad auf, um sich von einer Krankheit zu erholen. Damit ihn aber der laute Lärm der Gesellschaft nicht störte, machte er gern einsame Spaziergänge. So kam er einst auch auf einen Felsen, der nach einer Seite steil abfiel. Als er dicht am Rande des Abgrundes halt machte, um über das weite Meer zu schauen, stand plötzlich ein Mann neben ihm, der ihn mit seltsamem Lächeln ansah. Es war ein Wahnsinniger, der seinen Wärtern entlaufen war. „ Springe einmal da hinab ", sagte er zu dem Fremden, „ sonst werde ich dich hinabstürzen." Der Badegast schwebte in höchster Gefahr, denn der Wahnsinnige war augenscheinlich ein äußerst kräftiger Mann. Da hatte er einen guten Einfall, der ihm das Leben retten würde. Ohne seine Fassung zu verlieren, sagte er: „ Das ist keine Kunst. Aber wir wollen einmal hinuntergehen, damit ich von unten nach oben springe. Das kann nicht jeder." Der Wahnsinnige war einverstanden, und beide machten sich auf den Weg, um auf der anderen Seite langsam von dem Felsen herunterzusteigen. Der Badegast war gerettet; denn jetzt kamen auch die Wärter, um den Kranken wieder ins Irrenhaus zu bringen.

1. Wie war der Badegast, bevor er ins Seebad ging?
2. Woher wissen Sie, daß er den Lärm nicht gern hatte?
3. Wie war der Felsen?
4. Bis wohin ging der Badegast?
5. Wer muß einen Wahnsinnigen bewachen, und warum?
6. Warum schwebte der Badegast in höchster Gefahr?
7. Was wäre geschehen, wenn der Badegast nicht den guten Einfall gehabt hätte?
8. Woran erkennen Sie, daß der Badegast nicht aufgeregt war?

9. Womit war der Wahnsinnige einverstanden?
10. Wo fanden die Wärter den Wahnsinnigen?

1. Why had the visitor come to the seaside resort?
2. Why did he like walking on his own?
3. When did he stop and admire the view?
4. What happened when he stopped?
5. How had the man got there?
6. What did the man want the visitor to do?
7. What did the visitor manage not to betray?
8. What did he say he would do that was much more difficult?
9. How did the two men get down to the shore?
10. Where was the man the visitor had met taken to, and by whom?

Zum Nacherzählen (Umriß, S. 235)

32. *The rescue*

Ein ruhiger Abend, eine vollkommene Windstille versprachen das richtige Wetter für das nächtliche Fest, als auf einmal ein schreckliches Geschrei entstand. Erde hatte sich vom Ufer losgetrennt, man sah mehrere Menschen ins Wasser stürzen. Mit einigen Männern eilte der Hauptmann zur Stelle, trieb sogleich die Menge von dem Ufer fort, um denjenigen Platz zu machen, welche die Ertrinkenden herauszuziehen suchten. Schon waren alle, teils durch eigene Kraft, teils durch fremde Hilfe, wieder in Sicherheit, bis auf einen Knaben, der durch allzu ängstliche Anstrengungen statt sich dem Ufer zu nähern, sich davon entfernt hatte. Die Kräfte schienen ihn zu verlassen, nur einigemal kam noch eine Hand, ein Fuß in die Höhe. Unglücklicherweise war der Kahn auf der andern Seite mit Feuerwerk gefüllt: nur langsam konnte man ihn leer machen, und dadurch wurde Zeit verloren. Der Hauptmann handelte schnell und warf die Oberkleider weg; alle Augen richteten sich auf ihn, aber ein Schrei der Überraschung ließ sich hören, als er sich ins Wasser stürzte. Jedes Auge begleitete ihn; als geschickter Schwimmer erreichte er bald den Knaben und brachte ihn, scheinbar tot, an das Ufer.

Nach Johann Wolfgang von Goethe (1749–1832):
Die Wahlverwandtschaften

1. Zu welcher Tageszeit sollte das Fest stattfinden?
2. Warum entstand plötzlich ein Geschrei?
3. Woher wissen Sie, daß einige der Menschen nicht schwimmen konnten?
4. Was hätte die Rettung verhindern können?
5. Warum hatte der Knabe das Ufer nicht erreichen können?
6. Woran erkannte man, daß er seine Kräfte verlor?
7. Warum konnte man den Kahn nicht schnell bekommen?
8. Wodurch wurde Zeit verloren?
9. Warum schrien die Leute vor Überraschung?
10. Warum gelang es dem Hauptmann, den Knaben bald zu erreichen?

1. Why was the day of the firework-display well chosen?
2. Why did several people fall into the water?
3. Why was the crowd driven from the bank?
4. How did the people who had fallen in manage to get out to safety?
5. What mistake did the boy make?
6. What seemed to be happening to him?
7. Why was it necessary to empty the boat?
8. What did the captain do before springing into the water?
9. What happened at the moment he sprang into the water?
10. What did he succeed in doing?

Zum Nacherzählen (Umriß, S. 235)
Zum Fortsetzen (Umriß, S. 170)

33. *The will o' the wisps*

An dem großen Fluß lag in seiner kleinen Hütte, müde von der Anstrengung des Tages, der alte Fährmann und schlief. Mitten in der Nacht weckten ihn einige laute Stimmen; er hörte, daß Reisende übergesetzt werden wollten. Als er vor die Tür hinaustrat, sah er zwei große Irrlichter über dem angebundenen Kahn schweben, die ihm versicherten, daß sie große Eile hätten und schon am anderen Ufer zu sein wünschten. Der Alte zögerte nicht, stieß ab und fuhr, mit seiner gewöhnlichen Geschicklichkeit, quer über den Strom, während die Fremden in einer unbekannten Sprache miteinander redeten und hier und da in ein lautes

Gelächter ausbrachen, indem sie bald auf den Rändern und Bänken, bald auf dem Boden des Kahns hin und her hüpften.

„ Der Kahn schwankt! " rief der Alte, „ und wenn ihr so unruhig seid, kann er umschlagen; setzt euch, ihr Lichter! "

Darüber brachen sie in ein großes Gelächter aus, verspotteten den Alten und waren noch unruhiger als vorher. Er ertrug ihr schlechtes Benehmen mit Geduld und kam bald am anderen Ufer an.

„ Hier ist für Ihre Mühe ", riefen die Reisenden, und es fielen, indem sie sich schüttelten, viele glänzende Goldstücke in den Kahn.

Nach Johann Wolfgang von Goethe (1749–1832):
Das Märchen

1. Was tut ein Fährmann?
2. Warum schlief der Fährmann?
3. Hat er die ganze Nacht ununterbrochen schlafen können?
4. Wo war sein Kahn?
5. Woher wissen Sie, daß der Fährmann sofort in den Kahn stieg?
6. Woher wissen Sie, daß der Fluß schnell floß?
7. Warum verstand der Fährmann nicht, was die Irrlichter miteinander redeten?
8. Warum schwankte der Kahn?
9. Was befahl der Fährmann seinen Fahrgästen?
10. Woher wissen Sie, daß der Fährmann umsonst gesprochen hatte?

1. Where was the ferryman?
2. Why was he woken up?
3. Where were the two travellers?
4. What did they assure the ferryman?
5. What did they do every now and then while talking?
6. Where exactly did they hop about?
7. Why did the ferryman remonstrate?
8. What effect did this have on the passengers?
9. What sort of a man was the ferryman?
10. How did the passengers pay the ferryman?

Zum Nacherzählen (Umriß, S. 235)

34. *The strange duel*

Ralfson setzte sich ebenso wie der Amerikaner auf sein Pulverfaß.[1] Er nahm eine Zigarre heraus und zündete sie an. Er blickte zu seinem Gegner hinüber, der ihn gar nicht ansah. Die Lunte[2] brannte langsam, und Ralfson berechnete, daß sie in einer Viertelstunde das Pulver entzünden mußte. Er dachte an sein früheres Leben und hatte beinahe die Lunte vergessen. Als er sich nun bückte, um nachzusehen, hatte sie gerade den trockenen Zweig erreicht. Der nächste Augenblick mußte fatal sein. Ohne nachzudenken, riß er sein Taschentuch heraus und löschte den Funken aus. Dann rannte er zu dem Amerikaner und löschte auch das Feuer an dessen Lunte aus.

,, Mensch oder Teufel! '' rief er, ,, ich will Sie mit jeder Waffe bekämpfen, aber dies halte ich nicht aus! ''

,, Sie sind sehr mutig, wenige hätten so lange ausgehalten wie Sie '', sagte der Amerikaner, indem er sein Messer herauszog und die Schnur durchschnitt, mit der das Pulverfaß an den Baum gebunden war. Er stieß es mit dem Fuß um, und Ralfson sah sprachlos, wie Äpfel aus dem Faß rollten.

,, Ihr Faß enthält auch nur Äpfel. Ich bin vielleicht zu weit gegangen. Aber wenn Sie einverstanden sind, wollen wir quitt miteinander sein.''

Nach Friedrich Gerstäcker (1816–1872):
Das sonderbare Duell

1. Wie wollte Ralfson zeigen, daß er keine Angst hatte?
2. Was mußte geschehen, bevor das Pulver sich entzündete?
3. Warum vergaß Ralfson beinahe die Lunte?
4. Weshalb würde der nächste Augenblick fatal sein?
5. Warum riß Ralfson sein Taschentuch heraus?
6. Zu welchem Zweck rannte er zum Amerikaner?
7. Weshalb hielt der Amerikaner ihn für sehr mutig?
8. Warum zog der Amerikaner sein Messer heraus?
9. Warum war Ralfson erstaunt?
10. Was mußte geschehen, bevor sie quitt miteinander sein konnten?

1. What did Ralfson do immediately on sitting down?

[1] Das Pulverfaß: *powder-barrel.*
[2] Die Lunte: *match.*

2. What was his adversary doing?
3. How did Ralfson know he only had a quarter of an hour to live?
4. What did he do during that quarter of an hour?
5. At what moment did he look down?
6. What was his immediate reaction to what he saw?
7. What did he do after that?
8. What did he tell his adversary he was prepared to do?
9. What was the American's comment on Ralfson's behaviour?
10. Why had the American remained so cool?

Zum Nacherzählen (Umriß, S. 235)

35. *The visit*

Mark Twain [1] war umgezogen und wohnte seit einem halben Jahr in einer neuen Wohnung. Da erschien er eines Tages zur Stunde des Mittagessens in Hausschuhen und ohne Kragen bei der Familie, die ihm gegenüber wohnte.

Er wurde ins Besuchszimmer geführt und sagte dort zu den erstaunten Nachbarn: „ Es tut mir sehr leid, meine Herrschaften, daß es mir bisher nicht möglich gewesen ist, Ihnen einen Besuch zu machen, obgleich ich schon ein halbes Jahr in Ihrer nächsten Nähe wohne. Es ist immer wieder etwas dazwischengekommen. Endlich aber sagte ich mir heute: jetzt muß es einmal sein! Und da werden Sie sich, wie ich fürchten muß, wundern, daß ich nach so langer Zeit nun, statt in korrektem Anzug, in Hausschuhen und ohne Kragen zu Ihnen komme. Auch wird es Ihnen sonderbar vorkommen, daß ich die Stunde Ihres Mittagessens wählte. Aber ich hoffe, Sie werden mir verzeihen, wenn ich Ihnen den Grund nenne, warum ich Ihnen gerade jetzt meinen Besuch mache. Ich wollte Ihnen nämlich nur sagen, daß es bei Ihnen brennt und daß die Flammen bereits das Dach Ihres Hauses erreicht haben! "

1. Wann war Mark Twain umgezogen?
2. Was wollten seine Nachbarn machen, als Mark Twain erschien?
3. Warum wunderten sie sich?
4. Wann hätte er sie besuchen sollen?

[1] Mark Twain: amerikanischer Humorist, Verfasser von *Huckleberry Finn*.

5. Warum hatte er sie nicht vorher besuchen können?
6. War er in korrektem Anzug gekommen?
7. Welche Stunde sollte man vermeiden, wenn man einen
   Besuch macht?
8. Worauf hoffte er?
9. Hatte er guten Grund zu dieser Hoffnung?
10. Worin besteht der Humor dieser Geschichte?

1. How long had Mark Twain been living in his new flat?
2. How was Mark Twain dressed when he paid his first visit to
   his neighbours?
3. When did he pay this visit?
4. Where did his neighbours live?
5. What room was Mark Twain shown into?
6. Why hadn't he paid his neighbours a visit before?
7. What decision had he made that day?
8. Why did he think they would be surprised?
9. What did he hope they would do?
10. What exactly was happening to their house?

Zum Nacherzählen (Umriß, S. 236)

36. *Master and dog*

Also beschloß Herr Richtwin, den Hund das nächste
Mal sofort zu bestrafen. Bald danach lief der Hund noch
einmal hinter dem Reiter her und Richtwin hinter dem
Tier. Endlich stand der Hund und ließ, den Schwanz
zwischen den Beinen, seinen Herrn herankommen. Sobald
dieser sich aber auf zehn Schritt genähert hatte, lief Thasso
wieder fort. Herr Richtwin ging langsam, rief, pfiff und
machte ein freundliches Gesicht: der Hund kam herbei—
aber nur auf zehn Schritt; dann lief er wieder davon. Der
Herr eilte, schlich, stand wieder still—das Tier blieb immer
bei ihm, aber auch immer zehn Schritt von ihm entfernt.
Die Jungen lachten, und die ganze Straße lief an Tür und
Fenster, um zu sehen, wer denn endlich gewinne, Meister
Richtwin oder Meister Thasso. Der stolze Bürger zitterte
vor Wut und warf sogar mit Steinen nach dem Hund.
Thasso aber wich jedem Wurf wunderbar geschickt aus,
sprang dem Stein nach, apportierte ihn wie zum Spott mit
fliegender Hast und war schon wieder zwanzig Schritt
voraus, ehe sein Herr auch nur den Stock erhoben hatte.

Jeder Tag brachte neue Szenen ähnlicher Art. Der Hund benahm sich immer schlechter und wich immer geschickter den wohlverdienten Stockschlägen aus.

Nach Wilhelm Heinrich Riehl (1823–1897):
Der stumme Ratsherr

1. Was pflegte der Hund zu tun, sobald er den Reiter sah?
2. Wie wollte Richtwin das verhindern?
3. Woher wissen Sie, daß der Hund das Schlimmste erwartete?
4. Auf welche Weise vereitelte (=*frustrated*) der Hund die Absicht seines Herrn?
5. Woher wissen Sie, daß solche Szenen die Leute amüsierten?
6. Woran kann man erkennen, daß Richtwin sehr zornig wurde?
7. Was machte ihn noch zorniger?
8. Woher wissen Sie, daß dies mehr als einmal geschah?
9. Was verdiente der Hund?
10. Was hatte Richtwin in der Hand?

1. What did Herr Richtwin decide to do?
2. What did the dog do soon afterwards?
3. How near did Herr Richtwin get to the dog?
4. What did he do to lure the dog nearer?
5. What happened when he stopped?
6. Why did everybody living in the street dash to the window or door?
7. Why did Herr Richtwin throw stones at the dog?
8. What happened when Richtwin threw stones at the dog?
9. What hadn't his master time to do?
10. What went on happening every day?

Zum Nacherzählen (Umriß, S. 236)

37. *Help in need*

Ein Kaninchen lief an ihr vorüber, in den Berg hinein. Vittoria sprang ihm nach und warf einen buntgefärbten Ball, den sie bei sich trug, dem kleinen weißen Tier nach. Der Ball rollte den Hügel hinab nach dem Fluß zu, der sich hier in die Tiefe stürzte. Aus Furcht, der Ball möchte vom

Wasser fortgeführt werden, rannte sie so eilig hinab, daß sie, unten angekommen und sich zu eilig und tief nach dem glänzenden Spielzeug hinabbeugend, wirklich in das Wasser stürzte. Vor Schreck schrie Kamillo laut auf und stürzte sich ihr nach, erfaßte die junge Frau, die sich gerade noch an einem hervorragenden Stein festhielt, und sie fest umfassend, brachte er sie ans Ufer. Mit großer Mühe trug der Kleine die größere Gestalt fort, zwar nur wenige Schritte hinauf, aber doch weit genug vom Wasser entfernt, um in Sicherheit im Gras neben der Geretteten ruhen zu können. Blaß, aber still lächelnd, saß Vittoria im Gras, dankbar blickte sie ihren Retter an und reichte ihm die zitternde Hand.

Nach Johann Ludwig Tieck (1773–1853):
Vittoria Accorombona

1. Wo war Vittoria?
2. Wie viele Personen waren da?
3. Warum warf Vittoria ihren Ball?
4. Was wollte sie verhindern?
5. Warum stürzte sie ins Wasser?
6. Was machte sie, um nicht vom Wasser fortgeführt zu werden?
7. Was mußte Kamillo machen, um Vittoria zu retten?
8. Warum kostete es Kamillo große Mühe, Vittoria in Sicherheit zu bringen?
9. Wie zeigte Vittoria, daß sie ihrem Retter dankbar war?
10. Woran kann man erkennen, daß Vittoria Angst gehabt hatte?

1. What was the animal that ran past Vittoria?
2. What did Vittoria do?
3. What happened to the ball?
4. What did Vittoria fear might happen?
5. What did she do to prevent it happening?
6. How did Kamillo save her from drowning?
7. Who was the taller of the two, Vittoria or Kamillo?
8. How far did Kamillo carry Vittoria, and where?
9. What signs were there that Vittoria had been, but was no longer, afraid?
10. What was her feeling towards Kamillo?

Zum Nacherzählen (Umriß, S. 236)

38. *Not a minute too soon*

Andreas sollte zuerst hingerichtet werden; er bestieg mit dem Henker die Leiter, da schrie eine Frau auf und sank ohnmächtig einem alten Mann in die Arme. Andreas blickte hin, es war Giorgina; laut bat er Gott um Mut und Stärke. „Dort, dort sehe ich dich wieder, meine arme unglückliche Frau, ich sterbe unschuldig!" rief er, indem er den Blick zum Himmel erhob. Der Richter rief dem Henker zu, er solle sich beeilen, denn es entstand eine Unruhe unter dem Volk. Der Henker legte dem Andreas den Strick um den Hals, da rief jemand aus der Ferne: „Halt—halt, um Christus willen, halt!—der Mann ist unschuldig!—ihr richtet einen Unschuldigen hin!"— „Halt, halt!" schrien tausend Stimmen. Näher sprengte nun der Mann zu Pferde, der zuerst gerufen hatte, und Andreas erkannte auf den ersten Blick in dem Fremden den Kaufmann, mit dem er in Frankfurt zu tun gehabt hatte. Seine Brust wollte vor Freude zerspringen, kaum konnte er sich aufrecht erhalten, als er von der Leiter herabgestiegen war. Der Kaufmann sagte dem Richter, daß zu derselben Zeit, wo der Mord im Schlosse begangen worden sei, Andreas in Frankfurt, also viele Meilen davon entfernt, gewesen sei and daß er dies vor Gericht auf die unzweifelhafteste Weise durch Dokumente und Zeugen beweisen wolle.

Nach Ernst Theodor Amadeus Hoffmann (1776–1822): Ignaz Denner

1. Woher wissen Sie, daß Andreas nicht der einzige war, der hingerichtet werden sollte?
2. Warum schrie Giorgina auf?
3. Worauf hoffte Andreas?
4. Warum wollte der Richter, daß Andreas schnell hingerichtet werden sollte?
5. Warum verlangte der Fremde, daß Andreas nicht hingerichtet werden sollte?
6. Woher wissen Sie, daß sich eine große Menge dort befand?
7. Wo hatte Andreas den Reiter kennengelernt?
8. Warum konnte Andreas sich kaum aufrecht halten?
9. Wessen war Andreas angeklagt worden?
10. Warum konnte er das unmöglich begangen haben?

1. What was just about to happen?
2. What did Giorgina do?
3. What did Andreas call out to his wife?
4. What effect had his words on the crowd?
5. What was happening to Andreas when a shout was heard from afar?
6. Who had shouted first?
7. What effect had the man's arrival on Andreas?
8. What had happened at the castle?
9. Where was Andreas at the time?
10. What was the merchant prepared to do?

Zum Nacherzählen (Umriß, S. 236)

39. *A discovery*

Neulich konnte der Prinz nicht einschlafen. Da kein Klingeln den Kammerdiener erwecken konnte, entschloß er sich, selbst aufzustehen, um einen seiner Leute zu rufen. Er war nicht weit gegangen, als er plötzlich eine liebliche Musik hörte. Er ging wie im Traum der Musik nach und fand Biondello auf seinem Zimmer auf der Flöte blasend, seine Kameraden um ihn her. Er wollte seinen Augen, seinen Ohren nicht trauen und befahl ihm fortzufahren. Mit einer großen Geschicklichkeit spielte dieser nun dasselbe Adagio wieder. Der Prinz sagte, daß er unzweifelhaft in der besten Kapelle spielen dürfte.

„ Ich kann diesen Menschen nicht mehr behalten", sagte er zu mir am folgenden Morgen; „ ich selber kann ihn nicht reichlich genug belohnen." Biondello, der diese Worte gehört hatte, trat herzu. „ Gnädigster Herr ", sagte er, „ wenn Sie das tun, so rauben Sie mir meine beste Belohnung."

„ Du bist zu etwas Besserem bestimmt, als zu dienen ", sagte mein Herr. „ Ein solches Talent zu vernachlässigen— Nein! Ich darf es nicht erlauben."

„ So erlauben Sie mir, gnädigster Herr, daß ich es zuweilen in Ihrer Gegenwart übe."

Und dazu wurden auch sogleich Schritte unternommen. Biondello erhielt ein Zimmer neben dem Schlafzimmer seines Herrn, wo er ihn mit Musik in den Schlummer wiegen und mit Musik daraus erwecken konnte.

Nach Johann Christoph Friedrich von Schiller (1759–1805):
Der Geisterseher

1. Warum erschien nach der Meinung des Prinzen der Kammerdiener nicht?
2. Warum erschien in der Tat der Kammerdiener nicht?
3. Warum stand der Prinz auf?
4. Warum war er erstaunt?
5. Woher wissen Sie, daß der Prinz ein Liebhaber der Musik war?
6. Warum meinte der Prinz, daß Biondello in der besten Kapelle spielen sollte?
7. Warum glaubte der Prinz, Biondello nicht bei sich behalten zu können?
8. Was wollte Biondello vor allen Dingen vermeiden?
9. Würde Biondello sein Talent vernachlässigen, wenn er beim Prinzen bliebe?
10. Wann sollte er dem Prinzen in Zukunft vorspielen?

1. How did the prince try to wake up his valet?
2. Why did he decide to get up himself?
3. When did he hear the music?
4. What did he find Biondello doing?
5. What was Biondello's objection to the prince's decision?
6. What was the prince afraid might happen if Biondello remained in his service?
7. How did Biondello think that danger might be averted?
8. Where was Biondello to sleep in future?
9. On what occasions was he to play music?
10. What evidence is there that the prince liked music?

Zum Nacherzählen (Umriß, S. 236)

40. *Rare books*

In einem Laden in Piccadilly wurden im Jahre 1884 zwei Jungen mit Namen John Sherratt und Joseph Hughes angestellt. Zwölf Jahre später entschlossen sich diese beiden, eine eigene Buchhandlung zu eröffnen. Sie nahmen in Manchester den Laden, in dem noch heute die berühmte Buchhandlung zu finden ist. Viele wertvolle Bücher sind durch die Hände der beiden Buchhändler gegangen.

Eines Tages kam eine alte Frau mit einem Paket in den Laden und bot zwei Bücher für 10 Schilling zum Verkauf.

Sie erzählte, daß ihr verstorbener Mann ihr gesagt habe, sie solle diese Bücher nie verkaufen, ausgenommen wenn sie kein Brot habe. Sie erhielt zwei Schilling, und man schickte sie in ein nahes Restaurant, um ein ordentliches Mittagessen zu bekommen; danach sollte sie zurückkommen und sich ihre zehn Schilling holen. In der Zwischenzeit erkannte man jedoch, daß es sich um zwei frühe Werke Shelleys in der Originalausgabe handle. Als die Frau zurückkam, erfuhr sie, daß ihre Bücher 450 englische Pfund wert waren und daß eine Bank ihr jede Woche anderthalb Pfund sieben Jahre lang auszahlen würde. Als die Frau das hörte, fiel sie in Ohnmacht. Man schickte nach einer Flasche Kognak, um sie wiederzubeleben. Seit dieser Zeit gibt es immer eine Flasche Kognak bei Sherratt und Hughes.

1. Wie heißt ein Laden, in dem Bücher verkauft werden?
2. Warum wollte die Frau die Bücher verkaufen?
3. Was wollte die Frau für die Bücher haben?
4. Was sollte sie sich mit den zwei Schilling kaufen?
5. Was würde sie bekommen, nachdem sie gegessen hatte?
6. Woher wissen Sie, daß ihr verstorbener Mann die Bücher für wertvoll hielt?
7. Warum waren die Bücher wertvoll?
8. Warum fiel die Frau in Ohnmacht?
9. Womit versuchte man sie wiederzubeleben?
10. Warum gibt es seitdem immer eine Flasche Kognak bei Sherratt und Hughes?

1. What did the two men decide to do in 1896?
2. Who came one day to the shop, and with what?
3. What did the woman come to the shop for?
4. What had the woman's husband urged her never to do?
5. Where did the bookseller send the woman and why?
6. What was discovered in her absence?
7. What did she learn when she came back?
8. What effect had the news on her?
9. What was sent for, and why?
10. What is to be found even today at Sherratt and Hughes, and why?

Zum Nacherzählen (Umriß, S. 236)

41. *A mystery*

An Cardillacs Haus in der Straße Nicaise schließt sich
eine hohe Mauer mit Nischen [1] und alten, halb zerbrochenen
Statuen darin. Dicht bei einer solchen Statue stand
Olivier in einer Nacht und sah hinauf nach den Fenstern
des Hauses, die in den Hof gehen, den die Mauer einschließt.
Da bemerkte er plötzlich Licht in Cardillacs Werkstatt. Es
war Mitternacht, nie war sonst Cardillac zu dieser Stunde
wach, denn er ging gewöhnlich Punkt neun Uhr zu Bett.
Olivier klopfte das Herz vor Furcht. Doch gleich verschwand das Licht wieder. Er drückte sich an die Statue in
die Nische hinein, doch mit Schrecken fühlte er, wie die
Statue sich bewegte. In der Dämmerung bemerkte er nun,
daß die Statue sich langsam drehte und hinter derselben
eine finstere Gestalt hervorkam, die mit leisem Schritt die
Straße hinunterging. Olivier sprang an die Statue zurück,
sie stand aber wie zuvor dicht an der Mauer. Ohne es
eigentlich zu wollen, wie von einer inneren Macht getrieben,
schlich er hinter der Gestalt her. Gerade bei einem Marienbild sah die Gestalt sich um, der volle Schein der hellen
Lampe, die vor dem Bild brannte, fiel ihr ins Gesicht. Es
war Cardillac.

Nach Ernst Theodor Amadeus Hoffman (1776–1882):
Das Fräulein von Scuderi

1. Was war hinter der Mauer?
2. Woraus kann man schließen, daß die Mauer wahrscheinlich
   alt war?
3. Woher wissen Sie, daß Olivier Cardillacs Gewohnheiten
   (= *habits*) gut kannte?
4. Warum klopfte Olivier das Herz?
5. Wie lange war Licht in Cardillacs Werkstatt?
6. Warum erschrak Olivier?
7. Wie trat die Gestalt auf die Straße?
8. Warum sprang Olivier an die Statue zurück?
9. Warum folgte er der Gestalt?
10. Was war nötig, um die Gestalt zu erkennen?

1. Was there a wall surrounding Cardillac's house?
2. Where was Olivier standing, and when?

[1] Die Nische: *niche.*

3. Why was he surprised to see a light in Cardillac's workshop?
4. What was Olivier hoping to do?
5. Why did he squeeze himself against the statue?
6. What gave him a shock?
7. What must have happened immediately after the figure had emerged?
8. Why was Olivier disappointed?
9. What impelled him to follow the figure?
10. How was he able to recognize the person he was following?

Zum Nacherzählen (Umriß, S. 237)
Zum Fortsetzen (Umriß, S. 170)

42. *An irreconcilable enemy*

Sein Schlaf war vorbei—er ging daher auf die alte steinerne Galerie, die über eine tiefe bewaldete Schlucht hinausging, um dort den Morgen abzuwarten. Dort fand er auch den gefangenen Offizier, der in einer Ecke lag. Er setzte sich zu ihm auf das halb abgebrochene Geländer.

„ Das Unglück macht vieles wieder gut ", sagte er und reichte ihm die Hand. Der Offizier wickelte sich fester in seinen Mantel und antwortete nicht. „ Hast du denn alles vergessen ", fuhr Friedrich ruhig fort, „ was wir in der guten Zeit vorbereitet haben? Mir war es Ernst mit dem, was ich damals wollte. Ich war ein ehrlicher Narr, und ich will es lieber sein, als klug ohne Ehre." Bei diesen Worten sprang der Offizier, der Friedrichs ruhige Züge nicht länger ertragen konnte, auf, packte ihn bei der Brust und wollte ihn über das Geländer der Galerie in den Abgrund stürzen. Sie kämpften einige Zeit miteinander; Friedrich war vom vielen Blutverlust schwach geworden und war schon nah am Rand der Galerie. Da fiel ein Schuß aus einem Fenster des Schlosses; ein Soldat hatte alles mit angesehen. „ Jesus Maria! " rief der Offizier getroffen, und stürzte über das Geländer in den Abgrund hinunter. Da wurde es auf einmal still, nur der Wald rauschte tief unten. Friedrich wandte sich traurig von dem Ort.

Nach Joseph von Eichendorff (1788–1857):
Ahnung und Gegenwart

1. Was konnte man von der Galerie aus sehen?
2. Woraus kann man schließen, daß Friedrich sich mit dem
    Offizier versöhnen (*make it up with*) wollte?
3. Woher wissen Sie, daß der Offizier wach war?
4. Warum wickelte sich der Offizier fester in seinen Mantel?
5. Woraus kann man schließen, daß die beiden Männer sich
    schon lange kannten?
6. Warum sprang der Offizier auf?
7. Was hätte leicht geschehen können?
8. Woraus kann man schließen, daß Friedrich verwundet war?
9. Wo war der Soldat?
10. Warum wandte sich Friedrich traurig von dem Ort?

1. Why did Friedrich come into the gallery?
2. What did the gallery project over?
3. What did Friedrich sit down on?
4. What were the officer's reactions to Friedrich's gesture?
5. What would Friedrich rather be?
6. What was it that made the officer jump up?
7. What danger threatened Friedrich?
8. How was this danger averted?
9. What happened to the officer?
10. What was the only thing that could be heard afterwards?

Zum Nacherzählen (Umriß, S. 237)

43. *The three dollars*

Der junge Mark Twain, dem es noch sehr schlecht ging,
blieb vor einem Restaurant stehen und sah hungrig auf die
Speisekarte. Da kam ein schöner Hund zu ihm und legte
den Kopf an sein Knie, ging auch weiter mit, als Mark
Twain sich von der Speisekarte trennte.

Ein Offizier trat auf Mark Twain zu: „Sie haben da ja
einen sehr schönen Hund! Ist er vielleicht zu verkaufen?"

„Geben Sie mir drei Dollar", erwiderte Mark Twain.

Sogleich zog der Offizier die drei Dollar heraus, faßte
den Hund am Halsband und ging mit ihm in das Restaurant
hinein.

Kurz danach kam um die nächste Ecke ein aufgeregter
Herr, der fortwährend nach allen Seiten pfiff, rief und
suchte.

„Suchen Sie vielleicht einen Hund?" fragte Mark Twain.

„Jawohl. Haben Sie ihn gesehen?"

„Wenn Sie mir drei Dollar geben, verspreche ich, Ihnen den Hund sofort zu bringen." Der Herr versprach ihm bereitwillig die drei Dollar.

Mark Twain verschwand in dem Restaurant und kehrte nach wenigen Minuten mit dem Hund zurück. Er hatte dem Offizier seine drei Dollar zurückgezahlt, indem er dem Käufer erklärte, es sei ihm völlig unmöglich, sich von dem Hund zu trennen.

„ So hatte ich ", sagte Mark Twain, „ mein Gewissen wieder beruhigt und doch drei Dollar verdient! "

1. Warum ging Mark Twain nicht sofort ins Restaurant?
2. Was ist eine Speisekarte?
3. Woran erkennen Sie, daß der Hund Mark Twain gern mochte?
4. Wofür hielt der Offizier Mark Twain?
5. Was hoffte der Offizier?
6. Warum war der Herr aufgeregt?
7. Was war der Herr bereit zu tun?
8. Wie lange blieb Mark Twain im Restaurant?
9. Was mußte er tun, um den Hund wiederzubekommen?
10. Warum hatte er ein unruhiges Gewissen gehabt?

1. What was Mark Twain doing outside the restaurant?
2. Why didn't he go in?
3. How did the dog show his affection for Mark Twain?
4. What did the officer want to know?
5. How did the officer prevent the dog from following Mark Twain?
6. How was the owner of the dog trying to find it?
7. What did Mark Twain promise him?
8. What had Mark Twain to do in order to return the dog?
9. How did he explain his change of mind?
10. How did Mark Twain have the best of both worlds?

Zum Nacherzählen (Umriß, S. 237)

44. *A strange incident*

Nach Mitternacht weckte den Maler ein sonderbarer Klang, den er zuerst bloß im Traum gehört zu haben glaubte; bald aber konnte er sich völlig überzeugen, daß es Musik war, welche von dem linken Schloßflügel herüber zu tönen schien. Es war, als spielte man die Orgel, dann wieder klang es wie ein ganz anderes Instrument, immer nur unterbrochen, mit längeren und kürzeren Pausen. Bestürzt sprang er aus dem Bett, ohne zu wissen, was er tun, wo er zuerst sich hinwenden sollte. Er hörte zu, und immer wieder dieselben sonderbaren Töne! Leise auf den Socken, den Schlafrock umgeworfen, ging er vor seine Tür und schlich, sich mit den Händen an der Wand forttastend, den finstern Gang hin, bis in die Nähe des Zimmers, wo sich der Gärtner und Henni befanden. Er rief um Licht, der Gärtner eilte heraus, erstaunt, den Maler zu dieser Stunde hier zu sehen. Da nun weder Vater noch Sohn irgend etwas anderes gehört hatten als das wechselnde Pfeifen des Windes, welcher auf dieser Seite heftiger gegen das Haus wehte, so entfernte sich Nolten, scheinbar beruhigt, mit Licht, erlaubte aber nicht, daß man ihn zurückbegleitete.

Nach kaum einer Minute hörten der Alte und Henni vollkommen deutlich die oben beschriebenen Töne und gleich darauf einen starken Fall und einen lauten Aufschrei.

Nach Eduard Mörike (1804–75): Maler Nolten

1. Wo wurde gespielt?
2. Warum war der Klang sonderbar?
3. Warum sprang der Maler aus dem Bett?
4. Warum mußte er mit den Händen tasten?
5. Warum war der Gärtner erstaunt?
6. Was fragte der Maler den Gärtner?
7. Wie war das Wetter?
8. Warum fühlte sich Nolten beunruhigt?
9. Was wollten der Gärtner und Henni tun?
10. War Nolten der einzige, der die Musik hörte?

1. What did Nolten first think when he woke up?
2. Where did the sound of the music come from?
3. What was strange about the music?
4. What was Nolten uncertain about?
5. What was he wearing?
6. How did he find his way to the gardener's room?
7. What had the gardener and his son heard?
8. What was the effect on Nolten of the answer he received?
9. What did Nolten insist on?
10. What happened almost immediately after Nolten had gone?

Zum Nacherzählen (Umriß, S. 237)

45. The faithful dog

Eines Tages als Abdias nach Hause ritt, bemerkte er,
daß sein Hund, der ihn stets begleitete, große Unruhe
zeigte. Er sprang an dem Pferd empor, als wolle er es
anhalten. Dann schoß er wieder eine Strecke des Weges
zurück, den sie gekommen waren. Dabei glänzten seine
Augen ganz unnatürlich. Abdias erinnerte sich, daß sich
Fälle von Hundswut in der Gegend gemehrt hatten. Er
fürchtete, der Hund könne toll sein. Je weiter er ritt, desto
aufgeregter benahm sich der Hund, und schweren Herzens
entschloß sich Abdias, das Tier zu erschießen. Er sah, wie
der Hund getroffen zur Erde stürzte, und ritt dann eilig fort.
Nachdem er etwa eine halbe Stunde geritten war, vermißte
er seinen Geldsack. Nun erkannte er seinen Irrtum: er
hatte den Sack an einer Waldstelle, wo er geruht hatte,
liegen lassen. Der Hund hatte es bemerkt und hatte ihn
warnen wollen. Und er hatte das treue Tier zum Dank
dafür getötet. Er riß sein Pferd herum und ritt zurück.
Als er zu der Stelle kam, wo er den Hund erschossen hatte,
fand er ihn nicht dort. Abdias folgte einer Blutspur.
Endlich kam er zu der Waldstelle: dort lag richtig sein
Geldsack und davor der sterbende Hund. Als Abdias die
Wunde untersuchen wollte, versuchte der Hund, ihm die
Hand zu lecken. Er war aber schon zu schwach und starb.

Nach Adalbert Stifter (1805–1868): Abdias

1. Woran erkannte Abdias, daß sein Hund nicht normal war?
2. Woran erinnerte ihn das Benehmen seines Hundes?
3. Woraus kann man schließen, daß Abdias seinen Hund liebte?
4. Woran erkannte Abdias seinen Irrtum?
5. Warum hatte der Hund sich aufgeregt benommen?
6. Warum ritt Abdias zurück?
7. Wohin war der Hund gegangen?
8. Warum war der Hund dorthin gegangen?
9. Was hoffte Abdias?
10. Warum leckte der Hund seinem Herrn die Hand?

1. What did the dog seem to want?
2. What in the dog's behaviour aroused Abdias's suspicion?

3. Why did he shoot the dog?
4. What did he notice some time afterwards?
5. What did he realize he had done?
6. How did he now explain to himself the dog's behaviour?
7. What did Abdias then do?
8. Where did he expect to find the dog?
9. Where in fact was the dog, and in what state?
10. What did Abdias do when he found the dog?

Zum Nacherzählen (Umriß, S. 237)

46. *The secret button*

Vittoria saß nahe an der Mauer, die das Haus von der
Straße trennte.   Während sie schrieb, war es ihr schon oft
gewesen, als ob sie ein sonderbares Geräusch hörte.   Vittoria, die nicht ängstlich war, wollte das Fenster öffnen, um
hinauszusehen, was sich in ihrer Nähe so verdächtig
bewegte; aber das Fenster war von den Dienern zu fest
verschlossen, sie konnte es ohne Hilfe nicht aufmachen.   Sie
hörte an der Wand aufmerksam zu, und es kam ihr jetzt
ganz deutlich vor, als hörte sie das Atmen eines Schlafenden.
Sie konnte nicht länger zweifeln, da dieses Atmen bald zum
Schnarchen wurde.

Während sie so, nicht ganz ohne Angst, an der langen
Wand hin und her tastete, fühlte sie mit der Spitze des
Fingers plötzlich ein Knöpfchen nicht größer und dicker als
eine Erbse—und sobald sie den Druck stärker wiederholte,
öffnete sich ohne Geräusch die Wand.   Sie sah in der
Dämmerung, daß dort, wo sie die Straße glaubte, sich noch
ein schmales Zimmer befand, in welchem jetzt viel deutlicher das regelmäßige Atmen des fremden Schlafenden zu
hören war.   Sie zögerte einen Augenblick, ob sie die Diener
wecken solle; doch nahm sie nach kurzem Nachdenken die
Lampe in die Hand und schritt hinein.   Wie erstaunte und
erschrak sie, als sie dort ihren Bruder, den verbannten
Marcello, in einem Sessel schlafend fand.

Nach Johann Ludwig Tieck (1773–1853):
Vittoria Accorombona

1. Was hatte Vittorias Verdacht (= *suspicion*) erweckt?
2. Was hoffte sie durch das Öffnen des Fensters zu entdecken?

3. Wo stellte sie sich hin, und warum?
4. Was überzeugte sie, daß sie recht hatte?
5. Woraus kann man schließen, daß ihr Zimmer nicht hell erleuchtet war?
6. Was mußte zuerst gemacht werden, bevor die Wand sich öffnete?
7. Was hatte Vittoria nicht zu sehen erwartet?
8. Was wollte sie zuerst tun?
9. Warum nahm sie die Lampe in die Hand?
10. Warum erschrak sie, als sie ihren Bruder im Sessel fand?

1. Where exactly was Vittoria?
2. What had she seemed to notice while she was writing?
3. Why did she try to open the window?
4. What made her stop trying?
5. How did she discover where the noise came from?
6. What made her certain that there was somebody quite near?
7. What trick did she discover?
8. Why was it difficult at first to see who was in the next room?
9. What was her first impulse?
10. Why didn't she expect to find her brother there?

Zum Nacherzählen (Umriß, S. 238)
Zum Fortsetzen (Umriß, S. 170)

47. *An ugly situation*

Ein plötzlicher Regen zwang uns, in ein Kaffeehaus einzutreten, wo gespielt wurde. Der Prinz stellte sich hinter den Stuhl eines Spaniers und beobachtete das Spiel. Vor der Ankunft des Prinzen hatte der Spanier fortwährend verloren, jetzt gewann er auf alle Karten, und die Bank war in Gefahr, von ihm gesprengt zu werden. Der Venezianer, der sie hielt, sagte dem Prinzen mit beleidigendem Ton—er störe das Glück, und er solle den Tisch verlassen. Dieser sah ihn kalt an und blieb; dieselbe Ruhe behielt er, als der Venezianer seine Beleidigung französisch wiederholte. Daher stand er auf und wollte den Prinzen beim Arm ergreifen; dieser verlor hier seine Geduld, er packte den Venezianer mit starker Hand und warf ihn unsanft zu Boden. Das ganze Haus kam in Bewegung. Auf das

Geräusch stürzte ich herein, unwillkürlich rief ich ihn bei seinem Namen. „ Nehmen Sie sich in acht, Prinz ", fügte ich hinzu, „ wir sind in Venedig." Der Name des Prinzen gebot eine allgemeine Stille, woraus bald ein Gemurmel wurde, das mir gefährlich schien. All die Italiener, die dort waren, traten beiseite. Einer um den andern verließ den Saal, bis wir uns beide mit dem Spanier und einigen Franzosen allein fanden. „ Sie sind verloren, gnädigster Herr ", sagten sie, „ wenn Sie nicht sogleich die Stadt verlassen. Der Venezianer, den Sie so übel behandelt haben, ist reich und mächtig—es kostet ihn nur wenig Geld, Sie aus der Welt zu schaffen."

Nach Johann Christoph Friedrich von Schiller (1759–1805):
Der Geisterseher

1. Warum traten der Prinz und sein Begleiter in ein Kaffeehaus ein?
2. Auf welche Weise hatte der Prinz das Glück gestört?
3. In welcher Sprache redete der Venezianer den Prinzen zuerst an?
4. Was wollte der Venezianer?
5. Warum verlor der Prinz endlich die Geduld?
6. Wo war unterdessen der Begleiter des Prinzen?
7. Was hätte er nicht tun sollen?
8. Warum entstand eine allgemeine Stille?
9. Was rieten die Franzosen dem Prinzen?
10. Was drohte dem Prinzen?

1. What did the prince do on entering the coffee-house?
2. What had been happening before his arrival?
3. Why was he asked to leave the card-table?
4. Why did the Venetian repeat his remark in French?
5. What did the prince do when his patience was at an end?
6. What did the prince's companion say?
7. What appeared dangerous to the prince's companion?
8. What did all the Italians present do?
9. What would happen to the prince if he didn't leave the city immediately?
10. Why was he held to be in great danger?

Zum Nacherzählen (Umriß, S. 238)

48. *The second brew*

Als ich in den Bädern von Lucca war, lobte ich bei Lady Woolen den Hauswirt, der mir so guten Tee gab, wie ich ihn noch nie getrunken hatte. Diese Dame wunderte sich darüber um so mehr, da sie, wie sie klagte, trotz aller Bitten von unserem Hauswirt keinen guten Tee erhalten konnte, und deshalb gezwungen war, ihren Tee aus Livorno kommen zu lassen—,, der ist aber himmlisch! " fügte sie hinzu. ,, Milady ", erwiderte ich, ,, ich wette, der meinige ist noch viel besser." Die Damen, die zufällig da waren, wurden jetzt von mir zum Tee eingeladen, und sie versprachen am folgenden Tag um sechs Uhr zu kommen. Die Stunde kam, der Tisch war gedeckt, die Butterbrötchen waren geschnitten, die Damen unterhielten sich lebhaft— aber es kam kein Tee. Die Sonnenstrahlen beleuchteten nur noch die Gipfel der Berge—aber der Tee kam nicht. Endlich, endlich kam mein Hauswirt und fragte: ob wir nicht Limonade statt des Tees genießen wollten? ,, Tee! Tee! " riefen wir alle einstimmig. ,, Und zwar denselben ", fügte ich hinzu, ,, den ich täglich trinke." ,, Von demselben, Exzellenz? Es ist nicht möglich." ,, Weshalb nicht möglich? " rief ich zornig. Immer verlegener wurde mein Hauswirt, er stammelte, er zögerte und erst nach längerer Zeit erfuhren wir, warum wir heute keinen Tee haben konnten.

Mein Herr Hauswirt verstand nämlich die Kunst, den Teetopf, woraus schon getrunken worden war, wieder mit heißem Wasser zu füllen, und der Tee, der mir so gut geschmeckt hatte und den ich so gelobt hatte, war nichts anderes als der zweite Aufguß von demselben Tee, den Lady Woolen aus Livorno kommen ließ.

Nach Heinrich Heine (1797–1856): Der Tee

1. Warum lobte der Erzähler den Hauswirt?
2. Warum mußte Lady Woolen ihren Tee aus Livorno kommen lassen?
3. Wovon war der Erzähler überzeugt?
4. Wie wollte er das beweisen?
5. Woher wissen Sie, daß die Sonne bald untergehen würde?
6. Warum fragte der Hauswirt, ob die Gesellschaft lieber Limonade trinken möchte?

7. Worauf bestand der Erzähler?
8. Warum wurde er zornig?
9. Wer hatte immer den ersten Aufguß?
10. Auf welche Weise hatte der Hauswirt immer Tee für den
    Erzähler gemacht?

1. Why was Lady Woolen surprised?
2. What had she always complained of?
3. What had she been compelled to do?
4. How did the narrator propose to prove himself right?
5. What had been done in preparation for the visit?
6. What suggestion did the landlord make?
7. What was everybody unanimous about?
8. What were the signs of the landlord's embarrassment?
9. Why was the landlord embarrassed?
10. What had the narrator in fact been praising?

Zum Nacherzählen (Umriß, S. 238)

49. *The wager*

„Was denkt ihr von diesem Herrn?" fragte ich die
Gesellschaft. „Er sieht aus", antwortete einer, „als ob er
nicht mit sich spaßen lasse." „Und trotzdem", erwiderte
ich, „was wettet ihr, ich will ihn bei der Nase packen, ohne
daß mir deshalb etwas Übles geschieht; ja, er wird mir
sogar dafür danken." „Wenn du das kannst, Wilhelm",
sagte Raufbold, „so zahlt dir jeder eine Mark." „Abgemacht!" rief ich aus; „ich habe keine Zeit zu verlieren"
und sprang die Treppe hinunter.

Bei dem ersten Anblick des Fremden hatte ich bemerkt,
daß er einen sehr starken Bart hatte, und schloß, daß keiner
von seinen Leuten rasieren konnte. Ich bat den Kellner,
mich als Barbier anzumelden, nahm das Rasierzeug, das ich
im Haus fand, und folgte dem Kellner. Der alte Herr
empfing mich mit großem Ernst, sah mich von oben bis
unten an und sagte: „Verstehen Sie Ihr Handwerk?" Ich
versicherte ihm, daß ich es gut konnte, und machte mich
daran.

Das Zimmer war so gelegen, daß meine Freunde vom
Hof hereinsehen konnten, besonders wenn die Fenster offen
waren. Ich bat darum, die Fenster aufmachen zu dürfen,
was er erlaubte, und ich fing an, den starken Bart ein-

zuseifen. Als es an die Oberlippe kam, zögerte ich nicht, den Herrn bei der Nase zu packen und sie merklich herüber und hinüber zu biegen, wobei ich mich so zu stellen wußte, daß die Wettenden zu ihrem größten Vergnügen erkennen mußten, ihre Seite habe verloren.

„ Haben Sie vielen Dank ", sagte der alte Herr, nachdem er sich im Spiegel betrachtet hatte. „ Hier ist etwas für Ihre Mühe ", fuhr er fort, indem er mir eine Mark reichte. „ Nur eines merken Sie sich: daß man Leute von Stand nicht bei der Nase packt."

Nach Johann Wolfgang von Goethe (1749–1832),
Wilhelm Meisters Wanderjahre

1. Was für ein Mann war der Herr?
2. Wofür würde er Wilhelm danken?
3. Woher wissen Sie, daß niemand von der Gesellschaft außer Wilhelm das für möglich hielt?
4. Woraus schloß Wilhelm, daß niemand von den Leuten den Herrn rasieren konnte?
5. Warum sollte der Kellner Wilhelm als Barbier vorstellen?
6. Was wollte der Herr wissen, bevor er sich rasieren ließ?
7. Warum bat Wilhelm darum, die Fenster aufmachen zu dürfen?
8. Was machte er, damit seine Freunde erkennen mußten, daß sie die Wette verloren hatten?
9. Woher wissen Sie, daß der Herr mit Wilhelm zufrieden war?
10. Warum hätte Wilhelm den Herrn nicht bei der Nase packen sollen?

1. What did Wilhelm wager?
2. What agreement did the friends come to?
3. What had given Wilhelm the idea?
4. In what sort of building did this incident take place?
5. What suggests that the gentleman had his doubts as to Wilhelm's capacity to shave him?
6. How could Wilhelm's friends see what was happening?
7. At what stage was it clear that Wilhelm was going to win his bet?
8. How do you know that his friends were not disappointed at losing the wager?
9. What did the gentleman do before thanking Wilhelm?
10. What advice did he give Wilhelm?

Zum Nacherzählen (Umriß, S. 238)

50. *The flood*

Gegen Morgen wachte der Vater auf und wurde unruhig, denn ihm kam es vor, als bewege sich jemand im Hause. Er warf hastig den Schlafrock über und eilte hinauf. Zu seinem Erstaunen fand er seinen Sohn, der eben im Begriff war, einen schweren, eisernen Kasten, in welchem sich wichtige Dokumente und eine große Summe in Gold und Silber befanden, aufzuheben. „ Bist du toll? " rief der Vater. „ Ein Damm ist irgendwo gerissen", rief Wilhelm. „ Es ist höchste Zeit, das Wasser tritt schon in den Garten." Er hob den Kasten und trug ihn aus dem Zimmer. „ Anziehen! schnell! auch Mutter! und Elsbeth! " rief der Jüngling in der Tür, und der Vater hörte, wie er die ungeheure Last die Treppe hinuntertrug. Der Vater eilte in das Schlafzimmer zurück, wo er die Mutter und Elsbeth schon angekleidet fand. „ Nehmt um Gottes willen ", rief er, „ was ihr braucht, denn wir wissen nicht, was aus der Sache werden kann."

Man lief schnell durch alle Zimmer, man steckte Papiere ein, man wickelte Sachen in Bündel, Schlüssel wurden abgezogen, und schon hörte man aus der Ferne Stimmen durcheinander, die immer bestimmter und deutlicher wurden.

Sie standen unten, und schon war das Wasser ins Haus gedrungen. Fritz sprang ihnen entgegen und nahm Elsbeth auf den Arm, rannte durch den Garten, indem das Wasser schon über die Füße ging, und setzte sie in seinem Boot ab. Dann kam er zurück und trug ebenso die Mutter in sein Boot. Der Vater folgte ihnen, nur etwas langsamer, und stieg auch ein. Es dauerte nicht lange, so hob sich das Boot ganz von selbst, Wilhelm lenkte es, und als sie hinschwammen und den Garten verließen, sahen sie das Wasser schon durch die unteren Fenster in die Zimmer dringen.

Nach Johann Ludwig Tieck (1773–1853):
Der funfzehnte November

1. Warum wurde der Vater unruhig?
2. Warum war er erstaunt?
3. In welchem Stock war Wilhelm?
4. Wo wollte Wilhelm den Kasten hinbringen?
5. Wo war seine Mutter und was machte sie?

6. Warum mußte man eilen?
7. Woraus kann man schließen, daß andere Leute sich näherten?
8. Warum nahm Fritz Elsbeth auf den Arm?
9. Bis wann mußte man warten, bevor man abfahren konnte?
10. Wo war das Boot gewesen?

1. What caused the father to go upstairs?
2. What was his son doing?
3. What was in the safe?
4. Why was the family in danger?
5. What did Wilhelm tell everybody to do?
6. Where was Wilhelm going with the safe?
7. What last-minute preparations were made?
8. What did the family notice when they got downstairs?
9. How did Elsbeth get to the boat?
10. What indicates that they got there only just in time?

Zum Nacherzählen (Umriß, S. 238)
Zum Fortsetzen (Umriß, S. 170)

OUTLINES OF PASSAGES FOR REPRODUCTION

26.   (S. 203) *Divine inspiration*

Christ Church — College — Rentmeister — weltlicher Bankier — wird zum Essen eingeladen — fromme Redensarten des Mannes — Kanonikus fährt nach London — zieht alles Geld aus der Bank — Bank bankrott — Christ Church gerettet.

27.   (S. 204) *A deal*

Beutel — Goldstücke — abgemacht — Schatten — kniet nieder — löst Schatten — steckt in die Tasche — verbeugt sich — zieht sich zurück — lacht für sich — ich halte Beutel fest — Sonnenschein — stehe wie versteinert da.

28.   (S. 205) *The Tsar*

Zar — Tyrann — fremder Gesandter — erscheint mit bedecktem Kopf — grausame Strafe — Kühnheit des englischen Botschafters — Fragen des Zaren — Antwort des Botschafters — Repräsentant der Königin Elisabeth — Beleidigung — Rache — Lob des Zaren — vergleicht ihn mit seinen Hofleuten.

29. (S. 206) *Trapped*

Umweg — kürzerer Weg — Eingang — Gewölbe — Felix wird neugierig — Stufen — ebene Stelle — Schuß — eiserne Tore — Wilhelm und Felix eingesperrt — Fritz nicht — Ärmel nur gefaßt — wirft Jäckchen ab — entflieht.

30. (S. 207) *A near escape*

Tal — Fürstin — Gebüsch — Tiger — Fürstin sprengt den Berg hinauf — Honorio — Pistole — Schuß fehlt — Tiger rennt der Fürstin nach — Honorio hinter ihm her — Pferd der Fürstin stürzt zu Boden — Fürstin in Gefahr — Honorio schießt mit der zweiten Pistole — tötet Tiger.

31. (S. 208) *Presence of mind*

Badegast in Seebad nach Krankheit — einsame Spaziergänge — Felsen — Abgrund — Mann plötzlich da — Wahnsinniger — soll hinunterspringen — Badegast in Gefahr — Mann sehr stark — guter Einfall — gehen Felsen hinunter — Wärter kommen — Badegast gerettet.

32. (S. 209) *The rescue*

Ruhiger Abend — Fest — schreckliches Geschrei — Menschen stürzen ins Wasser — Hauptmann — treibt Menge fort — Ertrinkende werden herausgezogen — Knabe — Anstrengungen — entfernt sich — kraftlos — Kahn mit Feuerwerk gefüllt — keine Zeit zu verlieren — Hauptmann springt ins Wasser — bringt Knaben ans Ufer — tot?

33. (S. 210) *The will o' the wisps*

Fluß — Fährmann schläft — zwei Irrlichter wollen übergesetzt werden — große Eile — Fährmann zögert nicht — Unterhaltung der Fremden — Gelächter — hüpfen hin und her — Kahn schwankt — Fährmann warnt sie — sie benehmen sich schlecht — Fährmann verliert nicht die Geduld — man kommt an — Irrlichter schütteln sich — Goldstücke.

34. (S. 212) *The strange duel*

Ralfson und Amerikaner — Pulverfaß — Ralfson zündet Zigarre an — Lunte — Viertelstunde — sein früheres Leben — bückt sich — trockener Zweig — löscht Funken aus —

rennt zum Amerikaner — mutig — Amerikaner durch-
schneidet Schnur — Inhalt des Fasses — quitt?

35. (S. 213) *The visit*

Mark Twain — seit einem halben Jahr in neuer Wohnung — besucht Nachbarn um Mittag — nicht korrekt
angezogen — ins Besuchszimmer geführt — entschuldigt sich
— hätte früher kommen sollen — etwas ist immer wieder
dazwischengekommen — heute — Anzug — Wahl der
Stunde — hofft auf Verzeihung — Grund — Feuer.

36. (S. 214) *Master and dog*

Hund läuft hinter Reiter her — sein Herr beschließt, ihn
zu bestrafen — er versucht, den Hund zu fassen — läuft, ruft,
pfeift, schleicht — Hund bleibt immer zehn Schritt von ihm
entfernt — Zuschauer lachen — Wut des Bürgers — wirft
Steine — Hund apportiert — Szene wiederholt sich — Hund
weicht Schlägen aus.

37. (S. 215) *Help in need*

Kaninchen — Vittoria wirft Ball — er rollt den Hügel
hinab — Vittoria läuft ihm nach — stürzt ins Wasser —
Kamillo stürzt sich ihr nach — rettet sie — bringt sie in
Sicherheit — ruht — Dankbarkeit der Frau.

38. (S. 217) *Not a minute too soon*

Andreas — hinrichten — Henker — Giorgina — Richter
— Unruhe unter dem Volk — Strick um den Hals — Reiter
kommt herangesprengt — erklärt Andreas für unschuldig —
Andreas erkennt Kaufmann — Kaufmann bringt Beweise mit.

39. (S. 218) *A discovery*

Prinz kann nicht einschlafen — klingelt vergebens —
steht auf — Musik — Biondello bläst auf der Flöte — andere
Diener um ihn her — Prinz entzückt — Biondello zu etwas
Besserem bestimmt — Kapelle? — Biondello möchte nicht
fortgehen — Ausweg?

40. (S. 119) *Rare books*

Sherratt und Hughes — eigene Buchhandlung in Manchester — alte Frau — Paket — verlangt 10 Schilling —
erzählt von ihrem verstorbenen Mann — man schickt sie ins

Restaurant — Bücher als zwei frühe Werke Shelleys in der
Originalausgabe erkannt — Frau kommt zurück — 450
Pfund — anderthalb Pfund jede Woche — Ohnmacht —
Kognak — Flasche.

41. (S. 221) *A mystery*
    Cardillacs Haus — hohe Mauer — Nischen — Statuen —
Olivier — Werkstatt — Licht — Mitternacht — ungewöhnlich — Olivier klopft das Herz — Licht verschwindet —
Nische — Statue dreht sich — Gestalt — Straße — Olivier
sucht Eingang — alles wie zuvor — er folgt Gestalt — sie
sieht sich um — Lampe — erkennt Cardillac.

42. (S. 222) *An irreconcilable enemy*
    Friedrich wacht auf — Galerie des Schlosses — Schlucht
— Offizier — Geländer — Friedrich redet Offizier an —
keine Antwort — spricht weiter — Offizier springt auf —
packt Friedrich bei der Brust — will ihn in die Tiefe stürzen
— Kampf — Friedrich schwach von vielem Blutverlust —
Gefahr — Schuß — Offizier getroffen — stürzt in die Tiefe
hinunter — Stille.

43. (S. 223) *The three dollars*
    Mark Twain — Restaurant — Speisekarte — Hund —
geht mit — Offizier will Hund kaufen — drei Dollar — geht
ins Restaurant — aufgeregter Herr — pfeift, ruft, sucht —
Mark Twain will ihm Hund für drei Dollar bringen — geht
ins Restaurant — bekommt Hund wieder — drei Dollar —
Gewissen (=*conscience*) beruhigt.

44. (S. 224) *A strange incident*
    Maler — sonderbarer Klang — vom Schloßflügel? —
Orgel? — steht auf — Schlafrock — sich an der Wand
forttastend — findet Gärtner und Henni — Licht — Gärtner
erstaunt — hat nichts gehört — nur Wind — Maler entfernt
sich — beruhigt? — Musik — Fall — Schrei.

45. (S. 226) *The faithful dog*
    Abdias — reitet nach Hause — Hund benimmt sich son-
derbar — Hundswut in der Gegend — toll? — aufgeregter —
Abdias erschießt Hund — vermißt nachher Geldsack — erkennt Irrtum — reitet zurück — Blutspur — Geldsack —
sterbender Hund — Abdias untersucht Wunde — zu spät.

46. (S. 227) *The secret button*

Vittoria schreibt — sonderbares Geräusch — Fenster — Wand — das Atmen eines Schlafenden — Vittoria tastet an der Wand hin und her — Knöpfchen — Druck — Wand öffnet sich — schmales Zimmer — Vittoria zögert — geht hinein — erkennt Bruder.

47. (S. 288) *An ugly situation*

Regen — Kaffeehaus — Spiel — Spanier — Wechsel des Glücks — Bank in Gefahr — Venezianer — Beleidigung — Prinz verliert Geduld — Haus kommt in Bewegung — ,, Nehmen Sie sich in acht, Prinz! " — Stille — Gemurmel — Italiener verlassen den Saal — Warnung der Franzosen — Venezianer ist reich und mächtig.

48. (S. 230) *The second brew*

Bäder von Lucca — ich lobe Hauswirt wegen seines guten Tees — Lady Woolen erstaunt — findet seinen Tee schlecht — läßt ihren Tee aus Livorno kommen — ,, der meinige ist viel besser " — lade Damen zum Tee ein — Tee kommt nicht — wir warten — Hauswirt tritt verlegen ein — schlägt Limonade vor — alle wollen Tee — kein Tee da — Erklärung des Hauswirts.

49. (S. 231) *The wager*

Herr läßt nicht mit sich spaßen — Wette: Wilhelm will ihn bei der Nase packen; er wird ihm dafür danken — Freunde gehen Wette ein — starker Bart des Herrn — Kellner meldet Wilhelm als Barbier — Freunde können vom Hof hereinschauen — Wilhelm seift Bart ein — Oberlippe — biegt Nase herüber und hinüber — Vergnügen der Freunde — Herr dankt Wilhelm — gibt ihm eine Mark — Rat des Herrn.

50. (S. 233) *The flood*

Gegen Morgen — Vater wacht auf — jemand bewegt sich — eilt hinauf — Wilhelm — Kasten — Gold und Silber — warum? — Damm ist gerissen — Wilhelm trägt Last hinunter — ruft Mutter und Schwester — Vater folgt — man nimmt alles mögliche mit — Fritz trägt Frauen ins Boot — Vater folgt — Wasser steigt — Boot hebt sich — Wilhelm lenkt es — sie verlassen Garten.

SECTION VI

GERMAN VERSE FOR TRANSLATION
OR FOR EXERCISES IN COMPREHENSION

CHRISTIAN FÜRCHTEGOTT GELLERT (1715–1769)

1. The duckling

Die Henne führt die junge Schar,
worunter auch ein Entchen war,
das sie zugleich mit ausgebrütet.
Die Brut soll in den Garten gehn;
5 die Alte gibt's durch Locken[1] zu verstehn
und jedes folgt, sobald sie nur gebietet,
denn sie gebot mit Zärtlichkeit.

Die Ente wackelt mit, allein nicht gar zu weit;
sie sieht den Teich, den sie noch nicht gesehen,
10 sie läuft hinein, sie badet sich.
Wie, kleines Tier, du schwimmst? Wer lehrt es dich?
Wer hieß[2] dich in das Wasser gehen?
Wirst du so jung das Schwimmen schon verstehen?

Die Henne läuft mit struppigem Gefieder
15 das Ufer zehnmal auf und nieder
und will ihr Kind aus der Gefahr befrein.
Setzt zehnmal an[3] und fliegt doch nicht hinein,
denn die Natur heißt sie das Wasser scheun.
Doch nichts erschreckt den Mut der Ente;
20 sie schwimmt beherzt[4] in ihrem Elemente
und fragt die Henne ganz erfreut,
warum sie denn so ängstlich schreit.

1. Woraus bestand die junge Schar, die die Henne führte?
2. Wie war die Ente in die junge Schar gekommen?

[1] Das Locken: *enticement.*
[2] Heißen: befehlen.
[3] Ansetzen: *take a short run (before jumping), run up.*
[4] Beherzt: mutig.

239

3. Wohin wollte die Alte ihre Brut locken?
4. Weshalb folgten die jungen Hühner der Alten gern?
5. Warum wollte die Ente nicht auch in den Garten gehen?
6. Was können Enten tun, wenn sie zum ersten Mal ins Wasser gehen?
7. Wann hat eine Henne struppiges Gefieder?
8. Weshalb lief sie am Ufer auf und nieder?
9. Warum flog die Henne doch nicht ins Wasser?
10. Woran kann man erkennen, daß die Ente mutig war?

MATTHIAS CLAUDIUS (1740–1815)

2. The negro in the sugar-plantation

Weit von meinem Vaterlande
    Muß ich hier verschmachten[1] und vergehn,
Ohne Trost, in Müh und Schande;
    Ohhh die weißen Männer!! klug und schön!

5 Und ich hab den Männern ohn Erbarmen
    Nichts getan.
Du im Himmel! hilf mir armen
    Schwarzen Mann!

3. Lullaby

Schlaf, süßer Knabe, süß und mild!
    Du, deines Vaters Ebenbild!
Das bist du; zwar dein Vater spricht,
    Du habest seine Nase nicht.

5 Nur eben itzo[2] war er hier
    Und sah dir ins Gesicht
Und sprach: Viel hat er zwar von mir
    Doch meine Nase nicht.

---

[1] Verschmachten: *languish.*
[2] Itzo: jetzt.

Mich dünkt[1] es selbst, sie ist zu klein,
10   Doch muß es seine Nase sein;
Denn wenns nicht seine Nase wär,
Wo hättst du denn die Nase her?

Schlaf, Knabe, was dein Vater spricht,
Spricht er wohl im Scherz;
15 Hab immer seine Nase nicht,
Und habe nur sein Herz!

JOHANN WOLFGANG VON GOETHE (1749–1832)

4.   Elves' song

Um Mitternacht, wenn die Menschen erst schlafen,
Dann scheinet uns der Mond,
Dann leuchtet uns der Stern;
Wir wandeln und singen
5   Und tanzen erst gern.

Um Mitternacht, wenn die Menschen erst schlafen,
Auf Wiesen an den Erlen[2]
Wir suchen unsern Raum
Und wandeln und singen
10 Und tanzen einen Traum.

5.   The King of Thule

Es war ein König in Thule
Gar treu bis an das Grab,
Dem sterbend seine Buhle[3]
Einen goldnen Becher gab.

---

[1] Mich dünkt: mir scheint.
[2] Die Erle: alder.
[3] Die Buhle: die Geliebte.

5　Es ging ihm nichts darüber,
　Er leert' ihn jeden Schmaus[1];
　Die Augen gingen ihm über,
　So oft er trank daraus.

　Und als er kam zu sterben,
10 Zählt' er seine Städt' im Reich.
　Gönnt' alles seinen Erben,
　Den Becher nicht zugleich.

　Er saß beim Königsmahle,
　Die Ritter um ihn her,
15 Auf hohem Vätersaale,
　Dort auf dem Schloß am Meer.

　Dort stand der alte Zecher[2],
　Trank letzte Lebensglut,
　Und warf den heil'gen Becher
20 Hinunter in die Flut.

　Er sah ihn stürzen, trinken
　Und sinken tief ins Meer.
　Die Augen täten ihm sinken[3],
　Trank nie einen Tropfen mehr.

1. Was hatte dem König seine Geliebte gegeben?
2. Wann hatte sie es ihm gegeben?
3. Was hielt er davon?
4. Wozu diente der Becher?
5. Warum gingen ihm die Augen über?
6. Was hinterließ er seinen Erben?
7. Warum sollte niemand den Becher bekommen?
8. Wo aß der König zum letzten Male?
9. Warum trank er keinen Tropfen mehr?
10. Was beweist, daß der König treu bis an das Grab war?

[1] Der Schmaus: das Bankett.
[2] Der Zecher: der Trinker.
[3] Täten . . . sinken: sanken.

ADALBERT VON CHAMISSO (1781–1838)

6. The orphan

Sie haben mich geheißen
  Nach Heidelbeeren[1] gehn:
Ich habe nach den Beeren
  Im Walde nicht gesehn.

5 Ich bin hinausgegangen
  Zu meiner Mutter Grab,
Worauf ich mich gesetzet
  Und viel geweinet hab'.—

„Wer sitzt auf meinem Hügel,
10 Von der die Tränen sind?"—
„Ich bin's, o liebe Mutter,
  Ich, dein verwaistes Kind.

Wer wird hinfort[2] mich kleiden
  Und flechten mir das Haar?
15 Mit Liebeswort mir schmeicheln,
  Wie's deine Weise war?"—

„Geh hin, o liebe Tochter,
  Und finde dich darein[3],
Es wird dir eine zweite,
20 Statt meiner, Mutter sein.

Sie wird das Haar dir flechten
  Und kleiden dich hinfort,
Ein Jüngling wird dir schmeicheln
  Mit zartem Liebeswort."

1. Was hatte man der Waise befohlen?
2. Was war vor kurzer Zeit geschehen?

---

[1] Die Heidelbeere: *bilberry.*
[2] Hinfort: *in Zukunft.*
[3] Sich finden in: *resign oneself to.*

3. Woraus kann man schließen, daß die Waise traurig war?
4. Wo war das Kind?
5. Wodurch wurde die Mutter in ihrem Grab geweckt?
6. Woher wissen Sie, daß die Waise ein Mädchen war?
7. Woher wissen Sie, daß die Mutter das Kind liebte?
8. Was sollte die Waise in Zukunft tun?
9. Was würde das Kind nach der Meinung der Mutter finden?
10. Was ist ein Jüngling?

LUDWIG UHLAND (1787–1862)

7. *The boy's song of the mountain*

Ich bin vom Berg der Hirtenknab',
Seh' auf die Schlösser all herab;
Die Sonne strahlt am ersten hier,
Am längsten weilet[1] sie bei mir;
5 Ich bin der Knab' vom Berge!

Hier ist des Stromes Mutterhaus;
Ich trink' ihn frisch vom Stein heraus;
Er braust vom Fels in wildem Lauf,
Ich fang' ihn mit den Armen auf;
10 Ich bin der Knab' vom Berge!

Der Berg, der ist mein Eigentum,
Da ziehn die Stürme rings herum;
Und heulen sie von Nord und Süd,
So überschallt sie doch mein Lied:
15 Ich bin der Knab' vom Berge!

Sind Blitz und Donner unter mir,
So steh' ich hoch im Blauen hier;
Ich kenne sie und rufe zu:
Laßt meines Vaters Haus in Ruh!
20 Ich bin der Knab' vom Berge!

[1] Weilen: bleiben.

Und wann[1] die Sturmglock'[2] einst erschallt,
Manch Feuer auf den Bergen wallt[3],
Dann steig' ich nieder, tret' ins Glied[4],
Und schwing' mein Schwert, und sing' mein Lied:
25 Ich bin der Knab' vom Berge!

1. Wo hielt sich der Hirtenknabe auf?
2. Warum scheint die Sonne länger auf den Bergen?
3. Was ist das Mutterhaus eines Stromes?
4. Woher wissen Sie, daß der Knabe das Wasser liebte?
5. Was tat der Hirtenknabe, wenn der Sturm heulte?
6. Was konnte man manchmal unten sehen?
7. Warum hatte er keine Angst davor?
8. Wo wohnte der Vater des Knaben?
9. Wofür sind Sturmglocke und Feuer Zeichen?
10. Woran kann man seinen Mut erkennen?

8.   Captive's song

Wie lieblicher Klang!
O, Lerche! dein Sang,
Er hebt sich, er schwingt sich in Wonne[5].
Du nimmst mich von hier,
5 Ich singe mit dir,
Wir steigen durch Wolken zur Sonne.

O Lerche! du neigst
Dich nieder, du schweigst,
Du sinkst in die blühenden Auen[6].
10 Ich schweige zumal[7]
Und sinke zutal,
Ach! tief in Moder[8] und Grauen.

---

[1] Wann: wenn.   [2] Die Sturmglocke: *alarm bell.*
[3] Wallen: *swirl and billow.*   [4] Ins Glied treten: *join the ranks.*
[5] Die Wonne: tiefe Freude.   [6] Die Au(e): *water-mead.*
[7] Zumal: zugleich.   [8] Der Moder: *decay.*

9.   The crossing

Über diesen Strom, vor Jahren,
Bin ich einmal schon gefahren.
Hier die Burg im Abendschimmer,
Drüben rauscht das Wehr, wie immer.

5 Und von diesem Kahn umschlossen
Waren mit mir zween[1] Genossen:
Ach! ein Freund, ein vatergleicher,
Und ein junger, hoffnungsreicher.

Jener wirkte still hienieden[2]
10 Und so ist er auch geschieden,
Dieser, brausend vor uns allen,
Ist im Kampf und Sturm gefallen.

So, wenn ich vergangner Tage,
Glücklicher[3], zu denken wage,
15 Muß ich stets Genossen missen,
Teure, die der Tod entrissen[4].

Doch was alle Freundschaft bindet,
Ist, wenn Geist zu Geist sich findet;
Geistig waren jene Stunden,
20 Geistern bin ich noch verbunden.

Nimm nur, Fährmann, nimm die Miete,
Die ich gerne dreifach biete!
Zween, die mit mir überfuhren,
Waren geistige Naturen.

1. Was hatte sich seit der letzten Überfahrt nicht geändert?
2. Was konnte der Erzähler hören?
3. Wie viele Personen waren damals im Kahn?
4. Woher wissen Sie, daß sie nicht gleichaltrig waren?
5. Wie unterschieden sich die beiden Freunde?
6. Warum waren seine Freunde jetzt nicht hier?

---

[1] Zween: zwei.
[2] Hienieden: hier auf der Erde.
[3] Vergangner Tage, Glücklicher: vergangener, glücklicher Tage.
[4] Entrissen: entrissen hat.

7. Woraus schließen Sie, daß die drei Freunde sich gut verstanden?
8. Was für Gespräche hatten sie geführt?
9. Was bot der Erzähler dem Fährmann an?
10. Wie viele Personen hatte der Fährmann diesmal in der Tat
    übergesetzt?

10. The sword

Zur Schmiede ging ein junger Held,
Er hatt' ein gutes Schwert bestellt.
Doch als er's wog in freier Hand,
Das Schwert er viel zu schwer erfand[1].

5 Der alte Schmied den Bart sich streicht:
,, Das Schwert ist nicht zu schwer noch leicht,
Zu schwach ist euer Arm, ich mein',
Doch morgen soll geholfen sein."

,, Nein, heut! bei aller Ritterschaft!
10 Durch meine, nicht durch Feuers Kraft."
Der Jüngling spricht's, ihn Kraft durchdringt,
Das Schwert er hoch in Lüften schwingt.

11. Spanish legend

Mohrenkönigs Kind, Casilde,
    Eilte furchtsam übern Hof,
    Trug zu den gefangnen Christen
    In dem Korbe Wein und Brot.
5 Aldemon, der Mohrenkönig,
    Saß an des Palastes Tor:
    ,, Halt, mein Kind! wohin so eilig
    Mit dem wohlverdeckten Korb?
Bringst du noch den Christenhunden
10 Jeden Abend Wein und Brot,
    Nicht gedenkend, daß dein Vater
    Drauf gesetzt den bittern Tod? "

[1] Erfand: fand.

Und erblassend sprach Casilde:
„Ach! es ist nicht Wein und Brot,
15   Rosen sind es, frisch gepflücket,
Draus ein Kranz mir werden soll."
„Sind es Rosen, frisch gepflücket;—
Sprach der König Aldemon—
Laß die Rosen mich enthüllen,
20   Deren Duft mich laben[1] soll!"
Und der König zieht die Decke
Von der bangen Jungfrau Korb,
Der von Rosen überwallet[2],
Frischen Rosen, weiß und rot.

1. Wer war Casilde?
2. Wovor hatte sie Furcht?
3. Wohin hatte sie Wein und Brot gelegt?
4. Warum konnte man den Wein und das Brot nicht sehen?
5. Woher wissen Sie, daß der Vater die Christen haßte?
6. Woran können Sie erkennen, daß Casilde erschrak?
7. Wie versuchte Casilde sich zu retten?
8. Was wollte sie mit den Rosen machen?
9. Woher wissen Sie, daß Aldemon seiner Tochter nicht glaubte?
10. Was war geschehen?

12.   The sunken crown

Da droben auf dem Hügel,
Da steht ein kleines Haus,
Man sieht von seiner Schwelle
Ins schöne Land hinaus;
5   Dort sitzt ein freier Bauer
Am Abend auf der Bank,
Er dengelt[3] seine Sense
Und singt dem Himmel Dank.

[1] Laben: erfrischen.
[2] Überwallet: überfließt.
[3] Dengelt: schärft.

Da drunten in dem Grunde,
10 Da dämmert längst der Teich,
Es liegt in ihm versunken
Eine Krone, stolz und reich,
Sie läßt zunacht[1] wohl spielen
Karfunkel[2] und Saphir;
15 Sie liegt seit grauen Jahren,
Und niemand sucht nach ihr.

1. Was für ein Mann wohnte in dem kleinen Haus?
2. Warum konnte man von dem Haus weit ins Land sehen?
3. Was kann man mit einer Sense schneiden?
4. Warum mußte der Bauer die Sense dengeln?
5. Wo hatte er sich hingesetzt?
6. Wie kann man die Worte „ in dem Grunde " anders ausdrücken?
7. Was ist ein Teich?
8. Weshalb konnte man den Teich nicht mehr deutlich sehen?
9. Wie war die Krone in den Teich gekommen?
10. Woher wissen Sie, daß die Krone vergessen war?

JOSEPH VON EICHENDORFF (1788–1857)

13. The child's grave

Dort ist so tiefer Schatten,
Du schläfst in guter Ruh,
Es deckt mit grünen Matten[3]
Der liebe Gott dich zu.

5 Die alten Weiden neigen
Sich auf dein Bett herein,
Die Vöglein in den Zweigen,
Sie singen treu dich ein.

---

[1] Zunacht: nachts.
[2] Der Karfunkel: *carbuncle.*
[3] Die Matte: das Gras.

Und wie in goldnen Träumen
10 Geht linder Frühlingswind
Rings in den stillen Bäumen—
Schlaf wohl, mein süßes Kind!

14. Old age

Hoch mit den Wolken geht der Vögel Reise,
Die Erde schläfert[1], kaum noch Astern prangen,
Verstummt[2] die Lieder, die so fröhlich klangen,
Und trüber Winter deckt die weiten Kreise.

5 Die Wanduhr pickt, im Zimmer singet leise
Waldvöglein noch, so[3] du im Herbst gefangen[4].
Ein Bilderbuch scheint alles, was vergangen[5],
Du blätterst drin, geschützt vor Sturm und Eise.

So mild ist oft das Alter mir erschienen:
10 Wart' nur, bald taut es von den Dächern nieder
Und über Nacht hat sich die Luft[6] gewendet.
Ans Fenster klopft ein Bot' mit frohen Mienen,
Du trittst erstaunt heraus—und kehrst nicht wieder,
Denn endlich kommt der Lenz[7], der nimmer endet.

1. Warum reisen Vögel und wann?
2. Womit vergleicht der Dichter die Erde?
3. Wessen fröhliche Lieder sind verstummt?
4. Warum sang der Waldvogel wohl leise?
5. Warum nennt der Dichter das vergangene Leben ein Bilderbuch?

---

[1] Die Erde schläfert: die Erde will schlafen.
[2] Verstummt: verstummt sind.
[3] So: das.
[4] Gefangen: gefangen hast.
[5] Ein Bilderbuch scheint alles, was vergangen: alles, was vergangen ist,
   scheint ein Bilderbuch zu sein.
[6] Die Luft: der Wind.
[7] Der Lenz: der Frühling.

6. Wie ist das Wetter draußen?
7. Was würde über Nacht kommen?
8. Wer ist der Bote, der ans Fenster klopfen wird?
9. Warum würde der Dichter diesmal nicht zurückkommen?
10. Welche Jahreszeit scheint dem Dichter am besten zu
     gefallen?

15. Wayfarer's song

So ruhig geh' ich meinen Pfad,
So still ist mir zumut,
Es dünkt[1] mir jeder Weg gerad
Und jedes Wetter gut.

5 Wohin mein Weg mich führen mag,
Der Himmel ist mein Dach,
Die Sonne kommt mit jedem Tag,
Die Sterne halten Wach'.

Und komm' ich spät und komm' ich früh
10 Ans Ziel, das mir gestellt[2]:
Verlieren kann ich mich doch nie,
O Gott, aus deiner Welt!

16. The treasure-seeker

Wenn alle Wälder schliefen,
Er an zu graben hub[3],
Rastlos in Berges Tiefen
Nach einem Schatz er grub.

5 Die Engel Gottes sangen
Derweil[4] in stiller Nacht,
Wie rote Augen drangen
Metalle aus dem Schacht.

[1] Es dünkt mir: es scheint mir.
[2] Gestellt: gestellt ist.
[3] An . . . hub: begann.
[4] Derweil: unterdessen.

,, Und wirst doch mein!'' und grimmer
10 Wühlt er und wühlt hinab,
Da stürzen Steine und Trümmer
Über dem Narren herab.

Hohnlachen wild erschallte
Aus der verfallnen Kluft,
15 Der Engelgesang verhallte
Wehmütig in der Luft.

1. Zu welcher Tageszeit fing er an zu arbeiten?
2. Wie zeigte er seine Ungeduld?
3. Wonach gräbt man gewöhnlich?
4. Was wollten die Engel mit ihrem Singen?
5. Weshalb nahm der Gräber von ihnen keine Notiz?
6. Woher wußte er, daß Metalle im Schacht waren?
7. Woher wissen Sie, daß der Gräber unvorsichtig war?
8. Woher wissen Sie, daß jemand sich über den Tod des
Schatzgräbers freute?
9. Warum hörten die Engel auf zu singen?
10. Warum waren sie traurig?

17.   An old man's thoughts

Wie wird nun alles so stille wieder!
So war mir's oft in der Kinderzeit,
Die Bäche gehen rauschend nieder
Durch die dämmernde Einsamkeit,
5 Kaum noch hört man einen Hirten singen,
Aus allen Dörfern, Schluchten, weit
Die Abendglocken herüberklingen,
Versunken nun mit Lust und Leid
Die Täler, die noch einmal blitzen,
10 Nur hinter dem stillen Walde weit
Noch Abendröte an den Bergesspitzen,
Wie Morgenrot der Ewigkeit.

18. The mariner

Früh am Sankt Johannestag
Fiel ein Seemann in das Wasser.
—Was erhalt' ich, Schifferlein,
Wenn ich rette dich zum Strande?—
5 Geb' dir alle meine Schiffe
Samt der Gold- und Silberladung.
—Nicht nach allen deinen Schiffen,
Deinem Gold und Silber frag' ich,
Deine Seele, wenn du stirbst,
10 Will ich nur zum Lohne haben.—
Meine Seel' empfange Gott,
Und den Leib das salz'ge Wasser!

FRANZ GRILLPARZER (1791–1872)

19. The dancer

Ein Tänzer, hochberühmt in seinem Fach,
Ließ einst in einer Stadt sein Bestes sehen,
Er zog die Augen aller Kenner nach,
Wie[1] er erschien, stand alles auf den Zehen.
5 Ein Botengänger, drauß[2] vom Dorf herein,
Wollt' auch ein Zeuge so viel Wunders sein.
Er tritt ins Haus[3] und steht und staunt und schaut,
Zuletzt ruft er voll innern Grimmes laut:
O Unsinn, unerhört in diesen Landen[4]!
10 Da keucht und schwitzt der Tor die halbe Nacht
Und steht zuletzt am Fleck, wo er zuerst gestanden[5]:
Ich hätt' indes zwei Meilen wohl gemacht!
Der Künstler hört's, und mild, nach edlem Brauch,
Spricht er: Du hast wohl recht, allein ich auch;
15 Ein kleiner Unterschied macht hier das Ganze[6]:
Du gehst, mein Lieber, und ich tanze!

[1] Wie: sobald.
[2] Drauß: draußen.
[3] Das Haus: das Theater.
[4] In diesen Landen: *in these parts.*
[5] Gestanden: gestanden hat.
[6] Das Ganze: den ganzen Unterschied.

1. Woher wissen Sie, daß der Tänzer zu den besten gehörte?
2. Warum zog er die Augen aller Kenner nach?
3. Warum stand alles auf den Zehen?
4. Warum hatte der Botengänger heute sein Dorf verlassen?
5. Woher wissen Sie, daß der Botengänger etwas sah, was er nicht erwartet hatte?
6. Warum war er ärgerlich?
7. Was glaubte er besser machen zu können?
8. Woher wissen Sie, daß der Künstler nicht böse war?
9. Wer von den beiden war im Recht?
10. Was war der Unterschied zwischen beiden?

HEINRICH HEINE (1797–1856)

20. *The young herdsman*

König ist der Hirtenknabe,
Grüner Hügel ist sein Thron;
Über seinem Haupt die Sonne
Ist die große, goldne Kron[1].

5 Ihm zu Füßen liegen Schafe,
Weiche Schmeichler, rotbekreuzt;
Kavaliere sind die Kälber,
Und sie wandeln stolzgespreizt;

Hofschauspieler sind die Böcklein;
10 Und die Vögel und die Küh[2],
Mit den Flöten, mit den Glöcklein,
Sind die Kammermusizi[3].

Und das klingt und singt so lieblich,
Und so lieblich rauschen drein
15 Wasserfall und Tannenbäume,
Und der König schlummert ein.

[1] Die Kron: die Krone.
[2] Die Küh: die Kühe.
[3] Die Kammermusizi: die Kammermusiker.

Unterdessen muß regieren
Der Minister, jener Hund,
Dessen knurriges Gebelle
20 Widerhallet in der Rund[1].

Schläfrig lallt[2] der junge König:
„ Das Regieren ist so schwer;
Ach, ich wollt, daß ich zu Hause
Schon bei meiner Köngin[3] wär!

25 „ In den Armen meiner Köngin
Ruht mein Königshaupt so weich,
Und in ihren schönen Augen
Liegt mein unermeßlich[4] Reich! "

1. Wo saß der Hirtenknabe?
2. Mit wem wird der Hirtenknabe verglichen?
3. Warum hatten die Schafe rote Kreuze?
4. Was macht ein Hofschauspieler?
5. Auf welchem Instrument spielten die Vögel?
6. Wodurch wurde der König in den Schlummer gewiegt?
7. Wie verhinderte der Hund, daß die Schafe fortliefen?
8. Was mußte der Hund übernehmen, während der König
   schlief?
9. Warum wollte der Hirtenknabe zu Hause sein?
10. Wer wartete auf ihn zu Hause?

21. Calm at sea

Meeresstille! Ihre Strahlen
Wirft die Sonne auf das Wasser,
Und im wogenden Geschmeide[5]
Zieht das Schiff die grünen Furchen.

[1] Die Rund: die Runde.
[2] Lallt: spricht undeutlich.
[3] Die Köngin: die Königin.
[4] Unermeßlich: unermeßliches.
[5] Das Geschmeide: die Juwelen.

5 Bei dem Steuer liegt der Bootsmann
Auf dem Bauch, und schnarchet leise.
Bei dem Mastbaum, segelflickend,
Kauert der beteerte Schiffsjung.

Hinterm Schmutze seiner Wangen
10 Sprüht es rot, wehmütig zuckt es
Um das breite Maul, und schmerzlich
Schaun die großen, schönen Augen.

Denn der Kapitän steht vor ihm,
Tobt und flucht und schilt ihn: Spitzbub.
15 „ Spitzbub! einen Hering hast du
Aus der Tonne mir gestohlen! "

Meeresstille! Aus den Wellen
Taucht hervor ein kluges Fischlein,
Wärmt das Köpfchen in der Sonne,
20 Plätschert lustig mit dem Schwänzchen.

Doch die Möwe, aus den Lüften,
Schießt herunter auf das Fischlein,
Und den raschen Raub im Schnabel,
Schwingt sie sich hinauf ins Blaue.

1. Was für Wetter war es?
2. Warum vergleicht der Dichter das Meer mit einem Geschmeide?
3. Woher wissen Sie, daß der Bootsmann schlief?
4. Warum flickte der Schiffsjunge das Segel?
5. Woher wissen Sie, daß er sich nicht gewaschen hatte?
6. Woran kann man erkennen, daß er bald in Tränen ausbrechen wird?
7. Warum fluchte der Kapitän?
8. Was ist ein Spitzbub?
9. Warum tauchte das Fischlein aus den Wellen hervor?
10. Was wollte die Möwe mit dem Fischlein tun?

22. *King Richard*

Wohl durch der Wälder einödige Pracht
Jagt ungestüm ein Reiter;
Er bläst ins Horn, er singt und lacht
Gar[1] seelenvergnügt und heiter.

5 Sein Harnisch ist von starkem Erz,
Noch stärker ist sein Gemüte,
Das ist Herr Richard Löwenherz,
Der christlichen Ritterschaft Blüte.

Willkommen in England! rufen ihm zu
10 Die Bäume mit grünen Zungen—
Wir freuen uns, o König, daß du
Östreichischer[2] Haft entsprungen[3].

Dem König ist wohl in der freien Luft,
Er fühlt sich wie neugeboren,
15 Er denkt an Östreichs[4] Festungsduft—
Und gibt seinem Pferde die Sporen.

1. Warum spricht der Dichter von der „ einödigen Pracht"
der Wälder?
2. Zu welcher Jahreszeit ritt der König durch die Wälder?
3. Auf welche Weise ritt der König?
4. Wie zeigte er, daß er seelenvergnügt war?
5. Woran konnte man erkennen, daß er ein Ritter war?
6. In welches Land war er zurückgekommen?
7. Warum war er lange nicht da gewesen?
8. Was sind die „ grünen Zungen" der Bäume?
9. Warum fühlte sich der König wie neugeboren?
10. Was geschieht, wenn ein Reiter dem Pferde die Sporen
gibt?

[1] Gar: sehr.
[2] Östreichischer: österreichischer.
[3] Entsprungen: entsprungen bist.
[4] Östreichs: Österreichs.

23. The light fails

Der Vorhang fällt, das Stück ist aus,
Und Herrn und Damen gehn nach Haus.
Ob ihnen auch das Stück gefallen[1]?
Ich glaub, ich hörte Beifall schallen.
5 Ein hochverehrtes Publikum
Beklatschte dankbar seinen Dichter.
Jetzt aber ist das Haus so stumm,
Und sind verschwunden Lust und Lichter.

Doch horch! ein schollernd[2] schnöder[3] Klang
10 Ertönt unfern der öden Bühne;—
Vielleicht daß eine Saite sprang
An einer alten Violine.
Verdrießlich rascheln im Parterr[4]
Etwelche[5] Ratten hin und her,
15 Und Alles riecht nach ranzgem[6] Öle.
Die letzte Lampe ächzt und zischt
Verzweiflungsvoll, und sie erlischt.
Das arme Licht war meine Seele.

1. Wo fällt der Vorhang und wann?
2. Wie zeigt man, daß ein Stück gefallen hat?
3. Woher wissen Sie, daß der Dichter nicht sicher ist, ob das Stück gefiel?
4. Warum war das Haus so stumm?
5. Wodurch wurde die Stille unterbrochen?
6. Warum nennt der Dichter die Bühne öde?
7. Was machte die Ratten verdrießlich?
8. Was zeigt, daß dies kein modernes Theater war?
9. Wann ächzt und zischt eine Lampe?
10. Warum vergleicht der Dichter seine Seele mit der letzten Lampe?

[1] Gefallen: gefallen hat.
[2] Schollernd: *vibrating.*
[3] Schnöder: *hateful.*
[4] Das Parterr: das Parterre.
[5] Etwelche: irgendwelche.
[6] Ranzgem: ranzigem.

24. *The saviour*

Frohlockst, Plantagenet, und glaubst,
Daß du die letzte Hoffnung uns raubst,
Weil deine Knechte ein Grabmal fanden,
Worauf der Name „ Arthur " gestanden[1].

5 Arthur ist nicht gestorben, es barg[2]
Nicht seinen Leichnam der steinerne Sarg.
Ich selber sah ihn vor wenig Tagen
Lebendigen Leibes im Walde jagen.

Er trug ein Kleid von grünem Samt,
10 Die Lippe lacht', das Auge flammt'.
Er kam mit seinen Jagdgenossen
Einhergeritten[3] auf stolzen Rossen.

Wie allgewaltig sein Hifthorn schallt
Trara—trara—durch Tal und Wald!
15 Die Zauberklänge, die Wundertöne,
Sie sind verständlich für Cornwalls Söhne.

Sie melden: die Zeit ist noch nicht da,
Doch kommt sie bald—Trara—trara!
Und König Arthur mit seinen Getreuen
20 Wird von den Normannen das Land befreien.

1. Warum frohlockte Plantagenet?
2. Was hatte ihn zu diesem Glauben geführt?
3. Worauf hatte man gehofft?
4. Warum hatte Plantagenet zu früh frohlockt?
5. Was war in dem steinernen Sarge?
6. Was hatte Arthur vor einigen Tagen getan?
7. Woran kann man erkennen, daß Arthur große Freude an der Jagd hatte?
8. Wie gab er seinen Getreuen zu verstehen, daß sie hoffen durften?
9. Warum mußten Cornwalls Söhne noch geduldig sein?

[1] Gestanden: gestanden hat.
[2] Barg: enthielt.
[3] Einhergeritten: den Weg entlanggeritten.

25. Warning

Unsterbliche Seele, nimm dich in Acht,
Daß du nicht Schaden leidest,
Wenn du aus dem Irdischen scheidest;
Es geht der Weg durch Tod und Nacht.

5 Am goldnen Tore der Hauptstadt des Lichts,
Da stehen die Gottessoldaten;
Sie fragen nach Werken und Taten,
Nach Namen und Amt fragt man hier nichts.

Am Eingang läßt der Pilger zurück
10 Die stäubigen[1], drückenden Schuhe—
Kehr ein, hier findest du Ruhe,
Und weiche Pantoffeln und schöne Musik.

EDUARD MÖRIKE (1804–1875)

26. The landlord's lament

Da droben auf dem Markte
Spazier' ich auf und ab,
Den ganzen lieben langen Tag,
Und schaue die Straße hinab.

5 Es steht ein Regenbogen
Wohl über jenem Haus,
Mein Schild[2] ist eingezogen,
Ein andrer hängt heraus.

Heraus hängt über der Türe
10 Ein Hahn mit rotem Kamm;
Als ich die Wirtschaft führte,
Da war es ein goldenes Lamm.

Mein Schäflein wohl zu scheren[3],
Ich sparte keine Müh',
15 Ich bin heruntergekommen
Und weiß doch selber nicht wie.

[1] Stäubig: staubig.
[2] Der Schild: hier = das Schild.
[3] Sein Schäflein scheren: reich werden.

Nun läuft es mit Köchen und Kellnern
Im ganzen Hause so voll,
Ich weiß nicht, wem ich von allen
20 Zuerst den Hals brechen soll.

Da kommen drei Chaisen[1] gefahren!
Der Hausknecht springt in die Höh',
Vorüber, ihr Rößlein, vorüber,
Dem Lammwirt ist gar so weh!

1. Woran erkennen Sie, daß der Lammwirt viel Zeit hatte?
2. Warum sah er die Straße hinab?
3. Wann sieht man einen Regenbogen?
4. Warum war sein Schild eingezogen worden?
5. Wie hatte er reich werden wollen?
6. Woran erkennt man, daß er kein guter Wirt gewesen war?
7. Wie hatte sich das Leben im Wirtshaus geändert?
8. Was für ein Gefühl erweckte diese Änderung in dem alten Wirt?
9. Was muß ein Hausknecht tun, wenn Chaisen gefahren kommen?
10. Worüber klagte der Lammwirt?

FRIEDRICH HEBBEL (1813–1863)

27. *The young sailor*

Dort bläht ein Schiff die Segel,
    Frisch saust hinein der Wind;
Der Anker wird gelichtet,
Das Steuer flugs[2] gerichtet,
5   Nun fliegt's hinaus geschwind.

---

[1] Die Chaise: halboffener Wagen. (Dasselbe Wort auf englisch.)
[2] Flugs: schnell.

Ein kühner Wasservogel
   Kreist grüßend um den Mast,
Die Sonne brennt herunter,
Manch Fischlein, blank und munter,
10   Umgaukelt[1] keck den Gast.

Wär' gern hineingesprungen,
   Da draußen ist mein Reich!
Ich bin ja jung von Jahren,
Da ist's mir nur ums Fahren[2],
15   Wohin?   Das gilt mir gleich[3]!

28. *Two travellers*

Ein Stummer zieht durch die Lande[4],
   Gott hat ihm ein Wort vertraut,
Das kann er nicht ergründen
Nur einem darf er's verkünden,
5   Den er noch nie geschaut[5].

Ein Tauber zieht durch die Lande,
   Gott selber hieß ihn gehn,
Dem hat er das Ohr verriegelt,
Und jenem die Lippe versiegelt,
10   Bis sie einander sehn.

Dann wird der Stumme reden,
   Der Taube vernimmt das Wort,
Er wird sie gleich entziffern,
Die dunkeln göttlichen Chiffern[6],
15   Dann ziehn sie gen[7] Morgen fort.

[1] Umgaukelt: bewegt sich leicht hin und her um ihn herum.
[2] Mir ist nur ums Fahren: ich habe keinen anderen Wunsch als zu fahren.
[3] Das gilt mir gleich: das ist mir ganz einerlei.
[4] Die Lande: die Landschaft.
[5] Geschaut: geschaut hat.
[6] Chiffern: Chiffren.
[7] Gen: gegen.

Daß sich die beiden finden,
Ihr Menschen, betet viel.
Wenn, die[1] jetzt einsam wandern,
Treffen, einer den andern,
20   Ist alle Welt am Ziel.

1. Was ist ein Stummer?
2. Wen mußte der Stumme suchen?
3. Warum mußte er ihn suchen?
4. Was ist ein Tauber?
5. Von wem hatte er den Befehl bekommen?
6. Wer hatte ihn taub gemacht und wie?
7. Warum würden die beiden sprechen und hören können?
8. Nach welcher Richtung gingen die beiden?
9. Wie können die Menschen helfen, daß sich die beiden finden?
10. Schlagen Sie einen anderen Titel für das Gedicht vor.

29. A winter journey

Wie durch so manchen Ort
    Bin ich nun schon gekommen,
Und hab' aus keinem fort
    Ein freundlich Bild genommen[2].

5 Man prüft am fremden Gast
    Den Mantel und den Kragen,
Mit Blicken, welche fast
    Die Liebe untersagen.

Der Gruß trägt so die Spur
10   Gleichgültig-offner Kälte,
Daß ich ihn ungern nur
    Mit meinem Dank vergelte.

---
[1] Die: diejenigen, die.
[2] Fort . . . genommen: fortgenommen.

Und weil sie in der Brust
Mir nicht die Flamme nähren,
15 So muß sie ohne Lust
Sich in sich selbst verzehren.

Da ruf' ich aus mit Schmerz,
Indem ich fürbaß[1] wandre:
Man hat nur dann ein Herz,
20 Wenn man es hat für andre.

1. Woher wissen Sie, daß der Dichter viel gereist ist?
2. Woher wissen Sie, daß er nirgendwo freundlich aufgenommen wurde?
3. Wer war der fremde Gast?
4. Warum prüfte man an ihm Mantel und Kragen?
5. Warum konnte er die Leute nicht lieben?
6. Weshalb erwiderte er ihren Gruß ungern?
7. Womit hätten die Leute die Flamme in seiner Brust nähren können?
8. Was ist das für eine Flamme, die in der Brust des Dichters brannte?
9. Wie war dem Dichter zumute, jedesmal wenn er einen Ort verließ?
10. Was ist nötig, um ein Herz zu haben?

THEODOR FONTANE (1818–1898)

30. Gudbrandsdal

Die Felsen sind steil, die Schlucht ist schmal,
Der Snöhättan[2] blickt auf Gudbrandsdal.

Und weht es im Sommer heiß und schwül,
So halten die Felsen den Talgrund kühl,
5 Und starrt[3] es im Winter hoch oben von Eis,
So sprudeln unten die Quellen heiß,

---

[1] Fürbaß: weiter.
[2] Der Snöhättan: Name eines Berges.
[3] Es starrt von Eis: ist ganz mit Eis bedeckt.

Herbststürme ziehen darüber hin,
Nur Frühling und Friede wohnen darin,
Kein Fieber schleicht, keine Krankheit geht um,
10 „Tal des Lebens" heißt es drum[1].

Und die Menschen im Tal verlassen es nie,
Zu hohen Jahren kommen sie,
Keine Last, keine Sorge beugt ihre Gestalt,
Sie werden weiß, aber sie werden nicht alt.

15 Und drei Lebelang sehen dem Leben sie zu,
Da sind sie müd und verlangen nach Ruh,
Und sie rufen den Tod, der aber spricht:
„ Ihr müßt kommen, ich komme nicht."

Und sie steigen hinauf.   Und zum erstenmal,
20 Um zu sterben, lassen sie Gudbrandsdal.

1. Wo kann man eine Schlucht finden?
2. Warum ist das Wetter in Gudbrandsdal immer angenehm?
3. Was macht das Klima im Winter dort mild?
4. Wovor ist das „Tal des Lebens" geschützt?
5. Warum hat Gudbrandsdal den Namen, „Tal des Lebens" bekommen?
6. Wie kann man anders ausdrücken: „Zu hohen Jahren kommen"?
7. Woran kann man die älteren Leute im Tal erkennen?
8. Wie lange wollen die Leute im Tal gewöhnlich leben?
9. Wie unterscheidet sich ihr Tod von dem gewöhnlicher Menschen?
10. Wo finden die Talbewohner den Tod?

31. Ducks and drakes

Es fliegt ein Stein (die Hand warf ihn gut)
Kräftig, wagrecht[2] über die Flut.

[1] Drum: darum.
[2] Wagrecht: waagerecht.

Eine Säule steigt auf, und der Sonne Schein
Malt einen Regenbogen hinein.

5 Und weiter, ein zweites und drittes Mal,
Erhebt sich der siebenfarbige Strahl.

Aber je weiter vom Ufer entfernt,
Der Stein im Fluge das Fliegen verlernt.

Eine Schwere zieht ihn, es ebbt seine Kraft,
10 Der Strahl ermattet und erschlafft.

Ein Kräuseln noch einmal, ein Tropfen blinkt,
Und dann Ruh und Stille—der Stein versinkt.

32. *What does it matter?*

Heute früh, nach gut durchschlafener Nacht,
Bin ich wieder aufgewacht.
Ich setzte mich an den Frühstückstisch,
Der Kaffee war warm, die Semmel[1] war frisch,
5 Ich habe die Morgenzeitung gelesen,
(Es sind wieder Avancements gewesen).
Ich trat ans Fenster, ich sah hinunter,
Es trabte wieder, es klingelte munter,
Eine Schürze (beim Schlächter) hing über dem Stuhle[2],
10 Kleine Mädchen gingen nach der Schule—
Alles war freundlich, alles war nett,
Aber wenn ich weiter geschlafen hätt
Und tät von alledem nichts wissen,
Würd es mir fehlen, würd ich's vermissen?

---

[1] Die Semmel: das Brötchen.
[2] Eine Schürze hing über dem Stuhle: ein Zeichen, daß frische Wurst zu haben war.

33. *We leave it to others*

Ein Chinese ('s sind schon an[1] zweihundert Jahr)
In Frankreich auf einem Hofball war.
Und die einen frugen[2] ihn: ob er das kenne?
Und die andern frugen ihn: wie man es nenne?
5 „Wir nennen es tanzen ", sprach er mit Lachen,
„ Aber wir lassen es andere machen."
Und dieses Wort, seit langer Frist[3],
Mir immer in Erinnerung ist.
Ich seh das Rennen, ich seh das Jagen,
Und wenn mich die Menschen umdrängen und
10   fragen:
„Was[4] tust du nicht mit? Warum stehst du
      beiseit[5]? "
So sag ich: „ Alles hat seine Zeit.
Auch die Jagd nach dem Glück. All derlei[6]
      Sachen,
Ich lasse sie längst durch andere machen."

CONRAD FERDINAND MEYER (1825–1898)

34. *Two sails*

Zwei Segel erhellend
Die tiefblaue Bucht!
Zwei Segel sich schwellend
Zu ruhiger Flucht!

5 Wie eins in den Winden
Sich wölbt und bewegt,
Wird auch das Empfinden
Des andern erregt.

Begehrt eins zu hasten,
10 Das andre geht schnell,
Verlangt eins zu rasten,
Ruht auch sein Gesell.

---

[1] An: ungefähr.   [2] Frugen: fragten.   [3] Die Frist: die Zeit.
[4] Was: warum.   [5] Beiseit: beiseite.   [6] Derlei: solche.

35. After the Dutch manner

Der Meister malt ein kleines zartes Bild,
Zurückgelehnt beschaut ers liebevoll.
Es pocht. „ Herein."   Ein flämischer Junker ists
Mit einer drallen[1], aufgedonnerten[2] Dirn[3],
5 Der vor Gesundheit fast die Wange birst.
Sie rauscht von Seide, flimmert von Geschmeid[4].
„Wir habens eilig, lieber Meister. Wißt,
Ein wackrer Schelm stiehlt mir das Töchterlein.
Morgen ist Hochzeit. Malet mir mein Kind! "
10 „ Zur Stunde[5], Herr! Nur noch den Pinselstrich! "
Sie treten lustig vor die Staffelei:
Auf einem blanken Kissen schlummernd liegt
Ein feiner Mädchenkopf. Der Meister setzt
Des Blumenkranzes tiefste Knospe noch
15 Auf die verblichne Stirn mit leichter Hand.
—„ Nach der Natur? "—„ Nach der Natur. Mein Kind.
Gestern beerdigt. Herr, ich bin zu Dienst[6]."

1. Was tut ein Maler?
2. Womit malt er?
3. Woher wissen Sie, daß er mit seinem Bild zufrieden war?
4. Warum klopfte der Junker an die Tür?
5. Woraus kann man schließen, das der Junker ein reicher
   Mann war?
6. Warum sollte der Maler das Mädchen sofort malen?
7. Warum wollte der Junker ein Bild von dem Mädchen haben?
8. Was wollte der Maler tun, bevor er das Bild anfing?
9. Warum traten der Junker und das Mädchen vor die Staffelei?
10. Wo trug das Mädchen auf dem Bild den Blumenkranz?

[1] Drall: rund und fest.
[2] Aufgedonnert: überreich gekleidet.
[3] Die Dirn: das Mädchen.
[4] Das Geschmeid: Geschmeide.
[5] Zur Stunde: sofort.
[6] Zu Dienst: zu Diensten.

VOCABULARY

GERMAN—ENGLISH

Notes. (1) The plural ending—(*e*)*n* of feminine nouns of Group III is not indicated.

(2) Compounds whose constituent parts are already listed are omitted.

A

ab-brennen (a, a), burn down.
ab-drücken, fire.
der **Abend** (—e), evening.
das **Abendbrot** (—e), supper.
die **Abendglocke,** evening bell.
die **Abendröte,** sunset glow.
abends, in the evening.
der **Abendschimmer** (—), evening glow.
aber, but.
ab-fahren (ä, u, a), leave.
ab-fallen (ä, ie, a), fall.
abgebrochen, broken down.
ab-gehen (i, a): **geht ab,** exit.
abgelegen, remote.
abgemacht, agreed! done!
der **Abgrund** (—̈e), abyss, precipice.
ab-kommen (a, o), lose (one's way).
ab-nehmen (i, a, o), take off (hat).
ab-reisen, leave, go away.
ab-schrecken, deter.
ab-setzen, set down.
die **Absicht,** intention.
ab-stehen (a, a), protrude.
ab-stoßen (ö, ie, o), shove off.
ab-warten, wait for.
ab-werfen (i, a, o), throw off.
ab-ziehen (o, o), take out.
ach, oh.
acht: sich in — nehmen, take care.
ächzen, groan.
das **Adagio** (—s), adagio.
der **Adler** (—), eagle.

die **Adresse,** address.
ähnlich, similar.
die **Ähnlichkeit,** similarity.
all, all; —e, everybody; —es, everything, everybody.
allein, but; alone.
allgemein, general.
allgewaltig, all-powerfully.
der **Alltag,** daily routine.
alltags, on weekdays.
allzu, too, over-.
als, as, when; —(ob), as if.
also, so.
alt, old.
der **Alte** (—n, —n), old man.
die **Alte** (—n, —n), old hen.
der **Amerikaner** (—), American.
amerikanisch, American.
das **Amt** (—̈er), office.
amüsieren, amuse.
an, at, to, in, by, against.
an-bieten (o, o), offer.
an-binden (a, u), tie up, moor.
der **Anblick** (—e), sight; **beim ersten —,** at first sight.
an-blicken, look at.
ander, other, different.
ein **andermal,** another time.
sich **ändern,** change (*intr.*).
anders (als), differently (from), otherwise.
anderthalb, one and a half.
Andreas, Andrew.
die **Anekdote,** anecdote.
der **Anfang** (—̈e), beginning.
an-fangen (ä, i, a), begin.
angekleidet, dressed.
angenehm, pleasant.
angezogen, dressed.

269

die **Angst** (⁔e), fear; — **haben,** be afraid.
ängstlich, anxious(ly), nervous.
an-halten (ä, ie, a), stop.
der **Anker** (—), anchor.
an-klagen, accuse.
sich **an-kleiden,** dress (intr.).
*****an-kommen** (a, o), arrive.
die **Ankunft** (⁔e), arrival.
(sich) **an-melden,** announce, introduce (o.s.).
an-reden, address.
an-rühren, touch.
an-sehen (ie, a, e), look at; — **als,** look upon as.
an-setzen, make an attempt.
an-starren, stare at.
anstatt, instead of.
an-stellen, employ.
*****an-stoßen** (ö, ie, o) (**an**), stumble (against).
die **Anstrengung,** effort.
an-treten (i, a, e), start.
die **Antwort,** answer.
antworten, answer.
an-ziehen (o, o), put on; sich —, dress (intr.).
der **Anzug** (⁔e), dress.
an-zünden, light.
der **Apfel** (⁔), apple.
apportieren, retrieve.
arbeiten, work.
ärgerlich, irritable, angry.
arm, poor.
der **Arm** (—e), arm.
der **Ärmel** (—), sleeve.
die **Art,** kind.
der **Arzt** (⁔e), doctor.
die **Aster,** aster.
das **Atmen,** breathing.
auch, also, even, too.
die **Audienz,** audience.
auf, on, at, to, along, in; — **und ab** (**nieder**), up and down; — . . . **zu,** up to.
*****auf-bleiben** (ie, ie), remain open.
aufdämmernd, getting lighter.
der **Aufenthalt** (—e), stay.
*****auf-fallen** (ä, ie, a) (D), strike.
auf-fangen (ä, i, a), intercept.

aufgedonnert, all dressed up, dolled up.
*****auf-gehen** (i, a), open (intr.), rise.
aufgeregt, excited.
der **Aufguß** (⁔(ss)e), brew.
sich **auf-halten** (ä, ie, a), stay, stop.
auf-heben (o, o), pick up, raise.
auf-hören, stop.
auf-machen, open.
aufmerksam, attentive(ly); —*****sein auf,** pay attention to.
auf-nehmen (i, a, o), receive, resume.
auf-passen, watch out, pay attention.
aufrecht, upright.
die **Aufregung,** excitement.
auf-reißen (i, i), open wide.
sich **auf-richten,** struggle to one's feet.
auf-schlagen (ä, u, a), open.
auf-schließen (o, o), unlock.
der **Aufschrei** (—e), scream.
auf-schreien (ie, ie), scream.
auf-sehen (ie, a, e), look up.
*****auf-springen** (a, u), jump up, open suddenly.
*****auf-stehen** (a, a), get up.
*****auf-steigen** (ie, ie), fly up.
sich **auf-tun** (a, a), open (intr.).
*****auf-wachen,** wake up (intr.).
aufwärts, upwards.
auf-wecken, wake (tr.).
auf-ziehen (o, o), wind up.
das **Auge** (—n), eye; **unter vier —n,** without witnesses.
der **Augenblick** (—e), moment.
augenscheinlich, evidently.
aus, from, over, out of.
aus-blasen (ä, ie, a), blow out.
*****aus-brechen** (i, a, o), burst out, break out.
der **Ausbruch** (⁔e), outbreak.
aus-brüten, hatch.
aus-drücken, express.
aus-führen, take out.
*****aus-gehen** (i, a), go out.
ausgenommen, except.
aus-halten (ä, ie, a), stand.

aus-lassen (ä, ie, a), give vent
  to.
aus-löschen, extinguish.
aus-rufen (ie, u), cry out.
sich **aus-ruhen,** rest.
aus-sehen (ie, a, e), look.
außer (**sich**), beside (o.s.);
  except.
äußerst, extremely.
aus-sortieren, sort.
*__aus-steigen__ (ie, ie), get out.
aus-strahlen, radiate.
der **Ausweg** (—e), way out.
*__aus-weichen__ (i, i), dodge.
aus-zahlen, pay.
der **Autobus** (—se), bus.
das **Avancement** (—s), promotion.
die **Axt** (⁔e), axe.

B

der **Bach** (⁔e), stream, brook.
backen (gebacken), bake.
das **Bad** (⁔er), spa.
der **Badeanzug** (⁔e), bathing-suit.
der **Badegast** (⁔e), visitor.
baden, bathe.
der **Bahnhof** (⁔e), station.
bald, soon; — . . . —, now
  . . . now.
der **Balken** (—), beam.
der **Balkon** (—e), balcony.
der **Ball** (⁔e), ball.
bang, apprehensive.
die **Bank** (⁔e), bench.
die **Bank,** bank.
das **Bankhaus** (⁔er), banking-
  house.
der **Bankier** (—s), banker.
bankrott, bankrupt.
der **Barbier** (—e), barber.
der **Bart** (⁔e), beard.
der **Bauch** (⁔e), belly; **auf dem**
  —, flat on one's face.
der **Bauer** (—n/s, —n), peasant.
das **Bauernhaus** (⁔er), farm.
der **Baum** (⁔e), tree.
die **Baumwolle,** cotton.
beabsichtigen, intend.
der **Becher** (—), goblet.
sich **bedanken,** thank.
bedeckt, covered.
bedenklich, doubtfully.

bedeuten, mean.
der **Bediente** (—n, —n), servitor,
  official.
die **Bedingung,** condition.
sich **beeilen,** hurry.
beendigen, end.
beerdigen, bury.
die **Beere,** berry.
der **Befehl** (—e), order.
befehlen (ie, a, o), command,
  tell (to do).
sich **befinden** (a, u), find o.s., be,
  feel.
befreien, free, save.
sich **begeben** (i, a, e), go.
*__begegnen__ (D), meet.
begehen (i, a), commit.
begehren, desire.
der **Beginn** (—e), beginning.
beginnen (a, o), begin.
begleiten, accompany, go
  with, escort, follow.
der **Begleiter** (—), companion.
die **Begleitung,** accompaniment.
Begriff: im —*sein, be on
  the point of.
behalten (ä, ie, a), hold, pre-
  serve.
behandeln, treat, look after.
behangen, hung, draped.
beherzt, boldly.
bei, by, with, on, in, near, at
  (the house of).
beide, both, the two.
der **Beifall,** applause.
das **Bein** (—e), leg.
der **Beiname** (—ns, —n), nick-
  name.
beisammen, together.
beiseite, to one side.
bekämpfen, fight.
bekannt, well-known; **näher**
  —, very familiar.
beklatschen, applaud.
(*)**bekommen** (a, o), get; suit.
belebt, crowded.
beleidigen, insult.
beleidigend, insulting.
die **Beleidigung,** insult.
beleuchten, light.
bellen, bark.
belohnen, reward.
die **Belohnung,** reward.
bemerken, notice.

sich **benehmen** (i, a, o), behave.

das **Benehmen,** behaviour.

benutzen, use.

bequem, comfortably, in comfort.

berechnen, calculate.

bereit, ready.

bereits, already.

bereitwillig, willingly.

der **Berg** (—e), mountain.

die **Bergesspitze,** mountain-top.

das **Bergwerk** (—e), mine.

berichten, announce.

*****bersten** (i, a, o), burst.

beruhigen, appease, set at rest.

berühmt, famous.

beschauen, look at.

beschließen (o, o), decide.

beschreiben (ie, ie), describe.

die **Beschreibung,** description.

besessen, mad.

besetzt, full up.

besonder, special, separate.

besonders, especially.

besprechen (i, a, o), discuss.

best, best.

bestehen (a, a); **— auf,** insist on; **— aus,** consist of.

besteigen (ie, ie), climb up.

bestellen, order.

bestimmen, destine.

bestimmt, distinct.

bestrafen, punish.

bestürzt, dismayed, alarmed.

der **Besuch** (—e), visit.

besuchen, visit.

das **Besuchszimmer** (–), drawing room.

betäuben, deafen.

beteert, smeared with tar.

beten, pray.

(sich) **betrachten,** look at (o.s.).

betreten (i, a, e), enter.

das **Bett** (—s, —en), bed.

die **Bettdecke,** blanket.

der **Bettler** (—), beggar.

beugen, bow; **sich —,** bend, stoop.

beunruhigt, uneasy.

der **Beutel** (—), purse.

bevor, before.

bevor-stehen (a, a), be imminent.

bewachen, guard, watch over, look after.

bewachsen, overgrown.

bewaldet, wooded.

sich **bewegen,** move, stir.

die **Bewegung,** commotion.

bewegungslos, motionless.

beweisen (ie, ie), prove.

der **Bewohner** (—), inhabitant.

bewohnt, inhabited.

bewundernswürdig, remarkable.

bewußtlos, unconscious.

bezahlen, pay.

das **Bezahlen,** payment.

biegen (o, o), bend.

bieten (o, o), offer.

das **Bild** (—er), picture, image.

das **Bilderbuch** (—̈er), picturebook.

die **Binde,** bandage.

binden (a, u), tie, cement.

bis, until, as far as; **— auf,** except; **— zu,** down to, as far as.

bisher, hitherto.

bitte (sehr), please (do), don't mention it.

die **Bitte,** request.

bitten (a, e) **(um),** ask (for).

bitter, bitter.

blähen, swell, belly out.

blank, snow-white, gleaming.

blasen (ä, ie, a), play, blow.

blaß, pale.

blättern, turn leaves over.

blau, blue; **das Blaue,** blue sky.

*****bleiben** (ie, ie), remain, stay.

der **Blick** (—e), glance, view, gaze, eyes; **auf den ersten —,** at first sight.

blicken, look; **sich — lassen,** be seen.

blinken, flash.

der **Blitz** (—e), lightning.

blitzen, gleam.

bloß, merely, bare.

blühend, in bloom, flourishing.

der **Blumenkranz** (—̈e), wreath of flowers.

das **Blut,** blood.

die **Blüte,** flower.

blutig, blood-red.

die **Blutspur,** trail of blood.

der **Blutverlust,** loss of blood.

das **Böcklein** (—), kid.

der **Boden** ($\stackrel{\cdot\cdot}{-}$), ground, floor, bottom; **zu** —, to the ground, down.

das **Boot** (—e), boat.

der **Boots-mann** (-leute), boat-swain.

böse, angry, bad, serious.

der **Bote** (—n, —n), messenger.

der **Botengänger** (—), errand-boy, carrier.

der **Botschafter** (—), ambassador.

der **Brauch** ($\stackrel{\cdot\cdot}{-}$e), custom, wise.

brauchen, need.

braun, brown.

sich **bräunen lassen,** get sunburnt.

brausen, roar.

brausend, blustering.

brav, brave.

brechen (i, a, o), break.

breit, broad, wide.

brennen (a, a), burn, scorch; **es brennt,** (there's a) fire!

der **Brief** (—e), letter.

der **Briefträger** (—), postman.

bringen (a, a), bring, take, drive.

das **Brot** (—e), bread.

das **Brötchen** (—), roll.

die **Brotrinde,** crust of bread.

die **Brücke,** bridge.

der **Bruder** ($\stackrel{\cdot\cdot}{-}$), brother.

die **Brust** ($\stackrel{\cdot\cdot}{-}$e), heart, breast.

die **Brut,** brood.

das **Buch** ($\stackrel{\cdot\cdot}{-}$er), book.

der **Buchhändler** (—), bookseller.

die **Buchhandlung,** bookshop.

die **Bucht,** bay.

sich **bücken,** bend down.

die **Bühne,** stage.

das **Bündel** (—), bundle.

buntgefärbt, bright-coloured.

die **Burg,** castle.

der **Bürger** (—), citizen.

die **Butter,** butter.

das **Butterbrötchen** (—), small slice of bread and butter.

C

die **Chiffre,** cipher.

der **Chinese** (—n, —n), Chinese.

der **Christ** (—en, —en), Christian.

der **Christenhund** (—e), dog of a Christian.

christlich, Christian.

Christus, Christ.

das **College** (—s), college.

D

da, since, as; here, there, then, when; **jetzt** —, now that.

dabei, in the matter, in doing so, withal; present.

das **Dach** ($\stackrel{\cdot\cdot}{-}$er), roof.

das **Dachfenster** (—), attic window.

dadurch, through that.

dagegen, against it; **nichts — haben,** have no objection.

daher, so, therefore, consequently.

damalig, of that time.

damals, (at) that time.

die **Dame,** lady.

damit, so that; with those words.

der **Damm** ($\stackrel{\cdot\cdot}{-}$e), dike.

dämmern, grow dark.

dämmernd, dusky, twilight.

die **Dämmerung,** half-light.

danach, afterwards.

daneben, next to it.

der **Dank,** thanks; **zum** —, as a reward.

dankbar, gratefully.

die **Dankbarkeit,** gratitude.

danken (D), thank.

dann, then.

sich **daran-machen,** set to work.

darauf, thereupon, on this.

daraus, out of it.

darin, in it, in them, inside.

darüber, about that, at this; **ihm ging nichts** —, he prized nothing more.

darum, therefore.

daß, that.

das **Datum** (Daten), date.

dauern, last, take.

davon, away, from there.

***davon-jagen,** dash away.

davor, in front of it.

dazu, to that end; with it.

*__dazu-kommen__ (a, o), get as far as.

*__dazwischen-kommen__ (a, o), intervene.

die **Decke,** cover.

decken, lay.

sich **dehnen,** stretch.

dengeln, sharpen.

denken (a, a) (**an**), think (of).

das **Denkmal** (—̈er), monument.

denn, for; then.

der, who.

derselbe, the same; it.

deshalb, therefore.

deutlich, clear(ly).

deutsch, German.

der **Deutsche** (—n, —n), German.

Deutschland (*n.*), Germany.

der **Dialog** (—e), dialogue.

dicht, close, thick.

der **Dichter** (—), poet.

dick, thick.

der **Dieb** (—e), thief.

diejenigen, those.

dienen (D), serve, be a servant; **— zu,** serve as, do for.

der **Diener** (—), servant.

der **Dienst** (—e), service; **zu —en,** at your service.

dieser, this.

dies(es), this (*pron.*).

diesmal, this time.

das **Ding** (—e), thing.

die **Dissertation,** thesis.

doch, yet, however, still, nevertheless; after all, I hope.

der **Doktor** (—s, —en), doctor.

das **Dokument** (—e), document.

der **Dollar** (—), dollar.

der **Donner** (—), thunder.

das **Dorf** (—̈er), village.

dort, there.

drall, buxom.

draus, from which.

draußen, outside.

sich **drehen,** turn.

dreifach, threefold.

drein, into it.

*__dringen__ (a, u), force one's way; peer through.

drinnen, inside.

droben, up there.

die **Droschke,** cab.

drüben, over there.

der **Druck,** pressure.

sich **drücken,** squeeze o.s.

drückend, tight.

drunten, down.

der **Duft** (—̈e), scent.

dumm, stupidly.

dunkel, dark, obscure; **im Dunkeln,** in the dark.

dünn, thin.

durch, through, by.

durchdringen (a, u), fill, pervade.

durcheinander, in confusion, in all directions.

durch-nehmen (i, a, o), go through.

durchschlafen (ä, ie, a), sleep through.

durchschneiden (i, i), sever.

dürfen, see § 102.

E

ebben, ebb.

eben, just, level; **noch —,** just.

das **Ebenbild** (—er), image.

ebenso wie, just like.

das **Echo** (—s), echo.

die **Ecke,** corner.

edel, noble.

ehe, before.

der **Ehestand,** married state.

die **Ehre,** honour.

ehrwürdig, venerable.

eigen, (of its) own.

die **Eigenschaft,** property.

eigentlich, really, as a matter of fact.

das **Eigentum** (—̈er), property.

die **Eile,** hurry; **— haben,** be in a hurry.

*__eilen,__ hurry.

eilig, hurriedly; **es — haben,** be in a hurry.

einander, one another.

(*)__ein-brechen__ (i, a, o) (**in**), burgle.

der **Eindruck** (—̈e), impression.

einer, somebody, one; **— um den anderen,** one after the other.

eines, one (thing).

die **Einfahrt,** carriage entrance.

der **Einfall** (─̈e), idea.

*****ein-fallen** (ä, ie, a), occur.

der **Eingang** (─̈e), entrance, opening.

ein-händigen, hand.

einher, along.

einigemal, occasionally.

einige(s), some, a few.

der **Einkauf** (─̈e), purchase.

ein-kaufen, shop.

das **Einkaufen,** shopping.

*****ein-kehren,** put up (at an hotel).

ein-laden (ä, u, a), invite.

einmal, once, just, really; **auf** ─, all at once.

einödig, solitary.

ein-packen, stow.

*****ein-reiten,** ride (into).

ein-richten, construct.

einsam, lonely.

die **Einsamkeit,** solitude.

ein-sammeln, collect.

*****ein-schlafen** (ä, ie, a), fall asleep, go to sleep.

ein-schließen (o, o), shut in, enclose.

*****ein-schlummern,** doze off.

ein-seifen, lather.

ein-singen (a, u), sing to sleep.

ein-sperren, shut in.

einst, one day.

ein-stecken, put in one's pocket, post.

*****ein-steigen** (ie, ie), get in.

einstimmig, unanimously.

*****ein-treffen** (i, a, o), occur.

*****ein-treten** (i, a, e), come in, enter; ─ **lassen,** show in.

einverstanden: ─ *****sein,** agree.

ein-ziehen (o, o), take in.

einzig, only, single.

das **Eis,** ice.

eisern, iron.

die **Elektrizität,** electricity.

das **Element** (─e), element.

Elisabeth, Elsbeth, Elizabeth.

die **Eltern** (*pl.*), parents.

empfangen (ä, i, a), receive, welcome.

das **Empfinden,** feelings.

empor, up.

das **Ende** (─s, ─n), end.

enden, end.

endlich, at last, finally.

eng, narrow, very small.

der **Engel** (─), angel.

der **Engelgesang** (─̈e), angel's song.

England (*n.*), England.

der **Engländer** (─), Englishman.

englisch, English.

das **Entchen** (─), duckling.

entdecken, discover.

die **Ente,** duck.

sich **entfernen,** go away, get further away.

entfernt, away.

*****entfliehen** (o, o), flee.

entgegen, towards.

entgegengesetzt, opposite.

*****entgegen-springen** (a, u) (D), rush towards.

*****entgegen-treten** (i, a, e) (D), come towards.

enthalten (ä, ie, a), contain.

enthüllen, uncover.

*****entkommen** (a, o), escape.

entlassen (ä, ie, a), dismiss.

*****entlaufen** (äu, ie, au), escape.

sich **entschließen** (o, o), resolve.

entschlossen, resolute.

sich **entschuldigen,** apologise.

die **Entschuldigung: um ─ bitten,** beg pardon.

*****entspringen** (a, u), escape.

*****entstehen** (a, a), begin, arise, be given.

entziffern, decipher.

entzückt, delighted.

(sich) **entzünden,** ignite.

das **Erbarmen,** compassion.

der **Erbe** (─n, ─n), heir.

*****erblassen,** (grow) pale.

erblicken, catch sight of.

die **Erbse,** pea.

die **Erde,** ground, earth.

das **Erdgeschoß,** ground floor.

der **Erdhaufen** (─), mound.

der **Erdteil** (─e), continent.

erfahren (ä, u, a), learn, discover.

erfassen, seize.

erfreut, delighted.

erfüllen, fill.

ergreifen (i, i), seize, reach.

ergründen, fathom.

erhalten (ä, ie, a), get, be given; **sich —,** keep o.s.

erheben (o, o), raise; **sich —,** rise, get up.

erhellen, light up.

sich **erholen,** recover.

sich **erinnern,** remember.

die **Erinnerung,** memory, reminder.

erkennen (a, a) (**an**), recognize (by); **— für,** recognize as.

erklären, explain.

die **Erklärung,** explanation.

erlauben (D), allow, permit.

die **Erlaubnis,** permission.

erleben, experience, see.

das **Erlebnis** (—se), experience.

erleichtert, relieved.

erleuchten, light (up), illuminate.

***erlöschen** (i, o, o), go out, fail.

erlösen, deliver, put out.

***ermatten,** weaken, fade.

ermattet, exhausted.

ermüdet, tired out.

der **Ernst,** gravity; **es ist mir —,** I mean it seriously.

eröffnen, open.

erregen, excite.

erreichen, reach, attain.

***erschallen,** ring out.

***erscheinen** (ie, ie), appear, be here.

erschießen (o, o), shoot dead.

***erschlaffen,** flag.

***erschrecken** (i, a, o), be startled.

erschrecken, frighten, daunt.

erschreckt, startled.

erst, only, not until; first; right; **— ich,** and so am I.

***erstaunen,** be astonished.

das **Erstaunen,** astonishment.

erstaunt, astonished.

***ertönen,** ring out.

ertragen (ä, u, a), bear, stand.

der **Ertrinkende** (—n, —n), drowning man.

***erwachen,** wake up (*intr.*).

erwarten, expect, await.

erwecken, wake up (*tr.*), arouse.

das **Erz** (—e), bronze.

erzählen, tell, relate.

der **Erzähler** (—), narrator.

essen (i, a, e), eat.

das **Essen** (—), meal.

das **Eßzimmer** (—), dining-room.

die **Etikette,** etiquette.

etwa, about.

etwas, something, anything; **— anderes,** anything else.

Europa (*n.*), Europe.

europäisch, European.

die **Ewigkeit,** eternity.

das **Exam-en** (-mina), examination.

existieren, exist.

Exzellenz (*f.*), Excellency.

F

das **Fach** (—̈er), profession.

***fahren** (ä, u, a), go, travel, drift, sail, run.

das **Fahrgeld,** fare.

die **Fahrkarte,** ticket.

der **Fährmann** (—̈er), ferryman.

der **Fahrplan** (—̈e), time-table.

das **Fahrrad** (—̈er), bicycle.

der **Fahrschein** (—e), (bus) ticket.

der **Fall** (—̈e), case, fall.

***fallen** (ä, ie, a), fall; go off.

falten, fold.

die **Familie,** family.

fangen (ä, i, a), catch.

die **Farbe,** colour.

das **Faß** (—̈(ss)er), barrel.

fassen, catch, seize.

die **Fassung,** composure.

fast, almost.

fatal, awkward; fatal.

fehlen, miss, feel want of, be short.

der **Fehler** (—), fault.

***fehl-gehen** (i, a), miss.

feiern, celebrate.

fein, delicate.

der **Feind** (—e), enemy.

das **Feld** (—er), field.

der **Fels, Fels-en** (—ens, —en), rock, crag.

das **Fenster** (—), window.
die **Ferien** (*pl.*), holidays.
die **Ferne,** distance.
fest, tight(ly), solid, soundly.
das **Fest** (—e), celebration, fête.
sich **fest-halten** (ä, ie, a), cling to.
der **Festungsduft,** (musty) smell of fortress-prison.
das **Feuer** (—), fire, beacon.
der **Feuerlärm,** fire-alarm.
das **Feuerwerk** (—e), firework(s).
das **Fieber** (—), fever.
finanziell, financial.
finden (a, u), find; **sich —,** meet, find one's way.
der **Finger** (—), finger.
finster, dark, lowering.
das **Fischlein** (—), little fish.
flämisch, Flemish.
die **Flamme,** flame.
flammen, blaze.
flechten (i, o, o), plait.
der **Fleck** (—e), spot.
der **Fleischer** (—), butcher.
flicken, patch.
*****fliegen** (o, o), fly, speed along.
das **Fliegen,** power of flight.
*****fliehen** (o, o), flee.
*****fließen** (o, o), flow.
flimmern, glitter.
die **Flöte,** flute.
fluchen, curse.
die **Flucht,** flight; **die — er- greifen,** take to one's heels.
der **Flug** (—ͤe), flight.
der **Flügel** (—), grand piano.
flugs, instantly.
der **Fluß** (—ͤ(ss)e), river.
die **Flut,** water(s).
die **Folge,** consequence.
*****folgen,** follow, ensue.
folgend, following, next.
die **Form,** baking-tin.
fort, away, along.
*****fort-fahren** (ä, u, a), continue.
*****fort-kommen** (a, o), get away.
das **Fortsetzen: zum —,** for continuation.
fortwährend, continually.
die **Frage,** question.
fragen (**nach**), ask (about, for); **nicht — nach,** not to care for; **sich —,** wonder.

Frankreich (*n.*), France.
der **Franzose** (—n, —n), Frenchman.
französisch, in French.
die **Frau,** wife, woman, Mrs.
das **Fräulein** (—), young mistress.
frei, open, outstretched, unsupported.
die **Freiheit,** freedom.
frei-lassen (ä, ie, a), free.
fremd, foreign, unknown, other people's.
der **Fremde** (—n, —n), stranger.
die **Freude** (**an**), joy (in).
freudig, joyful.
sich **freuen** (**über**), rejoice (at), be pleased.
der **Freund** (—e), friend.
die **Freundin** (—nen), friend.
freundlich, friendly.
die **Freundschaft,** friendship.
der **Friede** (—ns, —n), peace.
friedlich, peaceful.
Friedrich, Frederick.
frisch, fresh(ly), strong.
Fritz, Fred.
froh, joyful.
fröhlich, merry, merrily.
frohlocken, rejoice.
fromm, pious, god-fearing.
früh, early.
früher, former(ly).
der **Frühling** (—e), spring.
der **Frühlingswind** (—e), spring breeze.
das **Frühstück** (—e), breakfast.
der **Frühstückstisch** (—e), breakfast table.
(sich) **fühlen,** feel.
führen, lead, take, run, guide, show, carry.
füllen, fill.
der **Funken** (—), spark.
für, for, as; **— sich,** to himself, aside; **was — (ein),** what sort of (a).
die **Furche,** furrow.
die **Furcht** (**vor**), fear (of).
fürchten, fear; **sich —,** be afraid.
fürchterlich, terrifying(ly).
furchtsam, timid(ly), anxious(ly).
der **Fürst** (—en, —en), prince.

die **Fürstin** (—nen), princess.
der **Fuß** (—̈e), foot; **zu** —, on foot.

G

die **Galerie,** gallery.
der **Gang** (—̈e), corridor, passage.
ganz, whole; quite, right.
gar, altogether, right, very;
   — **nicht,** not at all.
der **Garten** (—̈), garden.
der **Gärtner** (—), gardener.
die **Gasflamme,** gas-jet.
die **Gasse,** (narrow) street.
der **Gast** (—̈e), guest.
das **Gasthaus** (—̈er), hotel, inn.
die **Gebärde,** gesture.
das **Gebäude** (—), building.
das **Gebelle,** bark(ing).
   geben (i, a, e), give; **es gibt,**
      there is (are).
   gebieten (o, o), command,
      bring about.
   geboren, born.
   gebrauchen, use.
der **Geburtstag** (—e), birthday.
das **Gebüsch** (—e), bushes, shrub-
      bery.
der **Gedanke** (—ns, —n), thought.
   gedenken (a, a), remember.
das **Gedicht** (—e), poem.
das **Gedränge,** crush.
die **Geduld,** patience.
   geduldig, patient.
die **Gefahr,** danger.
   gefährlich, dangerous.
   gefallen (ä, ie, a) (D), please,
      like.
   gefangen, captured, captive.
das **Gefieder,** feathers.
das **Gefühl** (—e), feeling.
das **Gefürchtete,** what had been
      feared.
   gegen, against, towards.
die **Gegend,** district, locality.
   gegenüber, opposite.
die **Gegenwart,** presence.
   *****gehen** (i, a), go, walk; **wie
      geht es ihr,** how is she; **es
      geht ihm schlecht,** he is
      faring badly; — **in,** look out
      on to; **es wird** —, it will be
      all right.

gehorchen (D), obey.
gehören (D), belong.
der **Geist** (—er), spirit; **im** —
      fühlen, have a premonition.
   geistig, spiritual.
   gekleidet, dressed.
das **Gelächter,** laughter.
das **Geläute,** tinkling.
das **Geld,** money.
der **Geldsack** (—̈e), money-bag.
die **Gelegenheit,** occasion, oppor-
      tunity.
der **Gelehrte** (—n, —n), scholar.
die **Geliebte** (—n, —n), beloved,
      sweetheart.
   *****gelingen** (a, u) (D), succeed.
   gelten (i, a, o), **das gilt mir
      gleich,** that's all the same
      to me.
   gemeinschaftlich, together
      with everybody.
das **Gemurmel,** murmur(ing).
das **Gemüt** (—er), heart.
   genau, closely, exactly.
der **General** (—e), general.
   genießen (o, o), take (food).
der **Genosse** (—n, —n), com-
      panion.
   genug, enough.
das **Gepäck,** baggage.
   gerade, straight, just, precisely;
      — **noch,** just in time.
   geradezu, straight.
das **Geräusch** (—e), noise, sound.
die **Gerettete** (—n, —n), rescued
      woman.
das **Gericht** (—e), law-court; **vor**
      —, in court.
   gering, slight.
   gern, willingly; *see* § 113 (h).
der **Gesandte** (—n, —n), en-
      voy.
   *****geschehen** (ie, a, e), happen.
das **Geschenk** (—e), present.
die **Geschichte,** story.
die **Geschicklichkeit,** skill, dex-
      terity.
   geschickt, skilful(ly).
das **Geschmeide,** jewellery.
   geschwind, swiftly.
der **Geselle** (—n, —n), com-
      panion.
die **Gesellschaft,** company,
      group, society.

das **Gesicht** (—er), face.
das **Gespenst** (—er), ghost.
das **Gespräch** (—e), conversation;
 ein — führen, have a conversation.
die **Gestalt,** figure, body.
 gestehen (a, a), confess.
 gestern, yesterday.
 gestorben, dead.
 gesund, in good health, well.
die **Gesundheit,** health.
der **Getreue** (—n, —n), liegeman.
das **Gewicht** (—e), weight.
 gewinnen (a, o), win.
 gewiß, certain(ly).
das **Gewissen** (—), conscience.
 gewöhnlich, usually.
das **Gewölbe** (—), vault.
 gewunden, winding.
der **Gipfel** (—), top.
 glänzen, shine.
 glänzend, shining.
der **Glaube** (—ns), belief.
 glauben, believe, think.
 gleich, immediately; like, same.
 gleichaltrig, of the same age.
 gleichgültig, indifferent, nonchalantly, with indifference.
das **Glied** (—er), limb.
das **Glockengeläute,** tinkling of bells.
das **Glöcklein** (—), little bell.
das **Glück,** fortune, (run of) luck, happiness.
 glücklich, happy, safe and sound.
 gnädig: der —e Herr, the master; **—e Frau,** Madam; **—ster Herr,** Your Highness.
das **Gold,** gold.
 golden, golden.
das **Goldstück** (—e), gold coin.
 gönnen, not to grudge.
der **Gott,** God; **— sei Dank,** thank Heavens; **um —es willen,** for Heaven's sake, Heavens!
der **Gottessoldat** (—en, —en), soldier of God.
 göttlich, divine.
das **Grab** (—er), grave.
das **Grabmal** (—er), tomb.

 graben (ä, u, a) **(nach),** dig (for).
der **Graf** (—en, —en), count.
die **Gräfin** (—nen), countess.
das **Gras** (—er), grass.
der **Grasplatz** (—e), lawn.
 grau, grey, remote.
das **Grauen,** dread.
die **Grausamkeit,** cruelty.
 greifen (i, i), put one's hand (into).
 grimm, angry.
der **Grimm,** wrath.
 groß, big, great.
der **Großknecht** (—e), head man on farm.
die **Großmutter,** grandmother.
 grün, green.
der **Grund** (—e), reason; valley;
 aus welchem —, for what reason.
der **Gruß** (—e), greeting.
 grüßen, greet; **— lassen,** send one's regards.
 gut, good, safe, well.
 gut-machen, make amends for.
 gutmütig, good-naturedly.

H

das **Haar** (—e), hair.
die **Haft,** custody, prison.
der **Hahn** (—e), cock.
 halb, half.
 hallen, reverberate.
der **Hals** (—e), neck.
das **Halsband** (—er), collar (of dog).
 halt, stop!
 halten (ä, ie, a), hold, keep, halt; **— für,** consider to be; **— von,** think of; **sich —,** refrain.
die **Haltestelle,** stop.
 halt-machen, stop.
der **Hammer** (—), hammer.
die **Hand** (—e), hand.
 handeln, act; **sich — um,** be a matter of.
das **Handwerk** (—e), trade.
 hängen, hang (tr.).

hängen (i, a), hang (*intr.*); hover.

der **Harnisch** (—e), armour.

hassen, hate.

häßlich, ugly.

die **Hast**, haste.

(*)**hasten**, hasten.

hastig, hastily.

der **Haufe** (—ns, —n), crowd.

das **Haupt** (—̈er), head.

der **Haupt-mann** (—leute), captain.

die **Hauptstadt** (—̈e), capital.

die **Hauptstraße**, main road.

das **Haus** (—̈er), house; **nach—e**, home; **zu —e**, at home.

der **Hausknecht** (—e), boots.

der **Hausschlüssel** (—), front-door key.

der **Hausschuh** (—e), slipper.

die **Haustür**, front door.

der **Hauswirt** (—e), landlord, master of the house.

heben (o, o), lift; **sich —**, rise.

das **Heft** (—e), note-book.

heftig, violent(ly), vehement-(ly).

heilig, sacred.

heiraten, marry.

heiß, hot.

heißen (ie, ei), be called, be name of; bid; **das heißt**, that is to say.

heiter, cheerful, serene.

der **Held** (—en, —en), hero.

helfen (i, a, o) (D), help.

hell, bright(ly); **im Hellen**, in the light.

der **Henker** (—), hangman.

die **Henne**, hen.

Henni, Harry.

herab, down.

heran, up (to).

herauf, up.

heraus, out.

herbei, along.

der **Herbst**, autumn.

herein, (show) in, come in.

her-haben, get from.

der **Hering** (—e), herring.

der **Herr** (—n, —en), gentleman, master, sir, Mr.

die **Herrin** (—nen), mistress.

herrlich, splendid.

die **Herrschaften** (*pl.*): **meine —**, ladies and gentlemen.

herrschen, reign.

*(*)**her-springen** (a, u), dash over.

herüber, across; **— und hinüber**, from one side to the other.

herum, round; **rings —**, all round.

das **Herumirren**, wandering about.

herum-reißen (i, i), pull round sharply.

herunter, down.

*(*)**herunter-kommen** (a, o), come down in the world.

hervor, out.

*(*)**hervor-kommen** (a, o), emerge.

hervorragend, projecting.

hervor-tauchen, emerge.

das **Herz** (—ens, —en), heart.

herzlich, heartily.

herzu, up (to).

heulen, howl.

heute, to-day; **— abend**, to-night; **— früh**, this morning.

hier, here.

hierher, here.

das **Hifthorn** (—̈er), hunting horn.

die **Hilfe**, help.

der **Himmel** (—), heaven.

himmlisch, heavenly.

hin, thither, down, hence, over, along; **— und her**, to and fro, back and forth.

hinab, down.

hinauf, (go) up.

*(*)**hinauf-steigen** (ie, ie), go up.

hinaus, out.

*(*)**hinaus-gehen** (i, a), project.

hinaus-schieben (o, o), postpone.

hindern, prevent.

*(*)**hindurch-kommen** (a, o), get through.

*(*)**hindurch-schleichen** (i, i), steal through.

hinein, in, in it, into them.

hinfort, henceforth.

hin-halten (ä, ie, a), hold out.

hin-reichen, hold out.

hin-richten, execute.
hin-setzen, set down; **sich —
(zu),** sit down (beside).
sich **hin-stellen,** go and stand.
hinter, behind; **— . . . her,**
along behind.
das **Hinterhaus,** back of the house.
hinterlassen (ä, ie, a), be-
queath.
hinüber, across.
hinunter, down.
sich **hin-wenden** (a, a), turn to.
*__**hin-ziehen** (o, o), scurry
across.
hinzu-fügen, add.
hinzu-geben (i, a, e), add.
der **Hirt** (—en, —en), herdsman.
der **Hirtenknabe** (—n, —n),
young herdsman.
hoch, high, lofty, great (age).
hochberühmt, renowned.
höchst, most, greatest; **—e
Zeit,** high time.
hochverehrt, much esteemed.
die **Hochzeit,** wedding.
der **Hochzeitstag** (—e), wedding-
day.
der **Hof** (—̈e), court(-yard).
der **Hofball** (—̈e), court ball.
hoffen (auf), hope (for).
hoffnungsreich, hopeful.
die **Hofleute** (*pl.*), courtiers.
höflich, polite(ly).
der **Hofschauspieler** (—), court
player.
die **Höhe: in die —,** into sight.
das **Hohnlachen,** mocking laughter.
holen, come for; **— lassen,**
send for.
der **Holländer** (—), Dutchman.
horchen, listen.
hören, hear; **sich — lassen,**
can be heard.
der **Horizont** (—e), horizon.
das **Horn** (—̈er), horn.
das **Hotel** (—s), hotel.
der **Hügel** (—), hill, grave.
das **Huhn** (—̈er), chicken.
der **Humor,** humour.
der **Hund** (—e), dog.
die **Hundswut,** rabies.
der **Hunger,** hunger.
hungrig, hungrily.

*__**hüpfen,** hop.
husten, cough.
der **Hut** (—̈e), hat.
sich **hüten,** beware.
die **Hütte,** hut.

I

immer, always; **— noch,**
still; **— wieder,** again and
again.
immerfort: noch —, on and
on.
in, in(to).
indem, (by) —ing.
indes, in that time.
der **Inhalt** (—e), contents.
innen, inside.
inner, inner.
die **Inspiration,** inspiration.
das **Instrument** (—e) instrument.
interessant, interesting.
interessieren, interest.
das **Irdische,** life on earth.
irgendein, any.
irgend etwas, anything.
irgendwelche, some.
irgendwo, somewhere.
sich **irren,** be wrong.
das **Irrenhaus** (—̈er), lunatic
asylum.
das **Irrlicht** (—er), will o' the
wisp.
der **Irrtum** (—̈er), mistake.
der **Italiener** (—), Italian.

J

ja, yes; you know, after all.
das **Jäckchen** (—), short jacket.
die **Jagd,** hunt, chase, pursuit.
der **Jagdgenosse** (—n, —n),
fellow-huntsman.
(*)**jagen,** gallop; hunt.
das **Jagen,** scurry.
das **Jahr** (—e), year.
die **Jahreszeit,** season (of year).
das **Jahrhundert** (—e), century.
jawohl, yes indeed.
je . . . desto, the (more) . . .
the (more); **— weiter,** the
further.

jedenfalls, anyway.
jeder, every, each (one), any-body.
jedesmal, every time.
jedoch, however.
jener, that.
jenseits, on the other side.
Jesus, Jesus.
jetzig, present.
jetzt, now.
Johannestag, (St.) John's Day.
Julie, Julia.
jung, young.
der **Junge** (—n, —n), boy.
der **Jüngling** (—e), youth.
der **Junker** (—), squire.
das **Juwel** (—s, —en), jewel.

K

das **Kabinett** (—e), (powder) closet.
der **Kaffee,** coffee.
das **Kaffeehaus** (—̈er), coffee-house.
der **Kahn** (—̈e), boat.
das **Kalb** (—̈er), calf.
kalt, cold(ly).
die **Kälte,** cold(ness).
der **Kamerad** (—en, —en), com-rade.
der **Kamm** (—̈e), crest.
der **Kammerdiener** (—), valet.
der **Kammermusiker** (—), chamber-musician.
der **Kampf** (—̈e), fight, battle.
kämpfen, fight.
der **Kanal** (—̈e), canal.
das **Kaninchen** (—), rabbit.
der **Kanoni-kus** (—ker), dean, canon.
die **Kapelle,** orchestra.
der **Kapitän** (—e), captain.
der **Kardinal** (—̈e), cardinal.
die **Karte,** card.
das **Kästchen** (—), casket.
der **Kasten** (—̈), box.
der **Katarrh** (—e), catarrh.
kauern, squat.
kaufen, buy.
der **Käufer** (—), purchaser.

der **Kauf-mann** (—leute), mer-chant.
kaum, scarcely.
der **Kavalier** (—e), cavalier.
keck, audaciously.
kein, no.
der **Keller** (—), cellar.
der **Kellner** (—), waiter.
kennen (a, a), know;
—**lernen,** get to know.
der **Kenner** (—), connoisseur, expert.
die **Kerze,** candle.
die **Kette,** chain.
keuchen, pant.
das **Kind** (—er), child.
die **Kinderzeit,** childhood.
kindisch, childish.
kindlich, child-like.
das **Kino** (—s), cinema.
die **Kirche,** church.
das **Kissen** (—), cushion.
klagen, complain.
der **Klang** (—̈e), sound.
klar, clear.
das **Kleid** (—er), dress; (*pl.*) clothes.
klein, small, little, slight.
das **Kleingeld,** small change.
*****klettern,** climb.
klingeln, ring.
das **Klingeln,** ringing.
klingen (a, u), sound, ring out.
klopfen, knock.
die **Kluft** (—̈e), cavity, mine.
klug, clever, wise(ly).
der **Knabe** (—n, —n), boy, lad.
der **Knecht** (—e), (serving) man.
das **Knie** (—), knee.
knien, kneel.
das **Knöpfchen** (—), little button.
die **Knospe,** bud.
knurrig, growling.
der **Koch** (—̈e), cook.
das **Kochen,** cooking.
der **Koffer** (—), suit-case.
der **Kognak** (—s), cognac, brandy.
*****kommen** (o, a), come, get;
*****dazu**—, get as far, make it.
der **König** (—e), king.
die **Königin** (—nen), queen.
das **Königshaupt** (—̈er), royal head.

das **Königsmahl** (—e), royal banquet.

können, see § 102.

das **Konzert** (—e), concert.

der **Kopf** (—̈e), head, mind.

das **Köpfchen** (—), little head.

der **Korb** (—̈e), basket.

korrekt, proper.

kosten, cost.

die **Kraft** (—̈e), strength, vigour.

kräftig, strong, powerful(ly).

kraftlos, exhausted.

der **Kragen** (—), collar.

krank, sick, ill.

der **Kranke** (—n, —n), patient.

die **Krankheit,** illness.

der **Kranz** (—̈e), garland.

das **Kräuseln,** ripple.

der **Kreis** (—e), circle; area, space.

kreisen, circle.

das **Kreuz** (—e), cross.

der **Krieg** (—e), war.

die **Krone,** crown.

der **Kuchen** (—), cake.

die **Kuh** (—̈e), cow.

kühl, cool.

kühn, bold.

sich **kümmern** (**um**), worry (about).

die **Kunst** (—̈e), trick; **keine** —, nothing.

der **Künstler** (—), artist.

kurz, short(ly).

kürzlich, recently.

L

laben, refresh.

lächeln, smile.

das **Lächeln,** smile.

lächelnd, with a smile.

lachen, laugh.

das **Lachen,** laugh.

der **Laden** (—̈), shop.

die **Ladung,** cargo.

lallen, burble.

das **Lamm** (—̈er), lamb.

der **Lammwirt,** host of the Lamb Inn.

die **Lampe,** lamp.

das **Land** (—̈er), land, countryside; **an(s)** —, ashore.

die **Landschaft,** scenery, countryside.

lang, long, tall.

lange, (for a) long (time).

länger, fairly long.

langsam, slow(ly).

längst, long since, long ago.

sich **langweilen,** get bored.

der **Lärm,** noise.

lassen (ä, ie, a), let, leave, cause, let go; see § 102 (b).

die **Last,** burden.

der **Lauf** (—̈e), career.

*****laufen** (ä, ie, au), run, walk.

lauschen, listen.

laut, (a)loud.

lautlos, noiselessly.

das **Lebelang,** lifetime.

leben, live.

das **Leben** (—), life.

lebend, alive.

lebendig, living, astir, spoken.

die **Lebensglut,** glow of life.

die **Lebensweise,** way of life.

lebhaft, vivaciously.

lecken, lick.

das **Leder** (—), leather.

ledern, leather.

leer, empty.

leeren, empty.

legen, put, lay; **sich schlafen** —, go to bed.

lehren, teach.

der **Leib** (—er), body; **lebendigen** —**es,** in the living flesh.

der **Leichnam** (—e), corpse.

leicht, easy, light, dexterous.

leid: es tut mir —, I am sorry.

das **Leid,** sorrow.

leiden (i, i), suffer.

leider, unfortunately.

leise, noiseless(ly), soft(ly).

die **Leiter,** ladder.

lenken, steer.

lesen (ie, a, e), read.

letzt, last.

leuchten, shine, gleam.

die **Leute** (*pl.*), people.

das **Licht** (—er), light, candle, will o' the wisp.

lichten, weigh (anchor).

lieb, dear.

die **Liebe**, love.
lieben, love.
lieber, preferable, rather; *see* § 113 (*h*).
das **Liebeswort** (—e), word(s) of love.
liebevoll, lovingly.
der **Liebhaber** (—), lover.
die **Lieblingsbeschäftigung**, hobby.
das **Lied** (—er), song.
liegen (a, e), lie (about); be.
die **Limonade**, lemonade.
lind, soft.
die **Linie**, line.
link, left.
die **Lippe**, lip.
die **Liste**, list.
die **Literaturgeschichte**, history of literature.
das **Lob**, praise.
loben, praise.
der **Lohn** (—̈e), reward.
lösen, detach; buy.
sich **los-trennen**, break away.
das **Löwenherz**, Lion-Heart.
die **Luft** (—̈e), air, wind; (*pl.*) sky; **in Lüften**, aloft.
lügen (o, o), lie, tell lies.
die **Lust** (—̈e), joy, gaiety.
lustig, merrily, gaily.

M

machen, make, do.
die **Macht** (—̈e), force.
mächtig, powerful.
das **Mädchen** (—), girl.
der **Mädchenkopf** (—̈e), girl's head.
mager, lean.
das **Mal** (—e), time; **zum ersten** —, (for) the first time.
malen, paint.
der **Maler** (—), painter.
manch, many (a).
manchmal, sometimes.
der **Mann** (—̈er), man, husband.
der **Mantel** (—̈), cloak.
Maria, Mary.
das **Marienbild**, image of the Virgin.
die **Mark** (—), mark (coin).

der **Markt** (—̈e), market.
Markus, Mark.
Marthe, Martha.
der **Mast** (—es, —en), mast.
der **Mastbaum** (—̈e), mast.
die **Mauer**, wall.
das **Maul** (—̈er), mouth.
das **Meer** (—e), sea.
die **Meeresstille**, calm at sea.
mehr, more; **keine Note** —, not another note.
sich **mehren**, increase.
mehrere, several.
mehrmals, several times.
die **Meile**, mile.
meilenweit, for miles.
meinen, think.
der **meinige**, mine.
die **Meinung**, opinion.
meistens, mostly.
der **Meister** (—), master.
melden, announce.
die **Menge**, crowd, lot.
der **Mensch** (—en, —en), man; **ein** —, anybody.
die **Menschenstimme**, human voice.
sich **merken**, bear in mind.
merklich, appreciably.
das **Messer** (—), knife.
das **Metall** (—e), metal.
die **Miene**, face, air.
die **Miete**, fare.
mild, gentle, gently, mellow.
im **mindesten**, in the least.
der **Minister** (—), minister.
die **Minute**, minute.
missen, miss.
mißfallen (ä, ie, a) (D), dislike.
mit, with, by; — **unter**, together with the other(s).
mit-bringen (a, a), bring with one.
miteinander, together with one another.
das **Mitglied** (—er), member.
mit-nehmen (i, a, o), take with one.
mit-spielen, act a part.
das **Mittagessen** (—), lunch.
das **Mittelmeer**, Mediterranean.
die **Mitteltür**, middle door.

mitten (**in**) (**unter**), in the middle (midst) of.

die **Mitternacht** (-̈e), midnight.

mit-tun (a, a), join in.

***mit-wackeln**, waddle along with them.

modern, modern.

mögen, *see* § 102.

möglich, possible.

der **Mohrenkönig**, Moorish king

der **Moment** (—e), moment.

die **Monarchin** (—nen), monarch.

der **Mond** (—e), moon.

monoton, monotonous.

das **Moos** (—e), moss.

der **Mord** (—e), murder.

der **Mörder** (—), assassin.

morgen, to-morrow.

der **Morgen** (—), morning; east; **am anderen** —, the next morning.

das **Morgenrot**, red dawn.

die **Morgenzeitung**, morning paper.

die **Möwe**, sea-gull.

müde, tired.

die **Mühe**, trouble, toil.

die **Mühle**, mill.

der **Müller** (—), miller.

munter, frolicsome.

die **Musik**, music.

der **Musiklehrer** (—), music-master.

müssen, *see* § 102.

der **Mut**, courage.

mutig, brave.

die **Mutter** (-̈), mother.

das **Mutterhaus**, birthplace.

die **Mütze**, cap.

N

nach, after, to, towards, on; according to; — **und** —, gradually.

der **Nachbar** (—s,—n), neighbour.

nachdem, after (*conj.*).

nach-denken (a, a), reflect.

das **Nachdenken**, reflection.

das **Nacherzählen: zum** —, for reproduction.

***nach-gehen** (i, a) (D), follow.

nachher, afterwards.

nachmittags, in the afternoon.

die **Nachricht**, news.

nach-sehen (ie, a, e) (D), see.

***nach-springen** (a, u) (D), run after.

nächst, nearest, next.

***nach-stürzen** (D), plunge after.

die **Nacht** (-̈e), night.

nächtlich, that night.

der **Nachtwächter** (—), night-watchman.

nach-werfen (i, a, o) (D), throw at.

nach-ziehen (o, o), attract, draw.

nageln, nail.

nah(e), near, near-by; very.

die **Nähe**, vicinity.

***nahen** (D), approach.

sich **nähern** (D), approach, get nearer.

nähren, feed.

der **Name** (—ns, —n), name.

nämlich, you see; same.

die **Nase**, nose.

die **Natur**, nature; **nach der** —, from life.

der **Nebel** (—), mist.

neben, next to.

der **Neffe** (—n, —n), nephew.

nehmen (i, a, o), take (from).

sich **neigen**, sweep down.

nein, no.

nennen (a, a), call, indicate, give (name).

nervös, nervous.

das **Nest** (—er), nest.

nett, nice.

neu, new, modern.

neugeboren, newborn.

die **Neugierde**, curiosity.

neulich, the other day.

nicht, not; — **mehr**, no longer; — **mehr wieder**, never again.

nichts (**als**), nothing (except).

nicken, nod.

nie, niemals, never.

nieder, down.

sich **nieder-neigen**, descend.

nieder-stoßen (ö, ie, o), strike down.

niemand, nobody.

nimmer, never.

nirgends, nowhere; — **mehr,** no longer anywhere.
nirgendwo, nowhere.
die **Nische,** niche.
noch, still, even, yet, again, nor, a bit longer; — **einmal,** once more; — **nicht,** not yet; **nur** —, only... more ; — **einige,** a few more; — **mals,** once again.
der **Nord,** north.
normal, normal.
der **Normanne** (—n, —n), Norman.
die **Not** (—"e), trouble, misery, need.
die **Note,** note.
das **Notenblatt,** score, music.
nötig, necessary.
Notiz nehmen (i, a, o), take notice.
die **Nummer,** number.
nun, now.
nur, only, just; — **zu,** go on.

O

ob, (I wonder) whether.
oben, above, up(stairs), up above; **nach** —, to the top; **von** — **bis unten,** from top to toe.
ober, upper.
die **Oberkleider** (*pl.*), top clothes.
die **Oberlippe,** upper lip.
oberst, top.
obgleich, although.
öde, deserted.
oder, or.
der **Ofen** (—"), stove, oven.
offen, open, undisguised.
der **Offizier** (—e), officer.
(sich) **öffnen,** open.
die **Öffnung,** opening, entrance.
oft, often.
ohne, without.
die **Ohnmacht,** faint; **in** — ***fallen,** faint.
ohnmächtig, fainting.
das **Ohr** (—s, —en), ear.
das **Öl** (—e), oil.
Olivier, Oliver.
der **Onkel** (—), uncle.

das **Orchester** (—), orchestra.
ordentlich, proper.
ordnen, settle.
die **Ordnung,** order; **in** — ***sein,** be all right.
die **Orgel,** organ.
sich **orientieren,** get one's bearings.
die **Originalausgabe,** original edition.
originell, original.
der **Ort** (—e), place, spot, scene.
die **Osterferien** (*pl.*), Easter holidays.
Österreich (*n.*), Austria.
österreichisch, Austrian.

P

ein **paar,** one or two.
packen, seize.
das **Paket** (—e), parcel.
der **Palast** (—"e), palace.
der **Pantoffel** (—s, —n), slipper.
das **Papier** (—e), paper.
das **Parterre** (—s), pit.
der **Paß** (—"(ss)e), passport.
passen (D), fit.
die **Pause,** interval.
peinlich, embarrassing.
die **Person,** character.
der **Pfad** (—e), way, path.
pfeifen (i, i), whistle.
das **Pfeifen,** whistle.
das **Pferd** (—e), horse; **zu** —, on horseback.
der **Pferdejunge** (—n, —n), stable-boy.
pflegen, be wont to.
die **Pflicht,** duty.
das **Pfund** (—), pound.
die **Philologie,** philology.
picken, tick.
der **Pilger** (—), pilgrim.
der **Pinselstrich** (—e), stroke of the brush.
die **Pistole,** pistol.
das **Plateau** (—s), plateau.
plätschern, flip.
der **Platz** (—"e), room; — **nehmen,** sit down.
plötzlich, sudden(ly).
pochen, knock.

die **Post,** post (-office).
die **Postsachen** (*pl.*), mail.
die **Pracht,** splendour.
prangen, be resplendent.
der **Prinz** (—en, —en), prince.
die **Prinzessin** (—nen), princess.
prophezeien, prophesy.
die **Provinzstadt** (—̈e) provincial town.
prüfen, scrutinize.
das **Publikum,** public.
das **Pulver** (—), gunpowder.
der **Punkt** (—e): — **9 Uhr,** at 9 o'clock sharp.

Q

die **Quelle,** spring, source.
quer, obliquely.
quitt: — ***sein,** be quits.

R

die **Rache,** revenge.
rächen, avenge.
das **Rad** (—̈er), wheel.
der **Rand** (—̈er), edge, brim, brink.
ranzig, rancid.
rasch, quick(ly).
***rascheln,** scamper.
rasieren, shave.
das **Rasierzeug,** shaving-things.
rasten, rest.
der **Rat,** advice.
raten (ä, ie, a) (D), advise, give advice.
die **Ratte,** rat.
der **Raub,** prey.
rauben, rob of.
der **Rauch,** smoke.
rauh, harsh.
der **Raum** (—̈e), room, place.
rauschen, rustle, murmur, roar.
recht, right; — **haben,** be right.
das **Recht** (—e), right.
reden, talk, say, speak.
die **Redensart,** phrase.
regelmäßig, regular.
der **Regen,** downpour.

der **Regenbogen** (—̈), rainbow.
regieren, rule.
das **Regieren,** ruling.
regnen, rain.
regnerisch, rainy.
reich, rich.
das **Reich** (—e), realm.
reichen, hand, proffer, hold out.
die **Reihe,** row.
die **Reise,** journey, way; **auf der** — ***sein,** be travelling.
***reisen,** travel.
der **Reisende** (—n, —n), traveller.
die **Reisetasche,** travelling-bag.
das **Reiseziel** (—e), destination.
(*)**reißen** (i, i), snatch; give way.
***reiten** (i, i), ride.
das **Reiten: beim** —, when riding.
der **Reiter** (—), rider, horseman.
***rennen** (a, a), run.
das **Rennen,** running.
der **Renner** (—), runner.
der **Repräsentant** (—en, —en), representative.
repräsentieren, represent.
der **Respekt** (—e) (**vor**), respect (for).
der **Rest** (—e), rest.
das **Restaurant** (—s), restaurant.
(sich) **retten,** save (o.s.).
der **Retter** (—), rescuer.
die **Rettung,** rescue; **ohne** —, without fail.
richten, set, direct; **sich** — **auf,** turn towards.
der **Richter** (—), judge.
richtig, right, sure enough.
die **Richtung,** direction.
riechen (o, o) (**nach**), smell (of).
der **Riese** (—n, —n), giant.
rings, round.
der **Ritter** (—), knight.
die **Ritterschaft,** knights; chivalry.
der **Rock** (—̈e), coat.
die **Rolle,** part.
***rollen,** roll.
Rom, Rome.
die **Rose,** rose.
der **Rosengarten** (—̈), rose-garden.

das **Rosengebüsch,** rose-bushes.
das **Roß** (—(ss)e), steed.
das **Rößlein** (—), pony.
  rot, red.
  rotbekreuzt, marked with red crosses.
  röten, redden.
  rötlich, reddish.
  rudern, row.
der **Ruf** (—e), repute.
  rufen (ie, u), call (out), exclaim, shout, summon.
das **Rufen,** shouts.
die **Ruhe,** calm(ness), rest, peace.
  ruhen, rest, lie.
  ruhig, calm(ly), quiet, peacefully.
  rühren, move, stir.
  rund um, all round.
die **Runde,** round; **in der —,** all around.

S

der **Saal** (Säle), hall, (ball)room.
die **Sache,** thing, matter, business.
der **Sack** (—̈e), sack, bag.
die **Sage,** legend.
  sagen, say, tell; **— wollen,** mean.
die **Saite,** string (of instrument).
  salzig, salt.
  samt, together with.
der **Samt** (—e), velvet.
  sanft, gentle, softly.
der **Sang** (—̈e), song.
  Sankt, Saint.
der **Saphir** (—e), sapphire.
der **Sarg** (—̈e), coffin.
der **Satan,** Satan.
der **Sattel** (—̈), saddle.
die **Säule,** column.
das **Saumtier** (—e), pack-animal.
  sausen, blow hard.
der **Schacht** (—̈e), shaft (of mine).
der **Schaden** (—̈), hurt.
das **Schaf** (—e), sheep.
  schaffen, remove.
der **Schaffner** (—), conductor.
das **Schäflein: sein — scheren,** feather one's nest.
  schallen, resound.
die **Schande,** shame.

die **Schar,** troop.
der **Schatten** (—), shade, shadow.
der **Schatz** (—̈e), treasure.
der **Schatzgräber** (—), treasure-seeker.
  schauen, look, see.
das **Schauspiel** (—e), spectacle.
  *****scheiden** (ie, ie), depart, die.
der **Schein** (—e), light, rays; note.
  scheinbar, apparently.
  scheinen (ie, ie), seem, shine.
der **Schelm** (—e), rogue.
  schelten (i, a, o), call (abusively).
  schenken, present.
der **Scherz** (—e), jest.
  scheuen, shun.
  schicken, send.
  schießen (o, o), shoot, swoop.
das **Schiff** (—e), ship.
das **Schifferlein** (—), young mariner.
der **Schiffsjunge** (—n, —n), cabin-boy.
das **Schild** (—er), inn-sign.
der **Schilling** (—), shilling.
  schimpfen, swear.
der **Schlächter** (—), butcher.
der **Schlaf,** sleep.
  schlafen (ä, ie, a), sleep, be asleep; **— *gehen,** go to bed.
der **Schlafende** (—n, —n), sleeping man, sleeper.
das **Schlafengehen,** going to bed.
  schläfrig, sleepily.
der **Schlafrock** (—̈e), dressing-gown.
das **Schlafzimmer** (—), bedroom.
der **Schlag** (—̈e), blow.
  schlagen (ä, u, a), strike; leap.
die **Schlange,** queue.
  schlecht, bad(ly).
  *****schleichen** (i, i), steal (along), creep.
  schließen (o, o), shut; **— aus** conclude from; **sich —,** shut (*intr.*); **sich — an,** adjoin.
  schlimm, bad.
das **Schloß** (—̈(ss)er), castle, palace; lock.
der **Schloßflügel** (—), wing of castle.

die **Schlucht,** ravine, gorge, glen.
der **Schlummer,** slumber, sleep.
der **Schlüssel** (—), key.
 schmal, narrow, very small.
der **Schmaus** ($-$⸚e), banquet.
 schmeicheln, coax, caress.
der **Schmeichler** (—), flatterer.
der **Schmerz** (—es, —en), sorrow.
 schmerzlich, sad.
der **Schmied** (—e), smith.
die **Schmiede,** smithy.
der **Schmutz,** dirt.
der **Schnabel** ($-$⸚), beak.
der **Schnee,** snow.
 schneiden (i, i), cut.
 schnell, quick(ly).
 schnupfen, take snuff.
die **Schnur** ($-$⸚e), cord.
 schnurren, buzz.
 schon, already.
 schön, beautiful, fine, fair, lovely.
der **Schreck** (—e), terror, fright.
der **Schrecken** (—), terror.
 schreckhaft, frightening.
 schrecklich, terrible.
der **Schrei** (—e), shout.
 schreiben (ie, ie), write.
 schreien (ie, ie), shout, cluck.
* **schreiten** (i, i), stride, walk.
der **Schritt** (—e), step, yard.
der **Schuh** (—e), shoe.
der **Schuhmacher** (—), cobbler.
die **Schule,** school.
die **Schürze,** apron.
der **Schuß** ($-$⸚(ss)e), shot.
(sich) **schütteln,** shake (o.s.).
 schwach, weak, feeble, feebly.
 schwanken, rock.
der **Schwanz** ($-$⸚e), tail.
das **Schwänzchen** (—), little tail.
 schwarz, (in) black.
 schwarzgebrannt, charred.
der **Schwarzwald,** Black Forest.
 schweben, hang, be (e.g. in danger).
 schweigen (ie, ie), be silent, be hushed.
die **Schwelle,** threshold.
 schwer, heavy, hard.
die **Schwere,** gravity.
das **Schwert** (—er), sword.
die **Schwester,** sister.
* **schwimmen** (a, o), swim.

das **Schwimmen,** swimming.
 schwindlig, giddy.
 schwitzen, sweat.
 schwül, sultry.
die **See,** sea.
das **Seebad** ($-$⸚er), seaside resort.
die **Seele,** soul.
 seelenvergnügt, blissfully happy.
der **Seemann** ($-$⸚er), mariner.
das **Segel** (—), sail.
 segelflickend, patching sails.
 sehen (ie, a, e), see, look, find; — **nach,** look for; — **lassen,** show, give of.
 sehr, very (much), — **wohl,** right.
 seit, since; for (*prep.*).
die **Seite,** side.
 seitwärts, to one side.
 selber, myself, himself.
 selbst, my-, your-, himself; **von** —, of its own accord.
 seltsam, strange.
die **Sense,** scythe.
der **Sessel** (—), armchair.
 setzen, set, add; **sich** — (**zu**), sit down (beside), get (in).
 sicher, certain, sure.
die **Sicherheit,** safety.
das **Silber,** silver.
 singen (a, u), sing.
das **Singen,** singing.
* **sinken** (a, u), sink.
der **Sinn** (—e), sense.
 sitzen (a, e), sit.
der **Sklave** (—n, —n), slave.
 so, so (much), as, such a, then, like this, in this way, that's right, really; — ... **als,** as ... as.
 sobald, as soon as.
die **Socke,** sock.
 soeben, just.
 sofort, immediately.
 sogar, even.
 sogleich, immediately.
der **Sohn** ($-$⸚e), son.
 solange, while.
 solch, such.
der **Soldat** (—en, —en), soldier.
 sollen, see § 102.
die **Solvenz,** solvency.
der **Sommer** (—), summer.

sonderbar, strange.

die **Sonne,** sun.

sonnenhell, brightly sunlit.

der **Sonnenstrahl** (—s, —en), sun-beam.

der **Sonntag** (—e), Sunday.

sonst, or else, otherwise, as a rule.

die **Sorge,** worry; **— tragen für,** see to, take care of.

sorgen für, provide for.

der **Spanier** (—), Spaniard.

sparen, spare, save up.

spaßen, joke; **er läßt nicht mit sich —,** he is not to be trifled with.

spät, late.

***spazieren,** walk.

der **Spaziergang** (—̈e), walk.

die **Speisekarte,** menu.

die **Sperre,** barrier.

der **Spiegel** (—), mirror.

das **Spiel** (—e), play, game, gambling.

spielen, play, gamble; flash.

das **Spielzeug,** plaything(s).

spitz, pointed.

der **Spitzbube** (—n, —n), rascal, thief.

die **Spitze,** tip.

der **Sporn** (Sporen), spur.

der **Sportplatz** (—̈e), playing-ground.

der **Spott: zum —,** to make fun of.

die **Sprache,** language.

sprachlos, speechless with surprise.

sprechen (i, a, o), speak (to), say.

(*)**sprengen,** gallop; break (bank).

***springen** (a, u), jump, run, bound, snap.

***sprudeln,** gush forth.

sprühen, flash, flush.

die **Spur,** trace.

die **Staatsinquisition,** State Inquisition.

die **Stadt** (—̈e), town, city.

die **Staffelei,** easel.

der **Stall** (—̈e), stable(s).

stammeln, stammer.

der **Stand** (—̈e), rank.

stark, heavy, strong, powerful.

die **Stärke,** strength.

starren (**von**), be covered with.

der **Stationsvorsteher** (—), station-master.

statt, instead of.

statt-finden (a, u), take place.

die **Statue,** statue.

staubig, dusty.

staunen, marvel.

stecken, put; ***—bleiben,** get stuck.

stehen (a, a), stand, stop, be; **— vor,** be about to take; ***—bleiben,** stop.

stehlen (ie, a, o), steal.

***steigen** (ie, ie), climb, get, rise.

steil, steep(ly).

der **Stein** (—e), stone, boulder, rock.

steinern, stone.

steinig, stony.

die **Stelle,** spot, place.

stellen, put, set, ask; **sich —,** (go and) stand, station o.s.

***sterben** (i, a, o), die.

sterbend, dying.

der **Stern** (—e), star.

stets, always.

das **Steuer** (—), helm.

still, quiet(ly), at peace.

die **Stille,** stillness, silence; **in der —,** quietly.

stillschweigend, without saying anything.

die **Stimme,** voice.

die **Stimmung,** mood.

die **Stirn,** brow.

der **Stock** (—̈e), stick.

der **Stock** (—werke), floor; **im ersten —,** on the first floor.

der **Stockschlag** (—̈e), blow with a stick.

das **Stockwerk** (—e), floor.

stolz, proud.

stolzgespreizt, proudly strutting.

stören, disturb, intrude, upset.

der **Stoß** (—̈e), blow, push.

die **Strafe,** punishment.

der **Strahl** (—s, —en), ray (of light), beam.

strahlen, shine bright.

der **Strand,** shore.
die **Straße,** street, road.
die **Strecke,** bit (of road).
   streichen (i, i), stroke.
   streifen (an), brush against.
der **Streifen** (—), stripe.
der **Strick** (—e), rope, halter.
der **Strom** (—̈e), stream, river.
   *****strömen,** stream.
die **Strophe,** verse.
   struppig, dishevelled.
die **Stube,** room.
das **Stück** (—e), play, piece.
der **Student** (—en, —en), student.
   studieren, study.
die **Stufe,** step.
der **Stuhl** (—̈e), chair.
   stumm, silent.
der **Stumme** (—n, —n), dumb
   man.
die **Stunde,** hour, time; **zur —,**
   immediately.
der **Sturm** (—̈e), storm, gale.
die **Sturmglocke,** tocsin, alarm-
   bell.
   stürmisch, gusty.
(*)**stürzen,** dash, fall, crash
   down; push, fling; **sich —,**
   plunge, dash.
   suchen, look for, try; **— nach,**
   seek for.
der **Süd,** south.
die **Summe,** sum.
   süß, sweet.
die **Szene,** scene.

T

die **Tabaksdose,** snuff-box.
der **Tag** (—e), day.
der **Tagesanbruch,** daybreak.
die **Tageszeit,** time of day.
das **Tagewerk,** day's work.
   täglich, every day.
das **Tal** (—̈er), valley, vale.
das **Talent** (—e), talent.
der **Talgrund** (—̈e), valley bottom.
der **Tannenbaum** (—̈e), fir-tree.
der **Tannenwald** (—̈er), fir forest.
   tanzen, dance.
der **Tänzer** (—), dancer.
die **Tasche,** pocket, bag.

das **Taschentuch** (—̈er), handkerchief.
sich **tasten,** grope.
die **Tat,** deed; **in der —,** in fact.
der **Taube** (—n, —n), deaf man.
   tauen, thaw.
   täuschen, mislead.
das **Taxi** (—), taxi.
der **Taxifahrer** (—), taxi-driver.
der **Tee,** tea.
die **Teekanne,** tea-pot.
der **Teetopf** (—̈e), tea-pot.
der **Teich** (—e), pond, pool.
der **Teil** (—e), part.
   teils ... teils, some ... others.
das **Telefon** (—e), telephone.
   telefonieren, telephone.
   teuer, dear.
der **Teufel** (—), devil.
das **Theater** (—), theatre.
das **Theaterstück** (—e), play.
der **Thron** (—e), throne.
   tief, deep, low, late.
   tiefblau, deep blue.
die **Tiefe,** depth; **in die —,** down.
das **Tier** (—e), creature, animal.
der **Tiger** (—), tiger.
der **Tisch** (—e), table.
der **Titel** (—), title.
   toben, rage.
die **Tochter** (—̈), daughter.
das **Töchterlein** (—), little daughter.
der **Tod,** death.
   todblaß, deathly pale.
   tödlich, fatal.
   toll, mad.
der **Ton** (—̈e), note, sound, tone
   of voice.
   tönen, ring.
die **Tonne,** barrel.
das **Tor** (—e), gate.
der **Tor** (—en, —en), fool.
   tot, dead.
   töten, kill.
die **Totenstille,** death-like silence.
   tot-schießen (o, o), shoot
   (dead).
   *****traben,** trot.
   tragen (ä, u, a), carry, take;
   wear.
die **Träne,** tear.
   trauen (D), trust, believe.
der **Traum** (—̈e), dream.

traurig, sad(ly).
treffen (i, a, o), meet, befall, make, strike.
treiben (ie, ie), drive.
trennen, separate; **sich —,** part, drag o.s. away.
die **Treppe,** stairs, staircase, (flight of) steps.
***treten** (i, a, e), come, go (in), enter, step.
treu, faithful(ly).
trinken (a, u), drink.
trocken, dry.
die **Trompete,** trumpet.
der **Tropfen** (—), drop.
der **Trost,** consolation.
trotz, in spite of.
trotzdem, in spite of that.
trüb, gloomy.
die **Trümmer** (*pl.*), wreckage.
das **Tuch** (—̈er), hanging.
tun (a, a), do; put.
die **Tür,** door.
die **Turmspitze,** top of tower.
der **Tyrann** (—en, —en), tyrant.

U

übel, roughly; **etwas Übles,** any harm.
üben, exercise.
über, over, across, above.
***über-fahren** (ä, u, a), cross.
die **Überfahrt,** crossing.
überfliegen (o, o), survey.
***über-gehen** (i, a), well over.
überlegen, consider.
übernehmen (i, a, o), undertake; take over.
überraschen, surprise.
die **Überraschung,** surprise.
überreichen, hand.
überschallen, drown.
die **Überschrift,** heading.
über-setzen, ferry across.
***über-wallen,** overbrim.
überwältigen, overcome.
(sich) **überzeugen,** convince (o.s.).
übrigens, by the way.
übriggeblieben, remaining.
das **Ufer** (—), bank, shore.
die **Uhr,** clock.

um, at, about, round, for; — **so mehr,** all the more; — . . . **her,** round; — . . . **willen,** for the sake of; — . . . **zu,** (in order) to.
sich **um-blicken,** look round.
umdrängen, crowd round.
umfassen, seize round the waist.
umgaukeln, hover *or* flit around.
***um-gehen** (i, a), be abroad.
umgeworfen, flung around.
***um-kehren,** turn back.
um-reißen (i, i), demolish.
der **Umriß** (—(ss)e), outline.
***um-schlagen** (ä, u, a), capsize.
umschlossen, girt in.
sich **um-sehen** (ie, a, e) (**nach**), look round (for).
umsonst, in vain.
um-stoßen (ö, ie, o), kick over.
der **Umweg** (—e), detour.
***um-ziehen** (o, o), move (house); **sich —,** change clothes.
unabsehbar, as far as the eye could reach.
unangenehm, unpleasant.
unbefriedigt, unsatisfied.
unbekannt, unknown.
unbemerkt, unnoticed.
unbescheiden, immodest.
unbewohnt, uninhabited.
unehrlich, dishonest.
unerhört, unprecedented.
unermeßlich, immeasurable.
unerträglich, unbearable.
unfehlbar, unfailingly.
unfern, not far from.
unfreundlich, inclement.
die **Ungeduld,** impatience.
ungeduldig, impatient(ly).
ungefähr, about, more or less.
ungeheuer, huge, enormous.
ungern, reluctantly.
ungestüm, impetuously.
das **Unglück** (—e), calamity, misfortune.
unglücklich, unhappy.
unglücklicherweise, unfortunately.
unhöflich, impolite.

die **Universität,** university.
unmittelbar, immediately.
unmöglich, not possibly.
unnatürlich, unnaturally.
die **Unruhe,** (feeling of) restlessness, uneasiness.
unruhig, restless(ly), uneasy.
unsanft, violently.
unschuldig, innocent.
der **Unschuldige** (—n, —n), innocent man.
unsicher, uncertain.
der **Unsinn,** folly.
unsterblich, immortal.
unten, down below, downstairs, at the bottom.
unter, under, among, below, beneath; lower.
unterbrechen (i, a, o), interrupt.
unterbrochen, with interruptions.
*****unter-gehen** (i, a), set (of sun).
sich **unterhalten** (ä, ie, a), converse.
die **Unterhaltung,** entertainment.
das **Unterkommen,** accommodation, shelter.
die **Unterredung,** conversation.
untersagen, forbid.
sich **unterscheiden** (ie, ie), differ.
der **Unterschied** (—e), difference.
die **Unterschrift,** signature.
untersuchen, examine.
ununterbrochen, uninterruptedly.
unvorsichtig, imprudent.
unwillkürlich, involuntarily.
unzweifelhaft, indubitable (-ably).
uralt, very old, primeval.

V

der **Vater** (—͏̈), father.
vatergleich, like a father.
das **Vaterland,** native-country.
der **Vätersaal,** ancestral hall.
Venedig, Venice.
der **Venezianer** (—), Venetian.
sich **verabschieden,** take one's leave.
verbannt, banished.

verbergen (i, a, o), hide.
sich **verbeugen,** bow.
verbinden (a, u): **die Augen** —, blindfold.
verblichen, pallid.
verbogen, bent.
verborgen, concealed.
verbringen (a, a), spend.
verbunden, united.
verdächtig, suspiciously.
verdienen, earn, deserve.
verdrießlich, peevishly.
verfallen, dilapidated, collapsed.
der **Verfasser** (—), author.
verfolgen, pursue.
vergangen, past.
vergebens, in vain.
*****vergehen** (i, a), perish; pass.
vergelten (i, a, o), return, pay back.
vergessen (i, a, e), forget.
vergleichen (i, i), compare.
das **Vergnügen** (—), pleasure.
vergnügt, pleased.
*****verhallen,** die away.
verhindern, prevent, hinder.
sich **verirren,** lose one's way.
der **Verkauf** (—͏̈e), sale.
verkaufen, sell.
verkünden, proclaim.
verkürzen, while away.
verlangen, demand, ask, desire; — **nach,** yearn for.
verlassen (ä, ie, a), leave, abandon.
*****verlaufen** (äu, ie, au), go off.
verlegen, embarrassed, in embarrassment.
die **Verlegenheit,** embarrassment.
verlernen, forget, lose.
verlieren (o, o), lose; **sich** —, lose one's way, vanish.
vermeiden (ie, ie), avoid.
vermissen, miss.
vermögen (*cf.* mögen, § 102) be able to.
vernachlässigen, neglect.
vernehmen (i, a, o), hear.
vernünftig, sensibly.
*****verreisen,** go away.
verriegeln, bolt and bar.
der **Vers** (—e), verse.
die **Versammlung,** assembly.

verschieden, various.

(sich) **verschließen** (o, o), lock (o.s.) (in), shut.

*****verschwinden** (a, u), vanish, disappear.

versichern, assure.

versiegeln, seal.

die **Verspätung: — haben,** be late.

verspotten, mock at, scoff at.

versprechen (i, a, o), promise.

der **Verstand,** intelligence.

verständlich, understandable.

verstehen (a, a), understand.

versteinert, petrified.

verstorben, deceased.

*****verstummen,** cease.

der **Versuch** (—e), attempt.

versuchen, try.

versunken, sunk, engulfed.

verteidigen, defend.

vertieft, buried.

vertrauen, entrust.

verwaist, orphaned.

der **Verwalter** (—), steward.

verwundet, wounded.

der **Verwundete** (—n, —n), wounded man.

sich **verzehren,** consume o.s.

verzeihen (ie, ie), forgive, excuse.

die **Verzeihung,** forgiveness.

verzweiflungsvoll, despairingly.

viel, much; **—e,** many, a lot of; **—es,** much.

vielleicht, perhaps.

vielmals, very much.

vielmehr, rather.

die **Viertelstunde,** quarter of an hour.

Viktor, Victor.

die **Violine,** violin.

der **Vogel** (—̈), bird.

das **Vöglein** (—), little bird.

das **Volk** (—̈er), people.

voll(er), full, full of.

vollkommen, absolute(ly), quite.

vollzählig, complete.

von, of, from, about.

vor, in front of, before, for, to; ago.

*****voran-gehen** (i, a), go on ahead.

voraus, on ahead (of).

vorbei, past, over.

vor-bereiten, prepare.

die **Vorbereitung,** preparation.

*****vor-dringen** (a, u), advance.

der **Vorfall** (—̈e), incident.

der **Vorgänger** (—), predecessor.

der **Vorhang** (—̈e), curtain.

vorher, before.

*****vor-kommen** (a, o), seem.

vor-schlagen (ä, u, a), suggest.

*****vor-schreiten** (i, i), advance.

vorsichtig, careful(ly), cautious(ly).

vortrefflich, splendidly.

vorüber, (go) past.

*****vorwärts-kommen** (a, o), make progress.

das **Vorzeichen** (—), forewarning.

vor-ziehen (o, o), prefer.

W

waagerecht, horizontally.

wach, awake; **— *werden,** wake up.

die **Wache,** guard, watch.

wacker, brave.

die **Waffe,** weapon.

wagen, venture.

der **Wagen** (—), carriage, vehicle.

die **Wahl,** choice.

wählen, choose.

der **Wahnsinnige** (—n, —n), lunatic.

wahr, true; **nicht —,** *see* § 101.

während, while.

wahrscheinlich, probably.

die **Waise,** orphan.

der **Wald** (—̈er), wood, forest.

die **Waldstelle,** spot in the wood.

das **Waldvöglein** (—), little woodbird.

die **Wand** (—̈e), wall.

*****wandeln,** walk about.

*****wandern,** walk.

die **Wanduhr,** clock.

die **Wange,** cheek.
wann, when.
warm, warm.
die **Wärme,** warmth.
wärmen, warm.
warnen (vor), warn (against).
die **Warnung,** warning.
warten (auf), wait (for).
der **Wärter** (—), attendant.
warum, why; — **wohl,** why
on earth.
was, a fact which.
sich **waschen** (ä, u, a), wash (*intr.*).
das **Wasser,** water.
der **Wasserfall** ("–e), waterfall.
der **Wasservogel** ("–), sea-bird.
der **Wechsel** (—), change.
wechselnd, ever changing.
wecken, wake (*tr.*).
der **Wecker** (—), alarm-clock.
weder . . . noch, neither . . .
nor.
weg, away, off.
der **Weg** (—e), path, way, route;
sich auf den — machen,
set out, off.
wegen, because of.
weh: mir ist —, I feel
wretched.
wehen, blow.
wehmütig, sadly, melancholy.
das **Wehr** (—e), weir.
das **Weib** (—er), woman.
weich, soft.
die **Weide,** willow.
Weihnachten (*pl.*), Christmas.
die **Weihnachtszeit,** Christmas-
time.
weil, because.
weilen, tarry.
der **Wein** (—e), wine.
weinen, weep.
die **Weise,** way; **auf welche —?**
in which way?
weiß, white.
weit, far (away), a long way,
wide; — **und breit,** far and
wide.
weiter, further, on.
welcher, which, who, what.
die **Welle,** wave.
die **Welt,** world; crowd; **alle —,**
everybody.

weltlich, worldly.
sich **wenden** (a, a), turn.
(ein) **wenig,** (a) little; **—e,** few.
wenn, when(ever), if; — **erst,**
as soon as.
wer, who.
****werden** (i, u, o), become; —
aus, become of; — **zu,**
become.
werfen (i, a, o), throw.
das **Werk** (—e), work.
die **Werkstatt** ("–en), workshop.
wert, worth.
wertvoll, valuable.
weshalb, why.
die **Wette,** wager.
wetten, bet, wager.
der **Wettende** (—n, —n), better.
das **Wetter,** weather.
wichtig, important.
(sich) **wickeln,** wrap (o.s.).
****widerfahren,** befall.
wider-hallen, echo.
widerlegen, refute.
der **Widerschein** (—e), reflection.
sich **widersetzen** (D), resist.
wie, how, like; as; as though
(if); what!; what . . . like.
wieder, again, another.
wieder-beleben, revive.
wieder-erkennen (a, a), recognize (again).
das **Wiedererzählen : zum —,**
for reproduction.
wiederholen, repeat.
****wieder-kehren,** return.
****wieder-kommen** (a, o), come
back.
wiegen, lull.
wiegen (o, o), weigh.
die **Wiese,** meadow.
wieviel, wie viele, how much,
how many.
wild, wild.
Wilhelm, William.
willkommen, welcome.
der **Wind** (—e), wind.
die **Windstille,** calm.
der **Winter** (—), winter.
wirken, be active.
wirklich, really, actually, in
fact.
die **Wirkung,** effect.

der **Wirt** (—e), landlord.
die **Wirtschaft,** estate; inn.
das **Wirtshaus** (—"er), inn.
wissen (weiß, wußte, gewußt), know (how to).
wissenschaftlich, scientific (-ally).
die **Witwe,** widow.
wo, where; — . . . **hin,** where to.
wobei, during which time.
die **Woche,** week.
wodurch, by what.
wogend, billowy.
woher, where from; how.
wohin, where to.
wohl, well, of course, certainly, I'm afraid; **mir ist —,** I feel well.
wohl-tun (a, a): **mir tut es wohl,** I find it comforting.
wohlverdeckt, carefully covered.
wohlverdient, well-merited.
wohnen, dwell, live.
die **Wohnung,** flat.
das **Wohnzimmer** (—), sitting-room.
sich **wölben,** swell out.
die **Wolke,** cloud.
wolkenlos, cloudless.
wollen, see § 102.
womit, with what.
die **Wonne,** ecstasy.
worauf, whereupon, on what, on which.
woraus, from what, from which.
worein, into what.
das **Wort** (—e), word.
worunter, amongst which.
wühlen, burrow.
die **Wunde,** wound.
das **Wunder** (—), wondrous thing.
sich **wundern** (**über**), be surprised at.
der **Wunderton** (—"e), magic note.
wünschen, wish, like.
der **Wurf** (—"e), shot.
die **Wurst** (—"e), sausage.
wüst, desolate.
die **Wüste,** desolate spot.
die **Wut,** fury, wrath, rage.

Z

zahlen, pay.
zählen, count.
zahm, tame.
der **Zar** (—en, —en), tsar.
zart, delicate.
die **Zärtlichkeit,** tenderness.
der **Zecher** (—), toper.
die **Zehe,** toe.
zehnmal, ten times.
das **Zeichen** (—), sign.
zeigen (**auf**), point (to), show.
die **Zeit,** time; **zur rechten —,** in time; **— zu,** time for; **eine —lang,** some time.
*****zerbrechen** (i, a, o), break.
zerbrochen, broken.
*****zerspringen** (a, u), burst.
der **Zeuge** (—n, —n), witness.
(*)**ziehen** (o, o), draw, pull (at), withdraw; blow, wander, go; **sich —,** move; **darunter —,** fold in.
das **Ziel** (—e), goal, object, destination.
ziemlich, rather, fairly (long).
die **Zigarre,** cigar.
die **Zigeunerin** (—nen), gipsy woman.
das **Zimmer** (—), room.
zischen, hiss.
zittern, tremble, quiver.
zögern, hesitate.
der **Zoo** (—s), zoo.
zornig, angry, angrily.
zu, to, at; too.
zu-bringen (a, a), spend.
zucken, twitch.
zu-decken, cover over.
zuerst, first.
zufällig, by chance.
zu-flüstern (D), whisper to.
zufrieden, pleased, satisfied.
der **Zug** (—"e), train; feature.
der **Zugführer** (—), guard.
zugleich, at the same time.
zu-hören (D), listen (to).
die **Zuhörer** (*pl.*), audience.
*****zu-kommen** (a, o) (**auf**), come up to.
die **Zukunft,** future.
zuletzt, finally.
zu-machen, close.

zumute: wie ist ihm —? how does he feel?

zunacht, at night.

die **Zunge,** tongue.

sich **zurecht-finden** (a, u), know one's way about.

zurück, back.

zurückgelehnt, leaning back.

*__zurück-kehren,__ return, come back, go back.

zurück-rufen (ie, u), recall, restore.

sich **zurück-ziehen** (o, o), withdraw.

zu-rufen (ie, u) (D), call out to.

zusammen, together.

*__zusammen-gehen__ (i, a), keep time together.

zusammen-rollen, roll up.

das **Zusammentreffen,** meeting.

der **Zuschauer** (—), spectator.

zu-schlagen (ä, u, a), slam.

zu-schließen (o, o), lock.

zu-sehen (ie, a, e) (D), watch.

zutal, valley-wards.

*__zu-treten__ (i, a, e) (**auf**), come up to.

zuvor, before.

zuweilen, occasionally, sometimes.

zwar, it is true, and what's more, in fact.

der **Zweck** (—e), purpose.

der **Zweifel** (—), doubt.

zweifellos, undoubtedly.

zweifeln (**an**), doubt.

der **Zweig** (—e), branch, twig.

zwingen (a, u), compel.

zwischen, between, among.

die **Zwischenzeit,** interval; **in der —,** in the meantime.

VOCABULARY

(NOTE.—The plural ending—(e)n of feminine nouns of Group III is not indicated.)

A

able, to be, können, *irr.*
about, ungefähr; **to be — to** *see*
§ 102 (*b*) (vi).
abroad, to be —, im Ausland
*sein, *irr.*, **go —,** ins Ausland
*reisen.
absent, abwesend.
to **accept,** an-nehmen, *s.*
according to, nach (D).
accurate, genau.
acquaintance, der Bekannte
(§ 31).
across, über (A).
to **add,** hinzu-fügen.
advice, Rat, *m.*
aeroplane, Flugzeug (—e), *n.*
afraid, to be, sich fürchten; **—
of,** Angst (*f*) haben, sich
fürchten vor (D).
after, nach (D); nachdem (*conj.*).
afternoon, Nachmittag (—e), *m.*
afterwards, nachher.
again, wieder.
against, gegen (A).
age, Alter, *n.*
ago, vor (D).
ah, ach.
air, Luft (—̈e), *f.*
all, all (§ 74), ganz.
to **allow,** erlauben (AD).
allowed, to be, dürfen, *irr.*
almost, fast.
alone, allein.
along, entlang (A).
already, schon.
although, obgleich.
always, immer.
to **amuse o.s.,** sich amüsieren.

and, und; **— so,** deshalb.
angry, angrily, zornig.
animal, Tier (— e), *n.*
Anne, Anna.
another, noch ein; (= *different
one*), ein anderer.
to **answer,** antworten.
answer, Antwort, *f.*
anxious, ängstlich.
anybody: not —, niemand.
anything: not —, nichts.
appearance, Aussehen, *n.*
apple, Apfel (—̈), *m.*
arm, Arm (—e), *m.*
arrival, Ankunft (—̈e), *f.*
to **arrive,** *an-kommen, *s.*
artist, Künstler (—), *m.*
as, wie, da (§ 8); **— if,** als ob;
— soon —, sobald.
ashamed, to be, sich schämen
(G).
to **ask,** *see* § 114.
asleep: to fall —,*ein-schlafen, *s.*
astonishment, Erstaunen, *n.*
at, um (A), an (AD).
attentive(ly), aufmerksam.
aunt, Tante, *f.*
Austria, Österreich, *n.*
awake, wach.
to **awaken** (*intr.*), *erwachen.
aware: to be — of, sich (D)
bewußt *sein (G).
away, entfernt.

B

back, zurück; Rücken (—), *m.*
bad(ly), schlecht, schlimm.
bag, Koffer (—), *m.*
to **bake,** backen, *s.*

ball, Ball (-̈e), *m.*
bank, Ufer (—), *n.*
bath, Bad (-̈er), *n.*
to **bathe,** baden.
bathroom, Badezimmer (—), *n.*
beach, Strand, *m.*
to **beat,** schlagen, *s.*
beautiful(ly), schön.
beauty, Schönheit, *f.*
because, weil.
to **become,** *werden, *irr.*
bed, Bett (—s, —en), *n.*
bedroom, Schlafzimmer (—), *n.*
beer, Bier (—e), *n.*
before, vor (AD); bevor (*conj.*);
    vorher (*adv.*).
to **begin,** beginnen, *s.*
to **behave,** sich benehmen, *s.*
behind, hinter (AD).
belief, Glaube (—ns), *m.* (*no pl.*).
to **believe,** glauben.
to **belong,** gehören (D).
bench, Bank (-̈e), *f.*
Berne, Bern.
beside, neben (AD).
besides, außer (D).
better, besser.
between, zwischen (AD).
beyond, jenseits (G).
bicycle, Rad (-̈er), *n.*
big, groß.
bill, Rechnung, *f.*
bird, Vogel (-̈), *m.*
birthday, Geburtstag (—e), *m.*
black, schwarz.
blindly, blindlings.
to **bloom,** blühen.
to **blow,** blasen, *s.*
blow, Schlag (-̈e), *m.*
blue, blau.
boat, Boot (—e), *n.*, Schiff (—e), *n.*
body, Körper (—), *m.*
book, Buch (-̈er), *n.*
boot, Schuh (—e), *m.*
born, geboren.
to **borrow,** borgen.
both, beide (§ 43 (*e*)).
bottle, Flasche, *f.*
box, Kasten (-̈), *m.*
boy, Junge (—n, —n), *m.*
branch, Zweig (—e), *m.*
bread, Brot (—e), *n.*
to **break,** brechen, *s.*; — **into
pieces** (*intr.*), *zerbrechen, *s.*

breakfast, Frühstück (—e), *n.*
bridge, Brücke, *f.*
bright(ly), hell.
to **bring,** bringen (AD), *irr.*
brother, Bruder (-̈), *m.*
brown, braun.
to **build,** bauen.
building, Gebäude (—), *n.*
to **burn,** brennen, *irr.*
bus, Autobus (—se), *m.*
busy, beschäftigt.
but, *see* § 8.
to **buy,** kaufen.
by, an (AD), mit (D), von (D).

C

cake, Kuchen (—), *m.*
calm(ly), ruhig.
can, können, *irr.*
capital, Hauptstadt (-̈e), *f.*
car, Auto (—s), *n.*, Wagen (—), *m.*
card, Karte, *f.*
carriage, Wagen (—), *m.*
to **carry,** tragen, *s.*; — **out,** aus-
    führen.
case, Fall (-̈e), *m.*
to **cast,** werfen, *s.*
castle, Schloß (-̈(ss)er), *n.*
cat, Katze, *f.*
to **catch,** fangen, *s.*; — **train, person,** erreichen.
cathedral, Dom (—e), *m.*
Catherine, Katharine.
certain(ly), gewiß, sicher.
chair, Stuhl (-̈e), *m.*
to **change** (*tr.*), ändern; (*intr.*), sich
    ändern.
Charles, Karl.
cheap, billig.
cheese, Käse (—), *m.*
chicken, Huhn (-̈er), *n.*
child, Kind (—er), *n.*
choice, Wahl, *f.*
to **choose,** wählen.
Christmas, Weihnachten, *pl.*
church, Kirche, *f.*
cigarette, Zigarette, *f.*
cinema, Kino (—s), *n.*
circle, Kreis (—e), *m.*
city, Stadt (-̈e), *f.*
class, Klasse, *f.*
clear(ly), klar, deutlich.
clever, klug.

to climb, *klettern.

clock, Uhr, *f.*; **o'—,** Uhr.

closed, geschlossen.

closely, genau.

clothes, Kleider, *n. pl.*

cloud, Wolke, *f.*

coat, Mantel (-̈), *m.*; Jacke, *f.*

coffee, Kaffee, *m.*

cold, kalt.

to collect, sammeln.

Cologne, Köln.

colour, Farbe, *f.*

to come, *kommen, *s.*; **— back,** *zurück-kommen; **— in,** *herein-kommen.

comfortable, —ably, bequem.

companion, Gefährte (—n, —n), *m.*

compartment, Abteil (—e), *n.*

completely, ganz.

concern, Sorge, *f.*

concert, Konzert (—e), *n.*

consequence, Folge, *f.*

to consist (of), bestehen, *s.* (aus).

to contain, enthalten, *s.*

content, zufrieden.

to continue (*intr.*), fort-fahren, *s.*

conversation, Unterhaltung, *f.*

to cook, kochen.

cool, kühl.

cordially, herzlich.

corner, Ecke, *f.*

correct(ly), richtig.

to cost, kosten.

cottage, Hütte, *f.*

to count, zählen.

country, Land (-̈er), *n.*

courage, Mut, *m.*

of course, natürlich.

cousin, Vetter (—s, —n), *m.*

covered, bedeckt.

cow, Kuh (-̈e), *f.*

crowd, Menge, *f.*

to cry (= weep), weinen; (= **call out**), rufen, *s.*

cup, Tasse, *f.*

cupboard, Schrank (-̈e), *m.*

to cut, schneiden, *s.*; **— off,** ab-schneiden, *s.*

D

to dance, tanzen.

danger, Gefahr, *f.*

dangerous, gefährlich.

to dare, wagen.

dark, dunkel.

darkness, Finsternis (—se), *f.*

daughter, Tochter (-̈), *f.*

day, Tag (—e), *m.*; **one —,** eines Tages.

dead, tot.

deal: a good —, sehr viel.

dear, lieb (§ 31); (= **expensive**), teuer.

death, Tod, *m.*

December, Dezember, *m.*

to decide, beschließen, *s.*

deep(ly), tief.

to deserve, verdienen.

desire, Lust (-̈e), *f.*

desk, Schreibtisch (—e), *m.*

to die, *sterben, *s.*

different(ly), ander; anders (*adv.*).

difficult, schwer.

difficulty, Schwierigkeit, *f.*

to dig, graben, *s.*

diligent(ly), fleißig.

dining-room, Eßzimmer (—), *n.*

direction, Richtung, *f.*

dirty, schmutzig.

to disappear, *verschwinden, *s.*

dissatisfied, unzufrieden.

to distinguish, unterscheiden, *s.*

to disturb, stören.

to do, tun, *s.*

doctor, Arzt (-̈e), *m.*

dog, Hund (—e), *m.*

door, Tür, *f.*

Dorothy, Dorothea.

to doubt, zweifeln.

doubt, Zweifel (—), *m.*

downstairs, nach unten.

to draw, ziehen, *irr.*

drawer, Schublade, *f.*

dream, Traum (-̈e), *m.*

to dress (*intr.*), sich an-ziehen, *irr.*

to drink, trinken, *s.*

to drive (*intr.*), *fahren, *s.*; (*tr.*) (**car**), fahren, *s.*

drive, Fahrt, *f.*

during, während (G).

E

early, früh.

to earn, verdienen.

earth, Erde, *f.*
east, Osten, *m.*
Easter, Ostern, *pl.* (§ 81 (*j*)).
easy, easily, leicht.
to **eat,** essen, *s.*
edge, Rand (—̈-er), *m.*
effect, Wirkung, *f.*
elder, älter.
Elizabeth, Elisabeth.
Elsie, Else.
emperor, Kaiser (—), *m.*
empty, leer.
to **end,** enden.
end, Ende (—s, —n), *n.*
enemy, Feind (—e), *m.*
enough, genug.
to **entertain,** unterhalten, *s.*
Ernest, Ernst.
especially, besonders.
Europe, Europa, *n.*
even, sogar.
evening, Abend (—e), *m.* (§ 50);
— **-paper,** Abendzeitung, *f.*
ever, je.
every, jeder.
everybody, alle.
everything, alles.
everywhere, überall (§ 43 (*b*)
(iii)).
exact(ly), genau.
examination, Prüfung, *f.*
to **examine,** untersuchen.
example, Beispiel (—e), *n.*
exceedingly, äußerst.
except, außer (D).
excited, aufgeregt.
excursion, Ausflug (—̈-e), *m.*
exercise-book, Heft (—e), *n.*
to **expect,** erwarten.
expensive, teuer.
to **experience,** erfahren, *s.*
experience, Erfahrung, *f.,* see
§ 81 (*a*).
to **explain,** erklären.
explanation, Erklärung, *f.*
expression, Ausdruck (—̈-e), *m.*
extremely, äußerst.
eye, Auge (—s, —n), *n.*

F

face, Gesicht (—er), *n.*
in **fact,** in der Tat.
fairly, ziemlich.

fairy-tale, Märchen (—), *n.*
faithful(ly), treu.
to **fall,** *fallen, *s.*; — **asleep,** *ein-
schlafen, *s.*
family, Familie, *f.*
far, weit, fern.
farm, Bauernhof (—̈-e), *m.*
farmer, Bauer (—n/s, —n), *m.*
fast, schnell.
fat, dick.
fate, Schicksal (—e), *n.*
father, Vater (—̈-), *m.*
to **fear,** fürchten.
fear, Furcht, *f.*
feather, Feder, *f.*
to **feel,** (sich) fühlen.
to **fetch,** holen.
few, (nur) wenige; **a —,** einige.
field, Feld (—er), *n.*
to **fill,** füllen.
film, Film (—e), *m.*
finally, endlich.
to **find,** finden, *s.*; — **o.s.,** sich
finden.
fine, schön.
fire, Feuer (—), *n.*
firm(ly), fest.
first (*adj.*), erst; (*adv.*), zuerst;
at —, zuerst.
fish, Fisch (—e), *m.*
flat, flach.
flesh, Fleisch, *n.*
to **flow,** *fließen, *s.*
flower, Blume, *f.*
to **fly,** *fliegen, *s.*
to **follow,** *folgen (D).
fond: to be — of, lieben.
foolish, dumm.
foot, Fuß (—̈-e), *m.*
for (*prep.*), für (A); (*conj.*), denn.
to **forbid,** verbieten (AD), *s.*
to **force,** zwingen, *s.*
foreigner, Ausländer (—), *m.*
forest, Wald (—̈-er), *m.*
to **forget,** vergessen, *s.*
fortnight, vierzehn Tage.
fortunately, glücklicherweise.
Fred, Fritz.
free(ly), frei.
freedom, Freiheit, *f.*
French, Französisch, *n.*
fresh, frisch.
friend, Freund (—e), *m.*
friendly, freundlich.

to frighten, erschrecken.
from, aus (D), von (D).
in front of, vor (AD).
fruit, Obst, *n.*
fruit-tree, Obstbaum (—̈e), *m.*
full, voll.
furniture, Möbel (—), *n.*
further, weiter.
future, Zukunft, *f.*

G

gale, Sturm (—̈e), *m.*
game, Spiel (—e), *n.*
garden, Garten (—̈), *m.*
generally, gewöhnlich.
gentleman, Herr (—n, —en), *m.*
German (*adj.*), deutsch; (*noun*), der Deutsche (§ 31); Deutsch, *n.*
Gertrude, Gertrud.
to get, see § 114; — **up,** *auf-stehen, *s.*
ghost, Gespenst (—er), *n.*
girl, Mädchen (—), *n.*
to give, geben, *s.*; — **back,** zurück-geben; — **up,** auf-geben.
glad, froh.
glass, Glas (—̈er), *n.*
glove, Handschuh (—e), *m.*
to go, see § 114; — **away,** *fort-gehen, *s.*; — **out,** *aus-gehen.
gold, Gold, *n.*
good, gut.
goodness, Güte, *f.*
granddaughter, Enkelin (—nen), *f.*
grandfather, Großvater (—̈), *m.*
grandmother, Großmutter (—̈), *f.*
grandson, Enkel (—), *m.*
grass, Gras (—̈er), *n.*
grateful, dankbar.
gratitude, Dankbarkeit, *f.*
grave(ly), ernst.
great, groß.
green, grün.
to greet, grüßen.
grey, grau.
ground, Erde, *f.*
to grow, *wachsen, *s.*
guest, Gast (—̈e), *m.*

H

hair, Haar (—e), *n.*
half, halb; — **an hour,** eine halbe Stunde.
to hand, reichen (AD).
hand, Hand (—̈e), *f.*
handkerchief, Taschentuch (—̈er), *n.*
handsome, schön.
handwriting, Handschrift, *f.*
to hang (*intr.*), hängen, *s.*
to happen, *geschehen (D), *s.*; *vor-kommen, *s.*
happiness, Glück, *n.*
happy, glücklich.
harbour, Hafen (—̈), *m.*
hard, schwer; stark.
hardly, kaum.
hat, Hut (—̈e), *m.*
to have, haben, *irr.*; — **to,** müssen, *irr.*
head, Kopf (—̈e), *m.*
headache, Kopfschmerzen, *m. pl.*
health, Gesundheit, *f.*
healthy, gesund.
to hear, hören.
heart, Herz (—ens, —en), *n.*
heavy, schwer.
Helen, Helene.
to help, helfen (D), *s.*
help, Hilfe, *f.*
Henry, Heinrich.
here, hier (§ 40 (*a*) (i)).
to hide (*tr.*), verbergen, *s.*; (*intr.*), sich verbergen.
high, hoch.
to hike, *wandern.
hiker, Wandervogel (—̈), *m.*
hill, Berg (—e), *m.*, Hügel (—), *m.*
to hire, mieten.
history, Geschichte, *f.*
to hold, halten, *s.*
holidays, Ferien, *pl.*
home (*adv.*), nach Hause; **at —,** zu Hause.
homework, Schularbeit, *f.*
honour, Ehre, *f.*
to hope, hoffen; **I —,** hoffentlich.
hope, Hoffnung, *f.*
horse, Pferd (—e), *n.*
hot, heiß.

hotel, Hotel (—s), *n.*
hour, Stunde, *f.*
house, Haus (⸚er), *n.*; **—work,**
    Hausarbeit, *f.*
how, wie.
however, doch, aber.
hungry, hungrig.
to **hurry,** *eilen.
hurry, Eile, *f.*, *see* § 14 (*c*).
husband, Mann (⸚er), *m.*

I

if, wenn, ob (§ 8).
ill, krank.
illness, Krankheit, *f.*
immediately, sofort.
important, wichtig.
impossible, unmöglich.
in (*prep.*), in (AD); (*adv.*), ein,
    herein (§ 40 (*a*)).
inhabitant, Einwohner (—), *m.*
inn, Wirtshaus (⸚er), *n.*
innocence, Unschuld, *f.*
insect, Insekt (—s, —en), *n.*
instead of, (an)statt (G).
to **intend,** die Absicht haben, *irr.*
intention, Absicht, *f.*
to **interest,** interessieren.
interest, Interesse (—s, —n), *n.*
interesting, interessant.
into, in (A).
to **introduce,** vor-stellen (AD).
invitation, Einladung, *f.*
to **invite,** ein-laden, *s.*
iron, Eisen, *n.*
island, Insel, *f.*

J

Jack, Hans.
Joan, Johanna.
job, Stelle, *f.*
John, Johann.
journey, Reise, *f.*
joy, Freude, *f.*
joyful, fröhlich.
judge, Richter (—), *m.*
Julia, Julie.
to **jump,** *springen, *s.*
June, Juni, *m.*
just, *see* §§ 38, 39.

K

to **keep** (**word**), halten, *s.*
key, Schlüssel (—), *m.*
to **kill,** töten.
kind, lieb.
kindness, Güte, *f.*
king, König (—e), *m.*
kitchen, Küche, *f.*
knee, Knie (—), *n.*
knife, Messer (—), *n.*
to **knock,** klopfen.
to **know,** *see* § 114.

L

lady, Dame, *f.*
lamp, Lampe, *f.*
land, Land (⸚er), *n.*
landlord, Wirt (—e), *m.*
landscape, Landschaft, *f.*
language, Sprache. *f.*
large, groß.
to **last,** dauern.
last, letzt; **at —,** endlich, zuletzt;
    — night, gestern abend.
late, spät; *see* § 114.
later, später.
to **laugh,** lachen.
Laurence, Lorenz.
lazy, faul.
to **lead,** führen.
leaf, Blatt (⸚er), *n.*
to **learn,** *see* § 114.
at least, wenigstens.
to **leave,** *see* § 114.
leg, Bein (—e), *n.*
less, weniger.
lesson, Stunde, *f.*
to **let,** lassen, *s.*
letter, Brief (—e), *m.*
letter-box, Briefkasten (⸚), *m.*
library, Bibliothek, *f.*
to **lie,** *see* § 114.
life, Leben (—), *n.*
light (= **not dark**), hell; **—**
    green, hellgrün.
light, Licht (—er), *n.*
to **like,** mögen; gefallen (D); *see*
    § 113 (*h*).
like, wie; **— that,** so.
to **listen,** zu-hören (D).
little, klein; (= **not much**),
    wenig.

to live, leben; wohnen.
lonely, einsam.
long *(adj.),* lang; *(adv.),* lange.
no longer, nicht mehr.
to look, *see* § 114; — **forward to,** sich freuen auf (A); — **out,** hinaus-sehen, *s.*
to lose, verlieren, *s.*
lot, Menge, *f.*; **a — (of),** viel.
to love, lieben.
lovely, schön.
low, niedrig.
loyal, treu.
luggage, Gepäck, *n.*
lunch, Mittagessen (—), *n.*

M

magnificent, herrlich.
maid, Dienstmädchen (—), *n.*
to make, machen.
man, Mann (—̈er), *m.*; Mensch (—en, —en), *m.*
many, viele.
Margaret, Margarete.
mark, Mark (—), *f.*
to marry, heiraten.
Mary, Marie.
master, Herr (—n, —en), *m.*
matter, Sache, *f.*
Max, Max.
meadow, Wiese, *f.*
meal, Mahlzeit, *f.*
to mean, bedeuten.
meaning, Bedeutung, *f.*
meat, Fleisch, *n.*
to meet *(intr.),* sich treffen, *s.*; — **(at station),** ab-holen von (D).
to mend, reparieren.
merrily, lustig.
merry, fröhlich.
Michael, Michael.
mid-day, Mittag (—e), *m.*
middle, Mitte, *f.*
midnight, Mitternacht, *f.*
might, *see* § 102 *(b)* (ii).
mile, Meile, *f.*
milk, Milch, *f.*
minute, Minute, *f.*
Miss, Fräulein (—), *n.*
to miss, verpassen.
mistake, Fehler (—), *m.*
mistaken: to be —, sich irren.
moment, Augenblick (—e), *m.*

money, Geld (—er), *n.*
month, Monat (—e), *m.*
moon, Mond (—e), *m.*
more, mehr.
morning, Morgen (—), *m.*; **this —,** heute morgen (§ 50).
most, höchst.
mother, Mutter (—̈), *f.*
mountain, Berg (—e), *m.*
mouth, Mund (—̈er), *m.*
to move, bewegen.
moved, bewegt.
movement, Bewegung, *f.*
Mr., Herr (—n, —en), *m.*
Mrs., Frau, *f.*
much, viel, sehr, sehr viel.
music, Musik, *f.*
must, müssen, *irr.*
myself, selbst.

N

name, Name (—ns, —n), *m.*
narrow, eng, schmal.
natural, natürlich.
nature, Natur, *f.*
near, nah, in der Nähe (von).
nearest, nächst.
nearly, fast.
necessary, nötig.
neck, Hals (—̈e), *m.*
need, Not (—̈e), *f.*; **in —,** in der Not.
to need, brauchen.
neighbour, Nachbar (—n/s, —n), *m.*
neither: — . . . nor, weder . . . noch.
nephew, Neffe (—n, —n), *m.*
never, nie.
nevertheless, doch.
new, neu.
New Forest, Neuwald, *m.*
news, Nachricht, *f.*
newspaper, Zeitung, *f.*
next, nächst; neben (AD).
nice(ly), nett; schön.
niece, Nichte, *f.*
night, Nacht (—̈e), *f.*; **last —,** gestern abend (§ 50).
nightshirt, Nachthemd (—s, —en), *n.*
no, nein.
nobody, niemand.

noise, Lärm, m.
not, nicht; — at all, gar nicht;
— yet, noch nicht.
note (bank-), Schein (—e), m.
nothing, nichts.
to notice, bemerken.
now, jetzt.
nowadays, heutzutage.

O

to obey, gehorchen (D).
object, Gegenstand ("-e), m.
office, Büro (—s), n.
officer, Offizier (—e), m.
official, der Beamte (§ 31).
often, oft.
oh, ach.
old, alt.
once, einmal; at —, sofort.
only (adj.), einzig; (adv.), see
§ 114.
to open (tr.), öffnen, auf-machen;
(intr.), sich öffnen.
open(ly), offen; in the —, im
Freien.
opinion, Meinung, f.
opportunity, Gelegenheit, f.
opposite, gegenüber (D).
or, oder; — else, sonst.
to order, bestellen.
order, Ordnung, f.; in — to,
um . . . zu.
other, ander; the — day, neulich; —wise, sonst.
ought, see § 102 (b) (v).
out, aus, hinaus; — of, aus (D).
outside, draußen.
own, eigen.

P

to pack, packen.
page, Seite, f.
pain, Schmerz (—es, —en), m.
pair, Paar (—e), n.
pale, blaß.
paper, Papier (—e), n.,
(= newspaper), Zeitung, f.
parcel, Paket (—e), n.
parents, Eltern, pl.
to part (intr.), *scheiden, s.
part, Teil (—e), m.
particularly, besonders.

to pass, *vorüber-gehen, s.
past, Vergangenheit, f.
past, vorbei (§ 112 (b)).
patient, der Kranke (§ 31).
Paul, Paul.
Pauline, Paula.
to pay, zahlen (AD), bezahlen.
peace, Friede (—ns), m.
pen, Feder, f.
pencil, Bleistift (—e), m.
people, Leute, pl.; Menschen, m. pl.
perhaps, vielleicht.
person, Mensch (—en, —en), m.
picture, Bild (—er), n.
pipe, Pfeife, f.
place, Ort (—e), m.; Stelle, f.
plan, Plan ("-e), m.
to plant, pflanzen.
plant, Pflanze, f.
plate, Teller (—), m.
to play, spielen.
play, Stück (—e), n.; Spiel (—e),
n.
pleasant(ly), angenehm.
to please, gefallen (D), s.
please, bitte.
pleased, froh.
pleasure, Vergnügen (—), n.
pocket, Tasche, f.
poem, Gedicht (—e), n.
poet, Dichter (—), m.
policeman,   S c h u t z - m a n n
(-leute), m.
polite(ly), höflich.
poor, arm.
porter, Gepäckträger, m..
to possess, besitzen, s.
possible, möglich; as late as —,
möglichst spät.
post, Post, f.
postcard, Postkarte, f.
postman, Briefträger (—), m.
post-office, Post, f.
pound, Pfund (—), n.
to prefer, vor-ziehen, s; (see § 113(d)).
preparation, Vorbereitung, f.
to prepare, bereiten.
presence, Gegenwart, f.
to present, schenken (AD).
present, Geschenk (—e), n.;
Gegenwart, f.
pretty, hübsch.
to prevent, verhindern.
pride, Stolz, m.

prince, Prinz (—en, —en), *m.*
prisoner, der Gefangene (§ 31).
probably, wahrscheinlich.
professor, Professor (—s, —en), *m.*
to promise, versprechen (AD), *s.*
promise, Versprechen, *n.*
proud, stolz; — **of,** stolz auf (A).
Prussia, Preußen, *n.*
purchase, Einkauf (—̈e), *m.*
purpose, Zweck (—e), *m.*
to put, *see* § 114; — **on** (**clothes**), an-ziehen; (**hat**), auf-setzen.

Q

quarter, Viertel (—), *n.*; — **of an hour,** Viertelstunde, *f.*
queen, Königin (—nen), *f.*
question, Frage, *f.*
quick(ly), schnell.
quiet(ly), leise; ruhig (= **peaceful**).
quite, ganz.

R

raft, Floß (—̈e), *n.*
to rain, regnen.
rain, Regen (—), *m.*
raincoat, Regenmantel (—̈), *m.*
to raise, heben, *s.*
rare(ly), selten.
rather, ziemlich.
to reach (= **get to**), erreichen.
to read, lesen, *s.*; — **out,** vor-lesen.
ready, fertig; (= **prepared**), bereit.
really, wirklich, eigentlich.
reason, Grund (—̈e), *m.*
to receive, erhalten, *s.*
to recognize, erkennen, *irr.*
to recover, sich erholen.
red, rot.
to refuse, ab-lehnen.
reign, Regierung, *f.*
to remain, *bleiben, s.*; — **silent,** schweigen, *s.*; — **standing,** *stehen-bleiben, s.*
to remember, sich erinnern an (A).
to repeat, wiederholen.
to reply, erwidern, antworten.
request, Bitte, *f.*
rescue, Rettung, *f.*

to rest, ruhen.
restaurant, Restaurant (—s), *n.*
restless, unruhig.
rich, reich.
Richard, Richard.
to ride, *fahren, s.*; (**horse**), (*)reiten, *s.*
ride, Fahrt, *f.*
right(ly), recht, richtig.
to ring bell, klingeln.
river, Fluß (—̈(ss)e), *m.*
road, Straße, *f.*
Robert, Robert.
rock, Felsen (—), *m.*
room, Zimmer (—), *n.*; (= **space**), Platz (—̈e), *m.*
round (*adj.*), rund; (*prep.*), um (A).
to rub, reiben, *s.*
rucksack, Rucksack (—̈e), *m.*
to run, *laufen, s.*
Russia, Rußland, *n.*

S

sad(ly), traurig.
sailor, Matrose (—n, —n), *m.*
sake: for the — of, wegen, um . . . willen (G).
same, derselbe (§ 65).
sand, Sand, *m.*
Saturday, Sonnabend, *m.*
sausage, Wurst (—̈e), *f.*
to save, retten.
to say, sagen (AD).
scenery, Landschaft, *f.*
school, Schule, *f.*
schoolboy, Schüler (—), *m.*
schoolmistress, Lehrerin, *f.*
sea, Meer, *n.*; **at** (**to**) **the —-side,** am (ans) Meer; —-**shore,** Meeresufer (—), *n.*
to seat o.s., sich setzen.
seat, Platz (—̈e), *m.*
secret, Geheimnis (—se), *n.*
to see, sehen, *s.*
to seem, scheinen, *s.*; *vor-kommen (D), s.*
to sell, verkaufen (AD).
to send, schicken (AD); — **for,** schicken nach (D).
sentence, Satz (—̈e), *m.*
serious, ernst.
servant, Dienstmädchen (—), *n.*

to set (sun), *unter-gehen, s.
several, mehrere.
to sew, nähen.
  shade, Schatten (—), m.
  shadow, Schatten (—), m.
to shake (o.s.), (sich) schütteln.
  shame, Scham, f.
to share, teilen.
  sharp, scharf.
  sheep, Schaf (—e), n.
to shine, scheinen, s.
  ship, Schiff (—e), n.
  shirt, Hemd (—es, —en), n.
  shoe, Schuh (—e), m.
  shop, Laden (—̈), m.
  short(ly), kurz.
to show, zeigen (AD).
to shut, schließen, s.
  side, Seite, f.
  sign, Zeichen (—), n.; Spur, f.
  silent: to be —, schweigen, s.
  silly, dumm.
  simply, einfach.
  since (prep.), seit (D); (conj.), da.
to sing, singen, s.
  single, einzig.
to sink, *sinken, s.
  sister, Schwester, f.
to sit (down), see § 114.
  sitting-room, Wohnzimmer, n.
  situated: to be, liegen, s.
  situation, Lage, f.
  sky, Himmel (—), m.
to sleep, schlafen, s.; go to —,
    *ein-schlafen, s.
  sleepy, schläfrig.
  slow(ly), langsam.
  small, klein.
to smile, lächeln.
to smoke, rauchen.
  smoke, Rauch, m.
to snow, schneien.
  snow, Schnee, m.
  so, so; — that, so daß; and —,
    daher.
  soft, leise.
  soldier, Soldat (—en, —en), m.
  some, einige.
  somebody, jemand.
  something, etwas.
  sometimes, manchmal.
  son, Sohn (—̈e), m.
  song, Lied (—er), n.
  soon, bald; as — as, sobald.

sorry: to be —, leid tun (D), s.
south, Süden, m.
to speak (to), sprechen (mit), (D).
  speaker, Redner (—), m.
  special(ly), besonder(s).
  speech, Rede, f.
to spend (time), verbringen, irr.;
    (money), aus-geben, s.
in spite of, trotz (G).
to spoil, verderben, s.
  spot, Stelle, f.
  spring, Frühling (—e), m.
  stairs, Treppe, f.
  stamp, Briefmarke, f.
to stand, stehen, s.; — up, *auf-
    stehen, s.
  station, Bahnhof (—̈e), m.
to stay, *bleiben, s., sich auf-halten,
    s.; — up, *auf-bleiben, s.
to steal, stehlen, s.
  step, Schritt (—e), m.
  Stephen, Stefan.
  steps, Treppe, f.
  stern, streng.
  still (adj.), still; (adv.), noch.
  stillness, Stille, f.
to sting, stechen, s.
  stone, Stein (—e), m.
to stop, see § 114.
  story, Geschichte, f.
  stout, dick.
  straight, gerade.
  strange(ly), sonderbar.
  stranger, der Fremde (§ 31).
  street, Straße, f.
to strike, schlagen, s.
  strong(ly), stark.
  student, Student (—en, —en), m.
  stupid, dumm.
  subject, Gegenstand (—̈e), m.
to succeed, *gelingen (D); I suc-
    ceed, es gelingt mir.
  success, Erfolg (—e), m.
  successful, erfolgreich.
  such, solch.
  suddenly, plötzlich.
  sufficiently, genug.
  sugar, Zucker, m.
to suggest, vor-schlagen, s.
  suit, Anzug (—̈e), m.
  suit-case, Koffer (—), m.
  sum, Summe, f.
  summer, Sommer (—), m.; —
    holidays, Sommerferien, pl.

sun, Sonne, *f.*
Sunday, Sonntag (—e), *m.*
sunshine, Sonnenschein, *m.*
supper, Abendessen (—), *n.*
to **suppose,** an-nehmen, *s.*
sure, sicher.
to **surprise,** überraschen.
surprised: to be —, erstaunt
sein (irr.) über (A) (= **at**).
Susan, Susanne.
sweet(ly), süß.
to **swim,** *schwimmen, s.*
Swiss, Schweizer (—), *m.*
Switzerland, Schweiz, *f.*

T

table, Tisch (—e), *m.*
to **take,** *see* § 114; — **off,** aus-
ziehen, *s.*
to **talk,** sprechen, *s.*
tall, groß, hoch.
tea, Tee, *m.*
teacher, Lehrer (—), *m.*; Lehrerin (—nen), *f.*
tear, Träne, *f.*
to **tell,** sagen (AD); — **(a story to),**
erzählen (AD).
terrible, schrecklich.
than, als.
to **thank,** danken (D).
theatre, Theater (—), *n.*
then, *see* § 114.
there, da, dort (-hin).
thick, dick.
thing, *see* § 114; **that sort of —,**
so etwas.
think, denken, *irr.* an (A) (= **of**).
thirsty, durstig.
this, dieser.
though, obgleich.
thought, Gedanke (—ns, —n), *m.*
through, durch (A).
to **throw,** werfen, *s.*
ticket, Fahrkarte, *f.*
tidy, ordentlich.
tight, eng.
till (*conj.*), bis; (*prep.*), bis (A).
time, *see* § 114.
tired, müde.
to, zu (D), nach (D), an (A), in
(A); — **and fro,** auf und ab.
to-day, heute.
together, zusammen.

to-morrow, morgen.
to-night, heute abend.
too, zu; (= **also**), auch.
tooth, Zahn ($\ddot{\,}$e), *m.*
top (of hill), Gipfel (—), *m.*
torch, Taschenlampe, *f.*
tower, Turm ($\ddot{\,}$e), *m.*
town, Stadt ($\ddot{\,}$e), *f.*; — **hall,**
Rathaus ($\ddot{\,}$er), *n.*
train, Zug ($\ddot{\,}$e), *m.*
tram, Straßenbahn, *f.*
to **translate,** übersetzen.
to **travel,** *reisen, *fahren, *s.*
traveller, der Reisende (§ 31).
tree, Baum ($\ddot{\,}$e), *m.*
to **tremble,** zittern.
trouble, Mühe, *f.*
true, wahr.
truth, Wahrheit, *f.*
to **try,** versuchen.
Tuesday, Dienstag, *m.*
to **turn (round),** sich um-wenden,
irr.; — **to,** sich wenden (*irr.*) zu
(D).
two, zwei; **the —,** die beiden.

U

umbrella, Schirm (—e), *m.*
uncle, Onkel (—), *m.*
uncomfortable, unbequem.
to **understand,** verstehen, *s.*
unfortunately, leider.
unfriendly, unfreundlich.
unhappy, unglücklich.
university, Universität, *f.*
unknown, unbekannt.
unpleasant, unangenehm.
untidy, unordentlich.
until, bis.
unusual, ungewöhnlich.
unwise, unklug.
up, hinauf (§ 40 (*a*) (ii)).
upstairs, nach oben.
usual(ly), gewöhnlich.
to **use,** gebrauchen.
useful, nützlich.

V

in **vain,** umsonst.
valley, Tal ($\ddot{\,}$er), *n.*
various, verschieden.

very, sehr.
vicinity, Nähe, *f.*
village, Dorf (—er), *n.*
to visit, besuchen.
visit, Besuch (—e), *m.*
voice, Stimme, *f.*

W

to wait, warten auf (A) (= **for**).
waiter, Kellner (—), *m.*
to wake up (*intr.*), *erwachen; (*tr.*), wecken.
to walk, *gehen, *s.*
walk, Spaziergang (—̈e), *m.*
wall, Wand (—̈e), *f.*; (**exterior**), Mauer, *f.*
to want, wollen, *irr.*
war, Krieg (—e), *m.*
warden, Herbergsvater (—̈), *m.*
warm(ly), warm.
to warn, warnen.
to wash (*tr.*), waschen, *s.*; (*intr.*), sich waschen, *s.*
to watch, zu-sehen (D), *s.*
watch, Taschenuhr, *f.*
water, Wasser (—), *n.*
way (= **manner**), Weise, *f.*; **in this —,** auf diese Weise; (= **road**), Weg (—e), *m.*
weak, schwach.
to wear, tragen, *s.*
wearily, müde.
weather, Wetter (—), *n.*
week, Woche, *f.*
well (*adj.*), gesund; (*adv.*), gut; nun; **— -known,** bekannt.
wet, naß.
wheel, Rad (—̈er), *n.*
when, wann, wenn, als (§ 8).
whenever, wenn.
where, wo.
whether, ob.
while, während.
while, Weile, *f.*

to whistle, pfeifen, *s.*
white, weiß.
who, wer; der (*see* § 58).
whole, ganz.
why, warum; nun.
wife, Frau, *f.*
wild(ly), wild.
will, Wille (—ns), *m.* (*no pl.*).
William, Wilhelm.
to win, gewinnen, *s.*
wind, Wind (—e), *m.*
window, Fenster (—), *n.*
wine, Wein (—e), *m.*
winter, Winter (—), *m.*
to wish, wünschen (AD).
wish, Wunsch (—̈e), *m.*
with, mit (D), bei (D).
without, ohne (A).
woman, Frau, *f.*
wonder, Wunder (—), *n.*
wonderful, wunderbar.
wood, Holz (—̈er), *n.*; (= **forest**), Wald (—̈er), *m.*
word, Wort (—e), *n.*
to work, arbeiten.
work, Arbeit, *f.*
workman, Arbeiter (—), *m.*
world, Welt, *f.*; **— war,** Weltkrieg (—e), *m.*
worse, schlimmer.
to write, schreiben (AD), *s.*
wrong, unrichtig, falsch; **to be —,** unrecht haben, *irr.*

Y

yard, Schritt (—e), *m.*
year, Jahr (—e), *n.*
yellow, gelb.
yes, ja.
yesterday, gestern.
yet, doch; **not —,** noch nicht.
young, jung.
youth, Jugend, *f.*; **— -hostel,** Jugendherberge, *f.*

INDEX TO GRAMMAR SECTION

(Both pages and paragraphs are indicated.)